Political Economics in Retrospect

Adolph Lowe
(1893–1995)

Political Economics in Retrospect

Essays in Memory of Adolph Lowe

Edited by

Harald Hagemann

Professor of Economic Theory, University of Hohenheim, Germany and Life Member of Clare Hall, University of Cambridge, UK

and

Heinz D. Kurz

Professor of Economics
Karl-Franzens Universität Graz, Austria

Edward Elgar
Cheltenham, UK • Northampton, MA, USA

Published by
Edward Elgar Publishing Limited
8 Lansdown Place
Cheltenham
Glos GL50 2HU
UK

Edward Elgar Publishing, Inc.
6 Market Street
Northampton
Massachusetts 01060
USA

A catalogue record for this book
is available from the British Library

Library of Congress Cataloguing in Publication Data

Political economics in retrospect: essays in memory of Adolph Lowe /
   edited by Harald Hagemann, Heinz D. Kurz.
      Includes bibliographical references and index.
        1. Economics—Germany—History. 2. Economics—United States—
   History. 3. Lowe, Adolph, 1893– . 4. Economics. I. Hagemann,
   Harald. II. Kurz, Heinz-Dieter.
   HB107.L69P65 1997
   330—dc21   97–22600
                                                                          CIP

ISBN 1 85898 057 7

Printed and bound in Great Britain by
Biddles Ltd, Guildford and King's Lynn

Contents

Figures and Tables

FIGURES

TABLES

Contributors

Volker Caspari is Professor of Economic Theory at the Technical University of Darmstadt, Germany.

Betsy Jane Clary is Professor of Economics at the College of Charleston, South Carolina, USA.

Marion Countess Dönhoff is the Editor of the weekly newspaper *Die Zeit*, Hamburg, Germany.

Heiner Ganßmann is Professor of Sociology at the Free University of Berlin, Germany.

Christian Gehrke is Researcher at the University of Graz, Austria.

Harald Hagemann is Professor of Economic Theory at the University of Hohenheim in Stuttgart, Germany, and Life Member of Clare Hall, Cambridge, UK.

Joseph Halevi is Senior Lecturer of Economics at the University of Sydney, Australia, and Full Professor at the UFR Sciences Economiques at the Université Pierre Mendès France in Grenoble, France.

Robert Heilbroner is Norman Thomas Professor Emeritus and Senior Lecturer at the New School for Social Research in New York, USA.

Claus-Dieter Krohn is Professor of Modern History at the University of Lüneburg, Germany.

Heinz D. Kurz is Professor of Economics at the Karl-Franzens University in Graz, Austria.

Michael Landesmann is Professor of Economics at the Johannes Kepler University in Linz and Research Director of the Vienna Institute for Comparative Economic Studies, Austria.

Ferdinando Meacci is Professor of Economics at the University of Padova, Italy.

Edward J. Nell is Malcolm B. Smith Professor of Economics at the New School for Social Research in New York, USA.

Allen Oakley is Associate Professor of Economics at the University of Newcastle, Australia.

Roberto Scazzieri is Professor of Economics at the University of Bologna, Italy, and a Life Member of Clare Hall, Cambridge, UK.

Bertram Schefold is Professor of Economics at the Johann-Wolfgang-Goethe University in Frankfurt, Germany.

Ian Steedman is Professor of Economics at Manchester Metropolitan University, UK.

Introduction*

Harald Hagemann and Heinz D. Kurz

Adolph Lowe was born *Adolf Löwe* on 4 March 1893 in Stuttgart and died in Wolfenbüttel, Germany on 3 June 1995. He was Alvin Johnson Professor Emeritus of Economics of the New School for Social Research in New York where the Graduate Faculty had been founded as the *University in Exile* in 1933 to rescue emigré scholars in the social sciences from the jaws of fascism. Lowe had been among the first professors of the Goethe University in Frankfurt who were dismissed by the Hitler regime in April 1933. From 1911 to 1915 Lowe studied law, economics and philosophy at the Universities of Munich, Berlin and Tübingen where he received his doctorate in law in 1918. Having directed a study on economic demobilization as early as 1916, Lowe became a chief economic adviser to the government of the young Weimar Republic in November 1918. After short periods in the ministries of Demobilization and Labour, Lowe served as a Section Head in the Ministry of Economics from 1919 to 1924, where he was particularly involved with issues of socialization, inflation and reparation policy. From 1924 to 1926 he was Head of the International Division of the German Bureau of Statistics in Berlin before he accepted an offer by Bernhard Harms and became a Director of Research at the Kiel Institute of World Economics. There he established a new department of statistical international economics and research on international trade cycles, which included outstanding scholars such as Gerhard Colm, Hans Neisser, Fritz Burchardt, Wassily Leontief and Jacob Marschak, and soon obtained an international reputation. From Kiel, where he was appointed Professor of Economic Theory and Sociology at the University in February 1930, Lowe moved to Frankfurt in October 1931.

The first country in exile was the United Kingdom where Lowe was special Honorary Lecturer in economics and political philosophy at the University of Manchester from 1933–40. In England he also became a naturalized citizen on the day after the outbreak of the Second World War: *Löwe* mutated to *Lowe*. In summer 1940 he accepted a renewed offer from the New School for Social Research in New York where he served as Professor of Economics until his retirement in 1963 and also as Director of Research in the Institute of World Affairs between 1943 and 1951. Lowe not only continued teaching until the late 1970s but also remained as a very active researcher. This is best reflected in the fact that his two main works,

On Economic Knowledge (1965) and *The Path of Economic Growth* (1976), were published rather late. In March 1983, fifty years after emigrating, Lowe returned to Germany where, until his death, he lived with his daughter Hanna and her family in Wolfenbüttel, hosting a steady stream of visitors, including many of the contributors to this book, until he was almost 100 years old.

The idea for this book first came up when several of the contributors met on different occasions in spring 1993 to celebrate Adolph Lowe's 100th birthday: in Frankfurt, Bologna, New York, Philadelphia and Bremen. It then turned out that, although there had been numerous *Festschriften* before, the last three in connection with his 90th birthday,[1] with the exception of a special Lowe–Mahalanobis issue of the French journal *Economie Appliquée* (Vol. 47, No. 2, 1994), nobody had taken the initiative to publish a *Festschrift* in his honour on the very special occasion of his 100th birthday. On the other hand, there was an impressive international community of scholars who were attracted by Lowe's work and his considering economics as inseparable from social inquiry in general, and many of the participants attending the different Lowe symposia were so enthusiastically engaged that it was almost a natural outcome to put a collection of papers together which, on the whole, may give an answer on the legacy of his works and thought. Since Lowe was already very sick and could not participate himself in the events in his honour in 1993, the idea was present from the beginning that this volume might become a *Gedenkschrift*, a book in memory of a great scholar and *citoyen* whose long list of honours included two honorary doctorates, from the New School for Social Research (1964) and the University of Bremen (1983), the Veblen–Commons Award (1979), the Grand Cross of the German Order of Merit (1984), honorary citizenship of the Goethe University in Frankfurt and honorary membership of the German Sociological Association.

Part I of this *Gedenkschrift* contains personal recollections by two former students and then lifelong friends of Adolph: *Marion Countess Dönhoff*, editor of the German weekly *Die Zeit*, and *Robert Heilbroner*, Professor Emeritus at the Graduate Faculty of the New School for Social Research, New York, the university where Adolph Lowe had his last teaching appointment. In addition, there is an intellectual biography of Adolph Lowe by *Claus-Dieter Krohn*, covering Lowe's intellectual and sociopolitical formation in the Weimar Republic and the reflection of this formation in some of his later works.

Part II turns to the roots of Lowe's approach to economic problems in 'classical' political economy; it emphasizes his adoption and adaption of the method, scope and content of the latter. *Volker Caspari* focuses attention on Lowe's distinction between 'structural' and 'force analysis' and expounds critically his 'instrumental method', that is, his concept of economic and social planning in a democratic society. *Heinz D. Kurz's* starting-point is Lowe's observation that in classical analysis economic growth and development were essentially explained *endogenously*, whereas the standard neoclassical model assumes the long-term rate of (steady-state) growth to be given from outside the system. In the rest of the chapter various contributions to the so-called 'new growth theory' are scrutinized; it is shown that the contributions under consideration can broadly be described as models of endogenous growth and exogenous profitability. Several shortcomings of the models are pointed out. *Ferdinando Meacci* deals with a special, but important aspect in the theory of capital and of capital accumulation: the treatment of 'working' and of 'circulating' capital. He argues that the two notions must not be confused and belong to two different theories.

Part III deals with the field of traverse analysis in which Adolph Lowe was a pioneer. Stimulated by the works of Marx, Sombart and Schumpeter, Lowe emphasized the central role of technical progress for both the cycle and the long-run growth trend. With his contributions to business-cycle theory Lowe had a profound impact on the debate in the German-speaking area in the late 1920s. This holds in particular for his seminal Kiel habilitation thesis 'How is business cycle theory possible at all?' (1926) in which he raised the fundamental methodological challenge of how cyclical phenomena could be incorporated into the system of economic equilibrium theory with which they are in apparent contradiction. *Harald Hagemann* and *Michael Landesmann* discuss Lowe's contributions to business-cycle analysis in the context of the rather broad tradition which dominated continental European research since Tugan-Baranowsky's pathbreaking study from the late nineteenth century until the 1930s. The overriding concern in these contributions was to establish the link between changes in the industrial structure of an economy and macroeconomic fluctuations. Emphasis is also on the theories of Bouniatian, Aftalion and Spiethoff, who all tried to integrate structural aspects into their theories. This tradition had also heavily influenced the Austrian theory of the business cycle with its emphasis on disproportions in production linked to the effects of monetary expansion on the relative price structure as it was developed by Hayek who had been Lowe's main opponent in the late 1920s. Starting from Lowe's distinction of different phases of capitalist development, *Edward J. Nell* reflects on the stages in the development of the business cycle. It is emphasized that the economy behaved differently after the Second World War compared to the period prior to the First World War. Increasing standards of living, organized markets and new cultural attitudes have all undermined the pressure to act in accordance with the extremum principle, and, as a consequence, market behaviour can no longer be reliably calculated from simple maximizing models of rational market behaviour. Nell presents a survey of stylized facts for the 'old' and the 'new' trade cycle which he uses for a critical reexamination of Lowe's theoretical conclusions. In particular he criticizes Lowe's contention that capitalism had become disorderly and his rejection of the Keynesian analysis of capitalist instability. Integrating the latter into Lowe's theoretical analysis would make his approach sound.

Ian Steedman compares three similar, but different kinds of models that are prominent in the literature on value and distribution: the Samuelson–Hicks–Spaventa two-sectoral model, Lowe's three-sectoral model, and the three-machine Mathur model. It turns out that the first model is a special case of the second, and the second is a special case of the third model. He concludes that in the theory of value and distribution Lowe's (and Mathur's) model is to be preferred to the more widely used Samuelson–Hicks–Spaventa model. *Joseph Halevi* turns to the literature on economic development and relates Lowe's work to major contributions to it. He begins with a brief overview of the debates on capital accumulation and economic crisis among Russian and German Marxists around the turn of the century, placing special emphasis on Tugan-Baranowsky. He then deals with the problem of the traverse from a less-developed to a mature economy and closes with a critical discussion of the structural theories of development of Dobb, Feldman, Raj and Sen, and Naqvi. This assessment stresses the strategic role of the first machine-tool sector in Lowe's three-sector scheme for the development process. *Roberto Scazzieri* sees in Lowe, as well as in John Hicks, one of the few modern economists who have attempted to construct a theory of economic history, making use of appropriate analytical tools and economic methodology in the explanation of historical processes. His chapter is an investigation into the analytical structure of economic dynamics, particularly the decomposition of production structures. Scazzieri discusses changing forms of production organization as well as the emergence of new hierarchies among elements of the productive system which often characterizes qualitative structural change. *Christian Gehrke* asks the question why Lowe's more interesting approach to traverse analysis in terms of a circular flow model has received relatively less attention than Hicks's in terms of a neo-Austrian model of production. Special emphasis is on the flexibility of the production system due to the possibility of operating productive capacity at different degrees of utilization, a possibility commonly ignored in contributions to traverse analysis. The investment hypothesis implicit in Hicks's 'full performance' assumption is criticized. What is needed is the introduction of a proper investment hypothesis in a framework that allows for degrees of capacity utilization that differ from normal degrees.

Part IV contains contributions which deal with the work of the 'economic philosopher' as Lowe was once termed by Kenneth Boulding.[2] The concern with a viable order, both stable and free, permeated Lowe's entire work. His last book, *Has Freedom a Future?* (1988), which deals with the conditions under which freedom can be established and maintained *vis-à-vis* the radical transformation to which contemporary Western society is exposed, can be regarded as the culmination of thought and teaching of a great social scientist. Here we find Lowe pleading for a new communal ethic and a revitalization of the Western tradition of individualism properly understood, that is, individualism rooted in social responsibility. What is at stake is the problem of balancing the private and the public domain where the latter is conceived as the guardian of the viability of the former. In his inquiry into the conditions of political freedom, Lowe returned to the central ideas of the booklet *The Price of Liberty* (1937) which he had dedicated to his friend Paul Tillich on the occasion of the latter's fiftieth birthday. Here we find Lowe as a young emigré from Nazi Germany and a perceptive historical, political and sociological observer praising 'spontaneous conformity' of liberal England as 'the only mode of life through which a large-scale society can reconcile the conflict between freedom and order' (1937, p. 6). The price of liberty is individuals' readiness to conform to particular constraints and controls that are manifested as structures, institutions and rules. *Bertram Schefold* takes up the concept of spontaneous conformity, which for Lowe was central in balancing freedom and order, and emphasizes that in fact it is one of the oldest in mankind for which, however, each generation has to work out its own solution. In particular, in Schefold's view spontaneous conformity, which had already been a central theme of Aristotle's philosophy, characterizes an economic style, with its different dimensions: specific forms of rationality and economic dynamism, with an economic and social order and based on a certain level of technological development.

Betsy Jane Clary focuses on the friendship of Lowe with Paul Tillich. The latter was the intellectual leader of German religious Socialism, one of the most distinguished Protestant theologians and philosophers in Germany and a former colleague at the Goethe University in Frankfurt. In particular, Clary concentrates on the ecumenical conference of Christian churches which was held at Oxford University in the summer of 1937, examining the report of the Oxford conference concerning the economic order and exploring the early contributions of Lowe and Tillich to social economics. Another long-time friend and former Frankfurt colleague of Lowe had been Karl Mannheim to whom (and Franz Oppenheimer) he dedicated his first book published in British exile, *Economics and Sociology* (1935), an ambitious plea for interdisciplinary work in the social sciences, which was based on a series of lectures Lowe had presented at the London School of Economics in February 1935. *Heiner Ganßmann* reexamines the proposals for the division of labour and cooperation between economics and sociology which were made by Lowe and Mannheim in the mid-thirties. One of the driving forces is his dissatisfaction with the current debate about the relationship between economics and sociology which is very much centred around 'economic imperialism'. The author shows that going 'back' to the arguments developed by Lowe and Mannheim rewards the researcher with more substantive definitions of economics and sociology and distinctions between the two disciplines than those dominating the contemporary debate. In particular, the hope remains that the combination of economic and sociological arguments can generate a scientifically sound and practically relevant reasoning about the socioeconomic conditions of the modern age. Finally, *Allen Oakley's* discussion of the traverse as a problem of human agency is an attempt belonging to this line of approach. Oakley's reflections on the dimensions of the involvement of human agency in the traverse as a theoretical and practical policy management problem, which is greatly stimulated by the sociological analysis of Anthony Giddens, highlights the different dimensions of instrumental analysis as Lowe's central theoretical tool of political economics. In it, structural analysis has to be supplemented by force analysis which studies the behavioural and motivational patterns which will not only put the economy on a goal-adequate traverse but also has a special significance in market systems and raises economics above the level of a mere engineering science. The complexities of traverse processes in modern capitalist economies show the importance of the information and knowledge needs and uses of agents, their formation of expectations to the extent that their means and abilities allow, in order to absorb and implement processes of structural change.

NOTES

*   We are grateful to Manuela Merthan, Sonja Weber and Babette Mummert for secretarial assistance at various stages of this project and, above all, for their ability to unscramble and standardize the various word-processed files we received. Special thanks must go to Julie Leppard and Mary Murphy for copy-editing and to Dr Gerhard Mauch for preparing the index.

1.   E. Nell (ed.), 'Value, growth and economic policy: Essays in tribute to Adolph Lowe', *Social Research*, Vol. 50, No. 2, Summer 1983; I. Rima (ed.), 'Special issue in honor of Adolph Lowe', *Eastern Economic Journal*, Vol. 10, No. 2, April–June 1984; H. Hagemann and H.D. Kurz (eds), *Beschäftigung, Verteilung und Konjunktur – Zur Politischen Ökonomik der modernen Gesellschaft*, Festschrift für Adolph Lowe, Bremen: University Press, 1984.

Earlier volumes have been D. Schwartzman (ed.), 'Essays in economic theory in honor of Adolph Lowe and Hans Neisser', *Social Research*, Vol. 33, No. 2, Summer 1966 and R.L. Heilbroner (ed.), *Economic Means and Social Ends. Essays in Political Economics*, Englewood Cliffs, NJ: Prentice-Hall 1969, which documents the two symposia which took place in the year of Lowe's 75th birthday.

2. K.E. Boulding, 'Is economics obsolescent?', *Scientific American*, Vol. 212, May 1965, p. 139.

PART I

Personal Recollections

1. Adolph Lowe: A Portrait 1

Marion Countess Dönhoff

For me he will always be Adolf Löwe as he was in the old days at Frankfurt University, where I had the good fortune to have him as a teacher. He did not drop the two dots over the 'o' for the purpose of anglicizing his name, they were missing from the typewriter used by an English official for providing him with a new passport. He never changed this back because in his splendid independence he did not feel that his identity was dependent on two little dots.

Adolph Lowe lived through the entire century, now at its close, in all its phases: the monarchy, the First World War, Weimar, the advent of National Socialism, and then, from England and America, the Second World War, the victory of the West, and finally the collapse of Soviet Communism.

He soon realized that this collapse did not solve the problem which had occupied him all his life – the reconciliation of individual freedom with social stability. He believed that what is important is a harmonious combination of market and planned economy, of freedom and order. In his book *On Economic Knowledge* (1965), he examines the conflict between the demands for freedom and emancipation of the Age of Enlightenment and the establishment of a stable and equitable social order.

He starts with the question of how democratic freedoms can survive in the face of the political, psychological, economic and technological challenges. He describes a refusal to see this problem as a self-delusion of the bourgeois-liberal and also of later socialist freedom philosophy. Lowe concludes that the liberal belief in harmony through individual self-regulation should not be evaluated as solely positive, because it not only sets free innovative forces but has also created the bases for modern self-destruction.

His concern from the start was the decay of society-forming traditions. Not that he rejected in principle the powers of emancipation but he also saw its drawbacks. Basically he was always in favour of emancipation because it shakes off old shackles, but he also knew that this entailed the destruction of 'protective functions'. When, for example, family ties are loosened, the state has to help out by taking over care for the aged and setting up nursery schools; in place of the individual the state steps in and with it usually bureaucracy.

What he was concerned with was the balance between freedom and order. He thought that just as in the social sphere, established customs are also a precondition in the economic sphere for the stability of the whole. This is why the general disintegration, caused in his opinion by hedonism and nihilism in our civilization, was of such concern to him. The greatest threat today is 'the self-destruction of society'.

Lowe, in a thoroughly clairvoyant and at the same time profound manner, always understood the problems of this century and put forward suggestions for their solution. In the world economic crisis of the 1930s he was, in contrast to many of his colleagues, convinced that Hitler's regime would last because the National Socialists adopted precisely that policy of job creation which a group at the Kiel Institute of Economics headed by Adolph Lowe had suggested – the mobilization of the unused productive capacity by publicly-controlled demand. Only by recourse to public demand was private enterprise placed in a position where it could do what was necessary to overcome the depression.

In an interview which Matthias Greffrath, my colleague at the time, and I had with the 95-year-old man in May 1988, we asked him which in his opinion had been the most fatal development since the end of the war. He replied: 'I think that the following constituted a serious sin of omission by the Allies at the end of the Second World War: at that time it would have been in principle possible to make a democratic Europe out of the compulsory European union created by Hitler'.

Lowe went on to say: 'In the spring of 1943 – after Stalingrad – when it had become clear that the West would win and thoughts of peace order became a primary subject of discussion, I, together with my friends Paul Tillich, Hans Staudinger and Fred Pollock from the Institute for Social Research, had a conversation with President Roosevelt. We submitted to him a plan which envisaged no longer reconstructing the old European nation states as sovereign units but of forming out of this bankrupt estate a democratically united Europe. The President's answer was: "That's impossible. I have given an undertaking to the governments of the European states (most of which were in exile in England or America) to reestablish the old sovereignties." There was no point in arguing any further.'

In his book *Has Freedom a Future?* (1988) he criticizes the trend to reduce the view of man and society to the drive for economic maximization. After all, humanity strives for more; maybe it is even its primary aim to find purpose and meaning. It is impossible, in his opinion, to rely under present-day conditions solely on the self-determination of the individual; it is precisely this that leads to the necessity for planning and state control.

The present situation of unlimited expectations and demands (a higher standard of living every year, travelling further afield, more luxurious accommodation) at the expense of future generations cannot be continued *ad infinitum*, for this would inevitably lead to an authoritarian control of society. Only if people are prepared to accept voluntary restrictions, can authoritarian government be avoided in the long run. It would suffice – he said at the time in 1988 – if we contented ourselves for some time with what we have; we have no need to practise asceticism.

However, in the present late capitalist society the pursuit of long-term interests entails risks and sacrifices for the individual. In consequence, preference is given to short-term interests, the pursuit of which in its turn intensifies instability.

Hence it seems almost hopeless to preach self-restraint to a society like ours which is bent on instant gratification. The precondition for success would be a change in people's fundamental attitudes. They would have to realize that 'society is not composed of the people who are there today but society is a continuous process with both a future and a past'. Thus Lowe's formula is: 'We need a series of minor disasters to bring people to their senses'. This, he thought, would probably lead to a sort of 'solidarity in emergency'.

I knew from previous discussions with him that Lowe had always been very sceptical of the doctrine of pure *laissez-faire*. Although it pleased him that the nineteenth century had abolished control of the individual through the absolutism of monarchs, priests and guild masters, but, so he thought, the whole only continued to function because the superpersonal restraints of the preliberal tradition guaranteed order and stability: 'These superpersonal restraints brought about a conformity of behaviour patterns in public life. Precisely this was the basis of the nineteenth-century social stability'. Hence again: 'Stable economic and social development is not possible without social control'.

England, the first stage of his emigration, obviously made a great impression on him. He attached vital importance to the English maxim: 'Never pursue an argument to the bitter end, this upsets the community spirit'. England, with her inherited behaviour patterns for what is publicly allowed and sanctioned, had appealed to him.

How right he was with his admiration for this, as he calls it, 'spontaneous conformity' of the English, how justified was his concern for society's self-destruction in Germany – this is patently obvious to everybody today, but he sensed it very much earlier. He always said: 'Survival is only possible if a certain conformity of individual behaviour is assured'.

Lowe said in our interview: 'We are going through a technological revolution. It promises us rising mass affluence, and threatens us with mass destruction and mass unemployment. At the same time we are experiencing all over the world political upheavals; we are creating space for new democracies but also for new tyrannies. We are undergoing a worldwide industrialization. This is the precondition for the Third World to emancipate itself, but at the same time it leads to climatic disasters.' Hence the central issue of his last book is how can one resolve these contradictions and bring the constructive freedom-loving tendencies to victory – a victory, albeit, that can only be won with sacrifices.

'I consider that the problem is in principle solvable', he says, 'and by what I call democratic planning, that is, democratic controls which aim at public and private freedom and at the same time strive for social stability. The first great advance in this direction was the Beveridge Plan in England after the Second World War. Its aim was general social security and in connection with this fiscal and monetary measures for stabilizing the economy.'

'My opinion that democratic planning is a condition for the constructive solution of our problem', said Lowe, 'is contrary to government policy, at any rate of the major Western states and of the majority of their voters. They have opposed progress in public planning and demand a reduction of even the rather patchy measures of the welfare state.'

In 1988 we asked him: 'Haven't the socialist states organized affluence out of existence? How does your planning differ from that in the GDR or in Poland?' His reply: 'To put it in a nutshell: totalitarian planning *commands* under the penalty of destruction. Democratic planning *manipulates* by enticement with certain opportunities and by the closure of other options. But there are certain borderline cases where Western planning also has to be authoritarian. We forbid, for example, a wide range of medicines and psychopharmacological drugs. For the present and the immediate future I have no desire to strive for more than the political and economic stabilization of an organized capitalism which reflects freedom to the widest possible extent. The next step can only be taken on this basis. Determining its direction and developing the appropriate institutions I see as the task of another generation.'

I occasionally visited Adolph Lowe in a home for the aged in New York before his return to Germany in 1983. I was astounded how he managed, despite his cramped living conditions, to encompass, intellectually alert as ever, the whole wide world as a matter of course.

2. Adolph Lowe: A Portrait 2

Robert Heilbroner

1 FIRST ACQUAINTANCE WITH A MASTER SEMINARIAN

I first made Adolph Lowe's acquaintance just after the Second World War, when I registered at the New School for Social Research with vague intentions of taking some graduate courses in economics. I was drawn to Lowe's class by the course title – Theories of Economic Growth – rather than by his name, of which I had never heard, and I found myself with twenty-odd other students of various ages and appearances rather anxiously waiting to see what our professor would be like. Perhaps half, like myself, had studied economics before the war and were testing the water to see if graduate work seemed a propitious direction in which to go. A handful of 'older' men, in their forties and fifties, were identifiable as bankers or businessmen because they wore business suits. Many of them were German and, unlike myself, had come to hear the man, not to explore the subject. The rest were casual students who had drifted in more or less by accident, in search of a pleasant, interesting, not too demanding evening: few of this last contingent lasted for the second class.

At the table before us sat a small, trim, bespectacled man, already grey and bald, who looked at us with as much curiosity as we at him. He was sorting through the registration cards that we had filled out with the details of our past studies, our occupations, our intentions. We watched as he perused our brief biographies one by one, his face registering doubts, interest, and occasional consternation. Each of us wondered which expression was produced by our own card. The perusal once concluded, reading lists and a thin pile of notes were produced from an ancient briefcase, a professorial throat was cleared, and the lecture began. For myself and the other graduate students, and for the older contingent, there was no doubt from that moment that this was the course we were looking for.

Lowe was an extraordinary teacher. His notes were meticulously organized, with main divisions, subdivisions, and key words to indicate the points of the subject to be discussed, but as he spoke he seemed barely to glance at the outline; only after we studied our own notes later did we realize how perfectly organized was the underlying thesis. His delivery was easy and conversational, but like his expressive face it revealed his own appraisal of things all too clearly – eyebrows raised when he was presenting a doubtful case, the expression stern when he was himself deeply interested in the argument, eyes flashing when he was picking apart a specious argument. Much later, after I had myself gone beyond being his student, Lowe told me that in his own student days in Germany before the First World War, his nickname had been 'the monk'. I can guess the reason, especially in the light of what I have read of student life in Germany in those years. Half a century after that initial introduction I can still recall the sense of being inducted by a master seminarian into an undertaking that would require the devotion – although certainly not the unquestioning belief – of high theology. I was not the only one to feel the appeal of this passionate intellectuality. Within a month we were all Lowe's disciples, and most of us – bankers and businessmen, as well as students – remained that way for life.

2   'SOCIOLOGICAL' CHALLENGES TO ECONOMIC THEORY

Lowe's dramatic, yet carefully constructed style was the perfect vehicle for his intellectual message. That message had begun very much in the tradition of his most influential teachers, Franz Oppenheimer and Lujo Brentano. Its distinctive character was an attempt to illumine history by revealing within it the workings of a powerful, order-bestowing force. This was, of course, the force of economics, working its effects in the dynamics of accumulation and in the allocative pressures of the market, both of these effects tempered and shaped by technological and psychological influences generally grouped under the heading of 'sociology'.

This was a very far cry from the simple Keynesian economics that we students had learned during the late 1930s, when technology never entered our heads; and even more different from the economics of the 'older' students in Lowe's class who had never heard of liquidity preference. What Lowe added to our naive conceptions of economics was an understanding of the complications introduced by these 'sociological' considerations in two specific forms.

The first was a recognition of the effects of technological constraints and requirements on the accumulation process itself. This was an interest that Lowe had picked up from his studies of Marx, who was the first economist to divide all economic activity into two imaginary sectors – Department I occupied solely with producing capital goods, and Department II solely with consumption goods. Lowe now separated Department I into two subdepartments – Department Ia devoted to the production of self-reproducing capital goods (Lowe's exemplar was machine tools), and Department Ib devoted to the ordinary plant and equipment used by Department II. Later these subdivisions of Department I came to play a strategic role in Lowe's work on the path of economic growth and its 'traverses' from one trajectory to another. The second 'sociological' element was derived from Keynes and Hicks. It concerned the dependency of market outcomes on the expectations held by marketers – an approach that made it impossible to use 'supply and demand' as if they always produced the end results that simple neoclassical theory expected.

We did not then realize that this 'sociological' view was a considerable advance from Lowe's earlier work, such as his widely-known article 'Wie ist Konjunkturtheorie überhaupt möglich?' (1926). Lowe had answered the question by asserting that a theory of business-cycle fluctuations was possible only because 'laws' of behaviour imposed a dependable regularity over the flux of events. In those days Lowe himself had not yet fully grasped the relationship of that law-governed behaviour to the problems of expectations or structures of production. Indeed, even during the years when we encountered him at the New School, Lowe remained essentially within the general fold of 'positive' economic thought, in so far as the disruptive influences of 'sociology', although increasingly recognized as presenting unavoidable problems for the maintenance of orderly growth, were not seen as also posing profound challenges to economic theory itself.

That truly decisive change came during the late 1950s and early 1960s as Lowe began work on what would become *On Economic Knowledge*, first published in 1965. By that time I had moved from student to colleague and even intimate, and was engaged in an endless exchange of letters in which we reviewed and criticized each other's work. I was then working on *The Future as History* and my letters to Adolph (it had only taken me ten years to call him by his first name) were largely sighs of woe and frustration, to which his responses were sympathetic and encouraging. Lowe's letters were more analytic. I remember writing to him that I was charmed by the nymph EXPRI, an acronym – as I best remember – for the 'extremum principle' that was Lowe's phrase for maximization under conditions of static expectations.[1]

What I have not forgotten was the deeper concern beneath the search for analytical exactitude. The concern sprang from Lowe's dawning recognition that EXPRI would only be the prevailing form of behaviour in a society whose prevailing level of affluence and simplicity of production enforced very short-term horizons for both buyers and sellers. In a word, the 'sociology' of a well-working capitalist system required both uncomplicated production processes and markets in which there was no possibility of a postponement of sales on the part of producers, or of purchases on the part of buyers. To put it differently, the presence of destabilizing expectations could only be assured in a society whose production and consumption were both governed by immediate necessity. Summing up these conditions, Lowe wrote in *On Economic Knowledge*:

> Thus the claim to universal validity of traditional theory amounts to the hypothetical perpetuation of a society *in extremis*. But is this an economic *society*? Rather than freely and deliberately choosing among alternatives, its members are forced to respond in a pseudo-mechanical manner to pseudo-mechanical stimuli. Or to use another metaphor, they are supposed to behave like hungry rats driven through the windings of their maze by conditioned reflexes – not as men aware of a field of interaction with other men, in which all pursue freely chosen goals. Thus incorporation of the pertinent environmental factors into the (economic) model, far from contradicting its natural science origin, only confirms its affinity with the world of the subhuman. At the same time, it emphasizes once more the merely marginal significance of traditional theory as an explanatory and predictive tool, and the need for breaking through a logical framework in which human action and interaction are reduced to the play of blind natural forces.[2]

3   THE INSTRUMENTAL METHOD OF LOWE'S POLITICAL ECONOMICS

From this conclusion there follows logically the inversion of economic theory that lies at the core of Lowe's 'instrumental' economic theorizing. Traditional 'positive' economics starts from empirical givens, adds the impact of the economic variable(s) at play, and predicts the resulting changes in the system's configuration. This is a path that Lowe was no longer interested in pursuing, partly because of his scepticism with respect to the predictability of the system, partly for the moral and political reasons set forth above. *On Economic Knowledge* therefore goes in an entirely new direction. Its objective is not to clarify still further the shape of things to come. It is to deduce from the existing shape of things the steps needed to attain the goals that society sets for itself.

As the term 'instrumental' indicates, economics thereby changes the specification of its own theoretical mission from a means of prediction to one of goal attainment. This does not mean, of course, that the economist cannot warn against unattainable goals, or that he or she can guarantee the achievement of 'realistic' ones. It means only that the task of the economist is to *deduce* what flows of labour and capital will be required to move from an existing configuration of society to a desired one; then to specify what behavioural paths must be followed to give rise to these flows; and from that to prescribe the incentives and stimuli most likely to bring about that desired behaviour.

It is this last step that is crucial. Despite the redirection of economic theory from final ends to intermediate means, a predictive vulnerability remains. Suppose that society, through its political processes, opts for a policy of high-employment, low-inflation growth. But suppose further that the combination of monetary and fiscal measures calculated to attain this end does not produce the desired result. In itself, this would be tantamount to a predictive failure, much like that of positive economics.

There is, however, a saving element in the instrumental conception. It is the recognition that because policy prescriptions inevitably contain a predictive element with respect to their effectiveness, the design of policy must take the form of a spectrum of means. Thus instrumental economics would normally comprise a range of interventions, beginning with mild stimuli and constraints, but also encompassing a series of increasingly stringent means to achieve the desired end. At the limit would lie the maximum degree of direct intervention that the political process would permit – perhaps large-scale fiscal stimulation and direct public employment programmes; strong anti-inflationary tax measures, even price controls. The range of intervention would thereby be determined by political consent, just as would the initial decision to resort to policy determinations. In this way, the importance of economics is both reduced and enhanced under Lowe's instrumental vision – reduced in so far as its science-like status is considerably diminished; enhanced in so far as economics becomes the enabling agency of society itself.

4   BALANCING FREEDOM AND ORDER

Thus instrumental economics is quintessentially political, not only in its conscious awareness of the subordination of economic theory to political will, but also in its acute awareness that political economics, like any other form of social policy, must be kept within the bounds of democratic government.

Here biography and intellectual development served to reinforce one another. From the vantage point of an active economic official in the Weimar Republic, Lowe had watched with growing apprehension the economic deterioration of Germany. Thereafter he experienced at first hand the terrifying descent into fascism. During the early days of the Hitler regime, the Lowe family lived with bags packed, ready to leave the country at a moment's notice. The moment came in 1933 when Lowe's two daughters, Rachel and Hanna, were sent home from school because they were Jewish. The packed bags were thereupon picked up, and the family spent the night in a hotel. The following morning, together with his wife Beatrice and his two daughters, Lowe went to the station and uneventfully boarded the first train to Switzerland. On the following day he returned to Germany alone, went to his bank, withdrew the family's funds, and calmly returned to his Swiss refuge. In April 1933, Adolph Lowe was dismissed from his position at Frankfurt University – one of the first social science professors to be fired under a new law that permitted the authorities to let professors go for racial or political views. Adolph was always very proud of the fact that it was the second reason that was cited in his case.

I introduce this story to emphasize that Lowe was acquainted at first hand with the dangers of political power. Hence it may seem inconsistent that he should have advocated a redirection of economic theory that legitimated and expanded economic power, rather than one that subordinated it to the workings of unimpeded economic processes. The reason, as I hope the foregoing brief exposition has made clear, was his increasingly strong conviction that such a *laissez-faire* minimization of economic power would itself pose the very danger against which it was presumably the remedy – namely, economic dysfunction on a scale sufficiently large to create sociopolitical instability, with its ultimate threat of authoritarian and totalitarian 'solutions'.

For Lowe, instrumentalism was therefore a means of avoiding the economic frustrations from which political dangers sprang. But how to avoid, or at least minimize, the risks that obviously accompanied the deliberate strengthening of economic policy-making? Here once more a biographical note may serve a clarifying purpose. A few months after his successful flight to Switzerland, Lowe was able to secure a teaching position at the University of Manchester. In England he discovered a political climate very much to his liking. It was marked by what he called, in a famous pamphlet, *The Price of Liberty* (1937), a 'spontaneous conformity' that provided 'from within' the necessary orderliness that every viable society required.

That vision of a benign force of self-restraint as the basis for a successful democratic social order became an abiding reference point throughout Lowe's subsequent career. In his last book, *Has Freedom a Future?* (1988), Lowe spells out the political philosophy that undergirds his instrumental economic vision. We live, he tells us, in an age of 'emancipation' which has two contradictory effects. On the one hand, it enlarges our individual spheres of competence and freedom; on the other hand, it brings the spectre of anarchy, as the self-disciplining force of conformity weakens. The question is then posed as to how freedom is to be safeguarded in such a world. Lowe poses the answer in a paradox: '*Freedom is safe only so long as it is associated with certain constraints*.[3] The italics are his, not mine. In turn, these safeguards will only emerge in a society that performs well above the 'critical threshold of instability'. The welfare state, in which an instrumental economics establishes the central guide to policy and a disinterested civil service offers the advice on which a consensual public policy can be formed, then constitutes the framework within which a free society can be preserved.

5   A WORDLY PHILOSOPHER

This is no more than the briefest sketch of Lowe's political economics. I have not attempted to examine in depth the premises or the analytic apparatus of Lowe's argument, but only to lay out its basic structure as a whole. I should, however, add a word as to a consideration that may have crossed the reader's mind. It is not a difficult matter to criticize many of the arguments in both *On Economic Knowledge* and *Has Freedom a Future?*. That which is difficult is to find a better or more workable answer to the questions that Lowe poses – namely, how can economics best serve the aims of a democratic society, and what structure of society seems most likely to preserve a commitment to political liberty?

Let me now conclude on a personal note. In the spring of 1993, I spoke at Frankfurt University at a meeting to celebrate Lowe's 100th birthday. Lowe himself was too weak to be able to attend, but I heard many lovely words of praise at the ceremony; I spoke myself; and later I had the great pleasure of bringing to Lowe at his home in Wolfenbüttel, the Goethe medallion of which he had been designated as the first recipient.

When I spoke at Frankfurt, I began by asking how it was that a young man in Germany could have escaped military service in the tense days just before the First World War. The audience was silent. I then gave the answer that I had heard from Adolph Lowe himself. He had indeed been called up for military service, and was duly summoned for inspection by an Army doctor. After a thorough examination, the doctor turned to Lowe with a grave face. 'I regret very much to tell you', he said, 'that we cannot accept you into service. You have a very weak heart.' I said to the audience: 'Would that we all had such weak hearts!'. I did not speak only of my beloved teacher's longevity, but of his moral courage, his commitment to high goals, his sense of vocation.

One final personal reminiscence. After I had studied with Lowe for several years I conceived the idea of writing the history of the great economists, with special emphasis on the marvellous socioeconomic scenarios about which I had learned so much from Lowe himself. When I mentioned this to Lowe, he was aghast. Drawing himself up to his full height, his arms akimbo, he said to me with the immense authority that he embodied: 'That you cannot do!'. But I thought that perhaps I could, and without telling Lowe, I produced the first three chapters which I very nervously gave him one day after class.

It is my own favourite measure of the man that after the next class he called me to one side, produced my pages, and said with the same magisterial authority 'That you must do!'. With his help – half inspiration, half *Beckmesser* – that is what I did. In the most recent edition of that book, *The Worldly Philosophers,* I have had the immense pleasure of including Adolph Lowe himself, together with this anecdote (Heilbroner 1986:8). He does not appear as the last of the great scenarists of a self-steering economic society, for reasons that must be clear. He enters, instead, as the person who has sought to open a new chapter for economics as a means to help society find its way through the difficult challenges ahead.

NOTES

1.   A small portion of this correspondence, largely Lowe's letters to myself, is available in the library of the New School for Social Research.
2.   Adolph Lowe, *On Economic Knowledge*, New York: Harper & Row, 1965, pp. 126–7.
3.   Adolph Lowe, *Has Freedom a Future?*, New York: Praeger, 1988, p. XXVII.

REFERENCES

Heilbroner, R.L. (1961), *The Future as History*, New York: Grove Press.
Heilbroner, R.L. (1986), *The Wordly Philosophers. The Lives, Times, and Ideas of the Great Economic Thinkers*, Sixth edition, New York: Simon & Schuster.

3. The Shaping of a German Scholar – Adolph Lowe's Early Intellectual Biography

Claus-Dieter Krohn

1   INFLUENCING FACTORS OF LOWE'S EARLY INTELLECTUAL DEVELOPMENT

When forty years ago the walls of the hall of mirrors in Versailles shook with the enthusiastic cheers of four hundred voices after the imperial proclamation had been read out, its sound reached far beyond the borders of France, well into our homeland, and an inexpressible, outgoing and yet inward feeling of happiness moved our people. This was not the expression of a flush of victory, nor was it simply the expression of love for the aged sovereign and his heroes, rather, it was the sigh of relief after the relaxation of the pressure that had weighed upon us for centuries, the relieved wakening from a long and oppressive dream: the spirits were placated, our people had become united again. ... The significance of this reunification reached far beyond the countries directly involved. Europe now has a strong centre. A new, firmly established state has entered the circle of world powers with fresh strength, ready to devote its entire fortune to progress and culture. It was this national unification which helped us to become what the men of enlightenment hoped to achieve by dissolving all national ties: true citizens of the world.

Thus culminated the ceremonial speech delivered by the seventeen-year-old student Adolf Löwe[1] during the celebration organized by his Stuttgart Gymnasium on the occasion of the fortieth anniversary of the foundation of the German Reich on 18 January 1911. Those who are familiar with his later scientific work may be surprised by the national ardour. There was nothing missing from the terminological arsenal of the Wilhelminian middle class: the development of the idea of German unity under Prussian leadership, the weak German liberalism without tight organization or strong political will, the 'mighty despot' Bismarck as executor of the German unification, and, finally, 'the war with France (1870) which was forced on us for trivial causes' and in which German unity was 'cemented with blood'.[2]

This, Lowe's earliest written testimony, reflects in a terse and precise manner the socialization constraints of contemporary education through which even very young students were indoctrinated with the frozen, premodern patterns of the *Kaiserreich*'s intellectual mandarins: affirmative overaccentuation of state and nationality; the German unification, during

15

which freedom fell by the wayside; and although enlightenment is mentioned, it is also criticized for its neglect of 'all national ties'. Typical for this intellectual tradition of the nineteenth-century educated middle class was that it reduced the rational universalism of the enlightenment to the religious individualism of authoritarian Lutherism, which shaped the national unification under Prussian leadership. And it was not without reason that, even a few years later, in his writings on current political events during the breakdown of the *Kaiserreich*, Adolph Lowe was to take Luther as an example for the new social order: 'The present historic moment resembles in its grandeur the day on which the monk from Wittenberg pinned the charter of personality on the door of oppressive brotherhood'.[3]

At first sight, the statements of the young Lowe appear the more strange since he came from a liberal Southern-German family of Jewish descent. Yet, the 'Prussian view' was very common among assimilated German Jews, in particular, because to them Prussia symbolized not only the military and authoritarian society but also the constitutional rule which was the first of the later German Reich to accord equal status to Jews as citizens in the course of modernization 'from the top' initiated by the bureaucracy at the beginning of the nineteenth century. Despite the modern racial anti-semitism which determined the ideology of parts of the shaken middle classes since the 1870s, following the rapid takeoff of the industrial revolution, integration at the turn of the century had progressed so far that many Jews had cut their earlier religious ties. Therefore it was certainly not unusual that a student such as Lowe should present the ceremonial address on the anniversary of the foundation of the Reich.

The disruptions in the subsequent sociopolitical development in Germany – the breakdown of the *Kaiserreich* following the onset of the First World War, the crises of the short-lived Weimar Republic, and then the barbarism of National Socialism after 1933 – had a strong impact on Lowe's intellectual development. His future thinking was to reflect not only these constantly new experiences, which revealed to him that the world view he had been taught at school was one of great distortion. It was furthermore to be determined by a political understanding of science that went beyond the narrow limits of all specialization. It shows – and this is why his analyses are so interesting from today's point of view – that in future he would always remain sceptical about any traditions of thought restricted to specific disciplines and about conventional political ideologies. Thus, in order to describe his intellectual development the following variables have to be stressed: the intellectual traditions of his prescientific and scientific origins, the academic institutions at which he worked, as well as the different political systems or structures under which his work developed.

Lowe's early public commitment took a new turn when, as a young law student, he took part in the campaign of the *Fortschrittliche Volkspartei* (Progressive People's Party) for the election of the German *Reichstag* in 1912. This election is of historical importance because for the first time the left-wing liberal bourgeoisie entered into an alliance with the Social Democrats, who had until then been denounced as '*vaterlandslose Gesellen*' ('unpatriotic fellows') by the Wilhelminian authorities; this alliance was to become the backbone of the so-called Weimar coalition after 1918. Lowe's early political orientation also clearly influenced his novice scientific work. He went to Berlin to become a student of Franz von Liszt, one of the founders of sociological criminology, who also had represented the Progressive Party in the *Reichstag* since 1912. There, as early as in his sixth semester, he presented a study on the relation between unemployment and crime which was so important that it was published in book form in 1914, and which, so far, has lost nothing of its topicality. In this study Lowe furnished empirical proof that the abatement of violent crime since the end of the nineteenth century was not least due to the influence of the growing unions which, with their subscriptions, not only helped to alleviate social misery but which, through their organization, also had a positive influence on the workers' sociopolitical attitude. It is noteworthy that this study necessitated investigations in a field which also prepared Lowe's later scientific research: although exact criminal statistics were available in Germany, comparable surveys on unemployment and on social development were still lacking, so that through painstaking detailed work he had to collect these data from diverse economic indicators from the foundation of the German Reich onwards.[4]

2   A LEADING BUREAUCRAT IN THE YOUNG WEIMAR REPUBLIC

Lowe's study of economic problems grew more intensive during the First World War. After a short period of military service, from which he was discharged in 1915 for health reasons, one of his academic teachers, the theorist of cooperatism Franz Oppenheimer, found him a post as secretary with a private research group, the *Kriegswirtschaftliche Vereinigung* (Association of Wartime Economy), which dealt with issues of a future postwar order. Both this association and the *Volksbund für Freiheit und Vaterland* (People's Alliance for Freedom and Fatherland), a collective movement of representatives of the Progressive Party and unionists formed in protest at the *Vaterlandspartei* (Fatherland Party), founded in 1917 – a first pre-fascist German mass organization which had emerged against the background of the impending military defeat – brought him closer to both Social Democracy and the Unions.

As early as 1916, Lowe submitted a first study on *Wirtschaftliche Demobilisierung* (Economic Demobilization) to the *Kriegswirtschaftliche Vereinigung* and in numerous newspaper articles he presented this topic to a broader public. Contrary to the then widespread optimism with regard to a German victory (*Siegfrieden*) Lowe – as far as censorship allowed him to do so – repeatedly indicated that the war with its until then unimaginable dimensions would lastingly influence the future of every sphere of social and economic life, independent of its outcome. It is remarkable that these early works already suggested the topic of his later analyses. Demobilization for Lowe indicated not only the gradual removal of war economy but, rather, the maintenance of a public control system which was to regulate the future peace economy by setting macro-goals, that is, of what is nowadays understood by an infrastructure policy. This includes, for instance, public job creation and what was then referred to by the term 'inner colonization', namely agricultural reorganization.[5]

To this end a detailed scheme had already been developed in the spring of 1918, but its publication was prevented by the authorities. Representatives of both large-scale industry and the big landed property had heard about it and thought that through such proposals Socialism would be propagated throughout Germany. They contacted the Prussian ministry of war, which itself suspected that these schemes represented a defeatist interference with the German will to win.

The only result of this activity was that, at the breakdown of the *Kaiserreich*, Lowe was called to the demobilization office, set up by the provisional Social Democratic government in November 1918, after he had passed his examination in law in 1915 and finished his doctoral thesis in 1918. Thus began his seven-year career as a member of the *Reichsverwaltung* (administration of the Reich). In 1919 he exchanged his post in the demobilization office for that of an assistant to the new Minister of Labour, a former union leader, before entering the ministry of economics, which had also been newly created during the November Revolution. There he first took over the section for nationalization and then worked for the department of reparations, for which he wrote, for instance, the extensive memoranda submitted by the government of the German Reich to the Genoa conference on international economic problems in 1922 and to the Paris conference on the regulation of reparation payments (Dawes Plan) in 1924.[6] After the Social Democrats' loss of power during the years of inflation, the younger, more critical staff hardly stood a chance in the mostly conservative economic administration. Thus, in 1924, Lowe was transferred to the German Statistical Office in Berlin. There, he joined in the development of new quantitative approaches to the study of economic development modelled by Wesley C. Mitchell at the National Bureau of Economic Research in the United States. Because of his work in this field, Lowe was among those who founded the Institute for Business Cycle Research in 1925.

In the final stage of the First World War, Lowe experienced closely the failure of the Imperial Establishment, whose members did not want to admit their defeat and who – with the myth of the 'stab in the back' – tried to shuffle off their responsibility on to others. Furthermore, he witnessed the ethics of responsibility demonstrated by the Social Democrats, who, in November 1918, took on the political assets of a bankrupt Reich without having any administrative experience or being in any way prepared for this. This caused him to revise completely his previous views. That this intellectual clarification was rather existential is shown by a first programmatic article, the only one in his decade-long activity in which he deals self-critically with his Jewish origin. In it he severely takes to task the undesirable developments of the emancipation of Jews, which – although it had been an ambitious goal of Enlightenment – had only granted them human rights at the price of their identity. The ensuing assimilation had led to servile overadaptation, so that, by the turn of the century, no one was more deeply entangled in the ruling powers than the Jews.

However, the solution he defined was not that of a return to Jewry, the 'romantic way to the organism of the national community', or that of the national regeneration aimed at by Zionism, which for Lowe was nothing but a 'flight away from an infectious ailing Europe', but rather the active formation of a 'new human community', and this, to him, was Socialism. Whether this was achieved through 'dedication to the humiliated and offended of the world' or whether the new construction of a 'socialist communal life' was built from the ruins of the social order destroyed in 1918 was but a question of temperament.[7]

Lowe's deduction of Socialism from 'the sources of Judaic doctrine' is characteristic for it implied the repudiation of a concept of Socialism deduced by intellectuals of bourgeois origin, in particular, from the material promises of Liberalism that were never really redeemed. Lowe's rejection of the liberal construct of the *homo oeconomicus* exclusively oriented by material objectives, which became more emphatic in his later economic studies, is already manifest both in these early writings in which he defined his personal position and in his practical work. This liberal dogma and the pretence of a harmony based more or less on natural law, which deluded men into believing they all had equal opportunities, had been a 'lie'. The deformations of the uncoordinated boosting of technology and business made new moral demands: 'the limitation of the free development of the individual personality'. To put this into effect, Lowe called for 'social democracy', in which the political self-determination of the individual was to be combined with a responsible organization of the social environment. Here, Lowe for the first time hinted at the sociopolitical tension between liberty and order, which was to become the leitmotiv of his future economic work.

He wanted to start with having all parts of the society join in the vast task of transferring the war organization into a peace economy through 'direct democracy'. Therefore he propagated the socialist council constitution not only in his journalistic writings. As assistant to the Reich's Minister of Labour he also belonged to the advisers of the national assembly in Weimar at the beginning of 1919, and was largely responsible for the formulation of Article 165 of the new constitution of the Reich concerned with the workers' councils and the economic councils.[8]

Lowe's religiously substantiated concept of Socialism was also to lead him into the circle of the religious socialists which had begun to develop around the Protestant theologian Paul Tillich in early 1919. This group of brothers-in-arms who fought for the same ideas was active not only throughout the 1920s, but its members maintained their close ties after their emigration in 1933, with Tillich, Lowe, and the economist Eduard Heimann in New York as the main centre. Many socialists found their intellectual focus in this circle for, since the early 1920s, Social Democracy more and more wavered indecisively between the old Marxist doctrines and a pragmatic approach to political problems and, with its bureaucratically encrusted party apparatus, offered hardly any ideas regarding the design of the new German democracy. In this circle, concepts of a socialist reform policy were discussed which dealt both with the failure of the official Christian churches as regards the social question and with the determinist degeneration of socialist theory. They wanted to combine the emotional promises of Christian moral principles with the social theory of a real Marxism. Socialism was conceived as the prophecy of a secular religion which was oriented not by the hereafter of the kingdom of God but, rather, by the social responsibility and justice of the present.[9] This was also calculated to appeal to the subjective needs of wide sections of the middle classes, and it was to this end, in particular, that a journal was founded after the Great Depression of 1929: the *Neue Blätter für den Sozialismus*. However, it became apparent that, under economic threat, these groups which were used to the protection provided by the Wilhelminian authoritarian state sought refuge under authoritarian and fascist forms of organizations instead of forming the desired socialist alliance.

3   ACADEMIC CAREER IN KIEL AND FRANKFURT

Lowe's career as university teacher began in 1926, when he was offered a professorship by the director of the Kiel Institute of World Economics. He had already been working there as lecturer since 1924 which gave him the opportunity to use the Institute's extensive library to collect material for his work in the Statistical Office in Berlin. The Kiel Institute, founded in 1914, had probably accumulated the largest stock of books and journals on world economic issues in Germany; however, a scientific treatment of this material had as yet not been undertaken. Now the newly appointed professor was to set up a separate research apparatus for 'statistical world economics and international business cycle research'. To this end, Lowe, together with Gerhard Colm and Hans Neisser, hired several first-class experts who, just like him, had gathered practical experience with macroecomonic problems in the economic offices of the Reich. This Kiel group was complemented by the part-time cooperation of both the emigrated Russian Menshevik Jacob Marschak, who, during the 1940s, belonged to the founders of modern econometrics in the United States, and his compatriot, the future Nobel prize winner Wassily Leontief. Their work was so innovative that they soon won recognition well beyond the German borders. For instance, the Rockefeller Foundation, which – in view of the worldwide unresolved economic problems of the postwar years – had launched an international research project to combat the crisis, soon considered the Kiel Institute the 'Mecca' of German business-cycle research and gave not only extensive financial support, but also sent over younger American scholars for research purposes.[10] The practical orientation of the scientific concept of the Kiel Institute also induced the government of the Reich to coordinate the so-called 'Enquete Commission' it had established after 1926 at that same institute. Until the early 1930s, this commission carried out the first and largest general survey on the structure of the German economy ever to have been organized, published in more than 60 volumes.

The cooperation within the Kiel circle proved so stimulating and fertile that even fifty years later, Lowe still considered this period the height of his scientific career.[11] However, in 1931 he accepted an offer from the young University of Frankfurt, which had been founded after the war and which tried to impart modern social sciences in particular. There, he again met his friend Paul Tillich who had come from Berlin to Frankfurt shortly before Lowe's arrival. He also met again his former schoolfellow Max Horkheimer, director of the Institute of Social Research, which was to become very famous, and, finally, Karl Mannheim, founder of the sociology of knowledge. The university curator Kurt Riezler had carefully appointed this team of scholars to make Frankfurt a pathbreaking academic centre. Their numerous interdisciplinary projects and seminars prepared a cooperation which was to become an intellectually and emotionally important stabilizing factor during Lowe's exile after 1933.

The many phases of his entering into science, which led past diverse agencies of practical economic policy, already offer a key to the questions dealt with by Lowe and his friends. Furthermore, there is the state of affairs of economics in Germany at that time. The so-called '*Staatswissenschaften*' were often but an appendix to the Faculty of Law and were still represented by the champions of the old Historical School of economics as late as the 1920s. This trend was a typical product of the development of the German authoritarian state. Having its origins in the eighteenth-century tradition of feudal-absolutist mercantilism, this school was one of the harshest critics of Anglo-Saxon classical political economy and rejected any form of timeless economic laws. It considered the economy a function of the state, which was to prescribe the course of development through administrative regulations. However, this did not imply that the representatives of the Historical School discussed concrete and detailed perspectives of action as regarded public intervention. Rather, in their so-called 'theory of economic stages', they were concerned with observing the preceding developments and with the general phenomenology of forms of intervention. On the other hand, the small number of champions of modern economic theory, the neoclassicists, who, within the German-speaking area, flocked together mainly along the Austrian periphery, had hardly anything to contribute either to an up-to-date analysis of the economic process or to an adequate economic policy. Absorbed in a deductive model, they quarrelled until the end of the 1920s about the theory of values, the opposition of labour theory of value to that of marginal utility: only in 1929 did a first systematic article on the business cycle appear from the neoclassical viewpoint, in a supplement volume of the authoritative handbook of economics, the *Handwörterbuch der Staatswissenschaften*.[12]

Against this background it is not surprising that, in his first articles, the new professor at the Kiel Institute at first dealt severely with the self-sufficiency of the contemporary economic approaches. These early works focused on the formulation of a realistic theory which was to supply instruments for operational measures of economic policy.[13] Details will not be given here,[14] we shall merely note that as a basis for this his analyses centred on the cyclical movements, which he considered a typical endogenous form of industrial development. In contrast to the neoclassicists, who – if at all – only dealt with the cycle and its special variety of a crisis, for which they could only state exogenous reasons, for example, the subjective disposition of ingenious entrepreneurs (J.A.

Schumpeter) or monetary measures of the banking system (R.G. Hawtrey in Great Britain or F.A. Hayek in Austria), Lowe and his Kiel colleagues regarded technical progress as the decisive determinant of dynamic, cyclical changes. With this they took up the line of reasoning of the classicists and in particular of the theory of cycles first systematically described by Marx in his reproduction schema, according to which the capitalist production process continuously leads to disproportionalities and crises due, among other things, to technical innovations and the ensuing displacement of workers. As opposed to the neoclassicists, whose arguments were demand-oriented and based on the theory of marginal utility, the Kiel reform economists with their analysis of the production process are therefore nowadays designated as 'new classicists' or 'post classicists'. Their approach was empirically substantiated by the wave of rapid rationalization starting in the mid-1920s, with which the German economy tried to reduce the cost pressure following the phase of easy money during the inflation, a measure which led to chronic unemployment of more than one million people, with upward tendency, even before the outbreak of the Great Depression of 1929.

While, during the first years following the First World War, Lowe and his colleagues had been mainly occupied with collecting economic statistical data, they now used these as a basis on which to formulate a realistic theory of the economic process. Finally, in a third step, they drew the necessary politico-economic conclusions from this. Thus, they demanded an 'active business-cycle policy', that is, structural policy through which the 'unleashed dynamics of our age' were to be tamed. Through macroeconomic control mechanisms they wanted above all to canalize the decisions of private enterprise in order to achieve balanced growth in the different sectors, full employment, and a just income distribution.

Gerhard Colm, for instance, developed a detailed financial model in which the national budget, through government expenditures, was assigned an actively compensatory role in the economic process. This was trailblazing in that the traditional financial theory had merely considered the public income from the point of view of an undisturbed availability of taxes. Here, for the first time, a way was shown to overcome the procyclical negative effects of the national budget *vis-à-vis* the immensely increasing public responsibilities after the First World War. And ten years earlier than Wassily Leontief, Lowe's student Alfred Kähler, in his doctoral thesis, developed a first, simple input–output model.[15] Based on these works the Kiel circle, after the start of the Great Depression and singularly within German science, offered proposals concerning an active anti-cyclical policy for overcoming the crisis which later on, however, was internationally connected with the name of Keynes. Yet, their recommendations went far beyond what the British economist intended. Whereas Keynes in his model took the technical structure for granted and, through an effective increase in demand by means of public deficit spending, aimed at the elimination of unemployment, which he considered to be of short duration, the Kiel economists regarded the control of the technological structure of the economy as the basic problem. They did not interpret the worldwide unemployment in the industrial countries after 1929 as a cyclical phenomenon but, rather, as the expression of a far-reaching structural crisis.

For Lowe, therefore, it meant 'barking at the moon and misjudging the reciprocal structural connections of the capitalist economy and of the capitalist state if one tried to emancipate the political sphere without changing the economic structure'. While the German Social Democrats, referring ever more directly to Keynes, adopted the concept of the anti-cyclical policy, Lowe saw in this approach of merely reactive public intervention only a 'deformation' which brought about nothing but 'an increase in power of the big economic interests to which bureaucracy was now surrendered, too'. Instead, he demanded that fundamentally new horizons were to be opened up so as to be able to design the 'switch tower' of a new organizing model.[16]

This did not refer to the economy alone. Just as he had already emphasized the educational value of the trade unions in his early study on unemployment and crime (*Arbeitslosigkeit und Kriminalität*, 1914), Lowe, in his role as university teacher, repeatedly commented on educational topics, not only in Germany but also later on, in exile. In a more extensive study of 1931, for instance, he dealt with the state of affairs of the German universities which, in the tradition of the great reformer Wilhelm von Humboldt of the early nineteenth century, still preserved the ideal of the free humanist personality designed for a small elite and which failed to educate the young academics to become democratic citizens. Through a long overdue educational reform he expected to replace the until then unlimited freedom of learning by fixed curricula which qualified students for a realistic analysis and mastering of real social problems.[17] While the universities, constituted along authoritarian lines, traditionally allowed young students to make the most of academic freedom, only to adjust themselves the more quietly to a life as subjects later in their professional careers, Lowe wanted a critically active citizen who was to acquire at the university practical knowledge which was to qualify him or her for democratic participation. And it was not without good reason that he and his friends from Kiel or from the circle of the religious socialists belonged to those scholars who also spoke up for mass education outside of the university, at institutions of adult education or when addressing the trade unions.

However, the illusionary character of this commitment soon became evident. The universities offered no resistance to the rise of National Socialism. On the contrary, under the tacit benevolence of many professors, the German student body became the first nazified social group. And many of the scientific elites deliberately used the crisis for the disintegration of the unloved republic and for the reestablishment of an authoritarian rule. It is remarkable how Lowe's outlook radicalized in the final phase of the Weimar Republic. Because the economic crisis had lost its purifying function, owing to the existence of cartels and monopolies, and furthermore endangered the entire political system, the only thing he considered feasible was a radical reconstruction of the entire social order – 'the horse can only bolt to the front' – which was to start with the nationalization of big industry.[18]

Those were Lowe's last words in Germany at the end of 1932. They reveal the deep feeling of insecurity and disillusionment which had seized him and many others of the younger critical social scientists. At that time he already suspected that he might soon 'get thrown out'. A few weeks later the National Socialists came into power. On 2 April 1933, immediately after the first large-scale boycott of Jews organized by the new government, he left Germany with his family, thus anticipating his official dismissal through the so-called 'Law for the Restoration of the Professional Civil Service' in early April. The intellectual prominence Lowe had gained in Germany may be illustrated by the fact that among the expelled scientists he belonged to the small circle of those who were also officially expatriated by the National Socialists.[19]

4 REFLECTIONS OF LOWE'S EARLY INTELLECTUAL BIOGRAPHY IN HIS LATER MACROSOCIAL ANALYSIS

Since the autumn of 1932, Lowe had administered the affairs of the Frankfurt Institute of Social Research, taking over from Max Horkheimer, who had left for Geneva in anticipation of the imminent end of the Weimar Republic, there to set up emergency quarters. After his escape to Switzerland, Lowe continued to be paid by the Institute out of its private endowment funds, until he, as well as Karl Mannheim and Jacob Marschak, found a position with a British university in the summer of 1933. These contracts were financed out of a large-scale relief programme launched by the Rockefeller Foundation for the rescue of the scholars expelled from Germany.

Lowe accepted the offer by the University of Manchester shortly before he was invited by the New School for Social Research in New York, which planned to set up a complete university-in-exile there. As editor of the recently published comprehensive *Encyclopedia of the Social Sciences*, Alvin Johnson, the director of that institution, knew most of the expelled German scholars because he had been able to recruit them as well as other European scientists as collaborators. Especially from the younger German social scientists, who with their post-1918 publications had contributed to the establishment of the crisis-ridden Weimar Republic, he expected to give new intellectual impetus to an isolationist America and above all to the anti-crisis programme, the New Deal, launched by President Franklin D. Roosevelt, who had just acceded to his office. With Gerhard Colm and Alfred Kähler from Kiel, Emil Lederer from Heidelberg, and Eduard Heimann from Hamburg, the New School won over important spokesmen for reform economics as a first core group for that university-in-exile. Lowe and Marschak, however, only joined up with this circle of old friends at the outbreak of the Second World War, when the universities of Manchester and Oxford did not extend their contracts and the New School together with the Rockefeller Foundation started a renewed relief action for endangered European scholars.[20]

Thanks to the international help Lowe was to be able to continue his academic work after 1933 without major interruptions. However, he had to suspend his studies on economic problems, which he had begun in Kiel and Frankfurt. Economics at the University of Manchester was dominated by the neoclassicist John Jewkes, who looked upon Lowe's scientific approach with scepticism and soon relegated him to the department of political science. And even after his invitation to the New School, Lowe could not immediately continue his research. For there, because of his experience gathered in the debate on demobilization after the First World War, he was appointed director of the new Institute of World Affairs, set up in 1943. This institute coordinated the large number of research projects on the war effort and on a postwar organization of Europe carried out by the emigrants who had been saved by the New School and who, because of their knowledge of the European conditions, now often worked as a think-tank for the Washington administration because as non-naturalized Americans they could not be officially employed by the American authorities. It was only in the 1950s, that Lowe was able to return to his economic studies interrupted in 1933, which, together with the political studies carried out in Manchester, were then to add to his *magnum opus*, *On Economic Knowledge*, published in 1965.[21]

During the 1930s, Lowe had contacts with his discipline only in so far as he became an esteemed counsellor of the relief committees in both the United States and Great Britain. The Rockefeller Foundation, for one, considered him 'A–1, both scientifically and from the point of view of character', and therefore looked upon him as one of the most important informants with regard to the selection of high-quality scholars expelled from Germany who were to be placed with American institutions. He fulfilled the same function for the Academic Assistance Council/Society for the Protection of Science and Learning, founded in 1933 by the director of the London School of Economics, William Beveridge. Its staff, lacking detailed knowledge, also consulted him when hiring German economists for British universities.[22]

However, Lowe's work as a political scientist in Manchester seems to have been all but frustrating for him. It well illustrates the breadth of his scientific interests and his ability to acculturize in this new intellectual environment that, while in Manchester, he produced several remarkable studies which, on the one hand, met his penchant for macrosocial analysis and, on the other hand, similar to his work published after 1918, represented a critical reflection of the shocking experiences of 1933. This applies above all to his short book *The Price of Liberty*. It was characteristically published under the rather personal subtitle of *A German on Contemporary Britain* and went through several editions within a few months; as late as 1948, a new edition was published.

After a first study on *Economics and Sociology*, published in 1935, which drew on the tradition of classical political economy and pleaded for an interdisciplinary cooperation of economics and sociology, Lowe, in *The Price of Liberty*, put both to himself and to the British public the question[23] why a system such as the British, which – to the eye of the outside observer – was so obviously that of a class society still interspersed with many feudal relics, had at that time a far greater stability than the German society. The key explanation for this he saw in the 'spontaneous conformity', which was characterized by a cooperation of all classes, groups and individuals. In the motherland of constitutional self-commitment this conformity had developed in the course of slow, but steady social change and had increasingly extended the individual members' right to participate. Thus subjects turned citizens, to whom the social unity of the society was more important than the complete enforcement of the respective group or class interests. This social structure, for instance, also gave him a hint why, compared to his own reform group, Keynes, during the Great Depression, hardly had to consider more far-reaching sociopolitical consequences in his intervention model.

The German development differed completely, for there the processes of democratization had merely been the enforced, short-term and state-organized result of national catastrophes, as was shown by the Prussian defeat by the Napoleonic armies in 1807, the unsuccessful bourgeois revolution of 1848, or the end of the *Kaiserreich* in 1918. Because of the lack of emancipation, the German bourgeoisie had, since the nineteenth century, cultivated an intellectual and social extremism which had a disintegrating effect, so that social unity could only be maintained authoritatively, through the old bureaucratic–absolutist state apparatus.

The *Price of Liberty* reflects the witnessing of a democracy, namely the British, an experience which was completely new to Lowe. The few years of the Weimar Republic had been marked by traditional ideological camp mentalities, which did not allow compromises to be reached through discourse but, rather, from the very beginning paralysed the first democratic society in Germany through reciprocal antagonism. The behavioural patterns described with the concept of spontaneous conformity were regarded by Lowe as the expression of a mutual horizontal commitment of the citizens to the democratic society. This was governed by the promise of all citizens to vouch for the institutional guarantees of the rights of liberty. The civil self-regulation of the English constitution – and to an even greater extent of the American, which Lowe was to experience a few years later – was unheard of in Germany. Under the authoritarian structures that prevailed there, bonds and obligations could only develop vertically, not between citizens but, rather, between subjects and state power. Thus, Lowe's comparison of the British and the German system culminates in the phrase: 'Spontaneous conformity is the only mode of life through which a large-scale society can reconcile the conflict between freedom and order'.[24]

The systematic application of this insight to the economic and social order was undertaken by Lowe many years later in his major work, *On Economic Knowledge*.[25] The system of political economics developed there is, on the one hand, directed against the scientific fundamentals of the traditions of economic thinking, manifest in the rational principle of 'economic man'. On the other hand, it was made clear that the neoclassical market model had little empirical validity and had only gained significance because, within the political value system of the Western world, it corresponded largely to the ideal of the autonomous personality. Yet, men had never been autonomous in this sense of the word, rather, they were dependent on a large number of social, cultural, institutional and other factors.

Instead of the economic process with its one-dimensional aim of maximizing goods, which was dealt with in the economic sciences in isolation from the society, Lowe defined a competing 'pluralism' of possible production and distribution optima, the achievement of which was not merely a technical problem, but which had to be evaluated in a discourse on politico-social objectives. As an example, he cited the competing interests in handling the as yet unresolved ecological problems. In contrast to the 'positive' method of traditional economics which prognostically deduces a future state of the economy based on the knowledge of the initial data and of the uniform behavioural law of the market camps, Lowe's political economics tries to take the reverse path. First, a socially-desired final state was to be defined for the entire system in an estimable period of time within the democratic process. Afterwards the task of economics has to be that of analysing ways of achieving these goals as well as the necessary conditions. This method is defined in the model of instrumental analysis, which makes the appropriate process of adjustment, the behavioural and motivational variables pertaining to the system of private enterprise, and the adequate public operational controls the focus of its methodological apparatus.

It is the aim of Lowe's political economics to crack the mental sterility of the traditional theory which, with its seemingly causal laws, meant the mental perpetuation of a 'coercive society' which bound its members to a specific economic behaviour. Political economics, on the other hand, does not know any categorical economic imperatives; it does not take value decisions. Its instrumental method merely wants to provide the means for a synthesis of liberty and order. It points out ways not only of realizing stability and social justice and of protecting the endangered fundamentals of life in the process of modern nationalization based on a division of labour, but also of maintaining freedom and spontaneity.

NOTES

1. After his flight from Germany to Great Britain, Löwe was naturalized there at the beginning of the Second World War. The British authorities anglicized his name to Lowe. This version will be used throughout this chapter.
2. 'Festrede anläßlich des Sedantages 1911, gehalten von Adolf Löwe', Realgymnasium Stuttgart, manuscript.
3. A. Löwe (1919), 'Die neue Demokratie', *Der Spiegel*, **1**, pp. 8ff.
4. A. Löwe (1914), *Arbeitslosigkeit und Kriminalität. Eine kriminologische Untersuchung*, Berlin.
5. Labor and A. Lowe (1916), *Wirtschaftliche Demobilisierung*, ed. by the Kriegswirtschaftliche Vereinigung, Berlin; A. Löwe (1917), 'Rücksiedlung aufs Land', *Heer und Heimat*, **2** (28); A. Löwe (1918), 'Die Fragen der Übergangswirtschaft', *Die Woche*, **20**, pp. 612–3 and 637–8.
6. *Wirtschafts- und Handelsfragen Deutschlands im Rahmen der Weltwirtschaft* (1922), Berlin; *Material für ein Studium von Deutschlands Wirtschaft, Währung und Finanzen* (1924), Berlin.
7. A. Löwe (1920), 'Zur Soziologie der modernen Juden', *Der Spiegel*, **2** (14/15), pp. 8ff.

8. A. Löwe (1919), 'Die neue Demokratie', op. cit.; A. Löwe (1919), 'Die Arbeiter- und Soldatenräte in der Demobilmachung', *Europäische Staats- und Wirtschaftszeitung* **4**, pp. 89ff.
9. *Sozialismus aus dem Glauben. Verhandlungen der sozialistischen Tagung in Heppenheim a.B.* (1929), Zürich and Leipzig: Rotapfel.
10. Tracy B. Kittredge/Rockefeller Foundation, 'Social Sciences in Germany', 9 August 1932, Rockefeller Archive, R.G. 1.1/20, 186.
11. A. Lowe to David Clark, 19 December 1974: 'I still regard the years spent there [in Kiel] as the climax of more than half a century's teaching and research'.
12. A. Müller-Armack (1929), 'Konjunkturforschung und Konjunkturpolitik', *Handwörterbuch der Staatswissenschaften,* 4th ed., Suppl. Vol., Jena, pp. 645 ff.
13. A. Löwe (1925), 'Der gegenwärtige Stand der Konjunkturforschung in Deutschland', in Moritz Julius Bonn and Melchior Palyi (eds), *Die Wirtschaftswissenschaften nach dem Kriege. Festgabe für Lujo Brentano zum 80. Geburtstag,* Vol. 2, Munich and Leipzig: Duncker & Humblot, pp. 329ff.; A. Löwe (1926), 'Wie ist Konjunkturtheorie überhaupt möglich?', *Weltwirtschaftliches Archiv,* **24**, pp. 193ff.
14. A. Lowe (1989), 'Konjunkturtheorie in Deutschland in den zwanziger Jahren', in Bertram Schefold (ed.), *Studien zur Entwicklung der ökonomischen Theorie VIII.*, Schriften des Vereins für Socialpolitik, Vol. 115/VIII, Berlin: Duncker & Humblot, pp.75ff.; compare also the chapter by Hagemann and Landesmann in this book.
15. G. Colm (1927), *Volkswirtschaftliche Theorie der Staatsausgaben. Ein Beitrag zur Finanztheorie,* Tübingen: J. C. B. Mohr (Paul Siebeck); A. Kähler (1933), *Die Theorie der Arbeiterfreisetzung durch die Maschine. Eine gesamtwirtschaftliche Abhandlung des modernen Technisierungsprozesses,* Greifswald: Julius Abel.
16. A. Löwe to Alexander Rüstow, 25 October 1932, Rüstow papers 6, Bundesarchiv Koblenz; A. Löwe (1933), 'Der Stand und die nächste Zukunft der Konjunkturforschung', in G. Clausing (ed.), *Der Stand und die nächste Zukunft der Konjunkturforschung. Festschrift für Arthur Spiethoff,* Munich: Duncker & Humblot, pp. 154ff.
17. A. Löwe (1931), 'Das gegenwärtige Bildungsproblem der deutschen Universität', *Die Erziehung* 7, pp. 1ff.; compare Lowe (1937), 'The task of democratic education: Pre-Hitler Germany and England', *Social Research,* **4**, pp. 381ff.; Lowe (1940), *The Universities in Transformation,* London: Sheldon Press; Lowe (1971), 'Is present-day higher learning "relevant"?', *Social Research* **38**, pp. 563ff.
18. A. Löwe to Alexander Rüstow, 20 November 1932, op. cit.
19. Expatriation List No. 79 (14 November 1938), publ. in the German *Reichsanzeiger* No. 269 (18 November 1938).
20. C.-D. Krohn (1993), *Intellectuals in Exile. Refugee Scholars and the New School for Social Research,* Amherst: University of Massachusetts Press.
21. A. Lowe (1952), 'A structural model of production', *Social Research,* **19**, pp. 135ff.; Lowe (1954), 'The classical theory of economic growth', **21**, pp. 127ff.
22. Memo Rockefeller Foundation/Paris Office, 23 March 1934, Rockefeller Archive RG 1.1, 200/109/539; papers of the Academic Assistance Council, Bodleian Library, Oxford, file 164/4.
23. A. Löwe (1937), *The Price of Liberty. A German on Contemporary Britain,* 1st and 2nd edns, London: Hogarth Press; Löwe (1935), *Economics and Sociology. A Plea for Co-Operation in the Social Sciences,* London: Allen & Unwin.
24. *The Price of Liberty,* preface to the 3rd. edn. (1948).
25. A. Lowe (1965), *On Economic Knowledge. Toward a Science of Political Economics,* New York-Evanston: Harper & Row; enlarged edn. (1977), White Plains, NY: M.E. Sharpe.

PART II

Classical Roots of Lowe's Approach

4. Adolph Lowe's Distinction between Structural and Force Analysis and Classical Economic Theorizing*

Volker Caspari

On the occasion of Adolph Lowe's 90th birthday Edward Nell took up Lowe's distinction between structural and force (behavioural) analysis (Nell, 1984). He characterized classical theory as structural analysis and associated behavioural analysis with neoclassical theory. In general I subscribe to the views presented in his article, and therefore I would like to qualify some of his arguments by stressing in particular the behavioural aspects in classical theory.

Let me begin with a short remark on the distinction between structural and behavioural analysis. I try to elucidate the above-mentioned distinction by means of model-building, since it is, at least in economics, the best-known analytical device. Typically, we distinguish three kinds of relations: (1) the behavioural aspect is formulated by means of an objective function which is going to be maximized or minimized; (2) the structural aspects are to some extent a part of the constraints; and (3) some equilibrium conditions (market clearing) are established. This is the conventional way that microeconomic models are designed. In these types of models the structural aspects are contained in the different constraints; the emphasis is on the optimization of stipulated ends. In classical models (or what we regard as classical models) a matter of the utmost concern is the modelling of two interrelated circular flows: (1) the flow of production of commodities by means of commodities and labour and, (2) the flow of final demand (effective demand) generating income which is distributed according to some socially implemented rules. At first sight such models seem to work without any economic agent and if agents are introduced their behaviour is modelled on the basis of *ad hoc* hypotheses. One may refer to the strong version of the classical saving hypothesis, which states that all profits are saved and all wages are spent. Even profit maximization or cost minimization could be regarded as an ad-hocery, because it is not derived from more 'general' principles of human behaviour. Whether classical theory really takes these targets and aims as *ad hoc* hypotheses will be discussed in turn. Advocates of the classical approach may argue that it is a preliminary, though important, step in the analysis of the economic system to neglect the behaviour of agents and to study in the first place the 'structural' properties of the system. Structural analysis, therefore, deals with the technical conditions of production and reproduction as well as with the conditions which emerge from the 'laws' of the circular flows of income and distribution. Structural analysis is always macro and is a fundamental element of the analysis of long-period positions. The prototypes of structural analysis are Quesnay's *'Tableau Economique'*, Marx's 'schemes of simple and extended reproduction' and, of course, Lowe's 'Structural Model of Production', which is hybrid because it combines the classical concept of circular flows with the linear approach of the Austrians.

While in structural analysis a system of relations emerging from the circular flow of income and from the feasibility conditions of production and reproduction are examined, behavioural analysis of neoclassical theory is based on the principles of methodological individualism (Schumpeter, 1908). Accordingly, the explanation of social (economic) phenomena should be traced back to individual human action. This methodological approach is most advanced in modern neoclassical economics, but it is becoming more and more important in other branches of the social sciences such as sociology, political science and jurisprudence.

1   NEOCLASSICAL THEORY

In neoclassical theory, structural and behavioural aspects are combined in a well-known way. Economic behaviour of an individual is reduced to a special and definite form of rationality: it is rational choice, more exactly rational choice under constraints and some of these constraints (that is, the budget constraint) originate in the structural framework. Usually, the structural aspects of this framework are characterized by a given set of productive technologies and a given set of endowments. Further, the circular flow of income is modelled: the endowments owned by the agents evaluated at equilibrium prices plus the profits (due to decreasing returns in some firms) being distributed to the owners of these scarce factors form the income constraint of each individual agent.

As far as behaviour of individuals is concerned, traditional neoclassical analysis adheres to the concept of rational choice, although it is well known that 'people' may not have well-behaved preferences. They have lexicographic preference orderings, they violate the transitivity conditions or the assumption of convexity. Unorthodox neoclassical economists have accepted this challenge and developed concepts of bounded rationality. Very recently game theory was used to design experiments from which it was hoped to gain empirical insights into the real boundaries of rational choice. Nevertheless, except for some dissenters neoclassical economists maintain their well-developed concept of rationality. The main reason for this, as Vogt (1993) has argued in a recent paper, is due to the fact that neoclassical theory does not only want to explain the quantitative changes in economic magnitudes (falling or rising prices, wages, consumption, and so on), but according to the concept of methodological individualism those changes should be traced back to the behaviour of economic agents. But this is only one half of the story. If an economic magnitude changes, neoclassical economists want to know who will benefit and who will lose. Any allocation implies a welfare position and changes in welfare positions are the second half of the story. This should remind us that in neoclassical economics the 'normative' aspect as far as behaviour of agents is concerned is actually more important than the 'positive' aspect of the theory. I venture to assert that the main motive for searching 'Microfoundations for Macroeconomics' can be attributed to the normative aspect of neoclassical economics. But macroeconomic theory was not really challenged by microeconomic theory. In fact, it was just the other way round. (Macroeconomics provided inappropriate answers to relevant problems and microeconomics provided appropriate answers to irrelevant problems.) Nowadays macroeconomists can make use of a great variety of micromodels (adverse selection in credit markets, implicit contracts in labour markets, and so on) not only in order to explain sticky interest and/or nominal wage rates but also to justify them, because they are compatible with 'rational' behaviour. Before the age of microfoundation, the assumption of sticky prices was supposed to be an ad-hocery. Now we are informed, that sticky prices, may among other things be due to asymmetric information, risk aversion and incomplete contracts. Why many economists are not tempted to regard this device as another form of ad-hocery has something to do with their conviction that only explanations which are based on an individual benefit–loss calculation are true economic explanations.

2   CLASSICAL THEORY AND BEHAVIOUR

The normative and behavioural (actually, choice-theoretic) foundations of neoclassical economics are very well developed and it seems that classical theory cannot keep up with it. For two reasons I would not subscribe to this view. First, in classical economics not welfare but wealth is the essential notion. Second, although classical and neoclassical economics share an individualistic approach, in order to explain economic (and social) behaviour the classical approach towards behaviour differs from the neoclassical one in at least two significant ways. Before I elaborate on this, let me make a short remark of the first point of difference. While Ricardo focuses in his *Principles* on the question according to which rules the net product is distributed among the different classes of the society, the scope of Smith's *Wealth of Nations* is much broader. Besides distribution, Smith is particularly interested in the causes of the growth of wealth. In the first chapter of the *Wealth of Nations* he investigates the relation between the degree of the division of labour and the size of markets. The expansion of the size of markets is positively correlated with an increasing division of labour. This process is the source of the increasing wealth of nations and within this process technologies of production change, new commodities emerge and old ones disappear. In view of this, the assumption of stable or even stationary preferences seems neither plausible nor adequate. Therefore, the behavioural analysis of classical economics did (and does) not refer to given preferences and tastes. But from this does it follow that classical economics is in any way deprived of behavioural analysis? Obviously not, for classical economics focuses on the behavioural assumption of profit maximization and this has nothing to do with preferences, at least in classical economic theory. In order to clarify this second point we reexamine how Smith dealt with human behaviour in the 'economic sphere'. At the risk of asserting the obvious, I venture to recall Smith's notion of self-interest. In his 'butcher–brewer' example, Smith argues, that one should 'never talk to them of our own necessities but of their advantages' (Smith, 1976a, Vol. I, p. 27).

But what does Smith mean by advantages? The neoclassical economist is immediately inclined to interpret this as an individual impulse for each person to increase his or her utility through the exchange of beer against meat. But why did Smith not use utility as an analytical concept in his *Wealth of Nations* although he used it in his *Theory of Moral Sentiments*? The answer is rather simple. His concept of utility differs in a significant way from the neoclassical one. According to Smith, utility is not a relation between an object (material or immaterial) and an isolated individual but rather a relation between an object and an individual mediated by other individuals or even more a relation between individuals mediated by a certain object.

> To one who was to live alone on a desolate island it might be a matter of doubt, perhaps, whether a palace, or a collection of such small conveniences as are commonly contained in a tweezer-case [Smith refers to tooth-picks, ear-pickers, nail-scissors] would contribute most to his happiness and enjoyment. If he is to live in

society, indeed, there can be no comparison, because in this, as in all other cases, we constantly pay more regard to the sentiments of the spectator, than to those of the person principally concerned, and consider rather how his situation will appear to other people, than how it will appear to himself. (Smith, 1976b, p.182)

Following Smith's arguments I want to raise two questions. First, how did Smith cast the connection between self-love and socially-mediated preferences into economic categories? Second, what follows from Smith's concept of utility if it is transplanted into the neoclassical theory of consumer choice? Let me take up the second point first. In modern social choice theory Smith's impartial spectator has been taken into consideration (that is, Sen, 1979). Sen outlines a situation in which an individual considers the preferences of another when deciding on his or her own (the prudish and the lewd on who should be allowed to read *Lady Chatterley's Lover*). Sen examines under which conditions aggregation of individual preferences leads to a consistent social preference ordering. However, the point in Smith's story is the 'reversed' problem: what happens to individual rational choice if preferences of different individuals are not independent of each other? This leads to externalities in consumption. Allocations with consumption externalities are, in general, not Pareto efficient. By definition, such allocations can be improved if individuals cooperate (compare Güth, 1992, p. 85).

The erosion of social values and deteriorating forms of cooperation, the loss of 'spontaneous conformity', as Lowe calls it, is nothing but a different and, of course, an analytically less-elaborated representation of social preference ordering which is going to fall apart. As we know from his *On Economic Knowledge*, this has led him to reject the behavioural rules on which the homeostatic principle of markets rests. However, we should notice that it is essentially the preference or utility-maximizing principle which is under attack and we may ask: does not the same hold true for profit maximization? According to neoclassical economics, profit maximization is logically subordinate to utility maximization, while the historical development of economic analysis suggests the opposite. According to Lowe, both concepts are different,[1] although they only seem to be varieties of the extremum principle. In fact, there was one group of neoclassical economists, particularly the Austrians, who never ceased to maintain that utility maximization is the one and only principle of explanation in economics. This had already become apparent in Schumpeter's *Wesen und Hauptinhalt der theoretischen Nationalökonomie* (1908). There he argues that the laws of return have no significant impact on the determination of value, because they are ruled out by the utility maximization of the resource or factor owner (opportunity costs)

(Schumpeter, 1908, pp. 219–43). This argument rests on the assumption that the quantity of the resources is given and thus the amount offered is determined by the difference between the given quantity and reservation demand of the factor owner. Therefore, the amount offered follows directly from utility maximization of the factor owner. Offer is, therefore, not independent from the law of demand. There are no scissors; there is only one cutting blade. Neoclassical economists who follow the Marshall–Pigou tradition use utility maximization to characterize the behaviour of households (consumers) and maintain, without reflection, profit maximization as the conducting motive of firms. Under these conditions one and the same individual should be able to distinguish between his or her role as a utility-maximizing consumer and his or her role as a profit-maximizing entrepreneur.

This tradition, actually the textbook tradition, can be traced back to Marshall's attempt to create a powerful synthesis of classical economics and consumer demand; the latter being derived from the utility principle.

In classical economics, or at least in Smith, profit maximization is derived from tying together the principle of self-love with that of *sympathy*.[2] The impartial spectator's feelings of sympathy are asymmetrical. He or she has more sympathy for the joys than for the sorrows of other people. 'I will venture to affirm, that, when there is no envy in the case our propensity to sympathize with joy is much stronger than our propensity to sympathize with sorrow' (Smith, 1976b, p. 45).

According to Smith, this asymmetrical character of sympathy constitutes the cause for the constant striving of individuals to become wealthy. Being wealthy is associated with joy and happiness, poverty with sorrow and desperation. Wealth is exhibited, poverty is concealed. These are the reasons, says Smith, why people strive to better their material position:

> From whence, then, arises that emulation which runs through all the different ranks of men, and what are the advantages which we propose by that great purpose of human life which we call bettering our condition? To be observed, to be attended to, to be taken notice of with sympathy, complacency, and approbation, are all the advantages which we can propose to derive from it. (Ibid., p. 50)

Again, it is not the comfort of being wealthy which leads to the aspiration of wealth, but the sympathy which other members of the society offer to wealthy people. It is the 'socialisation of the individual', as Heilbroner has argued (Heilbroner, 1982, pp. 428–34) which leads to a more substantial understanding of Smith's principle of self-love, which is rather different from the neoclassical concept of utility maximization.

If one wants to adhere to the classical tradition in economics it is neither sufficient nor promising to confine oneself to structural analysis, like the

Brahman who confines himself to meditation. Behavioural analysis becomes necessary if classical economists want to contribute to policy issues, such as the challenging transformation of planned economies into market economies. (The most simple advice to give free play to the forces of supply and demand without taking into consideration institutional and ethical aspects of human behaviour can lead, as is plain from the daily news about the Russian economy, to disaster.)

3   STRUCTURE, BEHAVIOUR AND LOWE'S INSTRUMENTAL METHOD

Looking at Lowe's work, it is striking that the economist Lowe has gone a long way towards structural analysis, while the sociologist and political philosopher was concerned with human behaviour. However, in his instrumental analysis, structural and behavioural analysis meet in a way not very different from the method of welfare economics. In welfare economics the 'structural' problem is: what is an efficient allocation? And the 'behavioural' problem is: how can it be achieved? The traditional answer is given by the First Theorem of welfare economics. A Pareto-efficient allocation can be achieved by decentralization of decisions and perfect competition. However, it is well known that either planning or cooperation are possible alternative ways to solve this problem, but they are likely to fail because of the information problem. From Lowe's point of view decentralization and competition can be regarded as instruments to achieve the efficiency goal. So, one may ask, how does Lowe's view differ from that of neoclassical welfare economics? According to welfare economics, an allocation failure is in most cases due to imperfect markets or externalities. Lowe has drawn our attention to quite a different aspect. In asking which individual motives may lead to an efficient allocation, he implicitly presumes that individual agents may aim at ends leading to a market behaviour which will not lead to an efficient state even under perfect market conditions. According to Lowe, utility maximization as an individual end is a tautological approach (Lowe, 1965, pp. 203ff.) and, therefore, completely useless for instrumental analysis. For a market signal, for example a price reduction, may lead to any kind of behaviour, which can always (*ex post*) be interpreted as rational or utility maximizing (provided that no axiom of preference ordering is violated). Therefore, it comes as no surprise that in those parts of his *Path of Economic Growth* where he deals with force or motor analysis (Lowe, 1976, pp. 218ff.) preference maximization plays no role at all. Lowe relies soley on the classical extremum principle (profit maximization) and on some more or less plausible assumptions concerning expectations. Whether or not the behaviour of a firm is profit maximizing can be tested empirically; if not by economists, then at least by the firm itself. Rationality or preference maximization, on the other hand, cannot be tested by simple observation, since it cannot be perceived independent of actual behaviour.

But there is another aspect which leads to Lowe's rejection of the utility conception. Lowe starts from the observation that modern market economies have undergone a fundamental change in their capacity of self-regulation, which he believes to be deteriorating. He regards the deficiencies in fulfilling macroeconomic goals such as high levels of employment, stability of the price level and sustained growth as indicators of a tendency to destabilization of the economic system. Besides oligopolistic market structures, he considers the increasing number of different aims and targets on the level of the individual – the age of hedonism – as the main cause of this deficiency in the self-regulating properties of market economies. The multiplicity of individual aims and targets leads to 'chaotic' individual behaviour and the market performance of the consumer demand may become unpredictable. On the level of social behaviour the 'hedonistic tendencies' are complemented by the decay of 'spontaneous conformity' which undermines not only the 'economic sphere' but also the social coherence of human life. The decreasing capacity of self-regulation has led Lowe to reverse the nexus of means and ends. Because markets do not work like they used to do, one has to look for instruments to influence the behaviour of economic agents and the conduct of markets in order to reach the macro goals. The design of instruments and the analysis of their effects on individual behaviour and market performance is the subject of Lowe's instrumental analysis. Lowe advocates interventionism but not only confined to aggregate demand management. Unlike Keynes, Lowe has never restricted himself to the economics of the short period. From his structural approach it follows that interventions should always reflect the complicated process of reallocation of labour and formation of (fixed) capital. Besides subsidies one can imagine income policy as an instrument which may influence the performance of the markets for labour and capital and additional arrangements to stabilize expectations and to reduce the level of risk.

The recent experience with German reunification confirms Lowe's scepticism that such a process of transformation would succeed without interventions. If there was a clearcut policy at all, it was in fact an interventionist policy and by no means a 'free market-policy'. Looking from Lowe's concept of instrumental analysis at the transformation which is really carried out, this policy could be criticized for two reasons. (1) The property question – restitution instead of compensation – has not been solved in a way which would stabilize the expectations of private investors. (2) At its core the transformation of the old system into a competitive market economy calls for a gigantic process of capital formation. This process would have benefited from a cooperative incomes policy. This has been missed, and now lost ground must be recovered by negotiations between trade unions and employers in a situation of high unemployment.

It seems to me that the transformation of planned economies into market economies in general and the German reunification in particular are appropriate fields of application for Lowe's instrumental analysis. But beyond this, the time for instrumental analysis is yet to come. The problems to be solved by appropriate interventions pile up: ecological problems, traffic chaos, technological unemployment, and so on. The list seems endless.

NOTES

*   An earlier version of this chapter was presented at the annual meeting of the History of Economics Society in Philadelphia, 26–29 June 1993. The present version has benefited from helpful discussions with Heinz D. Kurz and W. Föttinger.
1. He argues that Jevons, Menger and Walras substituted the extremum principle with the utility principle. See A. Lowe, *On Economic Knowledge* (1965), pp. 200ff.
2. This line of argument is developed by H. Reich. See Reich (1991), *Eigennutz und Kapitalismus: Die Bedeutung des Gewinnstrebens im klassischen ökonomischen Denken*, Berlin: Duncker & Humblot, pp. 60ff.

REFERENCES

Güth, W. (1992), *Theorie der Marktwirtschaft*, Berlin, New York: Springer.
Heilbroner, R.L. (1982), 'The socialisation of the individual in Adam Smith', *History of Political Economy*, **14**, pp. 427–39.
Lowe, A. (1965), *On Economic Knowledge*, New York: Harper & Row.
Lowe, A. (1976), *The Path of Economic Growth*, Cambridge: Cambridge University Press.
Lowe, A. (1937), *The Price of Liberty. A German on Contemporary Britain*, 2nd edn, London: Hogarth Press.
Nell, E.J. (1984), 'Structure and behavior in classical and neoclassical theory', *Eastern Economic Journal*, **10**, (2), pp. 139–55.
Reich, H. (1991), *Eigennutz und Kapitalismus*, Berlin: Duncker & Humblot.
Ricardo, D. (1821), *On the Principles of Political Economy and Taxation*, 3rd edn in *The Works and Correspondence of David Ricardo* ed. P. Sraffa with collaboration of M.H. Dobb, Vol. I, Cambridge: Cambridge University Press 1951.
Schumpeter, J.A.(1908), *Das Wesen und der Hauptinhalt der theoretischen Nationalökonomie*, Berlin: Duncker & Humblot 2nd edn 1970.
Sen, A.K. (1979), 'Personal utilities and public judgements: or what's wrong with welfare economics?' *Economic Journal*, **89**, pp. 537–58.
Smith, A. (1976a), *An Inquiry into the Nature and Causes of the Wealth of Nations* (ed. R.H. Campbell and A.S. Skinner), Vols I and II, Oxford: Oxford University Press.
Smith, A. (1976b), *The Theory of Moral Sentiments* (ed. D.D. Raphael and A.L. Macfie), Oxford: Oxford University Press.

Sturn, R. (1990), 'Natürliche Freiheit und soziale Kontingenz – Individualismus und Kollektivismus der Smithschen Handlungstheorie', in H.D. Kurz (ed*.), Adam Smith (1723–1790) – Ein Werk und seine Wirkungsgeschichte*, Marburg: Metropolis, pp. 93–117.
Vogt, W. (1993), 'Über die Rationalität der ökonomischen Theorie', in *Ökonomie und Gesellschaft*, Jahrbuch 10, Frankfurt am Main: Campus, pp. 32–59.

5. The Path of Economic Growth Theory: Some Recent Developments*

Heinz D. Kurz

1   INTRODUCTION

A major concern of Adolph Lowe was with the dynamics of the economic system: its development, growth and structural change. This is well documented in several of his contributions, especially in the *magnum opus* of the period after his retirement from the New School for Social Research, *The Path of Economic Growth* (Lowe, 1976).[1] The *Path* contains the fruit of Lowe's lifelong endeavour to come to grips with what in old-fashioned language were called the 'laws of motion of modern society': the sources of economic expansion and structural transformation, the obstacles to socioeconomic development, the political means to foster rising levels of income per capita and to ward off destructive tendencies accompanying the process of modernization, such as mass unemployment caused by the labour-displacing effects of technological change.[2]

In one of his earlier works devoted to this grand theme he counterposed the 'classical' and the 'neoclassical' points of view on the problems of development and growth. He concluded:

> It is only fair to say that this modern notion of 'endogeneity' is but a dim reflection of a much more ambitious method of analysis that dominated an earlier epoch of theoretical economics. As a matter of fact, upon this issue of endogeneity versus exogeneity, rather than upon conflicting theories of value, hinges the main difference between genuine classical theory and post-Millian economic reasoning, including all versions of neoclassical analysis. (Lowe, [1954] 1987, p. 108)

This statement predates the publication of Robert Solow's famous growth model and Trevor Swan's less famous but equally important contribution to neoclassical growth theory by two years (see Solow, 1956, and Swan, 1956). It predates by thirty years the so-called 'new' growth theory (henceforth NGT), taking Paul Romer's doctoral thesis as the year of its birth. Its advocates taking pride in having replaced the old Solovian model of exogenous growth with 'endogenous' growth models (henceforth NGMs). The question is whether the NGMs pass 'Lowe's test', that is, whether their notion of 'endogeneity' is more than 'a dim reflection' of the notion we find in the classical authors and whether it adds substantially to our understanding of the process of economic growth and development then and now.

This chapter attempts to give a preliminary answer to this question. The answer is necessarily preliminary for two reasons. First, given the recent burst of activity in this field which is reflected in a large and still mounting wave of contributions to the NGT, only a subset of the relevant literature could be taken into account. Second, since the NGT is still in an infant stage, its potential is not yet fully exploited. Therefore it is premature to form a final judgement on its success, or otherwise. While some of its practitioners seem to consider it a major innovation which will revolutionize the way we think not only about sustained endogenous growth, but also about economics in general (see, for example, Grossman and Helpman, 1994), its critics discern little else than just another fashion: these fashions come with the sound of a trumpet – to go unnoticed after a while.

This chapter takes a critical view on NGMs. While there can be no doubt that these contributions have drawn attention to fundamental questions, the answers provided are largely unconvincing. None of the questions raised is really new. The attraction exerted by the NGT appears to derive not least from its resumption of what was considered to be a fundamental problem of social sciences in the time of the inception of systematic analysis in the seventeenth and eighteenth centuries: the explanation of human history. The NGT purports to provide, to use Hicks's term, a 'theory of economic history' (Hicks, 1969), as far as the growth and development of economies is concerned. The theory purports to extend, in one of its dimensions, over the whole world or at least large parts of it; in another, over the whole span of human history or at least significant parts of it. The more interesting contributions to the NGT can even be interpreted as making a new attempt to tackle what was considered to be the main difficulty in this project, that is, in the words of the Scottish philosopher Adam Ferguson (1793, p. 205), history is 'the result of human action, but not the execution of any human design'.

The structure of the chapter is as follows. Section 2 summarizes Solow's growth model and relates it to the NGT. According to widespread opinion, the original novelty of the NGMs consists of the incorporation of increasing returns to scale in the theory of production and growth; in this section a first argument is provided why this view is at best misleading. Section 3 provides a typology of NGMs which structures the following discussion. Emphasis will be on the factors conceptualized as determining the 'marginal product of capital', which in competitive equilibrium is taken to equal the rate of profit, and the relationship between the rate of profit and the 'rate of time preference'. It is shown that, in the NGMs which start from the assumption of intertemporal utility maximization, in order to get 'endogenous' growth the former rate must consistently exceed the latter. Section 4 deals with the class of 'linear models', which determine the rate of profit by technology alone and take it to be constant over time. Section 5 deals with models starting from a convex technology but assuming that the marginal product of capital has a lower boundary which is positive (and larger than the rate of time preference). Section 6 contains an excursus on the so-called 'threshold models' of growth and development which focus attention on technological externalities and 'critical' levels of certain state variables, such as the capital–labour ratio. Emphasis is on multiple equilibria and 'virtuous' or 'vicious circles' of development. Sections 7 and 8 return to the main argument of the chapter and discuss models focusing attention on positive externalities associated with the accumulation of capital that are said to counteract diminishing returns to capital. In Section 7 the emphasis is on the impact of human capital formation on growth and development, whereas Section 8 is concerned with the impact of the creation and accumulation of knowledge, that is, the process of 'innovation' triggered by firms' research and development. Both kinds of activities are said to have important spillovers to the economy as a whole. Much of the discussion is centred around the idea that these activities generate public or semi-public goods, that is, goods that are non-rival and/or non-excludable. It is pointed out that increasing returns to scale, although employed by several protagonists of the NGT, is not an essential ingredient of the stories told: the growth contemplated by the NGMs would be no less 'endogenous' if this assumption were to be abandoned. The chapter concludes, in Section 9, with an account of what I consider to be the most important deficiencies of the NGMs.

Before we turn to the main argument, two remarks are appropriate. First, the chapter focuses attention on what are considered to be the most prominent contributions to the literature under consideration, that is, those that triggered the literary avalanche of the NGT; obviously a complete survey cannot be the aim of the chapter.[3] Second, while some contributions convey the impression that one of the crucial features of the NGT is that saving behaviour is given 'microfoundations' in terms of the assumption that there is an immortal representative agent maximizing an intertemporal utility function over an infinite time horizon, it will be shown that this assumption is not essential: starting from a given propensity to save, as in the original Solow model, would not render the models under consideration exogenous growth models. Nevertheless, in much of the argument and in line with the respective literature, we shall retain the assumption of intertemporal utility maximization.

2   SOLOW'S GROWTH MODEL

To understand what the NGT is all about, it is useful to start from Solow's growth model (see Solow, 1956, 1957, 1970), which is the main point of reference of the literature under consideration. This is done in Subsection 2.1. While in the original formulation of the model the propensity to save is treated as a 'behaviouristic' parameter that is given from outside, in the majority of the NGMs saving behaviour is derived from intertemporal utility maximization of a representative agent. Subsection 2.2 grafts this assumption on Solow's model. This prepares the ground for the following discussion in which the novelty of the NGMs is highlighted in terms of the relationship between only two variables: the marginal product of capital on the one hand and the subjective rate of time preference attributed to the representative agent on the other. However, as has been indicated in the above, the discussion could also be carried out in terms of a given saving propensity (out of profits), that is, assuming a zero rate of time preference. Subsection 2.3 addresses the problem of whether assuming increasing returns to scale would render Solow's model a model of endogenous growth.

2.1   The Traditional Formulation

Solow introduced his famous 1956 paper in the following terms:

> All theory depends on assumptions which are not quite true. That is what makes it theory. The art of successful theorizing is to make the inevitable simplifying assumptions in such a way *that the final results are not very sensitive*. A 'crucial' assumption is one on which the conclusions do depend sensitively, and it is important *that crucial assumptions be reasonably realistic*. When the results of a theory seem to flow specifically from a special crucial assumption, then if the assumption is dubious, the results are suspect. (Solow, 1956, p. 65; emphases added)

Both the question of the (in)sensitivity of final results and of the 'realism' of crucial assumptions were at stake then and, as we shall see below, are at stake again nowadays.

The model Solow presented was said to adopt 'all the Harrod–Domar assumptions except that of fixed proportions' (ibid., p. 66). A crucial premise in Solow's formulation is an aggregate production function with variable proportions. Assuming (i) that the production function is of the now standard constant returns to scale sort and (ii) that technical progress is of the labour-augmenting type, this function can be written as

$$Y = F(K, A(t)L), \tag{5.1}$$

where Y is total net output, K is the stock of capital, L is the amount of labour (employed) and $A(t)$ is an increasing function of t, with $A(t)$ exponential:

$$A(t) = A(0)e^{\mu t}, \tag{5.2}$$

where μ is the rate of growth of labour efficiency. From a microeconomic perspective, the Solovian model retained the simplicity of *free competition*. This necessitated the further assumption, implied by equation (5.2), that technological advances are equally beneficial to all firms. For this reason technology is treated as a *pure public good*, that is, both non-rival and non-excludable.

In addition, it is assumed that labour is growing exponentially at rate λ,

$$L(t) = L(0)e^{\lambda t}, \tag{5.3}$$

and that a given fraction of output, s, is saved and invested:

$$sY = \dot{K}. \tag{5.4}$$

Differentiating the production function with respect to time gives

$$\dot{Y} = F_K \dot{K} + F_{AL}(\dot{A}L + A\dot{L}) = sF_K Y + ALF_{AL}(\hat{A} + \hat{L}).$$

Solving for the rate of growth of output, $g = \hat{Y} = \dot{Y}/Y$, yields

$$g = sF_K + (1 - \beta)(\mu + \lambda), \tag{5.5}$$

where

$$\beta = \frac{K}{Y} F_K \quad \text{and} \quad 1 - b = \frac{AL}{Y} F_{AL}.$$

(It goes without saying that β need not, but may be constant, as in the Cobb–Douglas case.) In steady-state equilibrium the rate of growth, g^*, equals the sum of the exogenously-given rate of growth of the efficiency parameter A and the exogenously-given rate of growth of the labour force:

$$g^* = \mu + \lambda. \tag{5.6}$$

Assuming that the Inada conditions hold true, the steady state is approached asymptotically by any optimal path from arbitrarily given initial conditions. Outside the steady state the rate of growth of output may be larger or smaller than $\mu + \lambda$, the difference being equal to

$$g - (\mu + \lambda) = sF_K - \beta(\mu + \lambda). \tag{5.7}$$

Given the premiss underlying Solow's growth model, g would gravitate towards g^*, which means that the *steady-state rate of growth of output* is exclusively determined by the *exogenous* growth rate $\mu + \lambda$. While the saving rate and thus agents' behaviour do have an impact on the rate of expansion of the economy outside the steady state, they are totally unimportant once this state is reached. There is no endogenous growth in the very long run. It should also be mentioned that while the steady-state rate of growth is exogenous, the corresponding rate of profit is endogenously determined. However, since in the conventional Solovian growth model the convergence to the steady-state growth path may take a long time – in fact, there is only asymptotic convergence – growth in such a model is for all practical purposes always endogenous.

Seen from this perspective, the main novelty of the NGMs consists of also rendering the steady-state rate of growth an endogenous variable. This is seconded in some papers by an argument *pro* focusing attention on steady states rather than on transitions between them, as in the Solovian tradition. It is in this latter respect that the 'microfoundations' of saving behaviour are said to be of crucial importance, because it can be shown that lengthy transitions from one steady-state path to another occur only if very low intertemporal substitution in consumption is assumed (see King and Rebelo, 1993). Abandoning that assumption involves swift convergence which, in turn, is considered to justify an almost exclusive concern with steady-state growth paths. We shall also see that, in a sense, the NGT reverses the practice in the Solovian model as to which variable, the growth rate or the profit rate, is the exogenous and which the endogenous one. Indeed, with not much of an exaggeration the NGT may be characterized as a *theory of exogenous profitability and endogenous growth*. While some of the NGMs strictly satisfy this characterization, in others, which allow for a choice of technique, things are slightly more complicated.

2.2 Intertemporal Utility Maximization Grafted on to Solow's Model

In the majority of NGMs it is assumed that there exists an immortal 'representative agent' who is concerned with maximizing an intertemporal utility function, $u = u(c(t))$, over an infinite horizon. Choosing the path that maximizes consumption involves maximizing the integral of instantaneous utility,

$$\int_0^\infty e^{-\rho t} u(c(t))dt, \tag{5.8}$$

where ρ (≥ 0) is the rate of time preference or discount rate. The utility function is commonly specified as follows

$$u(c(t)) = \frac{c(t)^{1-\sigma}}{1-\sigma}, \tag{5.9}$$

where σ^{-1} is the elasticity of substitution between present and future consumption ($1 \neq \sigma > 0$).[4] In the literature, the discount rate is occasionally dubbed 'required rate of return', since it gives the break-even level of the profit rate (interest rate): with the actual rate of profit larger (smaller) than the discount rate, savings will be positive (negative). To simplify matters, assume that the exogenous growth factors are absent, that is, $\lambda = \mu = 0$. Assume in addition the notorious linear homogeneous Cobb–Douglas production function, the per-capita version of which is

$$y = Ak^\alpha, \tag{5.10}$$

where y is output per worker (Y/L), k is capital per worker, or capital intensity (K/L), and α is the elasticity of production with respect to capital. Performing the intertemporal optimization, the optimal rate of growth of output (which, in the case under consideration, equals the rate of growth of output per head), g, turns out to be

$$g = \frac{\alpha A K^{\alpha-1} - \rho}{\sigma}. \tag{5.11}$$

The first term of the numerator of equation (5.11) gives the marginal product of capital, dy/dk, which equals the rate of profit, r. We may therefore write

$$g = \frac{r - \rho}{\sigma}.\qquad(5.12)$$

Figure 5.1 illustrates this relationship. Obviously, when the rate of profit is just equal to the rate of time preference, there will be no growth, since net savings in society as a whole are zero. The rate of growth of output per capita is positive (negative) if r is larger (smaller) than ρ; the magnitude of the growth rate, in absolute terms, is larger, the larger is the difference between the two rates of return.[5] There exist unique and stable steady-state equilibrium values for the capital–labour ratio, k^*, the output–labour ratio, y^*, the rate of profit, $r^* = \rho$, and the wage rate, $w^* = y^* - rk^*$. With the exogenous factors, population growth and technological change, taken to be dormant, the economy will end up in a stationary state.

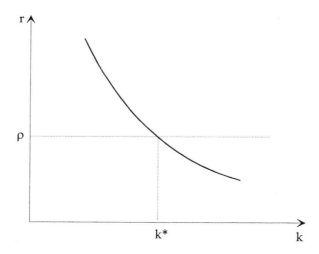

Figure 5.1   The growth rate in the Solow model

Continued technological change is thus necessary for sustained growth in the Solovian model. An increase in A, the efficiency parameter, at a constant rate μ would continuously shift the curve of the marginal product of capital in Figure 5.1 to the north-east. This technology-driven tendency of the rate of profit to increase would yield a steady stream of new opportunities for saving (and investment), that is, a positive rate of capital accumulation reflected in a positive rate of growth of output. In steady-state equilibrium these new opportunities are instantaneously and fully exploited, so that the tendency of the rate of profit to rise due to an increased efficiency is exactly offset by its tendency to fall due to capital accumulation. The rate of growth of output, capital and the wage rate in steady-state equilibrium would be equal to μ. With a constant capital–output ratio and a constant rate of profit, the share of profits in total income would also be a constant.

The question now is whether by assuming a production function with increasing returns to scale Solow's model would generate endogenous steady-state growth.

2.3   Increasing Returns

Let the production function be

$$Y = F(K, A(t)L^m),$$
(5.13)

where $F(.,.)$ is homogeneous of degree one and $m > 1$. This production function has increasing returns to scale in K and L: with $\varphi > 1$,

$$F(\varphi K, A(t)(\varphi L)^m) = \varphi F(K, \varphi^{m-1}A(t)L^m) > \varphi F(K, A(t)L^m).$$

If $A(t)$ grows at rate μ and labour L grows at rate λ, then a steady-state equilibrium, that is, a state in which both income Y and capital K grow at the same rate g^*, may exist only if

$$g^* = \mu + m\lambda.$$
(5.14)

This means, however, that the steady-state rate of growth is *not* endogenous, but determined by the technological and demographic parameters m, μ and λ. Hence, assuming increasing returns to scale would not help. Something else is needed, and to this something we now turn.

3   THE 'NEW' GROWTH MODELS: A TYPOLOGY

The last few years have seen the publication of a bewildering variety of NGMs. Despite all their differences, these models share some common features. However, it requires some effort to spot their 'core', so to speak. This is somewhat surprising, since all models have basically only three equations: (i) one to describe saving (alias investment) behaviour; (ii) one to describe the technology by means of which output is produced; and (iii) one to describe the mechanism that results in an 'endogenous' dynamics. The difficulty arises because in NGT, as in economics in general, there are two related tendencies at work, which Lowe has pilloried time and again. First, models are often differentiated artificially by changing aspects that are peripheral to the core of the argument. Second, it is the unfortunate habit of economists to shroud the simple meaning of their models in a fog of verbiage or more or less complicated mathematics. In the NGMs these tendencies concern mainly the second and the third 'equation', that is, the conceptualization and formalization of a self-propelling dynamics. Through this fog the NGMs can best be distinguished in terms of the different growth mechanisms contemplated or in terms of some special assumptions or special functional forms assigned to a given mechanism.

In what follows we shall distinguish between several classes of models. As was shown in the preceding section, in the Solovian model a marginal product of capital that is falling when capital accumulates is responsible for the exogeneity of the steady-state growth rate. The NGMs seek to do away with diminishing returns to capital and thus the tendency of the rate of profit to fall (see also Barro and Sala-i-Martin, 1995, p. 39). According to the interpretation given in this chapter the NGMs are best grouped in terms of the routes taken to accomplish this task (see also Kurz and Salvadori, 1995b and 1995c). Broadly speaking, the different NGMs will be summarized in an ascending order of difficulty or sophistication; as will become clear, this order deviates from the chronological one. We shall distinguish between:

i.   'linear models' which represent the simplest way to prevent the rate of profit from falling as capital accumulates by suspending the neoclassical mechanism of factor substitution;

ii.   models which preserve that mechanism but impose a lower boundary on the marginal product of capital;

iii.   models that envisage production technology as consisting of ranges with decreasing and increasing returns to scale;

iv.   models that focus attention on positive externalities of the accumulation of human capital; and

v.   models emphasizing positive externalities of the generation of new knowledge in research and development activities of firms.

From what has been said in Subsection 2.3, case (iii) cannot, by itself, lead to endogenous growth: in order for endogenous growth to obtain in such a framework one (or both) of the mechanisms contemplated in cases

(iv) or (v) must be added to the story. Nevertheless, case (iii) is included in the discussion because it deals with so-called 'threshold models' of growth which have gained some prominence in the literature. The reader may consider its treatment as a sort of excursus.

4   CONSTANT RETURNS TO CAPITAL

4.1   An Exceedingly Simple Model

The easiest way to get rid of a falling marginal product of capital is to set aside all factors of production that are non-accumulable, such as labour and land, and to take into consideration only accumulable inputs, that is, 'capital' of some kind. The simplest version of this class of models is the so-called '*AK* model', which starts from the premiss that there is a linear relationship between total output, *Y*, and a single factor capital, *K*, both consisting of the same commodity:

$$Y = AK, \tag{5.15}$$

where $1/A$ is the amount of that commodity required to produce one unit of itself. Because of the linear form of the aggregate production function, these models are also known as 'linear models'. The net rate of return on capital, *r*, is given by

$$r + \delta = \frac{Y}{K} = A, \tag{5.16}$$

where δ is the exogenously-given rate of depreciation. There is a large variety of models of this type in the literature. In the two-sector version in Rebelo (1991) it is assumed that the capital-good sector produces the capital good by means of itself and nothing else. It is also assumed that there is only one method of production to produce the capital good. Hence, *the rate of profit is technologically determined*. The consumption good is produced by means of the capital good and nothing else. Then the saving–investment mechanism jointly with the assumption of a uniform rate of growth, that is, a steady-state equilibrium, determines a relationship between the growth rate, *g*, and the rate of profit, *r*. Rebelo (1991, pp. 504 and 506) obtains either

$$g = \frac{A-\delta-\rho}{\sigma} = \frac{r-\rho}{\sigma}, \qquad (5.17)$$

or

$$g = (A - \delta)s = sr. \qquad (5.18)$$

Equation (5.17) is obtained when savings are determined on the assumption that the immortal representative agent maximizes function (5.8), as specified by equation (5.9), subject to constraint (5.15), and where $Y = c(t) + \dot{K}$. Equation (5.18) is obtained when the average propensity to save with regard to the 'social dividend', s, is taken as given.

Hence, in this model the rate of profit is given by technology alone and the saving–investment mechanism determines the growth rate. Figure 5.2 illustrates the first subcase (compare equations (5.16) and (5.17)). Provided that $A - \delta > \rho$, a unique steady-state equilibrium with a positive rate of growth is obtained. The marginal product of capital is constant irrespective of the amount of capital employed in the economy, and is consistently above that level of the rate of return above which savings are positive. The steady-state growth rate equals g^*.

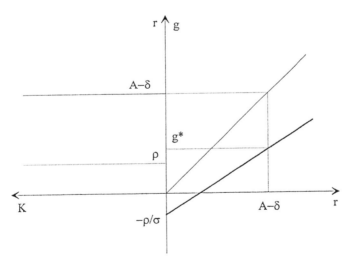

Figure 5.2   The growth rate in the Rebelo model

To understand better what this model amounts to, it is perhaps useful to compare it to the simplest model possible in the tradition of the 'classical' approach to the theory of growth and distribution, that is, the one in which corn is produced by means of corn and homogeneous labour on land of uniform quality.[6] In this model, which is a simple variant of Ricardo's 'corn model', the same commodity, corn, forms both the (circulating) capital input, consisting of the subsistence (in terms of corn) of workers plus seed corn, and the product.[7] The rate of profit in agriculture can therefore be determined as the ratio of the 'surplus product', or net output (exclusive of wages), and the capital advanced at the beginning of the production period, that is, as a ratio between two quantities of corn without any question of valuation. In order for a constant rate of profit to obtain in this model, two requirements must be fulfilled: (i) the corn wage per unit of labour must be given from outside and must be constant, irrespective of the levels of the state variables of the system such as the rate of growth or the size of the social capital; and (ii) land must be available in abundance, that is, it must be, and remain for ever, a non-scarce resource and thus a 'free good', as in von Neumann's famous growth model (see von Neumann, [1937] 1945). However, as Ricardo observed, with the system growing for a sufficiently long period of time, the point will come when land will become scarce, a rent will have to be paid to landlords and the rate of profit will decline.

Against the foil of the simplified 'classical' point of view sketched, the group of NGMs under consideration may now be reinterpreted as follows. First, these models assume implicitly that (simple) labour is a producible resource, whose cost of production is constant, that is, equal to the real wage rate: at the given wage labour is in elastic supply, and the supply is fully adjusted to the needs of capital accumulation.[8] Second, natural resources such as land are implicitly kept in a state of abundance by a sufficiently plentiful exogenous technical change of a resource-saving nature. Seen from this vantage point, the endogeneity of the growth rate is thus effected at the cost of an exogenous determination of the distribution of income coupled with the assumption of exogenous land-saving technical progress.

Before we turn to a somewhat more sophisticated variant of the type of NGMs under consideration, it should be noted that equation (5.18) is formally identical with the famous 'Cambridge equation' of the post-Keynesian theory of growth and distribution, championed by Nicholas Kaldor, Joan Robinson and Luigi Pasinetti. Its interpretation, however, is different: the direction of causality is reversed.[9] Post-Keynesians consider the growth rate as determined by 'animal spirits' of investors; the profit rate is then determined by the equilibrium condition that savings equal investment, where savings are taken to adjust to investment through changes in income distribution. (For a critical account of that mechanism, see Kurz, 1991.) Rebelo assumes, on the contrary, that what is not consumed will be invested, and since the rate of profit is determined by technology alone, the investment–saving mechanism determines the growth rate.[10]

4.2   A Somewhat Less Simple Model

Essentially the same avenue was followed by King and Rebelo (1990). The characteristic feature of their model is that instead of one kind of capital there are two kinds, real and human, both of which are accumulable. There are three lines of production, one for the social product, one for human and one for real capital. The production functions relating to the production of the two kinds of capital are given by

$$H = H(H_H, K_H) \tag{5.19}$$

and

$$K = K(H_K, K_K). \tag{5.20}$$

Both functions are assumed to be homogeneous of degree one and strictly concave. The composite capital good, consisting of human and real capital, is produced by means of itself only, and since each of the single capital items is produced in constant returns to scale production processes, the production of the composite capital good also exhibits constant returns. There are no diminishing returns to (composite) capital for the reason that there is no non-accumulable factor, such as simple or unskilled labour, that enters into the production of accumulable factors, that is, investment goods and human capital.[11] The rate of profit is uniquely determined by the technology and the maximization of profits. This follows from the *Non-substitution Theorem*, of which the model of Rebelo and that of King and Rebelo are special cases.[12] The Non-substitution Theorem states that taking the real wage rate as given, the rate of profit and relative prices are independent of the pattern of final demand provided (i) there are constant returns to scale, (ii) there is not more than one primary factor of production, and (iii) there is no joint production. In these conditions only one technique can be used in the long run, which gives the rate of profit and relative prices. The NGMs under consideration obviously satisfy these requirements with the special assumption that there is no primary factor, which is equivalent to assuming a zero remuneration of that factor (see Kurz and Salvadori, 1994). The growth rate of the system is then endogenously determined by the saving–investment equation. The larger the propensities to accumulate human and physical capital, the larger is the growth rate.

To conclude, some of the NGMs under consideration are characterized by a partial return to ideas that were prominent in growth theory prior to Solow's model. As regards technology, these models adopt considerably simplified versions of the 'classical' notions of production as a circular flow and of profits as a surplus product. As regards the prime mover of economic expansion, emphasis is on capital accumulation. However, in line with Solow's model and contrary to the post-Keynesian view, investment is taken to adjust to savings rather than the other way round, and 'Say's Law' is assumed to hold. The other genuinely neoclassical element of the approach consists of a concept of 'capital', the quantity of which can be ascertained independently of and prior to the determination of the rate of profit (and relative prices).

5   RETURNS TO CAPITAL BOUNDED FROM BELOW

Next there are models which preserve the dualism of accumulable and non-accumulable factors but restrict the impact of an accumulation of the former on their returns by a modification of the aggregate production function. Jones and Manuelli (1990), for example, allow for both labour and capital and even assume a convex technology, as in the Solow model. However, a convex technology requires only that the marginal product of capital is a decreasing function of its stock, not that it vanishes as the amount of capital per worker tends towards infinity. Jones and Manuelli stress: 'We want to show that a natural generalization of the standard convex technology used in the early analysis of growth models is sufficient to generate long-run increases in consumption per capita' (ibid., p. 1010). They assume that $h(k) \geq bk$ (each $k \geq 0$), where $h(k)$ is the per-capita production function and b is a positive constant. The special case contemplated by them is

$$h(k) = f(k) + bk, \tag{5.21}$$

where $f(k)$ is the conventional Solovian production function. As capital accumulates and the capital–labour ratio rises, the marginal product of capital will fall, approaching asymptotically b, its lower boundary. With a given propensity to save s and assuming capital to be everlasting, the steady-state growth rate g is endogenously determined: $g = sb$. Assuming on the contrary intertemporal utility maximization, then in order to guarantee unbounded growth it is necessary to assume that the technical parameter *b* is larger than the rate of time preference ρ. In the case in which it is, the steady-state rate of growth is given by equation (5.12) with *r* = *b*.

Jones and Manuelli then study the impact of parameters of tastes and technology and government policy variables on growth. They express some doubts as to recent attempts to attribute differences in growth rates between countries essentially to differences in tastes (reflected in the rate of time preference and the elasticity of substitution between present and future consumption). Although their own model is consistent with such an interpretation, the difficulty with this view is said to consist of explaining substantial variations in growth rates across time in a given country. This is why they suggest concentrating primarily on changes in government policy and their impact on the rate of return on capital to explain variations in the growth rate.

6   'THRESHOLD' MODELS

International evidence on growth rates of per-capita income reveals remarkable and persistent differences among nations. Some manage to sustain rapid economic growth over long periods of time, others expand at a low pace, while still others stagnate or even contract. The simple catchup hypothesis implicit in Solow's model, which maintains that, the larger the growth rate of a country is, the smaller is its per-capita income level, is not generally confirmed: while some poorer countries experienced accelerating growth and got closer to richer ones, others seem to be under the spell of a 'development trap' (see, for example, Baumol, 1986).

One attempt to explain persistent differences in national economic performance is in terms of a neoclassical model of economic growth augmented with a feature that is sufficient to produce multiple, locally-balanced growth paths in equilibrium. This avenue was taken by Azariadis and Drazen (1990). The feature under discussion is what they called 'technological externalities with a 'threshold' property': it permits returns to scale to increase, possibly substantially, whenever an economic state variable, such as physical or human capital per capita, exceeds a certain 'critical' value. To illustrate the basic idea, start from the intensive production function

$$y = A(k)k^{\alpha}. \tag{5.22}$$

In it the scale factor is taken to depend on *k*. Assume that *A*(*k*) depends on *k* in a very simple way: it is a step function with one jump at *k**:

$$A(k) = \begin{cases} A_0 & \text{for } k < k^* \\ A_1 & \text{for } k > k^*. \end{cases} \qquad (5.23)$$

Provided that the critical value k^* lies between the steady-state values of k that correspond to the scale factors A_0 and A_1, k_0 and k_1, there will be two locally-stable steady states. Azariadis and Drazen stress: 'Economies that start out with capital below the critical value k^* will converge monotonically to a steady state in which capital, consumption and income per head remain relatively low forever. ... The economy "takes off" toward $[k_1]$ if the initial capital per head is above k^*' (ibid., p. 509). The constellation under discussion is plotted in Figure 5.3; Figure 5.3a shows the technology, Figure 5.3b the relationship between the marginal product of capital and the capital–labour ratio.

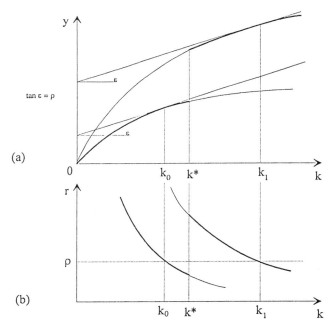

Figure 5.3   *Technology, the marginal product of capital and the capital– labour ratio in 'threshold' models*

If one is prepared to accept this, one might perhaps also be prepared to accept the idea of an 'interchange of increasing with decreasing returns to social inputs, that is, the existence of ranges for the state variables over which social returns to scale alternate from low to high as the size of production externalities varies' (ibid., p. 509).

There are several problems with this kind of approach. It is totally *ad hoc* and does not give convincing reasons why there should exist these 'critical' values of certain state variables and how their levels are to be ascertained. More important, it is not explained why economies are located on either side of the critical value. It is also unclear how economies which in the past were 'poor' managed to become 'rich'. Only explanations that are extraneous to the model provide some rationalization of actual development processes. These explanations generally have recourse to 'shocks' that are said to have shifted the economy's relevant state variable from the region to the left of the critical value to the region to the right of it. These shocks are traced back to wars, civil and other, or national catastrophes, such as floods, epidemics and so on. They are taken to cause the relevant state variable to jump, with important secular implications for the country's economic development. However, the model's contribution to a better understanding of the 'virtuous circle' of development and the 'vicious circle' of stagnation and decline is questionable.

In Subsection 2.3 it has been shown that a production function that exhibits increasing returns to scale is unable to do the job of rendering the Solovian growth model a model of endogenous growth. This result has implicitly been confirmed by the models sketched in this section. Something else is needed. As we already know, this something has to counteract any diminishing tendency of returns to capital. The following two sections are devoted to models contemplating *positive external effects* associated with the accumulation of capital that are taken to offset any fall in the marginal product of capital. There are essentially two kinds of external effects discussed: (i) those related to the formation of *human capital*; and (ii) those related to the generation of new *knowledge*. The most prominent representative of the first kind of approach is the model by Lucas (1988) and that of the second the model by Romer (1986).

7   ACCUMULATION OF HUMAN CAPITAL

7.1   Positive Externalities and Steady-state Growth

The gist of these models may be illustrated schematically in terms of the relationship between the two rates of return, r and ρ. If increasing returns in the process of formation of human capital or in R&D activities are sufficiently strong, the marginal product of capital will be an increasing function of the relevant state variable, ξ, as is illustrated in Figure 5.4. This raises the problem of (in)stability of steady-state equilibrium. If the economy starts to the right of ξ*, agents will want to accumulate human capital or to engage in research and development activities for ever, thus generating endogenous expansion. Growth will be a virtuous circle in the extreme sense that economic expansion will accelerate indefinitely. This has the disquieting implication of the economy producing an infinite output in finite time. (On the contrary, if the economy starts to the left of ξ*, agents will want to decumulate human and knowledge capital continuously, thus generating endogenous contraction.) In order to avoid this implausible consequence the advocates of these kind of models limit the increase of returns from above. This then yields a constellation such as the one depicted in Figure 5.5. It can be shown, setting aside the trivial solution (ξ = 0), that there are two steady-state equilibria: one defines a stationary economy (ξ = ξ*) and is unstable, the other a growing economy whose general rate of profit equals r^*.

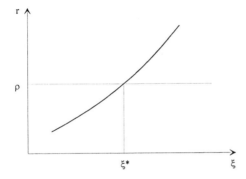

Figure 5.4   *Increasing returns and the (in)stability of steady-state equilibrium*

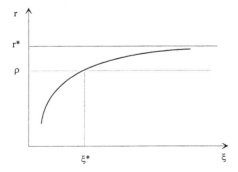

Figure 5.5   *Two steady-state equilibria*

7.2   Formation of Human Capital

An early attempt to generate sustained growth at an endogenous rate in a neoclassical framework was that of Uzawa (1965). In his model, the scale factor *A* is interpreted as representing human capital per worker. Its growth depends on the amount of labour services allocated to education. Emphasis is on optimal growth paths. With a linear utility function, Uzawa was able to show that the optimal path required that all investment was channelled either in physical or in human capital formation until after some time a steady state was reached characterized by uniform exponential growth in both physical and human capital per worker. Uzawa's model was the starting-point of several contributions to the NGT.

Lucas (1988) assumed that agents have a choice between two ways of spending their (non-leisure) time: to contribute to current production or to accumulate human capital. It is essentially the allocation of time between the two alternatives contemplated that decides the growth rate of the system. For example, a decrease in the time spent producing goods involves a reduction in current output; at the same time it speeds up the formation of human capital and thereby increases output growth. With the accumulation of human capital there is said to be an associated externality: the more human capital society as a whole has accumulated, the more productive each single member will be. This is reflected in the following macroeconomic production function

$$Y = AK^{\beta}(qhN)^{1-\beta}h^{*\gamma}, \qquad\qquad (5.24)$$

where the labour input consists of the number of workers, *N*, times the fraction of time spent working, *q*, times *h* which gives the labour input in efficiency units. Finally, there is the term h^*. This is designed to represent the externality. The single agent takes h^* as a parameter in his or her optimizing by choice of *c* and *q*. However, for society as a whole the accumulation of human capital increases output both directly and indirectly, that is, through the externality. Here we are confronted with a variant of a *public good* problem, which may be expressed as follows. The individual optimizing agent faces constant returns to scale in production: the sum of the partial elasticities of production of the factors he or she can control, that is, his or her physical and human capital, is unity. Yet for society as a whole the partial elasticity of production of human capital is not $1 - \beta$, but $1 - \beta + \gamma$.

Lucas's conceptualization of the process by means of which human capital is built up is the following:

$$\dot{h} = \upsilon h^{\zeta}(1-q), \qquad (5.25)$$

where υ and ζ are positive constants. (Note that equation (5.25) can be interpreted as a 'production function' of human capital.) Lucas hastens to add that it is not sufficient to assume $\zeta > 0$, for

> if we take $\zeta < 1$ in this formulation, so that there is diminishing returns to the accumulation of human capital, it is easy to see that human capital cannot serve as an alternative engine of growth to the [Solovian] technology term $A(t)$. ... This formulation would simply complicate the original Solow model without offering any genuinely new possibilities. (Ibid., p. 19)

Hence, it has to be assumed that $\zeta \geq 1$. Without much further discussion he postulates $\zeta = 1$. With this specification, the function (5.25) has a constant marginal product of human capital producing additional human capital. It deserves to be stressed that setting $\zeta = 1$ is not just a very special assumption consistent with endogenous growth, but the only assumption consistent with steady-state growth in Lucas's model. For if ζ were to be larger than unity, the growth rate would go up over time.

Interestingly, it can be shown that if there is *not* the above-mentioned externality, that is, if γ in equation (5.24) equals zero, and therefore returns to scale are constant and, as a consequence, the Non-substitution Theorem holds, endogenous growth in Lucas's model is obtained in essentially the same way as in the models by Rebelo (1991) and King and Rebelo (1990): the rate of profit is determined by technology and profit maximization alone; and for the predetermined level of the rate of profit the saving–investment mechanism determines the rate of growth. Hence, as Lucas himself has pointed out, the endogenous growth is positive *independently* of the fact that there is the above-mentioned externality, that is, independently of the fact that γ is positive. For a demonstration of this fact, see Kurz and Salvadori (1995b). Therefore, while complicating the picture increasing returns do *not* add substantially to it: growth is endogenous even if returns to scale are constant. If returns to scale are not constant then the Non-substitution Theorem does not apply. Therefore, neither the competitive technique nor the associated rate of profit is determined by technical alternatives and profit maximization alone. Nevertheless, these two factors still determine, in steady states, a relationship between the rate of profit and the rate of growth. This relationship together with the relationship between the same rates obtained from the saving–investment mechanism determines both variables. Thus, although the analysis is more complex, essentially the same mechanism applies as in the models dealt with in Section 4.

Finally, it should be noticed that in Lucas's model leisure time per unit of time is exogenously given. Hence, other than in standard neoclassical treatments leisure is not a good the amount of which can be chosen at will. More important, in a model in which actual employment is taken to coincide with full employment, the above premiss implies that all people who are idle are engaged in the production of human capital. Hence in this model it is of crucial importance whether it is a valid thing to assume full employment. If the answer happens to be 'No', then the model fails to assess correctly the loss in current output due to unemployment; it also wrongly takes those not employed as building up their human capital and thus contributing to a larger future output. Yet, the majority of those on the dole can safely be assumed to gradually lose their skills and dexterity. Hence, with regard to these people the theory misreads reality.

8   ENDOGENOUS TECHNICAL CHANGE

From the time of the classical economists onwards, technical change has always been regarded as at least partly endogenous. Important examples are Adam Smith's concept of the division of labour, Allyn Young's discussion of economies of scale and Nicholas Kaldor's 'technical progress function'.[13] While these contributions are generally given short shrift in the NGT literature, Arrow (1962) is considered an important precursor. In his paper on 'learning by doing' Arrow related the state variable 'level of technology' of a single firm to another state variable: the amount of capital accumulated in the economy as a whole. In a simplified form, output of firm i can be written as

$$Y_i = A(K) \, F(K_i, L_i), \tag{5.26}$$

where K gives the aggregate stock of capital and K_i and L_i denote the amounts of capital and labour employed in firm i. In this model the increase in A is an unintended byproduct of the experience accumulated while producing new capital goods. This learning by doing is taken to be purely *external to firms* producing or using the new capital goods. This strong assumption is analytically convenient in the sense that it allows one to avoid the important and difficult question of who gets rewarded for the increase in the scale factor A. While there is potential for endogenizing the rate of growth in Arrow's model, via a flexible saving rate, this was not used because he assumed a fixed share of income saved and a fixed capital coefficient, the ratio of which gives the growth rate.

Romer (1986) took Arrow's model as a starting-point. The acquisition of technological 'knowledge' is taken to be intimately tied to the accumulation of capital. Romer even assumes A to be proportional, and by an appropriate choice of units indeed equal, to K, the economy's total capital stock. As in Arrow, the growth in A is entirely external to firms that produce and use new capital goods. Romer's model differs from Arrow's essentially in only two respects: the adoption of a conventional neoclassical production function and the assumption of intertemporal utility maximization.

Attention focuses on the role of a single state variable: 'knowledge' or 'information'. The main idea is that the information contained in inventions and discoveries (which have become innovations) has the property of being available to anybody to make use of it at the same time. In other words, information is considered essentially a non-rival good. However, it is not taken to be totally non-excludable. Since those who make an economically significant discovery and the firms that market it typically control the access to the relevant information, they can, at least for some time, exclude others from using it. This power allows some people or firms to pocket extra or monopoly profits temporarily. It is around the two different aspects of publicness (non-rivalry and non-excludability) that the argument revolves.

Discoveries are made in research and development departments of firms. This requires that resources be withheld from producing current output. The basic idea of Romer's 1986 model is 'that there is a trade-off between consumption today and knowledge that can be used to produce more consumption tomorrow' (ibid., p. 1015). To this effect he postulates that there exists a (single) 'research technology' that produces 'knowledge' from forgone consumption. Interestingly, Romer conceives of 'knowledge' as a magnitude which does not depreciate and can be measured on a single scale as a continuous variable.[14] In other words it is like non-depreciating capital.

As regards the conceptualization of research activities, Romer stipulates a research technology that is concave and homogeneous of degree one,

$$\dot{k}_i = G(I_i, k_i), \tag{5.27}$$

where k_i is the current stock of private knowledge, I_i is an amount of forgone consumption in research by firm i, and $\dot{k}_i$ is the induced increase in the firm's knowledge. The production function of the consumption good relative to firm i is

$$Y_i = F(k_i, K, \mathbf{x}_i), \tag{5.28}$$

where K denotes the accumulated stock of knowledge in the economy as a whole and $\mathbf{x}_i$ all inputs different from knowledge. These inputs are assumed to be given and constant over time: 'factors other than knowledge are in fixed supply' (ibid., p. 1019). This premiss is comprehensible with respect to labour since 'a key distinguishing feature of this model is that population growth is not necessary for unbounded growth in per capita income. For simplicity it is left out' (ibid.). The premiss is also clear with respect to land of a single or of different qualities, whose powers, following Ricardo's approach, could be taken as 'indestructible'. But the premiss would not apply to exhaustible and renewable resources or to capital goods. The amounts available at each moment of time of these factors depend on the decisions of consumers and investors. Hence, their amounts cannot be kept constant by assumption. Strictly speaking, Romer's above assumption implies that there are neither exhaustible and renewable resources nor capital goods in the model. Put differently, there exists only labour, Ricardian land, and 'knowledge'. That is, 'knowledge' is the only existing quasi capital utilized in the production of the consumption good. (The forgone consumption good is, on the contrary, a capital good utilized in the production of 'knowledge'.) Spillovers from private research and development activities cause improvements in the public stock of knowledge K. It is assumed that the function is homogeneous of degree one in k_i and $\mathbf{x}_i$ and homogeneous of degree $\gamma > 1$ in k_i and K.[15]

Assuming, contrary to Romer, that the above production function (5.28) is homogeneous of degree one in k_i and K (that is, $\gamma = 1$), involves a constant marginal product of capital: the diminishing returns to k_i are exactly offset by the external improvements in technology associated with capital accumulation. In this case it can be shown that, as in the models previously dealt with, the rate of profit is determined by technology and profit maximization alone, provided, as is assumed by Romer, that the ratio K/k_i equals the (given) number of firms (see Kurz and Salvadori, 1995b). The saving–investment relation then determines endogenously the growth rate. Once again endogenous growth does *not* depend on an assumption about increasing returns with regard to accumulable factors. Growth would be no less endogenous if constant returns were to be assumed.

In the case in which $\gamma > 1$, the analysis is a good deal more complicated. First of all a steady-state equilibrium cannot exist. From the production function of the consumption good we obtain

$$\frac{\dot{Y}_i}{Y_i} = \gamma \frac{\dot{k}_i}{k_i} , \qquad (5.29)$$

which, in a steady state, should equal the growth rate of consumption and of forgone consumption. Then the ratio I/k should increase over time and therefore the profit rate r should also increase, which is inconsistent with a steady state.

Romer (1986) is of course not interested in a constellation, in which the growth rate goes up without limit. *A priori* theorizing cannot help much in determining the existence of a steady-state equilibrium, but some speculation is possible. Since forgone consumption I_i grows more quickly than 'knowledge' k_i, the rate of profit r, and therefore the growth rate of consumption output, increases over time. Hence an equilibrium may exist only if r is bounded from above. Romer is in fact forced to introduce *ad hoc* the assumption of 'a strong form of diminishing returns in research' (Romer, 1986, p. 1019), otherwise consumption would grow too fast and discounted utility would go to infinity.[16] To prevent this from happening he assumes that $G(I_i/k_i, 1) < \alpha$ for each I_i/k_i, $0 \leq I_i/k_i < \infty$, where α is a given constant. If

$$\lim_{I/k \to \infty} G(I/k, 1) = \alpha, \text{ then also } \lim_{I/k \to \infty} r = \alpha.$$

Obviously, in this way also the growth rate of consumption, which is related to r by the saving–investment relation, is bounded from above. As a consequence, all other growth rates are bounded and an equilibrium could obtain. Romer has indeed proved that such an equilibrium exists. Finally, it deserves to be mentioned that if $\gamma < 1$, then the rate of profit and all the growth rates would decrease indefinitely.

To conclude, a significant methodological difference between the treatment of capital in conventional long-period neoclassical models, including Solow's growth model, and that of 'knowledge' in Romer's construction should be noted. Conventional neoclassical theory starts from given initial endowments of all productive resources, including real capital, which define the set of intertemporal production possibilities of the economy. On the contrary, Romer assumes that there is no exogenously-given initial endowment of 'knowledge'. The quantity of the resource 'knowledge' available in the economy at any given moment of time is rather determined endogenously. Romer's approach thus shares a characteristic feature of 'classical' long-period analysis, which treats the size of social capital as an endogenous variable.[17]

In Romer (1987) the growth of the scale factor A is still directly linked to the growth of K, but the link between the two variables is conceptualized differently. Rather than reflecting learning by doing it is now considered the result of a greater variety of intermediate goods that render production more efficient. With expanding markets it pays the fixed cost incurred in the development of additional intermediate products which then raise productivity and foster growth. Romer incorporates the theory of optimal product variety of Dixit and Stiglitz (1977) in the growth model and tries to take into account monopolistic competition. It is assumed that each product is produced by a local monopolist and that there is a continuum of intermediate products, defined on the interval (0, A). The production technology gives final output as a function of labour and intermediate products

$$Y = L^{1-\beta} \int_0^A [x(i)]^\beta \, di, \quad 0 < \beta < 1, \qquad (5.30)$$

where $x(i)$ represents the input of intermediary good i. In a symmetric equilibrium $x(i) = x^*$ for all i. In equilibrium marginal revenue equals marginal cost for each monopolist. Marginal revenue equals the marginal product of each intermediate good and marginal cost comes from the production technology of intermediate goods each of which is taken to be produced by sacrificing one unit of the consumption good. Romer then constructs an aggregate production function

$$Y = bL^{1-\beta} A^{1-\beta} K^\beta, \qquad (5.31)$$

where b is a positive constant. The equilibrium value of A is determined by the zero-profit condition of free entry in the intermediate good industry; it depends on the fixed cost in each intermediate good sector and the stock of capital, K. The function (5.31) has increasing returns to scale. The main features of this model and a modified version of it (see Romer, 1990) are: (i) in the intermediate good industry there is imperfect competition which is reflected in monopoly rents yielded by successfully innovating firms; and (ii) increasing returns are incorporated in a steady-state model of endogenous growth.

9   CRITICAL REMARKS ON THE 'NEW' GROWTH THEORY

The NGMs are designed to contribute to a better understanding of actual growth processes both of industrialized and of developing countries. These models revolve around a few broad and rather obvious ideas that were spelled out time and again in the history of economic thought. What is new is the bold attempt to formalize these ideas within a macroeconomic steady-state framework. However, it can be doubted that the formalizations add significantly to our understanding of growth processes. This section points out what I consider to be some of the most important shortcomings of the NGT.

Nobody could sensibly deny that *structural aspects* play an important role in processes of economic growth and development. The various aspects of structural change are a major focus of attention in Lowe's *Path* (see Lowe, 1976). These aspects include (i) the endogenous change of the economy's institutional framework in the course of its growth and development, (ii) distributional shifts in output and employment between different sectors of the economy, and (iii) different forms of technical and organizational change. None of these aspects plays a role in the NGT.[18] It deserves to be stressed especially that as steady-state models the NGMs can only allow for Harrod-neutral technical progress, that is, progress of the *labour-augmenting* type. Hence, both the old growth theory of the Solovian variety and the NGT share an important feature: they contemplate only a *single* form of overall technical change. In regard to a proper treatment of technical change the steady-state framework turns out to be a strait-jacket that seriously limits the scope of the analysis.

As regards *preferences*, in most contributions to the NGT consumption is taken to be the sole end of economic activity. In some formulations not even leisure is considered to be a good that contributes to the consumer's utility. In these models saving is thus carried out, in a world of perfect foresight, solely for the purpose of changing the time pattern of the flow of consumption. Many eminent economists have provided reasons for doubting the validity of that crucial assumption (see Steedman, 1981). Even Irving Fisher, whose emphasis on a 'preference for early enjoyment income over deferred enjoyment income' (Fisher, [1930] 1977, p. 65) is frequently referred to in textbook treatments of time preference, was well aware of the existence of non-consumption enjoyments. As regards 'the benefits' deriving from 'property and wealth', Fisher expounded:

> a man may include in the benefits of his wealth the fun of running the business, or the social standing he thinks it gives him, or political or other power and influence, or the miserly sense of possession or the satisfaction in the mere process of further accumulation. (Ibid., p. 17)

When it is allowed that the holding and accumulation of wealth are desired for their own sake, then certain familiar results of time-preference theory that underlie most of the NGMs cease to hold. It is only recently that an attempt has been made to take into account the fact, emphasized by economists from Adam Smith, Ricardo, Marx, Max Weber, Frank Knight and Schumpeter to Keynes, that individuals also derive satisfaction from accumulating wealth (see Cole, Mailath, and Postlewaite, 1992). This is somewhat surprising since the strive to accumulate wealth, or some similar desire, would lead directly to an 'endogenous' explanation of growth, as is the case, for example, with Keynes's 'animal spirits'.

The process of economic growth is indissolubly intertwined with the emergence of *new methods of production* and *new goods*, the coexistence of different methods of production and the gradual disappearance of presently known methods and goods. *Variety* is an essential ingredient of growth. This fact is acknowledged in some versions of the theory of endogenous growth and is given special attention in others. Yet the way this is done involves reducing a world with heterogeneous goods, the variety of which may change, to a world with a single good only. Indeed, using Lancaster's term (Lancaster, 1969), all the different goods produced and consumed represent different amounts of a single *characteristic* only. For example, if a changing (increasing) variety of commodities due to product innovations is sought to be covered, however imperfectly, by intertemporal utility maximization it would have to be assumed that all goods to be invented only in the future are already allowed for in the current utility function. Alternatively, there must not be any genuinely new goods but only new products representing different amounts of a single characteristic.

An *aggregate production function* is designed to represent complex microrelations of production in simple terms. The quest for simplicity is certainly laudable. It should be noted, however, that from contributions to aggregation theory we learn that the conditions for consistent aggregation of micro relations of production to a macro relation are excessively restrictive, such that the aggregation conditions can safely be assumed never to be realized in reality; as Franklin Fisher (1971) pointed out, the conditions for any such derivation are 'far too stringent to be believable'. Despite this finding, the NGT uses aggregate production functions. Sometime this is defended on the grounds that these functions fit the data fairly well and their estimated marginal products approximate closely the observed 'factor prices', the wage rate (if labour is taken into account at all) and the profit rate. The claim itself is highly dubious, but even if it were justified, this must not be interpreted as rendering some *empirical* credibility to the aggregate production function. According to Fisher (1971) the seemingly good fit is simply an artefact of the constancy of the profit share. Hence there is neither theoretical nor empirical support for the aggregate production functions used in the NGMs.

It is an outstanding feature of many contributions to the NGT that *capital*, whether physical or human, is substantially upgraded as a factor of production relatively to (simple) labour and to natural resources; indeed, the latter is hardly ever taken into account and the former in some contributions only. In one class of models there is even only a single factor of production: 'capital'. The overwhelming weight attributed to that factor, its accumulation and incessant qualitative revolution consequent upon the growth in technical knowledge, would seem to have as a prerequisite the elaboration of a coherent long-period notion of capital. However, nothing even remotely resembling a serious attempt to come to grips with this problem is to be found in the NGT. On the contrary, the representatives of that theory simply ignore the results of aggregation theory and of the controversy in the theory of capital in the 1960s and 1970s.[19]

In his 1956 paper, Solow made it very clear that his analysis was based on extremely simplifying assumptions. In the concluding section of his paper, entitled 'Qualifications', he emphasized:

> All the difficulties and rigidities which go into modern Keynesian income analysis have been shunted aside. It is not my contention that these problems don't exist, nor that they are of no significance in the long run. My purpose was to examine what might be called the tight-rope view of economic growth and to see where more flexible assumptions about production would lead to a simple model. Underemployment and excess capacity or their opposites can still be attributed to any of the old causes of deficient or excess aggregate demand, but less readily to any deviation from a narrow 'balance'. (Ibid., p. 91)

The NGMs share this 'tight-rope view of economic growth', that is, they set aside economic fluctuations and assume that the economy follows a path characterized by the *full employment of all productive resources*.

Solow has repeatedly expressed his uneasiness about the general usefulness of this view.[20] Indeed, it is not only *vis-à-vis* current unemployment figures in the OECD that the assumption of full employment is difficult to sustain. As Edmond Malinvaud stressed a few years before the proper takeoff of the NGT:

> Students of economic growth will easily accept two ideas put forward ... namely that some disequilibria may be sustained over rather long periods, and that the existence of these disequilibria significantly reacts on the growth process, to speed it up, slow it down or change its course. (Malinvaud, 1983, p. 95)

However, what could easily be accepted by students of economic growth is not actually accepted by many practitioners of growth theory. The main problem with regard to much of growth theory, including the NGMs, is to be seen in the absence of a proper analysis of investment behaviour. As Malinvaud stressed:

> an essential part of any theory of economic growth should be the representation of investment, and it seems to me that both excess capacity and profitability have an

important role to play in this representation. ... [T]he investment equation ... should be the final outcome of the explanation. (Ibid., pp. 95–6)

It is a major shortcoming both of the Solovian model and of the NGT that no serious attempt is made to represent investment and to analyse the interplay between investment and saving. To assume that 'Say's Law of Markets' holds good is just not good enough.

NOTES

*   This paper was written in Spring 1994 and slightly revised in Spring 1996. Seminars I gave at the universities of Siena (Italy), Nice (France), Graz (Austria) and Cambridge (UK) were partly based upon it. I should like to thank the participants for useful discussions. I am especially grateful to Geoff Harcourt and Neri Salvadori for detailed comments. The paper is closely related to two papers co-authored by the latter and myself; see Kurz and Salvadori (1995b, 1995c).

1.   The *magnum opus* of the period prior to his retirement was, of course, his *On Economic Knowledge* (1964). It goes without saying that in Lowe's case the word 'retirement' did not have its usual meaning.

2.   For a summary account of Lowe's achievements, see Hagemann and Kurz (1990).

3.   For a more detailed account of the relevant literature, see Barro and Sala-i-Martin (1995).

4.   As will be seen in Section 9, this formulation leads to various difficulties, logical and other, which raise serious doubts about its usefulness. Solow, for perfectly good reasons it seems, does not think highly of the optimizing versions of the NGT: 'the use made of the intertemporally-optimizing representative agent ... adds little or nothing to the story anyway, while encumbering it with unnecessary implausibilities and complexities' (Solow, 1994, p. 49).

5.   In Fig. 5.1 the case of a given propensity to save would be represented by $\rho = 0$.

6.   On the classical theory of economic growth, see Lowe (1954 and 1976, pp. 5–7) and Kurz and Salvadori (1995a, Ch. 15, and 1995c).

7.   In this model $\delta = 1$, that is, only circulating capital is taken into consideration.

8.   This assumption is also entertained in the von Neumann model, which treats the two distributive variables, the wage rate and the rate of interest, *asymmetrically*: wages are given from outside the system of production and are included among the necessary advances of production, whereas the rate of interest is determined as a residual. The asymmetric treatment of the distributive variables is a characteristic feature of the classical approach to the theory of distribution and stands in striking contrast to the symmetric treatment of these variables in the neoclassical approach. On this, see Kurz and Salvadori (1993, 1995a, Chs. 1 and 14).

9.   This should be kept in mind when confronted with Bertola's observation that 'A relaxation of the representative-individual assumption to allow for heterogeneous income sources reveals a striking similarity between these models and post-Keynesian models of income distribution and growth' (Bertola, 1993, p. 1196).

10.   It should also be noted that Rebelo assumes a single capital good, whereas post-Keynesian economists generally allow for any number of capital goods; see the papers collected in Panico and Salvadori (1993). See also the generalization of the '*AK*-model' to any number of commodities by Kurz and Salvadori (1995d).

11.   The assumption that the formation of human capital does not involve any unskilled labour as an input is difficult to sustain: the whole point of education processes is that a person's capacity to perform unskilled labour is gradually transformed into his or her capacity to perform skilled labour. Adam Smith, for example, was perfectly aware of this. For an analytical treatment of the problem of human capital that takes his discussion as a starting-point, see Kurz and Salvadori (1995a, Ch. 11).

12.   The close relationship between some of the NGMs and the Non-substitution Theorem seems to have escaped the attention of the growth theorists.

13. On Smith's theory of growth, see Lowe (1954).
14. These assumptions are difficult to sustain. Knowledge is not a variable that can be measured on a single scale; it is in any case not cardinally measurable. It is intrinsically heterogeneous. Different kinds of knowledge are differently useful in production. New knowledge often renders previous knowledge obsolete.
15. As Romer later admitted, this formulation is inconsistent with the assumption that research is a nonrival good (see Romer, 1994, p. 15). He added that this 'may seem like a trifling matter in an area of theory that depends on so many other short cuts. After all, if one is going to do violence to the complexity of economic activity by assuming that there is an aggregate production function, how much more harm can it do to be sloppy about the difference between rival and nonrival goods?' (ibid., pp. 15–16). (It is unclear where to stop this process.)
16. In his discrete-time model of growth with only two periods he assumes a simple linear research technology by means of which one unit of forgone consumption produces one unit of knowledge; see Romer (1986, section IV). Obviously, this technology has constant returns.
17. For a detailed discussion of the classical approach, see Kurz and Salvadori (1995a).
18. While institutions, cultural norms etc. play no role in the formal part of the NGMs they are frequently invoked in the interpretative part. For example, different numerical values assigned to the rate of time preference are taken to reflect differences in the cultural setting. However, next to nothing is offered that would explain how these numerical values are arrived at. There is an abundance of *ad hoc* reasoning or, some critics might say, of prejudices garbed in scientific vocabulary.
19. For a discussion of that controversy, see, for example, Kurz and Salvadori (1995a, Ch. 14).
20. In his lecture delivered in Stockholm when he received the Nobel Prize in Economic Science Solow admitted with regard to his growth theory: 'I think I paid too little attention to the problems of effective demand' (Solow, 1988, p. 309). He also spoke of 'a standing temptation to sound like Dr. Pangloss, a very clever Dr. Pangloss. I think that tendency has won out in recent years' (ibid.).

REFERENCES

Arrow, K.J. (1962), 'The economic implications of learning by doing', *Review of Economic Studies*, **29**, pp. 155–73.
Azariadis, C. and A, Drazen (1990), 'Threshold externalities in economic development', *Quarterly Journal of Economics*, **105**, pp. 501–26.
Barro, R.M. and X. Sala-i-Martin (1995), *Economic Growth*, New York: McGraw-Hill.
Baumol, W.J. (1986), 'Productivity growth, convergence, and welfare: what the long-run data show', *American Economic Review*, **76**, pp. 1072–85.
Bertola, G. (1993), 'Factor shares and savings in endogenous growth', *American Economic Review*, **83**, pp. 1184–98.
Cole, H., G. Mailath and A. Postlewaite (1992), 'Social norms, savings behavior, and growth', *Journal of Political Economy*, **100**, pp. 1092–125.
Dixit, A. and J. Stiglitz (1977), 'Monopolistic competition and optimum product diversity', *American Economic Review*, **67**, pp. 297–308.
Ferguson, A. (1793), *An Essay on the History of Civil Society*, 6th edn (1st edn 1767), reprint 1966, Edinburgh: Edinburgh University Press.
Fisher, F.M. (1971), 'Aggregate production functions and the explanation of wages: a simulation experiment', *Review of Economics and Statistics*, **53**, pp. 305–25.
Fisher, I. (1977), *The Theory of Interest*, first published in 1930, New York: Macmillan.
Grossman, G.M. and E. Helpman (1994), 'Endogenous innovation in the theory of growth', *Journal of Economic Perspectives*, **8**, pp. 23–44.
Hagemann, H. and H.D. Kurz (1990), 'Balancing freedom and order: on Adolph Lowe's political economics', *Social Research*, **57**, pp. 733–53.
Hicks, J.R. (1969), *A Theory of Economic History*, Oxford: Clarendon Press.
Jones, L.E. and R.E. Manuelli (1990), 'A convex model of equilibrium growth: theory and policy implications', *Journal of Political Economy*, **98**, pp. 1008–38.

King, R.G. and S. Rebelo (1990), 'Public policy and economic growth: developing neoclassical implications', *Journal of Political Economy*, **98**, pp. 126–50.

King, R.G. and S. Rebelo (1993), 'Transitional dynamics and economic growth in the neoclassical model', *American Economic Review*, **83**, pp. 908–31.

Kurz, H.D. (1991), 'Technical change, growth and distribution: a steady-state approach to "unsteady" growth on Kaldorian lines', in E.J. Nell and W. Semmler (1991), *Nicholas Kaldor and mainstream economics. Confrontation or convergence?* London: Macmillan, pp. 421–48.

Kurz, H.D. and N. Salvadori (1993), 'Von Neumann's growth model and the "classical" tradition', *European Journal of the History of Economic Thought*, **1**, pp. 129–60.

Kurz, H.D. and N. Salvadori (1994), 'The non-substitution theorem: making good a lacuna', *Journal of Economics*, **59**, pp. 97–103.

Kurz, H.D. and N. Salvadori (1995a), *Theory of Production. A Long-period Analysis*, Cambridge, Melbourne and New York: Cambridge University Press.

Kurz, H.D. and N. Salvadori (1995b), 'The "new" growth theory: old wine in new goatskins', revised version of a paper presented at the workshop on 'Endogenous Growth and Development', at the International School of Economic Research, University of Siena, Italy, 3–9 July 1994. To be published in the proceedings of the conference.

Kurz, H.D. and N. Salvadori (1995c), 'Theories of "endogenous" growth in historical perspective', paper presented at the Eleventh World Congress of the International Economic Association, Tunis, Tunisia, 18–22 December 1995. To be published in the proceedings of the congress.

Kurz, H.D. and N. Salvadori (1995d), 'A multisector "AK-model" of endogenous growth', mimeographed, to be published.

Lancaster, K. (1969), *Introduction to Modern Microeconomics*, Chicago: Rand McNally.

Lowe, A. (1954), 'The classical theory of economic growth', *Social Research*, **21**, pp. 127–58. Reprinted in Lowe (1987).

Lowe, A. (1964). *On Economic Knowledge*, New York and Evanston; 2nd edn New York: M.E. Sharpe, 1977.

Lowe, A. (1976), *The Path of Economic Growth*, Cambridge: Cambridge University Press.

Lowe, A. (1987), *Essays in Political Economics: Public Control in a Democratic Society*, ed. Allen Oakley, Brighton: Wheatsheaf Books.

Lucas, R.E. (1988), 'On the mechanics of economic development', *Journal of Monetary Economics*, **22**, pp. 3–42.

Malinvaud, E. (1983), 'Notes on growth theory with imperfectly flexible prices', in J.-P. Fitoussi (ed.), *Modern Macroeconomic Theory*, Oxford: Basil Blackwell, pp. 93–114.

Neumann, J. von (1945), 'A model of general economic equilibrium', *Review of Economic Studies*, **13**, pp. 1–9. English translation of 'Über ein ökonomisches Gleichungssystem und eine Verallgemeinerung des Brouwerschen Fixpunktsatzes', in *Ergebnisse eines mathematischen Kolloquiums*, **8** (1937), pp. 73–83.

Panico, C. and N. Salvadori (eds) (1993), *Post Keynesian Theory of Growth and Distribution*, Aldershot: Edward Elgar.

Rebelo, S. (1991), 'Long run policy analysis and long run growth', *Journal of Political Economy*, **99**, pp. 500–521.

Romer, P.M. (1986), 'Increasing returns and long-run growth', *Journal of Political Economy*, **94**, pp. 1002–37.

Romer, P.M. (1987), 'Growth based on increasing returns due to specialization', *American Economic Review. Papers and Proceedings*, 77, pp. 56–72.

Romer, P.M. (1990), 'Endogenous technological change', *Journal of Political Economy*, **98**, pp. S71–S102.

Romer, P.M. (1994), 'The origins of endogenous growth,' *Journal of Economic Perspectives*, **8**, pp. 3–22.

Solow, R.M. (1956), 'A contribution to the theory of economic growth', *Quarterly Journal of Economics*, **70**, pp. 65–94.

Solow, R.M. (1957), 'Technical change and the aggregate production function', *Review of Economics and Statistics*, **39**, pp. 312–20.

Solow, R.M. (1970), *Growth Theory. An Exposition*, Oxford: Clarendon Press.

Solow, R.M. (1988), 'Growth theory and after', *American Economic Review*, **78**, pp. 307–17.

Solow, R.M. (1994), 'Perspectives on growth theory', *Journal of Economic Perspectives*, **8**, pp. 45–54.

Steedman, I. (1981), 'Time preference, the rate of interest and abstinence from accumulation', *Australian Economic Papers*, **20**, pp. 219–34. Reprinted in I. Steedman, *From Exploitation to Altruism*, Cambridge: Polity Press, 1989.

Swan, T.W. (1956), 'Economic growth and capital accumulation', *Economic Record*, **32**, pp. 224–361.

Uzawa, H. (1965), 'Optimum technical change in an aggregate model of economic growth', *International Economic Review*, **6**, pp. 18–31.

6. On Working and Circulating Capital

Ferdinando Meacci

'All capital is circulating capital'
(Marx, *Grundrisse*, p. 620)

The purpose of this chapter is to investigate whether the terms 'working' and 'circulating' capital are two different terms for the same concept or whether they should be considered two different terms for two different concepts.

This purpose will be carried out in two steps. First, we shall investigate the use of the term 'working' by Lowe himself. Second, the same attempt will be made with reference to Keynes. At the end of each of the two steps an assessment will be made of the use of this term by these economists. In both cases the assessment will be extended to the relationship, which was established both by Lowe and by Keynes via the notion of working capital, between their own treatment of this notion and two preceding streams of thought. These relationships run, in the first case, between Lowe and the Austrians; in the second, between Keynes and the classics (in Marx's sense).

These assessments will eventually converge towards the two main conclusions of the present chapter. One is that the terms 'circulating' and 'working' capital are *not* two different terms for the same notion. The other is that these two notions are different *because* they belong to two different theories.

The identification of these theories will be pursued in this chapter with more determination than the differentiation of the two notions if only because our aim is *not* to resort to what Shackle calls the 'bestiary' of our subject as if it were a 'taxonomy', or to the 'taxonomy' as if it were a 'machine'.[1]

1   LOWE

The notion of 'working' capital is introduced by Lowe on the assumption that this term is a modern substitute for the old classical term of 'circulating' capital:

Working capital is one of the neglected issues in neoclassical literature. As a matter of fact, very little of analytical use has been handed down to us even from classical writings. After two false starts by Smith and Ricardo, both trying to find a distinction between 'fixed' and 'circulating' capital, the latter concept became more and more identified with the 'wage fund' and, thus, with one of the most dubious constructs of classical economics. (1976, p. 48)

According to Lowe, the situation improved much later: first, through Taussig's *Wages and Capital* (1896) and Böhm-Bawerk's version of the structure of production (which according to Lowe 'is really a special model of the circulation of working capital'); second, through the works of some economists of the 1930s and particularly through that of Keynes.

Lowe's treatment of working capital starts from what he calls 'a census of an industrial community's wealth in physical terms'. This wealth is classified into *finished* and *unfinished* goods depending on whether these goods are 'ready for use' or not. Finished goods are in turn divided into the products of consumer-good industries (Sector II) which are *final* goods, and the products of equipment-good industries (Sector I) which are *finished*, but not final, goods. The equipment-good industries are in turn classified as industries that produce equipment for the consumer-good industries (Sector Ib) or for the equipment-good industries themselves (Sector Ia). The activities leading to a particular class of finished goods, whether final or not (say a dress, a loom or a steel mill), constitute a *sector*. This is depicted in Lowe's 'schema of industrial production' (along with the sectors producing the corresponding equipment goods and machine tools) as consisting of four *stages* with the N's, R's and F's standing for the stocks of labour, natural resources and fixed capital (and the n's, r's and f's for their annual flows) combined in fixed proportions to produce different flows of finished goods. There are as many sectors as finished goods and as many stages as unfinished goods. Lowe's theory of production is therefore an analysis of the physical flows of production resulting from the application of physical stocks of wealth. Hence Lowe's distinction between *fixed* and *working* capital: while fixed capital, according to this terminology, is the stock of the finished goods which are not final, working capital is the stock of the unfinished goods which correspond to the output of the stages of each sector. Accordingly, while *stage* analysis is the study of the transformations undergone by working capital within a particular sector, *sector* analysis is the study of the transformations of the fixed capital of one sector in relation to the transformations of the working capital of another. Stage analysis and sector analysis are combined by Lowe to show the conditions required for the *continuity of production*. These conditions are studied with regard to 'the circulation of fixed capital' and to the 'circulation of working capital'.[2] The first type of circulation is a prerequisite for the latter. Its possibility is derived by Lowe from the existence of a commodity which may be able to perform in an industrial system the same self-reproductive role played by corn in a corn economy. This commodity is found in *machine tools*, the typical output of sector Ia:

> Only if we can find in the mechanical sphere certain instruments that share with wheat and all other organic matter, including the human organism, the capacity for physical self-reproduction, can our problem be solved without historical regress. In other words, we have to look for some type of equipment that is technically suited, in conjunction with other productive factors, to reproduce itself as well as to produce other equipment. What we actually find is not one single such instrument but a comprehensive group of fixed-capital goods which are classified as *machine tools*. They are for industrial production what seed wheat and the reproductive system in animals are for agricultural production. (1976, p. 30)

According to Lowe, stage analysis and sector analysis are mixed up by the Austrians. He argues that these economists look at the production of equipment as 'a stage problem for the consumer-good sector' and concludes that this is 'equivalent to treating fixed capital as if it were working capital'.[3] This treatment of fixed capital is at the root of what Lowe calls the linear 'imperialism' of the Austrians, that is, their tendency (which is particularly clear in Böhm-Bawerk) to look at production as a one-way avenue from labour to consumption goods.

2   LOWE AND THE AUSTRIANS: AN ASSESSMENT

Lowe's elaborate scheme of production and use of the notion of working capital may be used as litmus paper for focusing, beyond Lowe's own horizon, on the Austrian theory of capital as well as on some differences between this theory and the theory of the classics. From this broader point of view it may be observed that Lowe's criticism of the Austrians boils down to an acknowledgement of a particular aspect of their theory; and that a shortcoming equivalent to what he believes to be a feature of their thought is embedded in the structure of his own scheme. In what follows this point will be developed in two stages: first, with regard to the Austrians; second, with regard to Lowe himself.

As for the Austrians: it should be acknowledged that their tendency to look at production as a one-way avenue from labour to consumption goods and, accordingly, their tendency to look at fixed capital as working capital descend from the method of vertical integration which they actually adopted in their scheme of thought (although they never mentioned it explicitly – as they did with the term 'working capital' itself). On the other hand, it should be noted that the method of vertical integration was tacitly adopted by the classical economists themselves, who, however, made a sharper use of it than the Austrians. To begin with, they were led by this method to focus on the economic, rather than on the technical, beginning of what the Austrians will call 'time-consuming methods of production'. This beginning is the *wages fund* (free capital) as command of productive labour, rather than labour and land (pure inputs) as original factors of production. In this sense the classical theory of production is essentially a theory of *reproduction* of the final goods (national revenue) of which the wages fund (the command of productive labour) is just a fraction. In the context of this theory capital presents itself as circulating or fixed depending on whether its reproduction occurs in a single period or in a longer span of time. Unlike the classical economics, the Austrians focused on time-consuming methods explicitly. They failed, however, to frame this concept in the context of reproduction of final goods. What they did was, rather, to confine their treatment of these methods to the context of what should properly be called the *production* (however vertically integrated) of these very goods.[4] This is the fundamental reason of the fact (noticed but left unexplained by Lowe) that the Austrians eventually dealt with (what was to be called) working capital as the only form of capital. From this point of view their real shortcoming consists less in what is claimed by Lowe, that is, in their looking at production as a one-way avenue from labour to consumption goods, than in their inability to give up their view of capital as working capital for the classical view of capital as circulating capital (an inability that Lowe is unable to grasp because of his inability to detect the difference between these two notions). This inability, it should be noted, descends from their broader failure to look at production in a classical sense, that is, as a *one-way avenue from consumption goods to consumption goods* (reproduction of national revenue). It has been a great misfortune that the Austrians neglected the classical theory of reproduction to which the notion of circulating capital essentially belongs.[5]

As for Lowe: his tendency to look at production as a whirlpool agitated by self-reproducing machine tools and, accordingly, his tendency to look at fixed capital as combined with working capital for the production of finished and unfinished goods, points to the method of horizontal, rather than of vertical, integration. Indeed, however much Lowe's analysis of the circulation of fixed and working capital may succeed in providing a view of capital contrasting with the linear 'imperialism' of the Austrians, and however much it may succeed in tracing the beginning of production back to the work of machine tools, it fails to go far enough to provide a view of capital similar to the view of the classics. For what, according to this view, does circulate is capital as circulating capital: which, in a vertically integrated economy, is nothing but the wages fund (free capital). Speaking of the methods of horizontal and vertical integration in the context of the theory of capital, it results that the distinction (which was introduced by Hawtrey in Keynes's footsteps and to which we shall return below) between *instrumental* and *working* capital[6] is to the method of horizontal integration what the distinction between *free* and *invested* capital (which was introduced by Jevons in the footsteps of the classical economists and which includes the distinction between *circulating* and *fixed*)[7] is to the method of vertical integration. The two methods, however, may be adopted with different intensities in the two cases. While, for instance, the method of horizontal integration may be pushed to the limit of leaving instrumental capital out of the picture, the method of vertical integration may be exploited to show the scope and sophistication of the classical notion of the wages fund. Now, leaving aside the weaknesses of, and the impoverishments undergone by, this 'dubious construct' it should be noted that at the core of the wages fund doctrine is the notion of the *labour market* as a meeting place between the supply of free capital for labour and of labour for consumption goods: hence the determination of the wage rate and the possibility that this rate may increase, remain constant or decrease as the 'funds destined for the maintenance of labour' vary with a given labour force.

There is no trace of the role of this market in Lowe's 'schema of industrial production'. It is true that the conditions for the 'continuity of production' are spelled out in his scheme as the conditions for the reproduction of fixed and working capital. But these conditions are relevant for the continuity of production as a technical, rather than as an economic, phenomenon: the coefficients n_a, n_b and n_z play in this model the role usually assigned to production coefficients in a von Neumann model. In this sense they reveal a closer similarity between Lowe and the Austrians than between Lowe and the classical economists. For production is viewed by the classics in the context of the reproduction of final goods (national revenue) and, therefore, in the context of a one-way (but circular) avenue going from the consumption goods exchanged for labour at the beginning (rather than from 'pure inputs' or 'machine tools') to the final (rather than finished) goods returned by labour at the end of time-consuming methods of production (roundaboutness in a classical sense). In this context all capital circulates (and therefore presents itself as circulating capital) while fixed capital is circulating capital of a special kind (a kind, that is, the circulation of which requires a longer period of time).

It goes without saying, however, that when the economist's point of view shrinks from the process of reproduction of national revenue to the section of it which is contained in a period of arbitrary length (period of production or period of process) the distinction between circulating and fixed capital vanishes. Then it is replaced by the distinction between instrumental and working capital (goods). The shift from the former to the latter distinction is associated with a change in the very meaning of the term *period*: while in the former case this is the period of *reproduction*, in the latter it becomes what has been called by Lowe (1976) a period of *observation* and by Hicks (1981–83, Vol. II, Ch. 18) an *accounting* period.[8] In the light of these distinctions it can be concluded that the more one departs from the method of the classics and the more one focuses on the functioning of an advanced economy the more the period of reproduction is replaced by the period of observation, the more the period of observation falls short of the average period of reproduction, and the more the distinction between circulating and fixed capital is turned into the distinction between instrumental and working capital (goods).

3   KEYNES

Lowe's 'census of an industrial community's wealth in physical terms' becomes in Keynes's *Treatise on Money* a census of the 'stock of real capital or material wealth existing at any time':

> We shall call goods in use *fixed capital*, goods in process *working capital*, and goods in stock *liquid capital*. Working capital is necessary because some goods take time to produce; and fixed capital is necessary because some goods take time to use or consume. Liquid capital is only possible when goods will 'keep'. (1930, Vol. 1, p. 116)

This distinction is formulated by Keynes in the light not only of his own distinction between *available* and *non-available* output (available, that is, for immediate consumption), but also of the distinction between *final* and *finished* goods mentioned above and shared by Keynes as well as by Lowe. In this sense the stock of real capital is entirely made up of non-available output (past and present) while that part of the unfinished goods which is not fixed capital consists partly of working capital and partly of liquid capital (by which Keynes means 'surplus stocks' only, that is, those stocks which are not regarded as belonging to working capital for they are not required for running an 'efficient business').

It is important to note that Keynes's distinction is first provided in Volume 1 of his *Treatise* and is later expanded in Volume 2, Book VI. The title of this Book 'The Rate of Investment and its Fluctuations' provides a clue for the rationale of such a distinction. This rationale stems from the very definition of the rate of investment given in Volume 1 as 'the net increment during a period of time of the capital of the community' and hinges on the different forces which, in the context of a disequilibrium between savings and investment in a monetary economy, affect the fluctuations of this rate when the capital to increase is of the fixed, working or liquid variety. After noting the close correlation between fluctuations in the amount of working capital and fluctuations in the volume of employment Keynes proceeds, first, to a discussion of the practical importance of changes in the working capital of a community, and, later on, to what he calls 'the theory of working capital' which ends up in two sections titled 'Productive and unproductive consumption' and 'The true wages fund'.

The classical terms of productive and unproductive consumption are reutilized by Keynes with a meaning which has nothing to do with the old framework. This meaning, however, is in perfect consistency with the new context of Keynes's analysis focused as it is on the functioning of a monetary economy with unemployment resulting from a disequilibrium between savings and investment. In this context those two terms are reutilized in connection with the different requirements of investment in working capital (with given fixed capital and unemployment) relative to the requirements of investment in fixed capital:

> An increase in working capital resulting from an increased volume of production and employment (and not from a lengthening of the productive process) does not involve an equal abstention from, or a reduction of, current consumption by the community as a whole, as does an increase in fixed capital, but mainly a redistribution of consumption from the rest of the community to the newly employed. Investment, which requires a redistribution of current consumption but no reduction in its aggregate, may be said to substitute productive consumption for unproductive consumption. (1930, Vol. 2, p. 111)

4   KEYNES AND THE CLASSICS: A FURTHER ASSESSMENT

Keynes's distinction between productive and unproductive consumption is confined to the relation between the rate of investment in working capital and the level of employment in the short run in which the structure of fixed capital is given. In dealing with this distinction and relation, however, Keynes goes so far as not only to distinguish (unlike Lowe) between his 'working capital' and the 'circulating capital' of the classics, but also to contrast these two concepts of capital in the light of what he believes to be 'the true wages fund'. This is suddenly done in a long and crucial passage which is worth quoting fully (sections are distinguished by letters to facilitate reference in the subsequent discussion):

> [a] Counsel has been darkened in this matter by a famous confusion of the classical economists and by the failure of their successors, who detected the confusion, to perceive the truth which lay, nevertheless, at the centre of the confusion. The classical economists emphasised the distinction between fixed capital and what they called 'circulating capital'. But they did not clearly distinguish my third category of capital, namely, 'goods in process' or working capital, which is not identical with their 'circulating capital'[a]. [b] They appreciated the necessity of a fund to support labour during the period of production [b]; [c] but they overlooked the *continuous* character of production and output [c] [d] and confused the working capital, which is provided by *continuously* feeding the flow of available income back into the machine of process, with the liquid capital or goods in stock at the *commencement* of any period of process [d]. [e] They did not clearly perceive that the capital to keep labour in employment is found, not in the stocks of goods *already* available [e], [g] nor by abstention from the consumption of available income, but by decisions which have the effect (a) of determining what proportions of the goods emerging from the machine of process are in fixed and in liquid form respectively [g], [h] and (b) of applying the flow of available income in one way instead of in another, namely, by supporting productive consumers instead of unproductive consumers [h]. (1930, Vol. 2, p. 114)

The issues raised in this passage are so far-reaching and the wording or the argument so questionable that they require a closer scrutiny. This will be done in four steps.

First, it should be noted that Keynes's notion of fixed capital as defined above is even more distant from the corresponding notion of the classics as their circulating capital is from Keynes's working capital itself (on which more below). While Keynes's definition is focused on the goods which 'take time to use or consume' and encompasses therefore all the goods that are *durable* (and nothing else, as required by the short-run theory of fluctuations and agreed upon by other economists of the 1930s including Hayek), the notion of the classics is best rendered by Jevons's observation whereby one should not say that 'a railway is *fixed capital,* but that *capital is fixed in the railway*' (1871, p. 264): a remark which invariably points to the wages fund as the typical form of capital at the beginning of its transformations (free capital). If Keynes were demanding from himself as much consistency as he calls for in classical theory, he should have abandoned the term 'fixed capital' (which was developed in a different context from his) for the more appropriate term of *instrumental* capital (which, indeed, was introduced by Hawtrey to contrast it with working capital in the context of the theory of fluctuations).

Second, it should be noted that Keynes's expressions 'machine of process' and 'period of process' in d–d above have nothing to do with the expression 'period of production' in b–b. Indeed a distinction between these two periods is so important that the very notion of working capital is either unnecessary or misleading without it. This distinction, although implied by Keynes himself in his treatment of working capital and of productive and unproductive consumption, is made explicit in a passage where Hawtrey speaks of the 'period of process' as distinct from – and indeed as a section of – the 'period of production':

> One part, which we shall call the period of process, is the time occupied by the productive processes applied to the material composing the commodity itself, without regard to the time taken in the construction of the instruments used in those processes. It is the period of production as it would be if every instrument were treated as an original factor of production and if the only capital were working capital. The rest of the period of production is that which is composed of the respective ages and periods of production of the instruments used. (Hawtrey, 1937, p. 11)[9]

Now it should be objected, with regard to Keynes's passage above, (i) that even Hawtrey's period of production is not the period of reproduction of the classics; (ii) that working capital is to the period of process what circulating capital is to the period of reproduction; and (iii) that working capital and the period of process belong to the analysis of the *short run* as much as circulating capital and the period of reproduction belong to the analysis of the *long run*. On the other hand, if it is true that Adam Smith (followed by many others) often speaks of circulating capital as if it consisted of the same goods which properly belong to what is called today 'working capital' this is not because of what Keynes believes. Rather, it stems from the fact that Smith used to deal with circulating capital sometimes from the point of view of an individual and sometimes from the point of view of the whole society. Unfortunately, the very meaning of the term 'circulation' changes in the two cases: it refers to a *change of hands* in the former case, to a *change of matter* (reproduction proper) in the latter. The beginning and end of circulation are consequently denoted by money capital and money income, in the former case; and by the final goods making up, respectively, the wages fund (free capital) and national revenue, in the latter. Furthermore, it is true that the point of view of the whole society is adopted by Keynes himself in most of his work. But even in this perspective the aims of Keynes and the classics remain very different. For while the purpose of Keynes is to investigate the fluctuations of production in a monetary economy where the structure of fixed capital is given (short run) the purpose of the classics (Smith) was to investigate the growth of national revenue in a real economy where the structure of fixed capital is still to be determined (long run).

Third, it can be argued that while stressing the confusion of the classics between circulating and working capital along with their confusion between the wages fund as a flow and the wages fund as a stock, Keynes ends up by confusing the two confusions. For it is true that the classics overlooked the continuous character of production and output as argued in c–c above. They were indeed more interested in *advance economics* than in *synchronization economics*. But the reason why they did overlook synchronization is, indeed, overlooked by Keynes himself. For the classics (Smith) focused on the causes of the wealth of nations, and therefore on the principles of change (accumulation) rather than, as Keynes eventually did, on the functioning of the economy or on the complications entailed in this functioning by change itself – and particularly by changes induced by money as a store of value. On the other hand, Smith's inclusion in his concept of circulating capital of goods which properly belong to the modern concept of working capital (an inclusion which, it must be admitted, did affect the thought of most other classics, excluding Marx)[10] is not due to the fact that he confuses a stock with a flow. Rather, it descends from his tendency to express himself against his own distinction between the individual and the social point of view. For the role which is played by a stock when the point of view is that of an individual is played by a flow when the point of view is that of society (as Smith himself implies when he argues that a man who neither consumes himself nor has others consume the 'stock which he possesses' – a stock, that is, of goods, and not of money in Keynes's sense – must be a fool). Furthermore, what is circulating capital from the point of view of an individual may not be circulating capital from the point of view of society.[11] Keynes, however, is so unaware of this confusion that he believes that Smith's general aim (the growth of wealth) is the same as his (the fluctuations of wealth), and that Smith's particular starting-point (the stock which a person possesses) is the same as his 'liquid capital' (which in d–d above is, however, identified, to confuse things further, with Keynes's own and different notion of 'normal' stocks). Thus what the classics 'did not clearly perceive' (e–e and f–f above) was what Keynes does here actually confuse, that is, the distinction between the period of process (in which instrumental capital goods are given) and the period of reproduction (in which the production of instrumental capital goods is considered as a step in the time-consuming reproduction of national revenue). But if 'they did not clearly perceive' this distinction it is, again, because they were concerned with (what happens to capital in) the period of reproduction and not at all with (what happens to unemployment in) Keynes's period of process.

Fourth, given Hicks's remarkable insight that our theories are like 'rays of light, which illuminate a part of the target, leaving the rest in a darkness' so that 'we must work, if we are to work effectively, in some sort of blinkers' (1975), it can be concluded that Keynes and the classics used to wear two different types of blinkers. Indeed, Keynes seems *himself* to be wearing two different types of blinkers in the passage quoted above: one for focusing on (what happens to unemployment in) the period of process, the other for preventing himself from realizing that the blinkers of the classics were aimed at a different target. If, however, all types (and particularly Keynes's second type) of blinkers are dropped it should be easily concluded (i) that Keynes's working capital is indeed different from the circulating capital of the classics; (ii) that even Keynes's fixed capital is, in spite of his belief and terminology, different from the classical concept (for fixed capital is to Keynes 'goods in use' and nothing else); and (iii) that the classical and Keynesian blinkers require two different notions of capital for capital is, according to Smith and the classics, not goods in use, or goods in process or goods in stock as Keynes implies in his classification (1930, p. 115). Rather, it is that part of available output (in the sense suggested by Keynes himself for very different purposes) which is advanced to labour for its reproduction in a more or less distant future. This basic difference is not understood by Keynes if only because his ray of light is focused on the fluctuations of wealth within a given period of time.

5   CONCLUDING REMARKS

In the light of the distinction between working and circulating capital discussed above and of the different theories to which these two notions belong it becomes possible, at this point, to single out some similarities among and differences between Lowe, Keynes, the Austrians and the classics. In particular, we can now identify some essential elements which, on the one hand, Lowe and Keynes have in common against the Austrians; and, on the other, Lowe and the Austrians have in common against the classics. This will be done in this section on the basis of the distinction, noted above, between period of *observation* and period of *maturation* as well as of the distinction, argued above, between period of maturation and period of *reproduction* (of national revenue).

Take the period of maturation first. This notion is essentially shared by Lowe and the Austrians but does not coincide with the period of reproduction of the classics. For the production of particular goods (including physical reproduction, such as that of plants through their falling seeds) is one thing (even when it is thought to start from 'pure inputs'); while the reproduction of national revenue (through the exchange of free capital for labour) is another. In this sense, however, the Austrians appear to be closer to the classics relative not only to Keynes (if only because their period of maturation is longer than the period of process and includes the production of 'durable goods') but also to Lowe (if only because they have their own theory of the labour market and their own notion, however wanting, of the wages fund).

Now take the period of observation. If its length were the same as that of the period of reproduction no room would be left for the distinction between working and instrumental capital goods. Since, however, the period of reproduction becomes longer and longer, or more and more differentiated from good to good, as the variety of final goods increases, and since the period of observation becomes accordingly shorter and shorter relative to the (average) period of reproduction, it should come as no surprise that the 'rays of light' of modern theories are focused more and more on 'working' and 'instrumental' and less and less on 'circulating' and 'fixed' capital. This helps us to understand the validity and limits of Lowe's observation on the 'imperialism' of the Austrians. For it is true that the Austrians lack the notion of circularity. Lowe's own notion, however, falls short of that of the classics. For the circularity that occurs in a given period of observation is one thing, and the circularity that occurs in a complete period of reproduction (from consumption goods to consumption goods) is another. The former may be called *whirlpool circularity*, the latter *pipeline circularity*: while the former concerns the interactions between the different molecules of water (finished and unfinished goods) once some of it is injected into a whirlpool of given size (period of observation), the latter concerns the flow of water through the 'hydraulic system' as a whole (time-consuming methods of production), that is, from the moment some water is injected into the whirlpool to the moment it returns increased to the point of injection.

Now it should be noted that what Lowe and Keynes (and many others) have in common against the classics is the focus on what happens in the period of observation rather than on what happens in the period of reproduction. While, however, the purpose of Lowe (and the Austrians) is to deal with *production* (rather than with reproduction), Keynes focuses on *fluctuations*. Furthermore, the period of observation is usually shorter in Keynes than in Lowe. For while Keynes is concerned mainly with what happens in the period of process, Lowe's concern is with the period of production (maturation). Lowe's period of production, however, falls short of the classical period of reproduction for, however long, it is not long enough to include the reproduction and reinvestment of the wages fund. In both cases the gap is theoretical: it is determined, in the first case, by the lack of the notion of reproduction of fixed capital (which is studied by Lowe and overlooked by Keynes); and, in the second case, by the notion of reproduction of free capital (which is studied by the classics and overlooked by Lowe).

To bring these conclusions to an end all the arguments above can be synthesized in the light of Hicks's methodological distinction between *Materialism* and *Fundism* (1974). If this distinction is applied to the authors discussed in this chapter, the following conclusions emerge: while Lowe and Keynes belong to Materialism, and the Austrians partly to Materialism and partly to Fundism, the classics belong fully to Fundism. On the other hand, if the distinction between Fundism and Materialism is applied to concepts and theories rather than to authors, a further regrouping becomes possible according to the following dichotomy: while the concepts of period of observation, period of production, period of process, horizontal integration, working and instrumental capital (goods) are benchmarks for, or belong to, Materialism (along with the theory of production, input–output analysis and the theory of fluctuations), the concepts of period of reproduction, vertical integration, free and invested capital, circulating and fixed capital are benchmarks for, or belong to, Fundism (along with the classical theories of capital, reproduction and growth).

NOTES

1. 'We need a "bestiary" – Shackle says with regard to what he calls 'linguistic economics' – 'and not merely a taxonomy, a taxonomy and not merely a machine' (1967, p. 293).
2. They are shown to be equal, in the first case, to

$$a' \geq f_{a'} + f_{b'}$$
$$b' \geq f_z$$
$$z' \geq n_{a'} + n_{b'} + n_{z'}$$

(where prime and double-prime signs indicate period 1 and period 2, the letters a, b and z the outputs of sectors Ia, Ib and II, and the letters n_a, n_b and n_z the goods necessary for the support of labour in the three sectors); and, in the second case, to $W = \Sigma w/2$ (where W is the stock of working capital and Σw is the aggregate of inputs over the whole period of maturation under conditions of a stationary flow of output). A closer analysis of the arithmetic of these relations is provided by Wyler (1953) who also focuses on the distinction (which is shared by Lowe and will be resumed below) between period of *maturation* (production) and period of *observation*. Wyler (like Lowe himself) conceives of the process of production in Robertson's sense of a sausage machine 'which it takes ten minutes to traverse, and which turns out one sausage per minute' (Robertson, 1959, p. 85). Robertson's simple arithmetic implies that each potential sausage remains in the machine for five minutes and is worth half a completed sausage so that the aggregate value of the 'amorphous objects' in the machine at a particular moment is the value of five completed sausages, or of five minutes' output.
3. This interpretation of the Austrians is quite common and is easily summed up in Haavelmo's words whereby 'the Austrian theory of capital tried to squeeze even the instruments of production into the framework of "final goods en route"' (Haavelmo, 1960, p. 79).
4. Schumpeter seems to be aware of this difference when he presents Jevons's theory of production as a bridge between the classics and the Austrians: 'Jevons knew better than to let labor be added to a growing intermediate product until a finished consumers' good emerges

that is consumed at once: as stated already, he included the process of 'uninvestment' so that his period was not simply a period of *production*' (1954, p. 908).

5.   This may be at the root of the recurring misuse of words and concepts in the language of economists with regard not only to 'working' and 'circulating' capital but also to 'period of production' and 'period of reproduction', not to speak of the distinction between 'finished' and 'final' goods. In this sense a non-contradictory use of the Austrian and classical concepts is badly needed. The following statement has been constructed with a careful selection of words so as to squeeze out the most recurring ambiguities: *the longer the period of production of finished goods (ploughs or corn) and the longer the period of reproduction of final goods (corn) the greater is the amount of capital circulating from the beginning to the end of this period, and the greater is the amount of working capital goods required at a particular moment of time to carry out the process of production of finished goods.*

6.   These two kinds of capital are contrasted with each other by Hawtrey (who sharply defines them with regard to a moment of time as well as in the context of time-consuming methods of production):

> Even if we conceive of the use of capital as essentially a device for utilizing the technical advantages of a more prolonged period of production, we still find a place for the conception of capital as an accumulated stock of wealth. At any moment of the productive process those productive operations which are already past will have left their mark in some material objects which embody their contribution to the process as a whole. These material objects fall into two broad classes, instrumental capital and working capital. (1937, p. 9)

Now it should be noted that it is from these 'material objects' that a theory of fluctuations must begin and that such a theory is necessarily focused on what happens in a predetermined period of time in which the structure of fixed capital is given. This point will be resumed below with regard to Keynes's and Robertson's treatment of working capital. See in particular note 9, below.

7.   It is interesting to note that while the first distinction properly runs between, and should be most correctly formulated in terms of, instrumental and capital *goods* the second distinction is most correctly formulated as it is normally used, that is, *without* the term 'goods' after the term 'capital. The analytical importance of this observation will become clear once it is acknowledged that the fate of capital proper (that is, free capital) is to be invested (and, consequently, to become either circulating or fixed in the sense implied in Jevons's railway example to be discussed below) whereas the function of capital goods is to cooperate with labour either as 'active' or as 'passive' tools of production.

8.   After noting in the article cited above that the task of dynamics is 'to superimpose the pattern of change, which is one time-pattern, upon the underlying pattern of capital-using production, which is another', Hicks argues that 'in all its main forms, modern economic dynamics is an accounting theory' (ibid., p. 221). See also note 10, below.

9.   The confusion between period of process and period of production seems to be at the root of the crucial misunderstanding between increases in working capital and increases in fixed capital in Hayek's trade-cycle model (Meacci, 1994). This misunderstanding is not absent from the mind of other economists. See for instance Robertson (1959, Ch. V) whose 'average period of production of goods' is, properly speaking, a period of process, and whose definition of what he calls 'circulating capital' is, properly speaking, a definition of working capital.

> There is in such a country at any moment a great mass of *unready* goods, on which labour and ingenuity of various kinds have been spent, but which are not yet ripe for the consumer's hands or mouth. This mass of *circulating capital*, as it is called, includes not only the stocks of shirts in the shop-window and the stocks of raw cotton in the warehouses and ships, but the half-worked fabric on its way through the spindles and the looms. (ibid., p. 85)

It is interesting to note that the chapter where these misunderstandings are committed is designed by Robertson to deal with the 'mechanics of banking' (ibid., p. 179) and particularly with the phenomena of credit and inflation, two typical ingredients of fluctuations.

10. From what is argued above it follows that Smith's confusion between circulating and (what will be called) working capital may be associated with his misunderstanding between what Marx calls 'circulating capital' and 'capital of circulation' and, more generally, between the 'material forms' of capital and its different 'economic functions' (see Meacci, 1989; 1991). The misunderstanding between the material forms and the different functions of capital, and therefore between circulating and working capital, has a long story and is, to a large extent, a matter of words. A most recent episode is provided by Blaug who presents Böhm-Bawerk's thought as follows:

> Most of his reasoning makes much better sense when it is realized that his 'capital' is only circulating capital, that is, funds tied up in the form of goods in process. The function of working capital is, not to cooperate with labour in production, but as it were to support labour during the interval between the application of inputs and the emergence of output. (1990, p. 499).

In view of the distinctions highlighted above this sentence should be reworded as follows (italics are used to stress differences): 'Most of his reasoning makes much better sense when it is realized that his 'capital' is only *working* capital, that is, funds tied up in the form of goods in process. The function of working capital is, *not to support* labour during the interval between the application of inputs and the emergence of output, but to *cooperate*, along with instrumental capital albeit in a difference sense, *with labour* in production'. Indeed Blaug's wording leads not only to an identification of circulating with working capital but also to a broader misunderstanding of the role of working capital in production for the role of the wages fund in reproduction. For a consistent use of the notion of working capital see, on the contrary, Hicks (1950, Ch. IV), and for a proper use of the terms circulating and working capital as pointing to two different notions belonging to two different theories, again see Hicks (1965, Part I, Chs IV and X in particular) and Hicks (1985). In this connection it may be added that Hicks's principle of self-containedness as discussed in these works is at the root of the notion of circulating capital in two different senses depending on whether this principle holds from the point of view of an individual (in which case capital presents itself as *money* capital at the beginning of its circulation) or of the whole society (in which case it presents itself as *free* capital).

11. See in this connection the preceding note and reconsider it in the light of Hawtrey's hitherto unnoticed (and unexplained) conception of circulating capital as made up of 'working capital and net cash resources' (1937, p. 139).

REFERENCES

Blaug, M. (1990), *Economic Theory in Retrospect*, Cambridge: Cambridge University Press.

Haavelmo, T. (1960), *A Study in the Theory of Investment*, Chicago: University of Chicago Press.

Hawtrey, R.G. (1937), *Capital and Employment,* London: Longmans.

Hicks, J. (1950), *A Contribution to the Theory of the Trade Cycle*, Oxford: Clarendon Press.

Hicks, J. (1965), *Capital and Growth*, Oxford: Clarendon Press.

Hicks, J. (1974), 'Capital controversies: ancient and modern', *American Economic Review*, **64** (2), pp. 307–16.

Hicks, J. (1975), 'The scope and status of welfare economics', *Oxford Economic Papers*, **27**, pp. 307–26. Reprinted in J. Hicks (1981–83, Vol. I, pp. 218–39).

Hicks, J. (1981–83), *Collected Essays on Economic Theory*, Oxford: Basil Blackwell, 3 Volumes.

Hicks, J. (1985), *Methods of Dynamic Economics*, Oxford: Oxford University Press.

Jevons, W.S. (1871), *The Theory of Political Economy*, London: Macmillan.

Keynes, J.M. (1930), *A Treatise on Money*, 2 Volumes, in *The Collected Writings of John Maynard Keynes*, London: Macmillan, 1971.

Lowe, A. (1976), *The Path of Economic Growth*, Cambridge: Cambridge University Press.

Marx, K. (1939), *Grundrisse der Kritik der Politischen Ökonomie*, Harmondsworth: Penguin Books, 1973.

Meacci, F. (1989), 'Different divisions of capital in Smith, Ricardo and Marx', *Atlantic Economic Journal*, **17**, pp. 13–21.

Meacci, F. (1991), 'The organic composition of capital and the falling rate of profit', in G. Caravale (ed.) (1991), *Marx and Modern Economic Analysis*, Aldershot: Edward Elgar, Vol. II, pp. 85–109.

Meacci, F. (1994), 'Hayek and the deepening of capital', in M. Colonna, H. Hagemann and O.F. Hamouda (eds), *Capitalism, Socialism and Knowledge. The Economics of F.A. von Hayek*, Aldershot: Edward Elgar, Vol. II, pp. 26–44.

Robertson, D. (1959), *Money*, Cambridge: Cambridge University Press.

Schumpeter, J.A. (1954), *History of Economic Analysis*, New York: Oxford University Press.

Shackle, G.L.S. (1967), *The Years of High Theory. Invention and Tradition in Economic Thought, 1926–1939*, Cambridge: Cambridge University Press.

Taussig, F.W. (1896), *Wages and Capital*, New York: Appleton.

Wyler, J. (1953), 'Working capital and output', *Social Research*, **20**, pp. 91–9.

PART III

The Economy in Traverse: Cycle,
Growth, Technology and Structural Change

7. Lowe and Structural Theories of the Business Cycle

Harald Hagemann and Michael Landesmann

1   INTRODUCTION

Adolph Lowe's contribution to the study of business cycles, to which the economics profession in Germany had increasingly turned in the 1920s, can hardly be overemphasized. With his seminal works on 'The current state of research on business cycles in Germany' (Lowe, 1925) and his 'brilliant article' (Kuznets, 1930b, p. 128) 'How is business-cycle theory possible at all?' (Lowe, 1926) Lowe had a profound impact on the debate on business-cycle theory in the German-speaking area. His leading role in this debate is also reflected in Hayek's *Geldtheorie und Konjunkturtheorie* (1929) in which the dispute with Lowe and his closest associate Burchardt (1928), who had launched an attack against monetary theories of the business cycle, plays a fruitful role. In particular, Hayek was challenged by Lowe's central methodological thesis 'that the incorporation of cyclical phenomena into the system of economic equilibrium theory, with which they are in apparent contradiction, remains the crucial problem of Trade Cycle theory' (Hayek, 1929; 1933, p. 33). Both authors also agreed on the importance of the underlying real structure of production and of changes in that structure over time.

The search for a dynamic conceptualization of the economic system, in which 'the polarity of upswing and crisis takes on the same position which the equilibrium had in the static system' (Lowe, 1926, p. 195), was at the centre of Lowe's research work, which was also characteristically stimulated by Schumpeter's and Sombart's emphasis on the role of technical progress and the interaction between long-run growth and cyclical fluctuations. However, Lowe's contributions before the Second World War to business-cycle analysis remained of a critical nature and the positive construction of a theoretical model of cyclical growth remained an unfinished job before the Nazis came to power in 1933; emigration then changed Lowe's research agenda for almost two decades.

In two articles published in the 1950s, however, Lowe's thought returned to his earlier direction of research, which he revived and developed against the background of the rise of modern growth theory stimulated by the works of Harrod and Domar. While Lowe's first paper 'A

95

Structural model of production' (1952) provides a more detailed exposition of the disaggregated framework he wanted to use, the second paper on 'Structural analysis of real capital formation' (1955) extends the analysis beyond the comparison of equilibrium positions to the analysis of the adjustment paths that the economy follows in response to once-and-for-all changes in one of the determinants of growth and to the capital stock adjustment problems related to continuous change. Half a century after his pathbreaking critical articles on business-cycle theory, Lowe's attempt to develop a theory of accumulation, technical progress, and structural change culminated in his *Path of Economic Growth* (1976). This book shows Lowe as the second pioneer in *traverse analysis*, after Hicks (1973).[1] One can define traverse analysis as an approach which specifies the rigidities inherent in the industrial structure and analyses how and to what degree these rigidities are overcome when a given 'structure' is exposed to dynamic 'impulses' or 'forces of change' such as technical progress, the supply of labour or natural resources. Typically, traverse analysis focuses on the stages in the structural adjustment processes in between steady states. Lowe's traverse analysis, in particular, illuminates

> the key position that 'real capital' holds in the growth of an industrial economy. It is this factor that, at all levels of industrialization, is responsible for the major bottlenecks when the rate of growth rises, and for waste of available inputs when it falls. For this reason our investigation will center on the *formation, application, and liquidation of real capital*. (Lowe, 1976, p. 10)

By the time Lowe returned to the study of structural economic dynamics, after the Second World War, the economics profession had shifted its interest from business-cycle analysis to growth theory and hence Lowe's later contributions, while picking up methodological tools and topics of economic dynamics which are clearly rooted in the interwar debates on business cycles, none the less fell short of reviving a 'structural approach' to business-cycle analysis and his later contributions belong more clearly to the study of structural adjustments in the process of longer-term economic growth. However, the fact that the later research line developed out of central concerns of the interwar business-cycle debate (particularly on the theme of 'technological unemployment' but also on defining the relative roles and relationships between 'real' and 'monetary' factors in economic fluctuations) shows that Lowe and a great number of his professional colleagues perceived the most fundamental and interesting features of business-cycle analysis as being related to industrial developmental change.

This focus of analysis meant that most of the important contributors to the continental European debate on business cycles chose analytical frameworks which allowed a representation of the interaction between *disaggregated (production) structures* of an economic system and macroeconomic fluctuations. This is in contrast to the highly aggregated frameworks adopted for theoretical business-cycle analysis in the post-Second World War contributions. Two types of representations of the production structure of a capitalist economy were available to the business-cycle analysts of the interwar years: the 'Austrian' tradition of viewing production as vertically differentiated stages of production and the Quesnay/Marx tradition of representing the horizontal interdependencies between sectors. We shall see later on that Lowe and his collaborators at Kiel chose a compromise between these two schemes as appropriate for their study of structural economic dynamics; Hayek (and others, such as Strigl, 1928) chose the Austrian representation.

Apart from the question of the representation of the structural features of a capitalist economy, there was also the question of *method of dynamic analysis*. Here, again, there were two traditions followed up by the contributors to business-cycle theory from the late nineteenth century onwards. One tradition goes back to Ricardo's famous chapter 'On Machinery' in the third edition of his *Principles*. Ricardo provides in this chapter probably the earliest example of a fully-fledged traverse analysis applied to the issue of temporary displacement of workers by machinery and then their reabsorption at higher levels of national income; the distinctive feature here was the analysis of a sequence of stages of an adjustment process. The other tradition goes back to the utilization of Marx's schemes of reproduction for the analysis of disproportional growth which can arise as a result of changes in the rate of growth and/or technical progress and/or shifts in expenditure structures due to income distributional shifts. Again, we can see that Lowe, in his contributions to structural economic dynamics, uses both of these methods of dynamic analysis, combining Ricardo's concern for a clear analysis of the sequence of stages in an adjustment process with Marx's concern for the problems of matching (sectoral) production structures, expenditure and income structures in the course of such a dynamic sequence.

In the following, we are going to discuss Lowe's contributions to business-cycle analysis in the context of the rather broad tradition which dominated continental European business-cycle research (Dennis Robertson was the one exception in England who also worked in this tradition) from the late nineteenth century up to the Second World War. We shall use the umbrella term 'structural theories of the business cycle' to characterize this tradition. The overriding concern in these contributions was, as mentioned above, to establish the link between industrial structural change and macroeconomic fluctuations. In our review of this tradition, we shall start with Michail Tugan-Baranowsky who, like Lowe, took Marx's schemes of reproduction as a major starting-point for his work on economic dynamics and who viewed cycles as an integral part of the process of capitalist development. Tugan-Baranowsky's early attempt to develop an endogenous theory of the business cycle had a strong influence on later authors such as Albert Aftalion, Joseph Schumpeter or Arthur Spiethoff and also provoked a lively discussion among the leading theoreticians of the Social Democratic Party in Germany, of which Lowe was well aware. Hansen goes as far as to state that Tugan-Baranowsky 'began a new way of thinking about the problem' of business cycles (Hansen, 1951, p. 281). Since Tugan-Baranowsky's seminal work had a strong influence on the modern literature, we shall start our investigation with the analysis of his theory, followed by some considerations of the business-cycle theories of Bouniatian, Aftalion and Spiethoff who have all tried to integrate important structural aspects into their theories. We shall then go on to discuss the debate between Adolph Lowe and Fritz (later Frank) Burchardt on one side, and their opponent from Vienna, Friedrich August Hayek, on the other side. Some of the central issues of that debate came up again after the Second World War when Lowe returned to the research programme of the Weimar years and completed his work on a theoretical model of structural economic growth, which focuses on technological change as the mainspring of destabilizing tendencies in industrial economies. Finally, we shall summarize our results and give an outlook on future research perspectives.

2   TUGAN-BARANOWSKY

The most elaborate early analysis – using the framework of Marx's schemes of reproduction – of the 'traverse path' of an economic system initiated by a change in the overall rate of growth or following a change in the techniques used in an economy was undertaken by the Ukrainian economist, Michail Tugan-Baranowsky (1865–1919).[2] He showed (Tugan-Baranowsky, 1901), that starting from a situation in which no growth occurs (but a positive surplus is produced), net investment of a part of the surplus would lead to a reallocation of productive resources (the stock of inputs) between the different sectors of the economy. In addition, he emphasized that in such circumstances, production would not grow (at least for some time) at the same rates in the different sectors.

> If social production grew in all production activities at the same rate, the capitalists would not have achieved their goal, that is, the accumulation of capital and the growth of their profits. Because in that case a significant portion of the produced commodities would not have been necessary, namely, an important part of the goods destined for capitalists' consumption. ... [A]t the same time, goods for which an

increased demand has been generated (that is, means of production and consumption goods for workers) would be supplied in insufficient quantities on the market. The embodiment of capitalists' profits in capital goods can thus only occur through a change in the distribution of social production.[3]

Tugan-Baranowsky first demonstrates that a redirection of productive activity across different branches is necessary when a change in the overall rate of economic growth, even with constant technology, takes place. He then shows that when technical change is introduced as well (he analyses the case of an increase in the 'technical composition of capital', which amounts to an increase in the degree of mechanization), the insights obtained from analysing a change in the overall rate of growth with constant technology can also be extended to cover the case of changing technology. Both unbalanced growth and the distinction of different stages in the adjustment process are established here as important components of an analysis of the transition to a higher rate of economic growth.

Another important point which was forcefully argued by Tugan-Baranowsky, and for which his analysis became best known, was the relative independence of investment activity from the demand for final consumption goods.

> From a comparison of the two cases, that of simple reproduction with that of expanded reproduction, one can draw the important conclusion that, in a capitalist economy, total demand for commodities is to some extent independent of the extent of social [final] consumption; total [final] consumption can fall and – at the same time – total demand for goods can rise ... (Tugan-Baranowsky, [1894] 1901, p. 25)

Emphasizing the Marxian statement that '[t]he *real barrier* of capitalist production is *capital itself*' (Marx [1894] 1959, p. 250) Tugan-Baranowsky denies the possibility of underconsumption crises (see also 1904, pp. 277ff.). The thesis that 'underconsumption' is the most important cause of economic crisis is 'utterly wrong' (*'grundfalsch'*, 1904, p. 279). According to Tugan-Baranowsky, this holds for all underconsumption theories whether developed by Sismondi, orthodox or revisionist Marxists or contemporary bourgeois economists. Although he also refutes Marx's theory of the falling tendency of the rate of profit, he sticks to the Marxian view that capitalist accumulation is an end in itself. 'Accumulate, Accumulate! This is Moses and the prophets' (Marx, [1867] 1954, p. 558), that is, capitalists derive utility from the mere possession of capital and its expansion. Tugan-Baranowsky thus is an adherent of the Marxian (and with some modifications also of the later Keynesian view) of the accumulation process, in which investment decisions dominate and can be taken as partially independent of individuals' time preferences. This contradicts the neoclassical view according to which the individual saving/consumption decisions dominate the course of events and investment is regarded as a medium for intertemporal distribution of consumption.[4]

On the expenditure side, Tugan-Baranowsky points out that, in so far as net accumulation leads to an increase in the employment of workers, consumption by workers will increase but not to the same extent as the consumption of capitalists has been reduced (relative to the situation in which all the surplus was consumed by the capitalists); the difference will be made up of increased production of capital goods.

The analysis of investment behaviour allows Tugan-Baranowsky to extend Marx's critique of Say's Law into a fully-fledged analysis of a credit economy.

> Credit frees the demand side from an immediate dependence upon current supply. Due to credit, demand can – independently from the contemporaneous supply – rise and fall significantly. ... In a credit economy, purchasing power is a complicated and elastic – but also unstable – item on top of the real monetary base; the purchasing power of the market can rise or fall independently of any change in the real conditions of the supply of commodities or money, simply dependent upon the inclinations of the buyers or sellers to make use of credit. Credit also reinforces to an extraordinary degree the natural dependence of individual enterprises .... Changes in the market take on a snowball effect: relatively insignificant events can exert a destructive effect on markets, since the original disturbance grows with its own propagation. ([1894] 1901, p. 30)

In such an environment expectations formation processes are extremely important:

> Commodity prices gain a particular instability as purchases and sales on credit gain in significance. They express a psychological element, that is, the calculations of trading partners are made with a view of not only the current but also the future conditions on the market, they depend on the general mood of the buyers and sellers, on the degree of speculation, and so on. (Ibid., p. 30)

A credit economy is thus prone to instability, the high mutual interdependence of firms (both in their expectations formation processes as well as through their credit links) results in a situation in which an initial disturbance can quickly gain momentum.

From the general case of analysing the effects upon disproportional growth of a change in the overall rate of growth or in the technology used in an economic system, as well as from his insights into the workings of a credit economy and the relative independence of investment behaviour, Tugan-Baranowsky puts together a full and consistent picture of the business cycle in a capitalist economy.

Having worked out carefully the consistency requirements which emerge from the study of an interdependent economy in which changes in the rate of growth and changes in technology occur over time, such an economy is bound to produce *disproportionalities*, that is, the overproduction of some commodities and/or shortages in the production of others (*partial* overproduction). Following from this, however, the high degree of interdependence of industrial activities and the snowball effects working both through credit links and through expectations formation processes could easily lead to a scenario of *general* overproduction:

> Achieving complete proportionality [in other words: complete matching between production decisions and demand requirements in a dynamic economy] is extremely difficult. Any other allocation of social capital would lead to the overproduction of some commodities. And since all production activities are closely interrelated, the partial overproduction of some commodities can easily lead to a general overproduction situation; unsold commodities accumulate and prices collapse. (Ibid, p. 234)

Tugan-Baranowsky, like many other cycle theorists of his time and after, relates an upswing to the increased rate of production of new fixed equipment and he observes, again like many others, that there are particularly severe fluctuations in the activity levels of the capital-goods-producing industries.

> Cyclical fluctuations are particularly strong in those branches of industry, such as shipbuilding, machinery production and related industries which W. Bagehot called the 'instrumental trades'. The total volume of national production fluctuates only little from year to year ... but even these small fluctuations, are sufficient to generate violent oscillations in those industries which produce the means of production. (Ibid., p. 238)

Tugan-Baranowsky then asks why the production of new fixed capital does not proceed in a continuous manner but in jumps. The reason for this he finds in the discrepancy between the accumulation of loanable capital (which proceeds in a continuous manner) and its use for productive investment. The accumulation and decumulation of loan capital do not play an active role in Tugan-Baranowsky's business-cycle analysis. It acts like a basin which receives a relatively continuous flow of funds, but the use of these funds in the form of productive investment proceeds in a non-continuous manner. The latter is subject to fluctuations because of the difficulty which capitalist accumulation has in adjusting to disproportional growth and changing resource allocation patterns.

> Loanable capital can be accumulated not only in periods of expansion but also when
> industrial production stagnates or is contracting. And ... in fact it does accumulate in
> such circumstances ... In our study of individual recessions and crises we have
> indicated the tremendous growth of the reserves of banks just after an economic
> crisis, when the economy is in recession. At the same time also private deposits in
> banks grow. This indicates an accumulation of free loan capital which is not invested
> in industry. In general, one can say that, just as the positive phases of the industrial
> cycle are characterized by the productive investment of loanable capital, the
> depressive phases are characterized by the accumulation of free, loanable capital.
> (Ibid., pp. 240–41)

Tugan-Baranowsky emphasizes here the continuation of the
accumulation of loanable 'money capital' throughout the different phases
of the industrial cycle. He argues, however, (p. 250) that the accumulation
of liquid funds is not the actual cause of the breakdown of an upswing but
is a reflection of the difficulties of the capitalist growth process in adjusting
to the (traverse) requirements for disproportional growth which the various
phases of an upswing or continuous expansion would demand.

As we have mentioned above, the 'proportions', that is, the relative
allocation of productive resources to the different sectors and their relative
production levels, have to change over the different phases of an expansion
process. At the beginning of an expansion, activity is concentrated in the
heavy capital-goods sector which is characterized by long gestation periods.
Economic activity then moves increasingly towards the provision of
'working capital' to utilize the new capacities once they have been
installed; finally, and to some extent simultaneously, production in
consumer-goods industries has to expand to satisfy the increasing demand
derived from increased employment levels, and the industries also have to
respond to the changing expenditure patterns which result from rising real
incomes. Tugan-Baranowsky traces the slowdown of the expansion process
and the emergence of first partial and then general overproduction back to
the inability of a capitalist economy to undertake adequately the structural
adjustment required by the disproportionate industrial growth pattern to be
followed by the economy in the course of an upswing. In particular, the
relative rigidity of fixed capital and long construction periods are the
causes of that inability. The following quotation provides us with the
sequence of his argument concerning the second phase of an upswing:

> In the various phases of an upswing the new durable social capital is being produced.
> Industrial production moves in a particular direction: the production of means of
> production becomes primary. Iron, machines, instruments, ships, building materials,
> will be produced in much larger quantities than before. At the end, the new fixed
> capital will be ready: new factories, new ships, new buildings are constructed and
> new railway tracks laid. After that, new foundations ('*Neugründungen*') will
> diminish. The demand for materials which were used for the construction of fixed

capital will diminish. The allocation of capital [across branches] requires new proportionalities: machines, instruments, iron, building materials will be less demanded since new foundations have become less. But since the producers of means of production cannot extract their capital from their enterprises, and because the size of the invested capital in terms of buildings, machinery, and so on, requires the continuation of production (otherwise idle capital will not yield any returns at all), an excess production of means of production will arise. And since industrial branches are mutually dependent upon each other, partial overproduction can easily lead to general overproduction – the prices of all commodities would fall and general stagnation of business activity can emerge ...

The reason for such a situation of general overproduction (which can – and often does – last for several years) lies in the absence of the [correct] proportionality between the different industrial branches. (Ibid., p. 250)

Tugan-Baranowsky clearly indicates here that the cause of the upswing coming to an end is the pattern of production built into the structure of capacities which have been built up during the economic expansion and which has become rigid; that is, it cannot adjust to the new production requirements at the end of an upswing. Partial and then general overproduction will result.[5]

However, Tugan-Baranowsky does emphasize the speculative nature which drives the expansion, particularly towards the end of an upswing and which makes a capitalist economy especially prone to 'disproportionalities' and consequently to economic crises:

The extension of production (levels) in the different industries proceeds in such periods [that is, particularly towards the end of an economic expansion] almost independently of the real conditions of demand, directed particularly by speculation and under the influence of manoeuvres at the stock exchange.

That is why, at the end of the expansionary phase of an industrial cycle, any proportionality in the distribution of social production activity is missing and [current proportions] can only be established through the destruction of a portion of the capital of those industries which have grown too much. (Ibid., pp. 250–51)

Summing up, Tugan-Baranowsky presents a concise picture of the cyclical growth process of a capitalist economy. As an economy embarks upon an expansion phase it proceeds through a well-defined sequence of operating different activities (departments or stages of production) at different rates. In a credit economy, investment gets an element of relative independence from the evolution of social consumption and thus provides the basis for overexpansion of capacities in certain sectors of the economy. Because of relative rigidities in adjusting allocation patterns and productive capacities to the requirements of the disproportionate growth process of an expanding economy and to adjust to situations where misallocations become apparent, brings with it the possibility – and, indeed, likelihood – of economic crisis. The economic crisis is itself the mechanism which –

with economic and social losses – brings about a readjustment of 'proportions' (the adjustment of productive capacities to the pattern of social demand) which, together with adjustments in the financial sphere and in income distribution, provides the basis for renewed capitalist expansion. Finally, it may be added that Keynes found himself 'in strong sympathy with the school of writers ... of which Tugan-Baranowsky was the first and the most original' (Keynes, 1930, p. 89), who based their theories of the credit cycle on fluctuations in fixed capital investment.

3   BOUNIATIAN

In the following we shall not present a comprehensive survey of Mentor Bouniatian's business-cycle theory but concentrate on those elements in his analysis which are innovative relative to the other authors discussed in this chapter.

Bouniatian starts his analysis of the business cycle at the deepest point of the depression and discusses what could cause demand to recover.[6] He thereby makes interesting and important observations concerning the importance of the evolution of demand structures. A revival of demand can stem from:

> [e]ither an increase in the demand following the development of social culture or result from innovations which result in the birth of new wants or which can better satisfy existing wants. (In recent times, examples of these are cars, electric light, the telephone, etc.). (Bouniatian, 1922, p. 251)

Another cause of demand picking up would be the industrial demand following the discovery of new methods of production, or export demand which could also be generated through credit links:

> an increase in the demand for industrial products following the discovery of new processes of production could also generate new capital spending; or it could be an increase in foreign demand for exported commodities ... this type of demand is often based on export credits granted by the exporting country. (Ibid., p. 252)

Bouniatian states, without detailed discussion, that the supply side of the economy is well able to respond to a new impulse of demand at the end of a depression: 'Whatever the cause of the expansionary movement, it will fall on fertile grounds in a period of depression, since at that moment an economy tries to develop its productive powers which have been compressed by the depression' (ibid., p. 252).

Attention is drawn, as in Tugan-Baranowsky, to the fact that an upswing is characterized in particular by the increased production and instalment of fixed capital equipment (Bouniatian speaks of a 'capitalisation intensifiée'). However, he also emphasizes a particular sequence in the generation of increased production activity in different industries as the upswing proceeds. This, of course, has implications for firms operating or being newly founded in the different industries:

> New firms of the type indicated above [that is, innovative firms] are being founded and develop hectic activities: companies in mining, metallurgy, in the construction of machinery, materials of various types, locomotives, etc. These firms give rise to a demand for production goods and initial production of accessory materials: coal, chemical products, etc., and also of materials destined to be used in the new factories and workshops. Due to the close relationship between the different industrial branches, intense demand pressures develop and, to satisfy these, productive capabilities are being fully stretched. (Ibid., pp. 253–4)

Bouniatian's crisis theory is essentially a theory of *overaccumulation* brought about by the intense drive towards accumulation typical for capitalist economies and a relative neglect of final consumption:

> The expansion in the capital goods and all the ancillary industries does not correspond to the actual consumption of consumption goods but is based on the expectation of future consumption and takes its impetus from the propensity [in a capitalist economy] to accumulate. As soon as consumption is unable to absorb the increased yield of the social process of production, i.e. as long as the purchasing power of the consumptive classes is disadvantaged and [production] is oriented towards increased capitalisation, a halt/slow-down of the entire process of reproduction will be unavoidable. (Bouniatian, 1908, pp. 119–20)

Bouniatian's crisis theory can be summarized as follows: the root cause of the crisis is 'overcapitalization', that is, the overexpansion of productive capacities in the face of limitations of final consumers' expenditure. The capitalization process is only loosely limited by consumers' expenditure since there can be an increase in the overall capital intensity of production processes. Furthermore such a limitation might not be felt immediately because of the gestation lag between the construction and utilization of productive capacities,[7] although eventually this limitation will make itself felt.

Overcapitalization can happen because the investment process is directed by future demand, which is a fact mentioned by many authors as a reason for an unrealistic and often speculative extension of productive capacities. Given an imperfectly competitive organization of industries, prices will be kept up for a while, allowing production to continue at the same level to add to inventories financed by means of credit. This additional demand for credit (not for additional capitalization but simply to maintain current production levels) will drive up interest rates. But Bouniatian insists that lack of credit is not the root cause of the crisis.[8]

> The increase in inventories will be assisted by the efforts of producers and traders to maintain the high prices which originally motivated production plans in spite of the difficulties of sales. For this purpose extensive use of credit facilities will be made if the internal resources of products are insufficient ... The producers need capital to maintain their inventories to honour their financial obligations and – if possible – to maintain production levels ... (Ibid., pp. 121, 123)

Bouniatian also contributed to the evolution of the accelerator principle in the economic literature.[9] He argued that fluctuations in 'backwardly linked' production goods and raw materials supplying industries would automatically be stronger than in the industries which produce final consumption goods:

> Even though overproduction might have its source in the consumption goods sector, this does not mean that overproduction will be strongest in that sector. Slight difficulties in the sales of consumption goods could cause stronger reverberations in the industries of 'higher order' and generates in the instrumental [capital goods and raw materials supplying] industries stronger overproduction. The stronger the previous expansion was and the further removed these goods are from the final fabrication stages and from final consumption the stronger their overproduction. (Ibid., p. 120)

In summary, Bouniatian combined a theory of overaccumulation with some interesting observations concerning the rate of the evolution of the structure of demand as an important element in causing an economic upswing. He also contributed to the development of the 'accelerator hypothesis' which was seen by authors at the time as one of the elements explaining economic fluctuations, and particularly the stronger cyclical pattern observed in the capital-goods industries. The accelerator mechanism fits well into his theory which uses underconsumptionist arguments (a lagging of wage incomes which reduces the growth of final consumption expenditure) and provides the basis for an understanding of the stronger fluctuations of the activity levels in capital-goods industries compared to those in the economy as a whole. Futhermore, we have seen that imperfectly competitive behaviour contributed substantially to the features of particular phases of the business cycle.

4   AFTALION

Central to Albert Aftalion's theory of the business cycle is that the structure of production activity is strongly affected by the system of relative prices and that, in turn, the movements of relative prices are themselves strongly influenced by the distribution of production activity across different sectors and by the characteristics of the techniques of production used in these sectors. In his detailed statistical investigation of the fluctuations of prices, incomes and costs, respectively, Aftalion also finds that the time series on aggregate production and the general price level do not coincide with the time series on production of fixed capital goods but lags behind it by a period of from one to three years. A central role is thus played by the leads and lags which characterize production activity and which transmit themselves into price movements. Such price movements in turn lead to production decisions which give rise to continuous cyclical movements of economic activity.

Hence, Aftalion's theory is built upon two main ideas:

1. that the price and quantity systems are never in a state of equilibrium and that excess supply and excess demand situations succeed each other over the various phases of the cycle;
2. that the 'objective' reason for such disequilibria is a *technological* one, that is, the long gestation times and longer-term effects of production decisions due to 'capitalistic' techniques of production, that is, techniques which use a strong element of fixed capital equipment.

The basic structure of his theory is supplemented by an analysis of 'secondary' factors, such as income share movements, credit and speculation, which are not the root causes (according to Aftalion) of cyclical movements but can extend and deepen their various phases.

Let us see how Aftalion states his theory:

> My principal thesis is that the chief responsibility for cyclical fluctuations should be assigned to one of the characteristics of modern industrial technique, namely, the long period required for the production of fixed capital ... My theory implies that the expectations of those directing production are alternately too optimistic and too pessimistic, a feature which it has in common with other theories. ... The system in expectations results from the capitalistic technique of production, the necessity to satisfy the needs of production of an industrial equipment requiring a long time for its construction. In other words, the system is a consequence of the long delay which often separates the moment when the production of goods is decided upon and a forecast is made from the moment when the manufacture is terminated, and the forecast is replaced by reality. (1927, p. 130)

In his book, Aftalion gives an illustrative example of why systematic 'errors' in expectations formation, and consequently in production decisions with long gestation lags occur. Take the example, he says, of a stove which takes some time to heat up after one has added coal. As the cold persists and the thermometer continues to indicate this, one is very tempted, while waiting for the room to heat up, to add additional coal to the fire. But if one is guided by current sensations and by the current thermometer reading one is likely to overheat the room. Similarly, after the room has been heated up one might stop adding coal even after a point has been reached when, to keep the room temperature at the required level, one should have proceeded to do so. (For this example, see Aftalion, 1913, pp. 360–61.)

Hence over- and underproduction are the direct result of systematic mistakes. But the reason why these mistakes are systematic and difficult to avoid is the nature of capitalistic techniques of production:

> It is owing to the conditions created by the capitalist technique of production [that is, fixed capital producing and using processes] that it is difficult to escape such errors. ... Too long an interval separates the ordering of new equipment and its delivery, between the moment when it starts producing and when it can satisfy wants. During this period ... excess demand and high prices persist. (Ibid., pp. 359–61)

Such high prices continue to induce entrepreneurs to invest more:

> So long as the industrial equipment in the course of construction is not finished, it does not adversely affect prices. Forecasts may remain optimistic. The insufficiency of ships or of electric lighting persists, in spite of the great number of ships on the way or of electric installations in progress. Prices rise further. And this rise of prices occasions new orders and a new increase of the production of fixed capital. (Aftalion, 1927, p. 131)

When the equipment goods in construction come on stream, price (and profit) movements start to reverse:

> when the new projects are finished, the new factories and electric installations completed, the new blast furnaces lighted, and the new looms, machines, locomotives, and ships delivered, prices begin to fall. Prosperity gives way to depression. For a certain time, however, large portions of the equipment previously ordered continue to be finished and delivered. These deliveries, even if they decrease slightly, are still very substantial. The fall of prices is accentuated and prolonged in spite of the great diminution of productive activity. (Ibid., pp. 131–2)

Just as in Bouniatian's analysis, an element of imperfectly competitive behaviour comes in to prolong the period of overproduction:

the long time required for the manufacture of the equipment means a high cost of this equipment. An effort is therefore made to avoid letting it lie idle. After a sudden diminution in the production of consumption goods during the first months of falling prices, production is resumed in spite of prices which afford little opportunity for profit. The resumption of production of these goods holds their prices at a low level. (Ibid., p. 132)

Credit and speculation are seen by Aftalion not as primary causes of cyclical fluctuations but they can contribute to lengthening and deepening the various phases thereof:

> The cyclical movement of credit, like that of incomes, is the effect and not the cause of the cyclical variations of prices and of forecasts. But the effect reacts on the cause, prolonging the duration and increasing the intensity of the cyclical movements of prices and production. For example, during prosperity credit favours the multiplication of purchases and orders, and allows optimistic forecasts to exercise fully their stimulating actions. Furthermore, by facilitating productive activity, it also causes an expansion of incomes, wages, and profits, without causing an immediately corresponding increase in the supply of finished goods, since it is principally in an enlarged reduction of fixed capital that credit resources are employed. Demand increases without, for the time being, an increase of supply and prices rise. ... Speculation acts in the same manner, by exaggerating price movements and, in particular, by multiplying, during the phase of prosperity, forward ordering and purchases on credit. ... Since the high prices of the prosperity phase cause a pronounced increase in the cost of production, the ensuing fall of prices makes the situation more difficult, diminishes profits, wipes them out, or even causes heavy losses. (Ibid., p. 133)

Summing up, Aftalion comes close to a unicausal explanation of industrial fluctuations. The root cause for the amplitude and the timing of the business cycle is for Aftalion a technological characteristic of a 'capitalistic' economy, that is, the long gestation lags of durable instruments of production. However, while being the fundamental cause, this characteristic alone would not lead to industrial fluctuations if there were perfect foresight. It is the long gestation period in the development of new productive capacities which leads entrepreneurs systematically to overestimate future demand at the beginning of an upswing when they face an excess demand situation. Similarly, it reduces further investment activity at the end of an upswing, when an excess supply situation is experienced, which pushes the economy into a recession. Finally, the over-retrenchment of production activity is realized and a new upswing starts.[10] The myopia of the expectations-formation process is reflected in the intertemporal price system which guides firms to overexpand production in the course of an upswing and to sharply contract production activity when an excess supply situation is experienced. Aftalion thus can be credited for further developing and integrating the *acceleration principle*, namely the idea that a relatively small increase (decrease) in the demand for consumption goods can produce a much larger increase (decrease) in the demand for capital goods, into a theory of the business cycle.

In addition, Aftalion weaves into his analysis of the nature of cyclical movements in a capitalist economy features of imperfectly competitive behaviour, speculation and the role of credit, all of which can reinforce the amplitudes and durations of the different phases of an industrial cycle.

5   SPIETHOFF

Arthur Spiethoff is probably the most prominent German business-cycle analyst at the turn and the beginning of this century. He was not only strongly influenced by Tugan-Baranowsky's seminal work, emphasizing overinvestment in the means of production as the dominant cause of modern fluctuations and rejecting Say's Law of markets as inappropriate to a monetary economy, but also by the German Historical School.[11] He differs from the other business-cycle theorists discussed so far in that he does not attempt to derive business fluctuations predominantly from a single cause or even from a tightly-knit analytical structure, but rather aims to synthesize the features of most of the prevalent business-cycle theories of his time in order to arrive at a comprehensive picture of industrial fluctuations. This allows him to develop his explanatory framework in much closer contact with the historically specific instances of particular business-cycle episodes. To a greater degree than the other authors discussed in this chapter he embeds his analysis in a detailed study of historical material.[12]

The careful use Spiethoff makes of elements of business-cycle analysis, which were often provided by other authors, can be seen from the following passage discussing the possibility of resumption of economic activity from a depressed state of the economy:

> During the depression, loanable funds find no outlet, the rate of interest falls continuously, whilst fixed interest rate securities rise. The decline in the yield of loan capital does not, however, lead to an expansion of fixed investment, because overproduction and the general tendency for prices to fall not only depress profits, but even constitute a danger of loss on investment. ... The fear of a loss on investments deflects more and more capital into loans and tends to reduce the rate of interest. Only when it has become plain for all to see that the rate of interest compares unfavourably with profit on investment, will expectations act as a stimulus for bigger investment. It is necessary for such a difference in yield to be demonstrated as vividly as possible by a few firms or by some branch of industry brought into being by courageous entrepreneurs. (Spiethoff, [1925] 1953, p. 148)

In this passage Spiethoff does take account of the accumulation of loan capital in the form of liquid funds in periods of depression, but he denies it the role attributed to it by other authors of being sufficient to initiate an upswing in economic activity. An upswing has to be generated by a confluence of a number of factors, some endogenous and some exogenous. For the latter he particularly emphasizes the role of innovations and the dynamics of particular expanding industries:

> For most upswings we are told of industries which served as a stimulus and a starting point for investment. Mining and steelworks, railways and electricity were large industries of this kind. In Germany, the 1840s showed clearly that good individual results were needed before the boom investments in railways started in 1844. ... Once some industry, e.g. the railways in this case, has proved its value, then it can always become a fresh focus as soon as new fields of application are found; in such industries expectations regarded as assured may suffice to act as a stimulus. The same was true also for mining, iron works, electricity works, etc. (Ibid., p. 149)

Spiethoff develops here what later became known as Schumpeterian themes, where industrial and interfirm differentiation as new technologies and new products are introduced become an essential part of the picture and the dynamic causing an economic upswing. An economic expansion starts – according to Spiethoff – from the success of a few firms in a particular industry (or group of industries) and then spreads as result of the confidence and successes experienced in these industries to related activities and industries where ' new fields of application ' can be found. Spiethoff develops here a 'network' idea of relationships between dynamic firms and industries which give each economic upswing its particular historical characteristic.[13] The element of innovation and technological transition (*'exogenous* stimuli') gives the economic expansion, furthermore, a feature of unpredictability with regards to its timing, duration and depth.[14]

Let us now return to Spiethoff's analysis of some of the *endogenous* elements in business-cycle behaviour. The following quotation continues the discussion of the forces which generate an upswing:

> The difference in yield between loans and fixed capital investment can largely be traced to the depression. The accumulation of idle funds depresses the rate of interest on loans and fosters a difference in yield. ... It is the pressure of the slump that drives people to fresh markets, to reduce costs of production and to encourage technical progress. The low prices of indirect consumption goods during the slump and the low wages and rates of interest reduce the construction cost of investment goods and increase the profit of invested capital. ... The downswing contains powerful self-annihilating forces and is thus itself, to a large degree, a cause for the subsequent upswing. (Ibid., p. 150)

Spiethoff develops here in a more detailed manner the theme mentioned briefly by Bouniatian (1922, p. 252) on why 'an expansionary movement ... will fall on fertile grounds in a period of depression'. Among the favourable conditions which develop in the course of a depression and which are conducive to the restart of an expansionary process are:

- low nominal rates of interest which support the opening of a gap between returns on interest-bearing financial assets and the (potential) returns on real investments as new investment opportunities become more apparent (see above); such a gap also results from
- a fall in the construction costs of new investment goods due to low wages and low interest rates in the course of the depression; and, furthermore,
- the new investment opportunities result from the efforts which existing businesses have to make in the difficult conditions of the depression to lower production costs through technological modernization and the search for new markets. To such new investment opportunities, enterprises can also more easily respond because of existing excess capacities, excess inventories and excess labour available in the course of a depression.[15]

The following passage shows the fragility of the initial phases of an upswing initiated by a transition to new techniques of production and accompanied by industrial reorganization:

> The improvement of productive facilities by the spread of the most recent techniques and the consequent reduction in the cost of production at first intensify competition, but in the long-run render low prices more bearable. Their effect is sometimes increased later by a disproportionately heavy fall in wages. The reconstruction of the weakest over-capitalised firms either through mergers or by new owners acquiring them at a low price has at first a paralysing influence owing to the capital losses involved, but the subsequent result is that these firms, too, find it easier to cope with the low prices. (Spiethoff, [1925] 1953, p. 148)

A very important component for an upswing to gain momentum – and, as we shall see later on, for the possibility of overproduction to arise – is the availability of 'credit'. Here Spiethoff emphasizes that if each enterprise had to finance its activities from earnings (either its own or other firms') the picking up of economic activity would be a much slower process. The extension of credit allows industry to bring unutilized capacities and unemployed labour into operation more quickly and also allows the process of new capital formation to proceed on a larger scale.

Credit is the indispensable means for an upswing. The services rendered to the upswing by credit are two-fold. Only with the help of credit is it possible to utilise capital in the way in which it is actually done and which is necessary. In the absence of credit, the owners of capital would be unable to use large parts of it, and the very formation of capital would be on a smaller scale. It is modern credit and banking institutions which now prevent a large part of savings from being withheld from production and used for hoarding as used to happen when stockings and mattresses served as banks. (Ibid.)

The availability of credit is especially important since an upswing usually starts in the investment goods industry, where the need for capital to finance economic activity is especially strong.

Spiethoff develops an interesting argument with respect to the role which produced flow inputs (such as iron, cement, steel, and so on) play in characterizing the features of an economic upswing, including the emergence of severe disproportionalities and overproduction. Spiethoff argues that the production of intermediate inputs (which he calls 'indirect consumption goods') could, in the course of an upswing, easily outstrip the formation of savings. Spiethoff thinks that such a *disproportion*:

is mainly due to the indirect consumption goods, but savings can also be responsible to some extent. ... Insofar as these [the intermediate inputs] are used to produce fresh indirect consumption goods they very greatly increase their own output rate and thus increase the need for purchasing power in the form of savings. Iron and building materials when used for steel furnaces, rolling mills and brickworks, have quite a different effect than if they are used for blocks of flats or for shoe factories. In the first case, the sale of the products of the new plant must always rely on savings, and may therefore easily come to exceed the latter. This fact is regularly overlooked by entrepreneurs in the extension of plant for the production of indirect consumption goods. (Ibid., pp. 157–8)[16]

There are a number of innovative features in Spiethoff's analysis here:

- The emphasis on indirect consumption goods is a precursor to the emphasis on the role of intermediate consumption in industrial production;
- Spiethoff emphasizes the circular aspect of intermediate goods production whose production can expand without there being – for some time – any restriction felt from the demand side (this is a version of the 'pigs' cycle' argument); furthermore,
- earlier restrictions which were due to the limited availability of natural resource inputs diminish in importance as technical change reduces the importance of natural resources, such as wood, as against produced inputs.

Characterizing the beginning of an upswing, Spiethoff develops an extensive multiplier analysis and emphasizes thereby the ability of a recuperating economy to generate the necessary savings:

> an upswing ... increasingly develops self-propagating and self-intensifying means. The increased employment of the available labour and productive resources furnishes goods for the expansion of production and increases the formation of savings for the augmented investment or, in other words, for the purchase of labour and of means of production, and thus for the creation of investment goods. ... An important stage is reached when prices begin to rise, for the rise in prices is the strongest incentive to expand production as well as a rich new source of net profit and thus of saving. The boom sets in when the spirit of enterprise grows so strong that the demand for capital raises rates of interest. A chain of upswing phenomena develops, each of which calls forth the next ... increased investment, increased consumption, rising prices and profits, together with the expansion of production and of capital formation and then again increased investment, etc. Once the unemployed have been absorbed, industry draws the additional labour it requires from agriculture and from undeveloped regions. The result is a constant spiral-like self-raising movement. (Ibid., p. 154)

Next, let us discuss Spiethoff's analysis of the 'end of the upswing' and the 'origin of overproduction'. The root of the possibility of overproduction for Spiethoff lies in the possibility that the production of investment goods and of produced inputs (intermediate consumption goods, as Spiethoff calls them) diverges from the volume of savings being generated. In particular, Spiethoff believes that towards the end of an upswing, the production of investment goods and of intermediate consumption goods might still continue at a relatively high rate while the volume of savings might come down; the latter is due to rising real wages and falling profits, rising raw material costs and, possibly, a fall in the expectation of returns on further investment. In certain periods of the upswing, savings temporarily cease to regulate the production and utilization of investment goods, and this allows the possibility of overproduction (and overaccumulation) to arise.

Spiethoff emphasizes that '[i]ndirect consumption goods and investment goods form part of complicated capital relationships, the study of which affords the key to the origin of *overproduction*' (ibid., p. 156). Spiethoff spells out the savings–investment relationships which constitute the basis of his analysis of 'overproduction' in the following way:

> Since the indirect consumption goods are only bought out of savings, indirect consumption depends on the investment of savings. The formation of savings proceeds quite independently of the production of the indirect consumption goods and of the construction of investment goods; at the same time, both are produced without entrepreneurs having any precise knowledge of the extent of capital formation or of the propensity to invest. If the makers of indirect consumption goods and the potential investors wanted to make production and the formation of savings keep pace with each other, then the two processes would have to be adjusted to each

other, in mutual knowledge. As such, knowledge is lacking and adjustment impossible, there is always the risk of one process lagging behind the other. This is decidedly the case during the last two stages of an upswing. During a boom there is so much saving destined for the purchase of indirect consumption goods that the latter prove to be in short supply. In the last stage of the upswing – that of capital scarcity – the relationship is reversed, and the supply of indirect consumption goods exceeds the demand from investment-seeking savings. At this point, overproduction has come into existence. (Ibid., pp. 156–7)

Behind this formulation is a critique of Say's Law which points not at an overall shortage of savings but of savings which are looking for productive investment; the difference between these must amount to investment into unproductive (or monetary) assets.[17]

To sum up, Spiethoff's business-cycle theory is formulated in a way which does not require overproduction or even an upswing to occur by necessity, but he describes a number of (endogenous) mechanisms which could easily lead to overproduction, crisis, and then to a situation which is favourable for a new upswing. For the latter to actually occur, new ('exogenous') impulses are necessary, such as the emergence of new technologies, new industries and new markets. The theory is thus a mixture of an analysis of endogenous mechanisms which could easily lead to business fluctuations, such as the credit mechanism in a developed capitalist economy, the importance of a self-feeding sector of intermediate input production, expectation formation and snowball effects, and exogenous impulses, such as new techniques of production, new areas of industrial activity.

Both these types of elements lead to a business-cycle theory in which the timing and the strength of the different phases of a cycle remain indeterminate and give rise to irregular patterns of industrial fluctuation.

6   LOWE, BURCHARDT AND HAYEK

Spiethoff's emphasis on the strategic role of capital investment in the explanation of business cycles, his approach of visualizing cyclical fluctuations as an entity and his search for endogenous mechanisms also gave major stimuli to Lowe's early work on business cycles. In his methodological examination of the logic of the existing business-cycle theories he classified Spiethoff, together with Aftalion and Cassel, as the leading representative of the 'method of circular reasoning', which in Lowe's view lies in between the non-theoretical view and a problem-adequate business-cycle theory (see Löwe 1926, pp. 177–80). He criticized Spiethoff for giving up the closedness of his system in his theory of the upswing by imputing the stimulating effect to two exogenous factors, namely the gaining of new markets and technological change, and by basing his crisis theory on the isolation of the sphere of productive goods from that of consumption goods.

In his 1926 paper, Lowe stated the central problem of business-cycle theory clearly: if economic theory is to explain the business cycle satisfactorily, it cannot do so simply by outlining the consequences of a disturbing factor exogenously imposed upon an otherwise static economy. Rather, it must seek some causal factor that is immanent to the system itself and can distort the set of equilibrium interrelationships. However, concerning the basic causal factor identified we find a decisive difference between Lowe and Burchardt on the one side, and Hayek on the other side. Although he dissociated himself from simplified versions of the quantity theory which only try to explain the absolute level of prices, Hayek nevertheless resorted to money and credit as the factors whose introduction distorts the rigid interrelations implied in the system of static equilibrium and makes endogenous fluctuations both possible and necessary. He not only regarded his trade-cycle theory most decisively as a monetary one but also emphasized that a theory of cyclical fluctuations other than a monetary one is hardly conceivable. Lowe (1928), on the other hand, in his critical evaluation of monetary explanations of the business cycle, came to the conclusion that nobody had succeeded in demonstrating the systematic nature of the monetary fluctuations themselves.[18] He regarded monetary factors as playing, at best, an intermediate causal role and as being likely to intensify any disequilibrium induced by non-monetary causes. Lowe saw the decisive endogenous disturbing factor to lie with technological change on the real side of the economy. From the very beginning he was deeply influenced by the Schumpeter–Sombart–hypothesis according to which technical progress is the central determinant of the cycle but also the essential factor influencing the long-run trend.[19] Lowe was supported by his closest collaborator, Fritz (later Frank) Burchardt (1928), whose paper on the history of monetary trade-cycle theory was even praised by his main opponent as 'very valuable in its historical part' (Hayek, 1929, p. 57). Burchardt showed how structural changes in economic history have altered the character of theory. During the nineteenth century crisis theory evolved into trade-cycle theory. Credit expansion and interest-rate movements became more important as features of the cycle. Recognizing monetary influences manifesting themselves especially through changes in the price level, Burchardt concluded that monetary factors alone cannot explain cyclical phenomena sufficiently. In his view non-monetary factors, and particularly technical progress, have to play an important role. With reference to Wicksell's influential theory, Burchardt emphasized that, although changes in the market rate of interest are important for movements of the price level, the real impulse for the disturbance of equilibrium of an economy is given by technical progress which leads to an increase of the natural rate (see Burchardt, 1928, p. 119). This was fully in line with Lowe's emphasis on the role of technical progress as the central determinant of both the cycle and the long-run growth trend.

Interestingly, in *Monetary Theory and the Trade Cycle* Hayek concedes that a discrepancy between the natural (or as he prefered to call it the 'equilibrium') rate and the money rate of interest does not presuppose any 'easy money' policy of central banks, and that technical progress may cause an increase in the natural rate which is not matched by an immediate adjustment of the money rate. Whereas he thus recognized the importance of technical progress as a starting point for cyclical fluctuations, he nevertheless viewed monetary factors as the ultimately necessary cause. Moreover, whereas Hayek ([1929] 1933, pp. 147 and 182ff.) explicitly supported Wicksell's view of a fluctuating natural rate which the banks cannot directly perceive, in *Prices and Production* technical progress as a possible cause of a disturbance of the initial equilibrium between the natural and the market rate of interest and thereby of cyclical fluctuations completely disappeared and Hayek retreated to Mises' traditional argument of making the monetary authorities the real villains of the piece.

On the other hand, Hayek (ibid., p. 41) added an interesting footnote to the English translation of *Geldtheorie und Konjunkturtheorie* in which he made the qualifying statement that he feels that his own theory of cyclical fluctuations, which emphasizes the real changes in the structure of production brought about by monetary causes, was much closer to certain structural theories of the business cycle than the latter are to other non-monetary explanations such as underconsumption theories or his own theory is to purely monetary explanations which superficially regard changes in the absolute level of prices as most important for determining cyclical fluctuations. Hayek explicitly mentioned Spiethoff and Cassel as those theorists who come closest to his own thinking.[20] Hayek's modifying statement is not surprising since from the very beginning he had emphasized that an important task for monetary theory is to explain changes in the structure of relative prices caused by monetary 'injections' and the consequential disproportionalities in the structure of production which arise because the price system communicates false information about consumer preferences and resource availabilities. While monetary factors cause the cycle, real phenomena constitute it. The changes in the real structure of production over time which constitute those fluctuations were developed by Hayek in *Prices and Production* on the basis of the famous triangles, in which the ordinate represents the length of the productive process and the abscissa measures the money value of the output of consumption goods. In this 'Austrian' representation of the structure of production or 'stages approach', which originally had been developed by Böhm-Bawerk, a sequence of original inputs is transformed into a single output of consumable commodities. No distinction is made between fixed and circulating capital; both types of capital are 'intermediate products' or 'working capital', that is, goods in process that sooner or later will be turned into consumers' goods. The production process is thought of as being unidirectional, that is, causal, rather than circular. This way of tracing back the production process to some original factor(s) – such as labour (and land) – leaves unexplained the reproduction and expansion requirements of the stock of fixed capital goods.

It was exactly this unsatisfactory treatment of fixed capital goods in the Austrian model of production which came under severe attack when Burchardt (1931–32) set out to compare, contrast and combine the two most important alternative ways of conceiving the production system, the schemes of the stationary circular flow in Böhm-Bawerk and Marx, and thus undertook the first synthesis of the vertical or stages model and the horizontal or sectoral (interindustry) model.[21] Burchardt criticized Böhm-Bawerk for mixing up two entirely different problems, namely the historical conditions of the original building up of a capital stock and the present conditions of reproduction of the existing capital stock. Second and most important, in an industrial economy the physical self-reproduction of some fixed capital goods is an essential technological characteristic, that is, a particular group of fixed capital goods, which Lowe later called 'machine tools' can be maintained and increased only with the help of a circular process in which these machine tools act as inputs. The role which these capital goods play in industrial production is thus analogous to the role of seed corn in agricultural production. It is therefore not technically possible to trace all finished goods back to nothing but labour (and land) and to treat fixed capital goods as the output of some intermediate stages in the vertical model, as Böhm-Bawerk and his 'Austrian' followers such as Hayek have suggested.

Hayek was not unimpressed by the critique of Burchardt which he regarded 'not only as the first but also as the most fruitful of all the recent criticisms of the "Austrian" theory of capital' (Hayek, 1939, p. 23). In the section 'The structure of capitalistic production' in his *Profits, Interest and Investment* Hayek even concedes that the stages concept, which he had used as the production-theoretic foundation for his theory of cyclical fluctuations in *Prices and Production*, 'gives the impression of a simple linearity of the dependency of the various stages of production which does not apply in a world where durable goods are the most important form of capital' (ibid., pp. 21–2). The stages concept may give an undue impression of linearity while in fact production relationships may in many respects be rather circular in character. However, Hayek persisted in giving preference to the vertical model of production.

Both Hayek and Lowe, in their subsequent writings, have been attracted by Ricardo's chapter 'On Machinery' (Ricardo, 1821: 1951, Ch. 31) in which the author discusses the employment consequences of the introduction of a different, more mechanized method of production. Hayek ([1931] 1935: 101ff.) traced the central idea of cyclical changes in the lengths of production periods leading to a 'concertina effect' back to Ricardo's doctrine of the conversion of circulating to fixed capital. In the framework of his business-cycle theory, the basic function of the Ricardo effect is to give a theoretical explanation for the upper turning-point. With consumer-goods prices running ahead of money wage rates, real wages will fall. As a consequence, entrepreneurs will be encouraged to substitute labour for capital. The change in the relative profitability of techniques that differ in the proportions in which they employ labour and capital will lead to a fall in the demand for investment goods and thereby to a reallocation of labour from 'higher' to 'lower' stages of production.

Whether Hayek's genealogical reference to Ricardo's machinery chapter is justified can be critically discussed (see, for example, Hagemann and Trautwein, 1996). Contrary to Hayek's formulation of the problem, Ricardo's structural adjustment problem does not arise from 'overinvestment' or even 'malinvestment' but from a change in the structure of the capital stock which changes its composition towards a greater proportion of fixed capital at the expense of circulating capital (the wage fund). Ricardo was a strict adherent of Say's Law, implying that the savings function was simultaneously also the investment function. Thus, the problem of capital accumulation running ahead of savings is clearly not a Ricardian theme. On the contrary, Ricardo identified the formation of additional real capital as the decisive factor that – in the long-run – can compensate for technological unemployment. Furthermore, Hayek's discussion of the Ricardo effect is restricted to the analysis of substitution processes between capital and labour which are induced by a change in factor prices; that is, Hayek operates with a flex-price model in which a variation of the real wage is the impulse causing a choice-of-techniques change. Ricardo, on the other hand, employs at first a numerical example in which the unemployment problem results from the capitalists' conversion of circulating into fixed capital, that is, the choice of a different technique out of an existing book of blueprints, with the real wage rate being fixed at an exogenously-given level. In the following passages, however, Ricardo emphasizes the sudden discovery of improved machinery, that is, an extension of the book of blueprints leading to technological change.

This explains why Ricardo's analysis of the machinery problem has become the starting-point for many subsequent analyses of technological unemployment as, for example, in John Hicks who, since the late 1960s had been fascinated by the Ricardo machinery effect. In *Capital and Time*, Hicks (1973) developed a traverse analysis based on a neo-Austrian representation of production structures to defend what he regarded as the central message of Ricardo's treatment of the machinery question: that there are important major innovations which can make the emergence of temporary technological unemployment highly likely if not unavoidable. On the other hand, increased investment in the wake of higher profits due to increased efficiency of the new techniques should lead to a path of higher output levels and return the economy to full employment in the long run.

Characteristically, Lowe, whose attention during more than sixty years of research was focused upon technological change as the mainspring of growth but also as a principal cause of destabilizing tendencies in that growth process and who was deeply affected by – what he perceived as – the spectre of high technological unemployment in the last years of the Weimar Republic, started his investigation of the macroeconomic consequences of technological change from Ricardo's analysis of the machinery problem (as did a number of other authors, some of whom were his collaborators and colleagues; see, for example, Neisser, 1942; for an overview of this literature see Gourvitch, 1940). He was centrally concerned to define the conditions at each stage of the 'traverse' such that an economy could move 'efficiently' back towards an equlibrium growth path, resolving thus the 'compensation problem' of Ricardo's machinery problem with least social disruption and extending this type of analysis to other 'forces of change', such as demographic change and environmental restrictions to growth. This type of analysis culminated in his *Path of Economic Growth* (Lowe, 1976).

7   LOWE AND THE STRUCTURAL ANALYSIS OF REAL CAPITAL FORMATION

Returning to Burchardt's seminal synthesis of the horizontal and the vertical model of production, this was first applied to genuine dynamic analysis by Lowe's PhD student Alfred Kähler in his study on the displacement of workers by machinery (Kähler, 1933). Lowe also drew heavily on Burchardt's two essays when in the early 1950s he set out to develop his structural analysis of real capital formation (see, for example, Lowe, 1952, pp. 142ff.). The central ideas of Burchardt also reappear in the 'schematic representation of industrial production'[22] which underlies Lowe's investigation of traverse processes. Lowe's scheme comprises not only three sectors but also four successive stages within each sector that lead up to the finished goods. Thus Lowe's category of equipment-goods industries includes not only the production of the final fixed capital goods but also the preceding stages of mining and the production of pig iron[23] and steel. Similarly, the consumer-goods sector includes not only the making of finished dress ready for sale to private households but also the preceding stages of cultivating cotton, spinning yarn and weaving clothes. The fact that all sectors are divided into stages representing the successive maturing of natural resources into final goods with the help of labour and fixed capital goods brings into light the often neglected role of working capital goods as goods in process and thereby introduces an element with a strong 'Austrian flavour' into the Lowe model. However, one important difference should not be overlooked. In accordance with the central point of critique which was raised by Burchardt against Böhm-Bawerk's concept of the structure of production, it is already the very *first* stage in which fixed capital goods in the Lowe model are to be applied in the production process, whereas in the models of Böhm-Bawerk and Hayek the output of working capital or intermediate goods of the preceding stage serves as an input in the subsequent stage only from the *second* stage onwards.

As has already been mentioned in the introduction, Lowe considered Marx's scheme of reproduction to be especially suited to the study of real capital formation – provided that three 'defects' are corrected (see Lowe, 1955, p. 586). The first correction consists in adding appropriate *stock* variables, such as blast furnaces and spindles at stage 2, because the equations in Marx's scheme make sense only if understood as describing *flows*. However, the respective stock variables play a significant role when processes of dynamic adjustment and structural change are to be analysed and the issue of 'bottlenecks' or rigidities comes into focus. Second, the two sectors of Marx's scheme have to be disaggregated into vertical stages so that the scheme can be applied also to working capital goods as goods in process. This was an essential element of Burchardt's synthesis and is incorporated into Lowe's fully developed scheme of industrial production. Finally, and most important, Lowe considered it necessary to extend the two-sectoral Marxian model to a *three*-sectoral scheme, through the splitting up of the key sector I of Marx's reproduction model, the one in which capital goods are produced, into two subsectors: one producing the equipment for the consumer-good industries and the other producing the equipment for the replacement and expansion of both equipment-good sectors. This need for a tripartite scheme, which is relevant for investigating the structural conditions for steady growth, but even more so for the study of traverse processes with their restructuring, was already stressed by Lowe as early as 1926 (p. 190). He thereby anticipated Hayek's later critique of a two-sectoral model where he viewed 'the crude dichotomy of industry into consumers' goods industries and capital goods industries' as 'certainly wholly insufficient to reproduce the essential features of the complicated interdependencies between industries in actual life' since the 'capital goods industries are ... further organised in a sort of vertical hierarchy' (Hayek, 1939, p. 21).

This vertical hierarchy, which implies a unique intertemporal complementarity in a stages model when processes of structural change are taking place, carries over to the three-sectoral Lowe model which can be constructed from the complete scheme by vertically integrating the various stage inputs and outputs of the three sectors in terms of certain aggregates of finished goods. This becomes obvious when we look at the methods of production as represented in the **A** matrix of machine-input coefficients a_{ij} and the **l** vector of direct labour coefficients.

$$\mathbf{A} = \begin{bmatrix} a_{11} & 0 & 0 \\ a_{12} & 0 & 0 \\ 0 & a_{23} & 0 \end{bmatrix} \qquad \mathbf{l} = \begin{bmatrix} l_1 \\ l_2 \\ l_3 \end{bmatrix}$$

Lowe's model of industrial production has two characteristic features. First, there exists a definite hierarchy of sectors, from 1 via 2 to 3, which gives even this sectoral model some Austrian flavour. Second, the abandonment of the single capital-good assumption leads to a special mixture of flexibility, arising from the dual utilization of machines which therefore can be transferred between sectors 1 and 2, and rigidity because the equipment goods of the second type are exclusively used in the production of consumption goods in sector 3. When changes in the major growth stimuli – labour supply and technical progress – occur, the ability of the economy to react to these changes is limited by the inherited stock of fixed capital goods.[24] The production of machine tools in sector 1 is the bottleneck which any process of accelerated accumulation must overcome. The necessary adjustment path requires both time and costs, and faces difficulties which arise from disproportions between sectors and misleading market signals causing expectational problems. As far as the structural processes are concerned, the compensation process for technological unemployment arising from pure labour-displacing innovations introduced in the consumption-goods sector resembles the adjustment pattern of the traverse to a higher rate of growth of labour supply. Thus from a structural point of view it is irrelevant whether the labour increment originates outside or inside the economic system. However, things look quite different concerning force analysis which studies the behavioural and motivational patterns which will put the economy on a goal-adequate traverse. Lowe's force analysis shows that the technologically-induced profits of the innovating firms provide an alternative source of investment funds besides the decreasing wages emerging from excess supply in the labour market, thus reducing investors' risk compared to the case of an increase in the rate of growth of labour supply.

8   OUTLOOK

The aim of this chapter has been to show that Lowe's work on business cycles (and growth) grew out of a rich tradition of business-cycle analysis which might be summed up under the name *structural theories of the business cycle*. These theories occupied the centre stage in the analysis of business-cycle phenomena since Tugan-Baranowsky's pathbreaking study from the late nineteenth century until the 1930s and had as their distinct feature the analysis of the interrelationship between changes in the industrial (particularly production) structure of an economic system and macroeconomic fluctuations. After the Second World War this tradition, which had also heavily influenced the Austrian theory of the business cycle with its emphasis on disproportions in production linked to the effects of monetary expansion on the relative price structure as developed by Hayek, was discontinued because of the pre-eminence of short-run macroeconomic analysis following the publication of Keynes's *General Theory* and the divorce of most of growth theory from business-cycle phenomena. In the area of business-cycle analysis, research shifted largely to an understanding of simple formal models based on the multiplier-accelerator mechanism. The careful emphasis of the earlier models on the interaction between industrial structural change and macroeconomic fluctuations and the rich discussion of the role of the banking sector in influencing intertemporal allocation patterns, expectations formation and shifts in income distribution over the different phases of the business cycle was lost. In the English-speaking world it was mainly Robertson (1915, 1926) who was influenced by structural approaches to business-cycle analysis, in particular the theories by Tugan-Baranowsky and Aftalion.[25] Although Robertson shared Hayek's later concern with the integration of 'real' and 'monetary' aspects of the business cycle, he was the first British economist to emphasize the role of *real* factors in the cycle.

Recently there has been renewed interest in the medium- to longer-term aspects of business-cycle phenomena, both in the form of a revival of long-wave ideas and what is referred to as 'real', 'new classical' or 'equilibrium' business-cycle theory (for the former, see Freeman et al., 1982, Kleinknecht et al., 1992 and Solomou, 1987; for the latter, see Kim, 1988, and contributions in Kydland, 1995). However, the former lacks the theoretical approach adopted by the earlier theorists, and the 'equilibrium business-cycle theory' research programme started by Lucas in the 1970s cannot be seen as a continuation of a 'structural approach' in the sense adopted in this chapter but has to be regarded as another, modern attempt to solve the fundamental methodological dilemma of business-cycle theory, namely the integration of cyclical phenomena into the system of equilibrium theory, with which they are in apparent contradiction. This is the point which had been elaborated by Lowe in his 1926 article and accepted by Hayek as the fundamental challenge.[26] Although formally complex, the economic content of most of the 'real' business-cycle models is highly stylized, based mostly upon the assumption of representative agents which means that they cannot give an account of many of the distributional and compositional factors relevant in the older business-cycle theories.

Thus, while the older theories discussed in this chapter did not achieve the degree of analytical rigour associated with modern economics, the richness of their observations, the demonstration of the complex interrelation between real and monetary as well as structural change factors in economic systems and the close association between the historical and analytical methods typical of their analyses, still provide a fertile source of inspiration for business-cycle analysis. In our view the rigorous pursuit of central ideas developed in the older 'structural' theories of the business cycle – many of which are still unavailable in the English language – still represents a most promising line of business-cycle research.

The strengths and weaknesses of Lowe's contribution to the 'structural approach' to business-cycle analysis can be summarized as follows.

First, he mounted with his 1926 article, an important methodological challenge to traditional general equilibrium theory to generate an appropriate theory of economic fluctuations. The paucity of the current state in business-cycle analysis proves the validity of his methodological position. Second, he himself favoured a particular method of dynamic economic analysis to study non-steady (fluctuating) movements in economic activity. The method he elaborated on was traverse analysis, based on a tradition going back to Ricardo, which emphasizes the relevance of structural rigidities as an economy's dynamic unfolds. Lowe also used a distinct method of decomposing the economic structure of an economy such that important structural features of adjustment processes could be brought to the fore. His research suggests that he believed that important aspects in the study of growth and of economic fluctuations require the use of the same method; there is no sharp break in the study of growth and of (structural aspects of) business cycles. On the critical side, we might remark that Lowe abandoned the fruitful integration of 'real' and 'monetary' aspects of business-cycle analysis which was central to many of the important contributions to the 'structural theory of the business cycle' as the survey of some of these contributions in this chapter shows; he focused in his analysis entirely upon the 'real side'. His focus on technical progress as the dominant factor requiring structural adjustment and causing major adjustment problems, is rich and the analysis is well worked out within his chosen analytical framework of decomposition of an economy. This decomposition, which integrates in a fruitful manner a focus on horizontal (reproductive) and vertical (time structure) aspects of interdependencies, could no doubt be further refined and hence the analysis of economic adjustment processes could be further enriched. More importantly, though, he pays exclusive attention to the rigidities which the material structure of production (capital stock and materials-in-process flows) imposes upon the process of economic change. He neglects the importance of the structure of human capital/skills/education which is increasingly seen as an at least equally important factor in the adaptability and growth capacity of economic systems. Furthermore, in the light of recent contributions to 'endogenous growth', his analysis could gain from an at least partial endogenization of the locus, speed and spread of technological innovation.

Finally, while Lowe and many other contributors to structural business-cycle analysis followed Schumpeter in emphasizing the importance of technical and organizational change as a crucial factor both in the cyclical and growth dynamics of capitalist economies, they did not follow him in analysing the relationship between market structure and the dynamics of innovation and diffusion of new technologies and products. The neglect of firm interactions and market organization in existing structural models which focus on techniques, industries, sectors, stages of production, and so on, but neglect the actual competitive process between firms, limits them from obtaining a comprehensive picture of capitalist economic dynamics. None the less, we believe that the existing body of 'structual theories of the business cycle' is still a greatly stimulating and promising starting-point for further analysis of the medium- and longer-run aspects of economic fluctuations.

NOTES

1. For a more detailed analysis, see Hagemann (1992) and Gehrke and Hagemann (1996).
2. For an elaborate assessment of Tugan-Baranowsky's contribution to the development of economic thought, see Amato (1984).
3. Tugan-Baranowsky ([1894] 1901), p. 22. All the quotations from German or French texts have been translated by the authors of this chapter.
4. For an excellent comparison of Tugan-Baranowsky's 'bubble' with the conventional neoclassical bubble, putting emphasis on these totally different views of the capitalist accumulation process, see the most recent contribution by Mainwaring (1995).
5. In this process, Tugan-Baranowsky asserts that: 'The disturbances in the area of monetary and credit relationships are only secondary occurrences, which can only emerge on the basis of a lack of proportionalities' ([1894] 1901, p. 250).
6. See particularly Part III in Bouniatian (1922); this section is entitled 'Analyse des Cycles Economiques et leurs Causes'.
7. See Bouniatian (1908), p. 120.
8. Bouniatian foreshadows in this respect the concern with imperfectly competitive behaviour in the wake of economic crisis which was an important component of interwar analyses of industrial fluctuations. See also Landesmann (1987).
9. The essence of the idea of the acceleration principle can already be found in Carver (1903).
10. The lifting of an economy out of a trough is a weak point in many business-cycle theories, and Aftalion's theory is no exception to this. The most satisfactory approach to this question seems to us to be a Schumpeterian-type analysis which introduces product and technological innovations as an important factor generating a sustained economic expansion. Schumpeterian-type features are included in Bouniatian's (see above) and Spiethoff's (below) accounts of business cycles.
11. Tugan-Baranowsky's Magister dissertation on industrial crises in contemporary Britain which was published in Russian in 1894 came out in a German translation in 1901. Spiethoff who had already published a first major paper on crisis theory in 1902 wrote a long review on Tugan-Baranowsky's book (Spiethoff, 1903) which formed an outline to his famous entry on 'Krisen' to the *Handwörterbuch der Staatswissenschaften* (1925: English translation 1953).
12. For a methodological justification of his approach, see Spiethoff (1952).
13. See also Dahmen's (1970) interesting study which develops a fuller analysis of this type.
14. 'It is in periods of economic and technical transition that the big exogenous stimuli most easily appear: the triumph of the large-scale machine industry, steam, electricity and other sources of power, the opening up of potash and of coal, new methods in steel making, the reorganisation of great industries such as mining and iron. Since such stimuli are incalculable, the beginning of a new upswing is equally incalculable' (ibid., p. 151).
15. Among the factors which facilitate and support an economic upswing, Spiethoff mentions: 'available savings, and not only available labour but available productive capacity and stocks of commodities. An explanation of upswings must proceed from this state of affairs. ... Cash holdings and commodity stocks played a greater role in former times - even though they are still present - and idle labour and productive resources have gained in importance' (ibid., p. 153).
16. Spiethoff also makes the interesting point that particular patterns of technological change have increased the likelihood of this type of disproportionality:

> The excessive extension of productive capacity for indirect consumption goods has been greatly facilitated by the most recent technical development which first made it possible for them to be overproduced. It is of the essence of the new techniques that they have made indirect consumption independent of the slow organic processes of growth and enabled man to increase it arbitrarily: I mean the replacement of wood by iron and bricks, and the subsequent further increase due to iron, bricks and cement being produced by the aid of coal instead of wood. ... Thus it now happens, and only has (this) been possible since the 19th century, that the indirect consumption goods increase so strongly during every upswing as to exceed the savings seeking investment' (ibid., p. 158).

17. 'Any formation of monetary capital which culminates in hoarding induces a downswing, as it leads to a corresponding quantity of goods becoming unsaleable and thus to overproduction' (ibid., p. 153).
18. Lowe's contribution to the 1928 meeting of the *Verein für Sozialpolitik* in Zürich was based on a lecture entitled *'Gibt es eine monetäre Konjunkturtheorie?'* which he had delivered on 26 March at a meeting of the Austrian Economic Society in Vienna where Hayek was present. For a more detailed analysis of the Lowe–Hayek connection, see Hagemann (1994).
19. Lowe's retrospective view on the debate in the German-speaking area in the late 1920s is particularly clear on this issue. See Lowe (1989).
20. In developing the main elements of his theory of cyclical fluctuations, Cassel (see *The Theory of the Social Economy*, Book IV) drew heavily on the ideas of Tugan-Baranowsky and Spiethoff. Consequently, Reijnders in a more recent paper goes as far as classifying Cassel as a 'Tugan Baranowskyan' (see Reijnders, 1996, pp. 16–19).
21. Lowe (1955, p. 590) complains of a complete disregard of Burchardt's 'happy synthesis' in the controversy on the theory of capital between Knight and Kaldor 1937–38, but Nurkse (1935) is a countervailing example which shows that the importance of Burchardt's work was at least recognized by some authors in the English-speaking world. For detailed comparisons of the advantages and drawbacks in vertical and horizontal models of production in modern literature see the contributions in Baranzini and Scazzieri (1990).
22. For a graphical exposition see Lowe (1952, p. 150) and Lowe (1976, p. 32).
23. Prices and quantities of pig iron production which fluctuated with great regularity were taken as the best single indicator of the condition of industry in many business-cycle theories, from Tugan-Baranowsky to Cassel.
24. We abstract here from possibilities of overutilization or underutilization of fixed capital goods. For a detailed discussion of the flexibility of the production system, which arises from the variability in the degree of capacity utilization, in the context of traverse analysis, see the contribution of Gehrke in this book (Chapter 12).
25. See also Robertson's review article (1914) on Aftalion (1913) and the French edition of Tugan-Baranowsky's classical study. Interestingly, for a British author Robertson was critical of Tugan-Baranowsky's putting too much weight on monetary factors. For a careful analysis of Robertson's study and alternative theories of industrial fluctuations, see also Presley (1979, Part I).
26. A closer look into the passage in Hayek's *Monetary Theory and the Trade Cycle* ([1929] 1933, p. 33, fn.), which is referred to in Lucas's well-known statement (1977, p. 7), clearly reveals the close link between Hayek's business-cycle analysis and the central methodological problem pointed out by Lowe. For a detailed comparison of modern real business-cycle theory with the earlier debate in the German-speaking area, particularly the contributions by Hayek and Lowe but also those of Schumpeter and Lutz, see Rühl (1994).

REFERENCES

Aftalion, A. (1913), *Les Crises Périodiques de Surproduction*, 2 vols., Paris: Marcel Rivière.
Aftalion, A. (1927), 'The theory of economic cycles based on the capitalistic technique of production', *Review of Economic Statistics*, 9, pp. 165–70.
Amato, S. (1984),. 'Tugan-Baranovsky's theories of markets, accumulation and industrialization: their influence on the development of economic thought and modern historiographic research', in I.S. Koropeckyj (ed.), *Selected Contributions of Ukrainian Scholars to Economics*, Cambridge, Mass.: Harvard University Press, pp. 1–59.
Baranzini, M. and R. Scazzieri (eds) (1990), *The Economic Theory of Structure and Change*, Cambridge: Cambridge University Press.
Bouniatian, M. (1908), *Wirtschaftskrisen und Überkapitalisation (Studien zur Theorie und Geschichte der Wirtschaftskrisen, I)*, Munich: E. Reinhart.
Bouniatian, M. (1922), *Les Crises Economiques*, Paris: M. Girard.
Burchardt, F.A. (1928), 'Entwicklungsgeschichte der monetären Konjunkturtheorie', *Weltwirtschaftliches Archiv*, 28, pp. 78–143.
Burchardt, F.A. (1931–32), 'Die Schemata des stationären Kreislaufs bei Böhm-Bawerk und Marx', *Weltwirtschaftliches Archiv*, 34, pp. 525–64 and 35, pp. 116–76.

Carver, T.N. (1903), 'A suggestion for a theory of industrial depressions, *Quarterly Journal of Economics*, **17**, pp. 497ff.

Cassel, G. (1918), *Theoretische Sozialökonomie*, English translation *The Theory of Social Economy*, London 1923: Fisher Unwin.

Dahmen, E. (1970*), Entrepreneurial Activity and the Development of Swedish Industry*, Homewood, Ill.: Richard D. Irwin.

Feldman, G.A. (1928–29),'On the theory of growth rates of national income, I and II', in N. Spulber (ed.), *Foundations of Soviet Strategy for Economic Growth. Selected Soviet Essays, 1924–1930*, Bloomington 1964: Indiana University Press, pp. 174–99 and 304–31.

Freeman, C., J. Clark and L. Soete (1982), *Unemployment and Technical Innovation: A Study of Long Waves and Economic Development*, London: Pinter.

Gehrke, C. and H. Hagemann (1996),'Efficient traverses and bottlenecks: a structural approach', in M. Landesmann and R. Scazzieri, *Production and Economic Dynamics*, Cambridge: Cambridge University Press, pp. 140–66.

Gourvitch, A. (1940), *Survey of Economic Theory on Technological Change and Employment*, Philadelphia; reprint, New York: Augustus M. Kelley.

Hagemann, H. (1990),'The structural theory of economic growth', in M. Baranzini and R. Scazzieri (eds), *The Economic Theory of Structure and Change*, Cambridge: Cambridge University Press, pp. 144–71.

Hagemann, H. (1992), 'Traverse analysis in a post-classical model', in J. Halevi, D. Laibman and E.J. Nell (eds), *Beyond the Steady State. A Revival of Growth Theory*, London: Macmillan, pp. 235–63.

Hagemann, H. (1994), 'Hayek and the Kiel School: some reflections on the German debate on business cycles in the late 1920s and the early 1930s', in M. Colonna and H. Hagemann (eds), *Money and Business Cycles. The Economics of F.A. Hayek*, Vol. I, Aldershot: Edward Elgar, pp. 101–20.

Hagemann, H. and H.M. Trautwein (1996), 'Cantillon and Ricardo Effects. Hayek's Contributions to Business Cycle Theory', University of Hohenheim, Department of Economics, Discussion Paper no. 119, Stuttgart.

Hansen, A.H. (1951), *Business Cycles and National Income*, London: Allen & Unwin.

Hayek, F.A. (1929), *Geldtheorie und Konjunkturtheorie*, Vienna: Hölder–Pichler–Tempski, English edition *Monetary Theory and the Trade Cycle*, London 1933: J. Cape, Reprint New York 1966: Augustus M. Kelley.

Hayek, F.A. (1931), *Prices and Production*, 2nd edn, London 1935: Routledge & Kegan Paul.

Hayek, F.A. (1939), *Profits, Interest, and Investment*, London: Routledge.

Hicks, J. (1973), *Capital and Time. A Neo-Austrian Theory*, Oxford: Clarendon Press.

Kähler, A. (1933), *Die Theorie der Arbeiterfreisetzung durch die Maschine*, Greifswald: Julius Abel.

Keynes, J.M. (1930), *A Treatise on Money, Vol. 2, The Applied Theory of Money*, The Collected Writings of John Maynard Keynes, Vol. VI, London 1971: Macmillan and Cambridge University Press.

Kim, Kyun (1988), *Equilibrium Business Cycle Theory in Historical Perspective*, Cambridge: Cambridge University Press.

Kleinknecht, A., E. Mandel and L. Wallerstein (eds) (1992), *New Findings in Long-wave Research*, Basingstoke: Macmillan.

Kuznets, S. (1930a), 'Equilibrium economics and business-cycle theory', *Quarterly Journal of Economics*, **44**, pp. 381–415.

Kuznets, S. (1930b), 'Monetary business cycle theory in Germany', *Journal of Political Economy*, **38**, pp. 125–63.

Kydland, F.E. (ed.) (1995), *Business Cycle Theory*; Aldershot: Edward Elgar.

Landesmann, M.A. (1987), 'Views on economic crisis, international economic relations and trade policy in inter-war Germany', *Osaka Journal of Economics*, **88**, pp. 3–33.

Landesmann, M.A. and R. Scazzieri (1990), 'Specification of structure and economic dynamics', in M. Baranzini and R. Scazzieri (eds), *The Economic Theory of Structure and Change*, Cambridge: Cambridge University Press, pp. 95–121.

Löwe, A. (1925), 'Der gegenwärtige Stand der Konjunkturforschung in Deutschland', in M.J. Bonn and M. Palyi (eds), *Die Wirtschaftswissenschaft nach dem Kriege. Festgabe für Lujo Brentano zum 80. Geburtstag*, Vol. 2, Munich and Leipzig: Duncker & Humblot, pp. 329–77.

Löwe, A. (1926), 'Wie ist Konjunkturtheorie überhaupt möglich?', *Weltwirtschaftliches Archiv*, **24**, pp. 165–97, English translation as 'How is business cycle theory possible at all?' in *Structural Change and Economic Dynamics*, **8**, 1997, pp. 245–70.

Löwe, A. (1928), 'Über den Einfluß monetärer Faktoren auf den Konjunkturzyklus', in K. Diehl (ed.), *Beiträge zur Wirtschaftstheorie. Zweiter Teil: Konjunkturforschung und Konjunkturtheorie*, Schriften des Vereins für Sozialpolitik, 173 II, Munich and Leipzig: Duncker & Humblot, pp. 355–70.

Lowe, A. (1952), 'A structural model of production', *Social Research*, **19**, pp. 135–76.

Lowe, A. (1955a), 'Structural analysis of real capital formation', in M. Abramovitz (ed.), *Capital Formation and Economic Growth*, Princeton, NJ: Princeton University Press, pp. 581–634.

Lowe, A. (1955b), 'Technological unemployment reexamined', in G. Eisermann (ed.): *Wirtschaft und Kultursystem – Festschrift für Alexander Rüstow*, Stuttgart and Zürich: Eugen Rentsch Verlag, pp. 229–54.

Lowe, A. (1976), *The Path of Economic Growth*, Cambridge: Cambridge University Press.

Lowe, A. (1989), 'Konjunkturtheorie in Deutschland in den zwanziger Jahren', in B. Schefold (ed.), *Studien zur Entwicklung der ökonomischen Theorie VIII*, Berlin: Duncker & Humblot, pp. 75–86.

Lucas, R.E. (1977), 'Understanding business cycles', in K. Brunner and A.H. Meltzer (eds) *Stabilization of the Domestic and International Economy*, Carnegie-Rochester Conference Series on Public Policy, Vol. 5, Amsterdam: North-Holland, pp. 7–29.

Lundberg, E. (1930), 'On the concept of economic equilibrium', *Ekonomisk Tidsskrift*, **32**; English translation in E. Lundberg, *Studies in Economic Instability and Change*, Stockholm 1995: SNS Förlag, pp. 13–47.

Mainwaring, L. (1995), 'Tugan's 'bubble': underconsumption and crisis in a Marxian model', *Cambridge Journal of Economics*, **19**, pp. 305–21.

Marx, K. (1867), *Capital. A Critique of Political Economy*, Vol. I, London 1954: Lawrence & Wishart; Vol III (1894), London 1959: Lawrence & Wishart.

Neisser, H. (1942), '"Permanent" technological unemployment', *American Economic Review*, **32**, pp. 50–71.

Nurkse, R. (1935), 'The schematic representation of the structure of production', *Review of Economic Studies*, **2**, pp. 232–44.

Presley, J.R. (1979), *Robertsonian Economics. An Examination of the Work of Sir D.H. Robertson on Industrial Fluctuations*, London: Macmillan.

Reijnders, J. (1996), 'Early endogenous theories of the business cycle: Tugan-Baranowsky and his influence on Spiethoff and Cassel', paper presented at the Annual European Conference on the History of Economics, Lisbon, 9–10 February.

Ricardo, D. (1821: 1951) *Principles of Political Economy and Taxation*; 3rd edn; *The Works and Correspondence of David Ricardo*, ed. P. Sraffa, Vol. I, Cambridge 1951: Cambridge University Press.

Robertson, D.H. (1914), 'Review of M. Tugan-Baranowsky *Les Crises Industrielles en Angleterre* and A. Aftalion *Les Crises Périodiques de Surproduction*', *Economic Journal*, **24**, pp. 81–9.

Robertson, D.H. (1915), *A Study of Industrial Fluctuation*, London: P.S. King & Son.

Robertson, D.H. (1926), *Banking Policy and the Price Level*, London: P.S. King & Son.

Rühl, C. (1994), 'The transformation of business cycle theory: Hayek, Lucas and a change in the notion of equilibrium', in M. Colonna and H. Hagemann (eds), *Money and Business Cycles. The Economics of F.A. Hayek*, Vol. I, Aldershot: Edward Elgar, pp. 168–202.

Solomou, S. (1987), *Phases of Economic Growth, 1850–1973: Kondratieff Waves and Kuznets Swings*, Cambridge: Cambridge University Press.

Spiethoff, A. (1902), 'Vorbemerkungen zu einer Theorie der Überproduktion', *Jahrbuch für Gesetzgebung, Verwaltung und Volkswirtschaft im Deutschen Reich*, **26**, pp. 721–59.

Spiethoff, A. (1903), 'Die Krisentheorien von M. Tugan-Baranowsky und L. Pohle', *Jahrbuch für Gesetzgebung, Verwaltung und Volkswirtschaft im Deutschen Reich*, **27**, pp. 679–708.

Spiethoff, A. (1925), 'Krisen', in *Handwörterbuch der Staatswissenschaften*, **VI**, pp. 8–91, English translation as 'Business Cycles' in *International Economic Papers*, **3**, 1953, pp. 75–171.

Spiethoff, A. (1952), 'The "historical" character of economic theories', *Journal of Economic History*, **12**, pp. 131–9.

Strigl, R. (1928), 'Die Produktion unter dem Einflusse einer Kreditexpansion', in K. Diehl (ed.), *Beiträge zur Wirtschaftstheorie. Zweiter Teil: Konjunkturforschung und Konjunkturtheorie*,

Schriften des Vereins für Sozialpolitik, 173 II, Munich and Leipzig: Duncker & Humblot, pp. 185–211.

Tugan-Baranowsky, M. (1894), *Promyshlennye krizisy v sovremennoi Anglii* (Industrial crises in contemporary Britain), St. Petersburg; German translation *Studien zur Theorie und Geschichte der Handelskrisen in England*, Jena 1901: Gustav Fischer; French translation from the 2nd Russian edn as *Les Crises Industrielles en Angleterre*, Paris 1913: Giard and Brière.

Tugan-Baranowsky, M. (1904), 'Der Zusammenbruch der kapitalistischen Wirtschaftsordnung im Lichte der nationalökonomischen Theorie', *Archiv für Sozialwissenschaft und Sozialpolitik*, **19**, pp. 273–306.

Tugan-Baranowsky, M. (1905), *Theoretische Grundlagen des Marxismus*, Leipzig: Duncker & Humblot.

8. Stages in the Development of the Business Cycle

Edward J. Nell

Lowe began his work in economics asking the question, how is the business cycle possible? He answered that the business cycle was made possible by the structure of the economy, which directs behaviour in ways that lead the system to expand, but in a fluctuating pattern. According to his view, later developed in depth by Fritz Burchardt, the same forces that generate expansion cause the cycle, and these forces are inherent in the system. Neither growth nor fluctuations are the result of outside factors impinging on an essentially stationary system. The working of capitalism had to be understood as essentially dynamic. The vision of stationary equilibrium disturbed by outside forces – articulated by Hayek in Lowe's time, and a part of the conventional wisdom of economists ever since – was wholly at odds with the viewpoint of Lowe and Burchardt.

Lowe and Hayek did agree, however, that the interaction of the agents in the economy tended to produce a definite outcome. For Hayek, this was an equilibrium, stable and stationary; growth was the adjustment of the capital stock to the equilibrium level, or to a new level caused by exogenous changes in parameters, while fluctuations were caused by exogenous 'shocks', which set off oscillatory responses. By contrast, for Lowe the outcome was growth, resulting from forces inherent in the system, the result of 'spontaneous' interaction. Market pressures caused firms to invest – and to innovate – but this took place in the form of waves of investment, followed by waves of retrenchment. These were the outcomes of normal market interaction. Growth followed a wave-like path; fluctuations were the norm, and took place in a regular and predictable manner. There was no need to call on outside forces to explain the cycle.[1] Nor should economic processes be analysed only in the mechanistic format of fixed responses to prefigured stimuli favoured by Hayek and formalistic schools. Spontaneous innovations, particularly technological progress, but also new lifestyles, must be included because they spring up as the result of market pressures, and form a part of the wave-like process.

From this perspective, government regulation can be seen to have an important role. Growth needs to be directed and fluctuations to be controlled and limited. Policy can greatly improve the performance of the economy, in terms of providing for the well-being of the population in an equitable manner. To put it more strongly – *not* to intervene, not to develop economic policy, would be irresponsible, since the normal working of the economic system swings from optimistic exuberance to depression, disrupting the orderly flow of commerce and preventing people from going about the business of everyday life.

But in the 1950s Lowe became increasingly uneasy over the role of policy. For one thing it appeared to work much less well than anticipated. A related problem was that prediction turned out to be practically impossible. At this point he came to a remarkable conclusion: the system had changed – as it became richer, it had become less regular. People were no longer subject to pressures of poverty and misery, capital was more available, and business less subject to strict market discipline. With more leeway, both households and business could afford to experiment, to try out new approaches. The system had become one which was no longer orderly or predictable. [2]

1   GROWTH AND STABILITY

Lowe's view regarding the stability of capitalism seems to be ambivalent. On the one hand it generates cycles endogenously. But on the other, prior to the Great Depression, the cycle is regular and within limits predictable. Furthermore, he argues that it could be controlled by suitable policy. After the Second World War both capitalism and government policy have changed. He rejects the view that postwar capitalism is inherently unstable, but he welcomes an activist government, since he regards the market mechanism as deficient. In *The Path of Economic Growth* (1976), he examined the ability of the market to guide an economy from one path of full-employment growth to a higher or lower growth path. In general, he argued, the market would not give the correct signals. The chief reason for this is that in a change from one growth path to another, the two parts of the capital-goods sector have to move in opposite directions, initially. For example, a lower rate of growth requires a higher level of consumption, to maintain full employment, so the subsector producing capital goods for the consumer-goods sector will have to expand, while the basic capital-goods subsector contracts – and conversely for a higher rate of growth. (The two cases are not fully symmetrical, in Lowe's account.) In a detailed set of scenarios he shows how difficult it would be for the price mechanism to provide adequate signals.

However, these scenarios are strongly dependent on two assumptions. The first is that full employment is to be maintained, and the second is that there are strict capacity constraints, with no excess capacity at full employment. In the postwar period, however, employment has seldom been full, and even at full employment there always existed excess capacity. Indeed, it can be argued that excess capacity is built into the system. Hence in this period the constraints that characterize Lowe's scenarios, and which require the inverse movements of the two parts of the capital-goods sector when the growth rate changes, do not appear to hold. This would suggest that the postwar period might have greater stability than earlier periods; the reverse of what Lowe wants to argue.

The most celebrated instability claim is that implied by the Harrod–Domar analysis of Keynesian growth. When the actual rate of growth deviates from the warranted rate – the rate that balances aggregate demand with aggregate capacity – the incentives to invest will be such as to drive the actual rate still further away.[3] This would provide endogenous instability, but Lowe regards the analysis as flawed. Because Harrod considers only capital goods and consumer goods, he fails to see that within the capital-goods sector there will be divergent patterns of movement, in adjusting to a new growth path. These divergent patterns will prevent the emergence of the radical instability suggested by the model.

However, Lowe's response is not really to the Keynesian problem. Lowe examines the movement required to maintain full employment; hence he assumes that changes in savings are exactly matched by corresponding changes in investment – an altogether unacceptable procedure from a Keynesian point of view.[4] His neglect of Keynesian questions, his view that cycles were orderly, and his rejection of the Harrodian approach cut him off from developing a theory of endogenous instability. Hence when he came to the view that postwar capitalism posed more serious problems than conventional theory was willing to recognize, he could not explain these problems by appealing to fundamental instability.

2   DISORDER OR INSTABILITY?

[A] general diagnosis of instability ... has been the constant theme of critics ... from Marx to Keynes. Now what unites these ... and even allies them with the champions of capitalist stability, is their *belief in an inexorable mechanism* which is supposed to direct all market motions. The critics differ from theoretical orthodoxy only in the manner in which they see this mechanism operate. It is the conviction of ... orthodoxy that market processes bear all the characteristics of a *negative feedback mechanism*, which automatically corrects any deviation from stability. The critics, on the other hand, point to certain .. factors ... which are alleged to produce *positive feedbacks*, amplifying partial distortions into general disequilibrium. (Lowe, 1987, p. 238)

Lowe considers but rejects the position of the critics. He allows that such 'positive feedbacks' may be 'contributory sources of destabilization'. But he finds the principal cause of the problem to lie 'in a weakening of the *behavioural* forces – those forces which, in the early stages of capitalism sustained the operation of negative feedbacks'.

In earlier eras, Lowe argued, economic behaviour had been more strongly constrained, partly by the pressure of poverty, which pressed down the working class, and partly by social pressures which affected the bourgeoisie. These external non-economic constraints channelled economic activity in ways that made such behaviour predictable. But the very success of capitalism in raising productivity and living standards undermined these constraints. Once they ceased to govern behaviour reliably, the motion of the economy could no longer be predicted.

He distinguished three phases of capitalist development. At the beginning of the first, production was still organized in small units, family firms and family farms, based on animal and human power, abetted by wind and water. Steam and mechanical power were developed and the forces of production expanded. But poverty remained the lot of the masses, while the attraction of wealth drew the newly-emerging stratum of entrepreneurs and business leaders into fierce competition. In the second period, evolving gradually out of the first, and lasting until the First World War, the factory system developed, and small firms began to grow into large corporations. But the pressures on the masses remained, and competition intensified as new markets opened and innovations began to develop more rapidly. In these two closely-linked periods, the pressures of poverty on the one hand, and competition, driven by the lure of wealth and success, on the other, channelled behaviour in such a way that 'the extremum principle', in Lowe's terms, correctly described the activities of agents in the market. Hence, in principle, the system was orderly and predictable.

Not so in the third period. First, the rise in living standards has reduced the pressure of poverty. Second, there has been a closing of what Lowe called 'escapements', ways of channelling excess savings, for example, investment in colonies and dominions. Third, organized markets – oligopolies – have limited competition, and finally, new cultural attitudes have arisen, condemning the ruthless and single-minded pursuit of profit. In response, government regulation has developed, controlling and limiting competitive strategies, and at the same time assuming responsibility for the level of overall employment and rate of inflation. All these developments undermine the pressure to act in accordance with the extremum principle, and, as a consequence, market behaviour can no longer be reliably calculated from simple models of 'rational maximizing'.

Not only do other motivations replace profit and utility maximizing, but motivation may change at any time. There is no longer any reason to expect regularity in behaviour. As they become wealthier, people grow and change. And so do institutions, once the pressure of competition has been lifted. Hence *at any time* motivations and behaviour may change.

This, then, explains the failures of prediction – and also the limited success of many policy initiatives. In the era of organized capitalism, roughly following the First World War (but Lowe considers the interwar period to be somewhat of a transition period), behaviour is not subject to the constraints that make it predictable. Hence the economy is liable to fluctuate wildly and is kept from doing so largely by government intervention. Yet this intervention is based on an economic theory which assumes that market behaviour is orderly and predictable, and will move towards an equilibrium. Policies are designed to assist the market in this process. Since markets are not moving towards equilibrium, and in fact are not even orderly, government policies are likely to go wrong, as indeed they do, in his view.

Lowe's solution is to invert the problem, in what he calls an 'instrumentalist' approach. Instead of assuming that the data and motivations, when properly understood by theory, are such as to define an equilibrium – the desired end-state – which it will be the job of policy to help the system reach, policy must define the desired end-state, and theory must then devise the required data and motivations, which will suffice to bring about that end-state. This requires the state to develop practical incentive schemes that will induce economic agents to behave in the required manner. [5]

3   STYLIZED FACTS AND LOWE'S POSITION

Before going further into Lowe's proposed solution, let us examine his claims. There seem to be two major contentions. First, the economy behaves differently prior to the First World War, and after the Second World War (treating the interwar period as a transition). Second, the chief cause of these differences lies in a breakdown of orderly behaviour, specifically that maximizing behaviour is no longer enforced by external conditions.

The first, we shall see, can be supported. It seems that the economy *did* behave differently prior to the First World War. But the second is more difficult to support. The postwar economy is not so much disorderly, as *unstable*. This instability can quite well account for the difficulties in predicting, and for the problems in policy. However, Lowe's policy approach may still be justified, at least in part, and, as well, a central difficulty in it can be resolved.

3.1   The Two Periods

It is difficult to make general claims about the economy – there are many extraneous influences and there will always be exceptions. Nevertheless, a number of general propositions can be developed about the behaviour of the economy, and these claims can be separated into two groups, applying roughly to Lowe's two historical periods, so that each group provides an approximately accurate picture over most of its period. The two pictures present a striking contrast on issues central to economic analysis; prices, money wages, employment, productivity, expenditure and money. Sources and brief explanations will be given, but no attempt will be made here to justify the claims in detail. The first group of propositions presents a portrait of what we shall term the 'old trade cycle' of the nineteenth century, running roughly from the Napoleonic Wars to the First World War, although respectable data only exist after about 1860 – and even then much is questionable. The second covers the post-Second World war period, the 'new trade cycle'.[6]

The old trade cycle
Business units tended to be small, operating relatively inflexible methods of production, meaning that the factory or shop could either be operated or shut down, but could not easily be adjusted to variable levels of output. Prices, on the other hand, were flexible in both directions, as were money wages. The price mechanism appeared to operate. The cycle could be seen in price data.

Prices and money wages

1.   The trend of prices was downwards over the whole period. By contrast, the trend of money wages was more or less flat in the first half century, then moderately rising.[7]
      Sources: Sylos-Labini (1989, especially Table I, II; 1993, esp. Table I, Appendix I.); Pigou (1927, especially Charts 3, 11, 14, 15, 16); Phelps Brown and Hopkins (1981, Chs 7, 8; especially Fig. 1, p. 183). There was an upturn in prices in the 1860s, and a smaller one just before the First World War, but the trend is dominant. The latter half of the nineteenth century shows a slight upward trend in money wages, becoming more pronounced after 1900.[8]

2. Both prices and money wages changed in both directions. Changes in raw materials prices (deviations from the trend) were greater in both directions than changes in manufacturing prices, which in turn were greater than changes in money wages. [9]
    Sources: As above, plus Pedersen and Petersen (1938), who focus on the contrast between flexible and relatively inflexible prices. Most of their most flexible prices were raw materials. It is noticeable, however, that even their 'inflexible' prices (prices that remain unchanged for more than one year, a number of times over the century) exhibit a downward trend (p. 222).

Employment and real wages

3. Changes in unemployment (proxy for output) were less than the changes in prices; changes in unemployment were 'small'.
    Sources: As above. Double-digit unemployment was rare, compare Pigou (1927, Charts 18, 19). Hoffmann (1965) provides an output index based on 43 series, which Phelps Brown adapts for 1861–1913. Pigou uses unemployment as a proxy for output. Sylos-Labini (1984) compares changes in prices, wages and output.
4. Putting these together, it can be seen that real wages, or more particularly product wages, moved countercyclically. That is to say, real wages varied directly with unemployment.
    Sources: Pigou (1927, especially Charts 16, 18, 20); Michie (1987). Michie recalculates the work of Dunlop (1938) and Tarshis (1939), and finds that product wages moved countercyclically before the First World War (Ch. 8).[10] (This will be a major point of contrast with the postwar era, although international comparisons are so difficult that it is hard to generalize. But some periods of procyclical movement will be evident.)

Productivity and output

5. Output as a function of labour, both for individual plants and for the economy as a whole, was believed by virtually all contemporary – and later – economists to exhibit diminishing returns. Actual evidence, however, is weak, although a good case can be made for extensive diminishing returns. Productivity, on the other hand, is closely correlated with short-run variations in output in many industries, and positively correlated in general, and varies in both directions more than employment.

Sources: Pigou (1927, Ch. 1, pp. 9–10); Aftalion (1927), Keynes (1939). Calculations made from Hoffmann's data on nineteenth century Germany show the strong correlations between productivity and output in the short run, and the greater variation of productivity compared to employment.[11]

6. Long-run productivity growth (measured in moving averages) was irregular and unpredictable, although substantial. It was transmitted to the economy through falling prices, with stable money wages. The rise in long-run real wages is closely correlated to productivity growth.
    Sources: Sylos-Labini (1993); Pigou (1927); Phelps Brown and Hopkins (1981)

Besides these strictly economic trends and relationships there are a number of important institutional facts that have changed dramatically. These, of course, are harder to substantiate with hard data. Nevertheless the historical record seems to support a set of generalizations – with the caveat that there may be many exceptions.

Business organization, finance and the state

7. Business was organized and operated by family firms. Firms invested to achieve an optimum size, at which they would then remain, varying their output around the least cost-level.
    Sources: Pigou (1927); Chandler (1977, 1990) examines the rise of large-scale corporations, beginning in the late nineteenth century. These early corporations are clearly the exceptions. Firms grew to their optimum size and remained at that level thereafter (Robinson, 1931).

8. Once firms reached their optimum size, they did not retain earnings for investment; profits were distributed, saved (or spent) and then loaned for investment by new firms. Finance for investment was thus predominantly external, raised through issuing bonds.
    Sources: As above. The bulk of investment represented borrowed savings, and was carried out by new firms (Clark, 1899; Urquhart, 1965).

9. Governments tended to play a passive role in economic affairs; the 'Night Watchman State' intervened little and planned less. Most intervention took the form of subsidizing development. Government spending and transfers together normally amounted to less than 10 per cent of GNP, in some cases near 5 per cent, and showed no trend until just before the First World War.
    Sources: Maddison (1984, especially Table 1; 1991); Hoffmann (1965), Urquhart (1965), Gemmell (1993).

Money and interest

10. The quantity of money behaved as if fixed exogenously.
    Sources: Eichengreen (1992); Pigou (1927). By mid-century the economies of Europe had shifted to the gold standard, prior to which they had operated on bimetallist principles. It is generally agreed that the gold standard behaved as if the economy relied on 'outside' money, that is, an exogenous money supply (Patinkin, 1965). To be sure bank checking deposits were beginning, and note issue by country banks was not closely bound by reserves, either in the US or the UK. But in a loosely organized banking system, without clearly defined policies governing the lender of last resort, prudent financial management required tightening reserves and raising the discount rate in the face of expansion and rising prices, and vice versa in times of falling prices. (Pigou, 1927, p. 279). Money may not have been strictly exogenous, but prudent management required the banking system to behave as if it were.

11. Investment booms were accompanied by over-eager financial expansion, leading to crises and crashes; these precipitated investment slumps and financial contraction. Variations in employment and prices closely matched expansions and contractions of credit.
    Sources: Hicks (1989, Ch. 11); Mill (1848, Book III, Ch. 12); Pigou (1927); Kindleberger (1978, especially Chs 3, 4, 6, 8 and Appendix). Interest rates and prices rose together in the upswing and fell together in the downswing. The financial crash was usually the signal for the expansion to collapse.

12. The long-term rate of interest was fairly stable, from the mid-nineteenth century until the First World War, and after the war continued to be moderately stable until the 1930s. What Keynes termed 'Gibson's Paradox' held for more than a century – levels and changes in the interest rate were closely correlated with levels and changes of the wholesale price index, and the long rate was more closely correlated than the short rate. Both contrast markedly with the postwar era.
    Sources: Kalecki calculates deviations from a nine-year (cycle-long) moving average of UK consols, and shows that they are very small (Osiatynski 1990, p. 297, Table 16). Kalecki considers this sufficient justification to treat the long rate as a constant in developing models of the business cycle. Keynes (1930, Vol. 2), discusses 'Gibson's Paradox'.

The new trade cycle

The family firm has been superseded by the modern corporation, operating mass-production technology, which enables it to lay off labour and adapt output and employment easily to changing sales. The price mechanism is no longer in evidence. The cycle appears in relations between quantities. But there is a clearly discernible pattern.

Prices and money wages

1. The trend of prices was upward the whole period, and the trend of money wages rose even more steeply. Neither prices nor money wages turned down.
   Sources: As above.
2. Raw materials prices fluctuated more than manufacturing prices, and occasionally fell, though less (in proportion) than in the old trade cycle. Money wage changes were proportionally greater than price changes. Real prices showed great stability, changing only with changes in productivity.
   Sources: As above, plus Neild (1963), and Coutts, Godley and Nordhaus (1978). Ochoa (1986) demonstrated the strong stability of real prices using 86 x 86 input–output tables.

Employment and real wages

3. Changes in unemployment and output were greater proportionally than changes in prices or money wages; changes in unemployment were large.[12]
   Sources: As above, especially Sylos-Labini (1984).
4. Changes in real wages (product wages) tended either to be mildly procyclical, or not to exhibit a distinct pattern. For the US a weak procyclical pattern has been 'largely confirmed' (Blanchard and Fischer, 1989, p. 17).
   Sources: Michie (1987, Chs 4, 5, 6); Blanchard and Fischer (1989, Ch. 1, pp. 17–19).

Productivity and output

5. Output as a function of employment tends to exhibit constant or increasing returns, according to Okun's Law, supported by Kaldor's Laws.
   Sources: Lavoie (1992); Lowe (1976, especially Ch. 10).

6. Productivity growth is transmitted to households through money wages rising more rapidly than prices. It tends to move procyclically and is the major source of increasing per-capita income; the trend over the cycle was stable until the 1970s; its decline since then has led to stagnant real incomes.
   Sources: Sylos-Labini (1993); Michie (1987), Okun (1981).

Business organization, finance and the state

7. The modern multidivisional corporation has replaced the family firm, as the organizing institution through which most of GNP is created. Growth is carried out largely by existing firms. Under conditions of mass production there are economies of scale and technological progress accompanies investment. Firms must invest continually just to keep up. It is no longer possible to define an optimal size for firms; the question has become their optimal rate of growth.
   Sources: Eichner (1976); Wood (1975); Penrose (1954; 1974).

8. Finance for investment has come to be largely internal, raised through retained earnings, for expansion projects carried out by existing firms.
   Sources: As above. In the 1960s the ratio of corporate debt to assets rose, then fell in the 1970s, but rose again very steeply in the 1980s. (Semmler and Franke, 1992). Gross investment is largely financed by retained earnings, but it could be argued that a large part of net investment is financed by borrowing. Gross investment is the relevant figure for growth, however, since replacements incorporate technical innovations. Moreover, much of the growth of corporate debt in the 1980s is connected with takeovers and mergers (Caskey and Fazzari, 1992).

9. Government intervention and planning became a regular feature of the postwar economic scene. Government expenditures plus transfers had risen to more than a third of GNP after the war, and continued to rise as a percentage of GNP throughout the period, faltering only in the 1980s.[13]
   Sources: Gemmell (1993); Nell (1988).

Money and interest

10. The supply of money is endogenous, responding to demand pressures.
    Sources: Moore (1988); Wray (1990); Nell (1992b). 'Endogenous money' has many meanings, but the point is that the money supply is not a constraint on real expansion.

11. Financial booms and crises became more loosely linked with the movement of prices, unemployment and output. Real booms generated financial expansion, but this proved able to continue in sluggish and even slumping conditions. Credit crunches sometimes but not always appeared to slow inflation, and sometimes but not always slowed expansion. Crashes no longer led to immediate slumps.
    Sources: Hicks (1989, Ch. 11); Wolfson (1986); Wray (1990).

12. The long-term rate of interest varied substantially in the postwar era. From the early 1950s to the early 1960s, the real long-term rate rose from near zero in both the US and the UK; it then fell to nearly zero in 1975, then rose steeply to over 7.5 per cent in 1985, and fell again thereafter. Thus it fell during the inflation of the 1970s, and rose during the early 1980s, as inflation declined. Real interest rates were high in the slump of the early 1980s, and even higher in the mid-1980s boom; they were low in the Korean War boom, and in the early 1960s, and also in the slump of the mid-1970s. Real interest rates are not highly correlated with either inflation or output.[14]
    Sources: Calculated from CitiBase, with five-year moving averages (the length of the postwar cycle) from 1950–90 (Nell, 1988).

There is a marked difference between the two periods, but there does not seem to be any evidence that the second period is more 'disorderly'. It simply exhibits a different pattern. But let us look further.

3.2   Structural Differences

The preceding points concern the nature of firms and the way markets work. Besides these differences there are others which describe the changes in the structure of the economy between the two eras. Two are particularly noticeable: the relationship between sectors changed, and so did the character of costs.

All through the period of the 'old trade cycle', labour flowed out of agriculture and primary products into manufacturing and services. Output grew in the latter two sectors more rapidly than in agriculture. As labour moved out of the primary sector it settled in large towns and cities, which grew rapidly. In the period of the 'new trade cycle', labour continued to leave agriculture, but employment in manufacturing slowed and then ceased to grow, relatively to other sectors, while services changed character and became the fastest expanding sector. Urbanization ceased, the cities stagnated, and even declined. But the suburbs expanded, as did the large metropolitan areas.

Table 8.1 shows the approximate size of sectors as proportions of GDP. It includes government under services. Separating it out is revealing, (Table 8.2). Labour costs have fallen in all sectors as a proportion of total costs; they were higher in the earlier era in every sector, but they have fallen as fast in agriculture as in manufacturing (Table 8.3).

Table 8.1   Size of sectors as proportion of GDP

	'Old trade cycle'	'New trade cycle'
Sectors	Craft-based factories	Mass production
Agriculture	40 – 50%	5 – 10%
Services	35–50%	40 –60%
	Mostly personal	Mostly business
	Low-tech, unproductive	Increasingly hi-tech
Manufacturing	10 –15%	35 – 50%
	Increasing	Stable or decreasing

Table 8.2   Government sector as proportion of GDP

	'Old trade cycle'	'New trade cycle'
Government	10%	40 – 55%
	Included in services	Services and manu-facturing
	Stable	Rising

Table 8.3   Labour costs as proportion of total costs

	'Old trade cycle'	'New trade cycle'
Agriculture	2/3–3/4	1/5–1/4
Services	3/4	1/3–2/3
Manufacturing	2/3	1/5–1/4

In the earlier period blue-collar labour costs made up between one-half and two-thirds of all labour costs. In the era of mass production, blue-collar work has fallen to much less than half of total labour costs.

In the earlier period, plant was designed to produce a certain level of output; varying production was costly and difficult. In the later period, employment and output could be varied more easily, so that average variable cost curves contained a long flat stretch (Lavoie, 1992, pp. 118–28).

4   PRICE QUANTITY ADJUSTMENTS

In the earlier era, markets evidently adjusted through price changes; in the later, however, prices are no longer changing in relevant ways. Instead, employment and output are adjusted when demand fluctuates. These two patterns of market response are significantly different. The first is stabilizing, the second, however, is not.[15]

4.1   Market Adjustment in the Pre-First World War Era

In the earlier era, when production was carried out with an inflexible technology, a decline in autonomous components of aggregate demand – investment or net exports – would lead prices to decline; since output could not easily be adjusted, it would have to be thrown on the market for whatever it would fetch. For similar reasons employment could not easily be cut back; hence there would be little or no downward pressure on money wages in the short run. As a consequence, when the current levels of the autonomous components of aggregate demand fell, real wages rose, in conditions in which employment remained generally unchanged. Hence – to put it compactly – when investment declined, consumption spending rose. Investment and consumption moved inversely to one another.

For *relatively small* variations in autonomous demand this is a stabilizing pattern of market adjustment. For *large* – and prolonged – collapses of demand, however, the relative inflexibility of output and employment can lead to disaster. Unable to cut current costs, or unable to cut them in proportion, and facing declining prices, firms will eventually have to shut down. When prices fall to the breakeven point, all their employees will be out of work. Under conditions of falling revenue, the firm would have to meet its fixed charges out of reserves, including the pay of its fixed labour force, and when these are exhausted, it would have no choice but to close its doors. If, in addition, its reserves are insufficient to meet contractual payments on borrowings, it will face bankruptcy. Shut-downs, of course, reduce both consumption and investment, thus tending to magnify an initial contraction. For small variations in autonomous demand, the price mechanism produces a stabilizing response, for large variations, a destabilizing one.

Similarly, a rise in the autonomous components of demand leads to a bidding up of prices, but not, initially of money wage rates. Hence the real wage falls. With employment fixed, consumption declines in real terms. Again, consumption and investment spending move inversely. In addition, the fall in the real wage makes it possible for employers to absorb the costs of reorganizing work, and thus, in the longer term, to hire additional employees. But so long as the proportional increase in employment is less than the proportion decline in the real wage, consumption will fall.

Such a fall in consumption following a rise in investment can be expected to exert a dampening influence on investment. Similarly the rise in consumption following a decline in investment activity can be expected to provide a stimulus.

These stabilizing influences are reinforced by the behaviour of interest rates. When demand falls, prices fall, and interest rates follow suit. We saw that according to 'Gibson's Paradox' interest rates were highly correlated with the wholesale price index. Hence a decline in investment will be followed by a fall in interest rates, just as consumption spending picks up. The effect will be to provide a stimulus. By contrast, in a boom, interest rates will rise, just as consumption spending turns down.

Of course, the impact of these countervailing tendencies will be reduced by bankruptcies and capacity shrinkage in the slump and by the formation of new firms and the expansion of capacity in the boom. When demand falls sharply and closures and bankruptcies reduce the number of firms, output shrinks, and the pressure on prices seems to be reduced. But bankruptcies and closures reduce employment, and therefore consumption demand. So demand declines further, and prices continue their downward course, pulling interest rates down with them. Falling prices and low interest rates make replacement investment attractive. At some point it will be worthwhile shifting replacement forward in time. This could then start an upswing. In the same way, capacity expansion will tend to inhibit the rise in prices in the boom – but building new capacity itself increases demand, which will feed the pressure on prices. Interest rates will continue to rise; at some point interest and prices will be sufficiently above normal for it to seem worthwhile to postpone replacement. This could then prove the start of the downturn.

In short, the pattern of market adjustment provides endogenous mechanisms that could bring a boom to a close, and lead to recovery from a slump. The system is self-adjusting, and capable of generating an endogenous cycle around a normal trend, just as Lowe suggested. The three internal processes just described contribute to this – real wages, and therefore consumption, move countercyclically, replacement investment moves countercyclically, while the interest rate moves procyclically. These combine to provide pressure on net new investment to eventually turn against the cycle, perhaps – or probably – with a variable lag that depends on circumstances. Whether such a cycle actually manifests itself, and what its characteristics, amplitude, and so on, will be, of course, will depend on the current parameters of the system, and on historical conditions.

146 The Economy in Traverse

4.2   Market Adjustment in the Post-Second World War Era

The mechanism of market adjustment in the earlier era rested on the countercyclical movement of real wages, coupled with the procyclical movement of interest rates. Neither of these patterns is observable in the postwar era. The mechanism just does not exist.

In this period, prices no longer vary with demand; instead prices are driven by inflationary pressures, partly generated by the new process of transmitting productivity gains through increases in money wage rates. This tends to upset socially important income relativities. If these are restored as a result of social pressures, costs will be increased without corresponding gains in productivity, thereby leading to price rises, setting off a wage–price spiral.[16]

But the system does respond to variations in autonomous demand. Mass production processes can easily be adjusted to changes in the level of sales. Employment and output will vary directly with sales. Hence when investment rises or falls, employment will also rise or fall, while prices and money wages remain unchanged. In the simplest case, consumption depends on the real wage and employment; as a result consumption will vary directly, rather than inversely, with investment. This is a version of the multiplier (Nell, 1992b).

Multiplier expansions and contractions of demand, if substantial and/or prolonged, will tend to induce further variations in investment in the same direction. This is the accelerator, or capital stock adjustment principle.

Early in the postwar era many Keynesian trade-cycle theorists argued that the endogenous processes of the modern economy were fundamentally unstable.[17] The plausible range of values for the multiplier and accelerator seemed to imply either exponential expansion and contraction, or, if a lag were introduced, anti-damped cycles. To develop a theory of the business cycle, it was necessary to postulate 'floors' and 'ceilings', which these movements run up against. The floor was set by gross investment; it could not fall below zero, and arguably it could not fall to zero, since existing capital had to be maintained, which required replacement. Full employment and supply bottlenecks of all kinds provided ceilings. Once the explosive movement was halted, various factors were supposed to lead to turnarounds (which might be endogenous in the case where the multiplier-accelerator generates anti-damped movements). Thus the business cycle was seen to be made up of three parts – an unstable endogenous mechanism, which runs up against external buffers, slowing movement down or bringing it to a halt, at which point various *ad hoc* factors come into play, leading to a turnaround and unstable movement again but in the opposite direction. In short, a mixture of endogenous and exogenous.[18]

The floors and ceilings, however, in practice seemed elastic; depressions could keep sinking, and full employment did not reliably stop booms. Nor was it clear why when an expansion or contraction hit a ceiling or floor, it should turn around. Many suggestions were offered, yet no single explanation, or combination of accounts, appeared convincing. It was suggested that different cycles might rest on different factors (Duesenberry, 1958). Yet however unsatisfactory the theory as a whole might have been, the argument that the endogenous mechanism was unstable appears to be sound.

It has been suggested that the financial system might stabilize an otherwise unstable economy. In a boom, interest rates will be pulled up, dampening investment and expenditure on consumer durables; in the slump interest rates will fall, encouraging investment and spending on durables. But, in practice, real interest rates do not appear to move procyclically, and investment has not shown itself to be interest-elastic. Moreover the theory is questionable; if the money supply is endogenous – adapts to the needs of trade – interest rates need not rise with expansion. And if investment is financed largely from retained earnings, it will be far more sensitive to the firm's competitive needs, than to the opportunity cost of funds.

In fact, rather than floors and ceilings, it has been politics that has provided the turning-points. Booms led to balance-of-payments crises or to inflationary wage–price spirals. Pressure from business interests would lead to an induced recession. Full employment also threatened – or was perceived to threaten – work discipline. On the other hand, slumps threatened governments at the ballot box. The actual business cycle of the postwar era had a distinctly political character.

4.3   Changes in Technology

The technological contrasts between the two eras are as striking as the economic ones, and it can be argued that the former helps to explain the latter[19] (Nell, 1992a, Chs 16, 17; 1993). The main features of the old trade cycle are all related, directly or indirectly, to the characteristics of the technology of the period. Until comparatively recently, technology was developed by and for small-scale operations, run largely by households or groups of households. These evolved into family firms. The first Industrial Revolution brought the shift from small craft operations to factories, which, however, were based on essentially the same technologies. Even though, at the end of the nineteenth century, great advances were made as steam power and steel were brought into widespread use, enabling substantial expansions in the size of plants, reaping economies of scale, the technologies still largely operated on the principles of 'batch' production, rather than continuous throughput. In many cases the use of steam power simply permitted a large number of work-stations, each organized according to older principles, to run at the same time off a central power source. The power, in turn, ran essentially the same tools that had previously been operated by hand. Operatives had to be present at all work-stations in order for any production to take place. Even where continuous throughput developed, start-up and shut-down costs were high.

These limitations had economic consequences. Any economy faces continuous shocks from the outside world. Of particular importance are exogenous fluctuations in sales. Firms could not easily vary output to match changes in sales – a firm could produce or shut down. Craft technologies were inflexible in terms of adapting output and employment (and so costs) to changes in the rate of sales. As a consequence, when demand rose (fell) output could only be increased (decreased) by varying productivity, that is work effort. The technology required team effort among workers, generally performing on a small scale, so that changes in output could only come with changes in effort – or by reorganizing the work team. But neither labour nor capital was willing to change work norms, except temporarily. Hence the level of employment would have to change, but this in turn would be costly in terms of disruption, and would take place only if compensated by higher prices, at least for a time. Thus a rise in demand would drive up prices, lowering the real wage, thereby leading to an expansion of employment. Inflexibility thus can help to explain the characteristic patterns of variations in prices, output, wages and employment.

Family firms operating craft technologies do not require extensive government oversight or intervention. A private enterprise financial system will serve this kind of economy well, except in hard times, when it will prove unstable.

By contrast, mass-production technology permits easy adaptation of employment and output to changes in sales, while leaving productivity unaffected. Variable costs will thus be constant over a large range. Prices will therefore tend not to vary with changes in demand. Mass-production technology also permits expansion to reap economies of scale, leading to larger firms, differently organized, and motivated to grow. Under mass production, productivity will tend to grow regularly, and will be reflected in wage bargains. Rising wages for production workers will create tensions with other social groups, leading to pressure to raise their incomes, creating inflationary pressures. Large growing corporations cannot tolerate a financial system prone to crisis; mass production requires government oversight and intervention in many related dimensions. As a consequence the new trade cycle differs in every one of the above respects.[20]

How can this be reflected in elementary economic theory? The production function has traditionally been the basic analytical tool of neoclassical theory in regard to pricing, employment and output. This discussion suggests that changes in technology are a primary cause of the changes in the behaviour of economic variables from the old to the new trade cycle. As a useful preliminary step, such a shift in technology can perhaps be represented as a change from a production function with a pronounced curvature, so that the slope declines, to one that is a straight line with a constant slope[21] (Nell, 1992a).

5   IMPLICATIONS FOR LOWE'S ARGUMENT

Lowe's insight that the economy worked differently before the First World War and after the Second World War appears to have been sound. But not because the 'extremum principle' no longer holds sway, or because competition no longer drives firms to invest and innovate. It is rather that in the earlier era, the price-adjustment mechanism seems to have provided a limited, but definite, degree of stability to the system, whereas in the later period, the (probably modified) multiplier-accelerator mechanism appears to set up destabilizing patterns of movement. These have to be corrected by policy – and as Lowe observed, the policy programmes may not always have been adequate to the tasks.

Part of the reason for this inadequacy, Lowe felt, was that policies were designed on the assumption that the economy was orderly. Hence they assumed that only a small degree of intervention was called for, that a little push would be enough to set the system in motion towards equilibrium. Unfortunately Lowe rejected the Keynesian analysis of capitalist instability, and committed himself to a questionable contention that capitalism had become disorderly. Yet if the economy is endogenously unstable, although not disorderly in Lowe's sense, the same criticism of policy holds. Policies devised on the assumption that a small push will nudge the system into a path headed for equilibrium are not likely to be adequate when the system is unstable.

Even if equilibrium exists, in the technical sense, it is irrelevant for policy if the system is unstable, for there will be no tendency towards that equilibrium. Under these conditions Lowe's 'instrumental' proposal makes good sense. The political process must define the goals – the growth rate, the desired level of employment, the acceptable inflation rate, the desired distribution of income and wealth, and so on. The first task of theory will be to make sure that these are compatible and feasible, given the available technology, natural resources, skills of the labour force, existing stock of plant and equipment, and so on. If they are not, then the political process will have to review the goals and come up with a feasible set. Once the objectives are clear, then policies – taxes, subsidies, controls, regulations, government expenditures – must be devised so as to generate appropriate incentives to ensure that economic agents act to bring about the realization of the objectives. This requires coordinating what the agents do and ensuring consistency; their actions must not lead to paradoxical or unintended results (Nell, 1988, Ch. 10).

At this point Lowe's own argument faces the problem that if the development of the system has undermined *motivation*, then the usual set of material incentives that the state can bring into play may not be sufficient. If agents are no longer maximizers, then tax and spending policies may have no bite. But if the problem is not disorder, but instability, then no such difficulty arises. The incentives, if properly chosen, can be expected to induce the desired behaviour; the new problem, however, will be to make sure that the resulting patterns of behaviour are macroeconomically stable. This will have to be addressed explicitly. The state cannot plan policy with a model that assumes stability, when macro-processes are endogenously unstable. The incentives must be arranged so that they create a dynamic process that moves in the desired direction.

In other words, theory has a further task, which does not appear in Lowe's account, namely to devise ways to neutralize the multiplier– capital–stockadjustment mechanism, or, today, perhaps the productivity growth–capital stock adjustment mechanism. This must be done to ensure that policies will not set off destabilizing patterns of reaction. With this addition, then, Lowe's approach can be judged sound. The two periods are different, and the second is unstable in ways that call for a policy to set the goals for the economy, and arrange for incentives that will systematically move the system towards them, rather than merely nudging it in the direction of an assumed 'natural' equilibrium, to which it will automatically be attracted.

NOTES

1. Note that Lowe (for the prewar economy) and Hayek (for all economies) both hold that the endogenous market mechanism establishes an equilibrium that is stable in the sense that movements away from it will be reversed, in what Lowe later terms a 'negative feedback system'. However, for Hayek the movement will eventually converge on the (stationary) equilibrium, whereas for Lowe the fluctuations could continue indefinitely around a growing path.
2. As examples, he cited the failures of the economic profession to foresee, on the one hand, the strong showing of the US economy following the Second World War – most experts predicted a deep slump – and on the other, the effectiveness of controls in preventing

inflation during the Korean War (Lowe, 1965, pp. 51–3). But these were examples; he encouraged a student to make a comprehensive survey. The result (Schoeffler, 1955), covers virtually the whole of economics, and painstakingly catalogues the repeated, major failures to foresee what lay just ahead.

3. For example, when $g = I/K < s/v$, this implies that $I/s < K/v$, which says that aggregate demand is less than capacity output. There is excess capacity, so why build more? The incentive is to cut back investment, pulling I/K down further.

4. Lowe's critique (Lowe, 1976, pp. 96–100) follows Kurihara's presentation, and starts from an equilibrium path, whereupon, by assumption, the saving ratio falls. The actual rate of growth is now $> s/v$. Kurihara concludes that there will be a *deficiency of capital all around*, and it is to this that Lowe takes exception (p. 97). He agrees that the fall of savings implies a rise in consumer demand, leading to an enhanced derived demand for capital goods in the consumer sector. But in the basic capital-goods sector ('machine tools') 'The fall in savings which, in our equilibrium model, is equivalent to a fall in investment, means that demand for the output of Sector Ia is bound to fall'. Hence equipment can be transferred from Sector Ia to Sector Ib, and the transition can be made without difficulty. A rise in the saving ratio initially appears to pose more difficulty, but in this case, Lowe argues, money wages will be bid up by the rising growth rate, and this will bring the saving ratio back down (pp. 99–100). He concludes, 'under the motorial conditions stated, which ... are the same as those assumed by Harrod, dynamic equilibrium displays genuine stability, and dislocations from equilibrium evoke forces that will pull the system back to the equilibrium path'(p. 99). But if saving is *not* automatically equal to investment, then when the saving ratio falls, the demand for investment cannot be assumed to decline. Hence there *will* be a shortage of capacity all around, and the Harrodian problem is still there to plague us.

5. Note the difficulty here: if economic agents no longer reliably act in accord with material incentives, how is government to induce them to act in the desired manner? The disorder that Lowe cites arises from a breakdown at the most fundamental level of behaviour. How can the government design policies if they do not know what incentives will work?

6. Evidence on both periods for the US, Canada, Germany, and Japan, showing the patterns described here as the old and the new trade cycles, is presented in Nell (1994).

7. Measuring trends presents notorious problems. In most of what follows segmented linear trends have been fitted. See Nell (1994).

8. These trends are consistent with the patterns of the previous centuries. In the latter part of the eighteenth century prices rose dramatically as a result of the French Revolution and the Napoleonic Wars. From 1600 to 1775, however, prices of consumables in Southern England were more or less flat, with a slight downward trend from 1650 on, broken only by sudden upturns due to wars. Builder's wages rose very moderately, staying flat for long periods, from 1600 to 1775, then rose steeply up to 1815, then went flat until the last quarter of the nineteenth century. (Phelps Brown and Hopkins, (1981 p. 170.)

9. Since money wages are less flexible than money prices, it is implied that real wages are flexible. Since primary products are more flexible than manufacturing goods, it is implied that the real price of primaries in terms of manufactures changes. Other real price variations can be calculated from the data.

10. Ray Majewski has examined these figures in a dissertation, using *Shipping and Commercial List*, and the *Aldrich Report* for pre-1890 prices, as a check on Warren and Pearson's Wholesale Price Index. The BLS provides a historic Index of Wages per Hour, and Angus Maddison has developed (1982) an index of real GNP, based on Gallman's (1966) study, which in turn is based on Kuznets (1961). Kuznets has been criticized by Romer (1989) and defended/revised by Balke and Gordon (1989). Neither the Romer nor the Balke and Gordon data change the result that there is a counter-cyclical pattern evident in the US data. See Nell (1994).

11. If the relationship between output and employment were described by a well-behaved neoclassical production function, then output and productivity should be related *inversely*, rather than directly. The widespread evidence of a positive relationship makes it clear that the countercyclical movement of product wages does not 'confirm' traditional marginal productivity theory. Nevertheless, the traditional theory appears to have been 'on to something', and the object here is to find out what that was.

12. That is, even *with* countercyclical government intervention, the variations in employment are large in the postwar cycle. They would be far greater in the absence of such policies.

13. In addition, it should be noted that state expenditure in relation to GNP was high and rising during the period, in both military and civilian categories. It rose and/or remained high, in spite of explicit and politically-inspired attempts to cut it back.

14. Thanks to Tom Palley for calculations verifying this point.

15. This discussion concerns the 'normal' behaviour of 'stylized' actual market agents, for example family firms or modern corporations, working-class or middle-class households. It is not concerned with the 'idealized rational agents', conceived independently of social context, that are found in the models of much contemporary economic theory. The normal behaviour of stylized actual agents may well involve maximizing subject to constraints, and will generally be 'rational' in some sense. But it is shaped and determined by context and institutions (Nell and Semmler, 1991, 'Introduction').

16. In many areas productivity will appear to rise because 'output' will be measured in terms of factor cost. When lawyers raise their fees to maintain their position relative to auto workers, the value of their services rises. Output and cost move together; productivity measured as revenue per hour has risen. But the effect is to raise the cost of living, creating pressure for a further wage increase.

17. Hicks (1950), examined the plausible ranges of values of the multiplier and capital–output ratios, and concluded that, empirically, the system had to be either unstable or generate anti-damped cycles. Matthews (1959) reviews the literature, and appears to regard models with an unstable endogenous mechanism, running up against buffers, as the most reasonable. A related school of thought argued that advanced capitalist economies had an inbuilt propensity to stagnate, which would have to be offset by government expenditure (Kalecki, 1971; Steindl, 1976), possibly abetted by various kinds of private 'unproductive' expenditure (Baran and Sweezy, 1966). In this case, the instability is seen to hold in one direction only – or chiefly – namely downwards. But it is denied that there are any 'self-correcting' adjustment mechanisms.

18. In the second half of the postwar era, changes in the economy may have affected the adjustment mechanism. Multiplier effects seem less pronounced, but changes in productivity appear to interact with investment in a destabilizing manner – for example, a slowdown in productivity reduces growth in incomes, which slows the growth of consumer demand, leading to a cutback in investment. This in turn further weakens growth in productivity. The multiplier-accelerator may be less in evidence, but the pattern of market adjustment still appears to be unstable.

19. These technological changes did not just happen; they were themselves the product of market incentives and pressures, brought about by the problems and opportunities faced by firms in their everyday business. This is the subject of the theory of *Transformational Growth*, but the issues are separate from those under discussion here (Nell, 1992a and 1993).

20. For further elaboration, compare Nell (1992a, Chs 16, 17) and Nell (1993) and the references cited there. Howell (1992), proposes a similar classification. Nell (1994), provides a fuller discussion of all these points.

21. Assuming for simplicity that all and only wages are consumed, the crucial dividing line occurs when the curvature of the production function is such as to give rise to a marginal product curve of unitary elasticity. At this point the proportional decline in the real wage is exactly offset by the proportional rise in employment. If the curvature were greater, the rise in employment would not offset the fall in the real wage – so that consumption would *decline* as a result of a rise in investment demand that led to a bidding up of prices. If the curvature were less, then a rise in investment, bidding up prices, would lead to such a large rise in employment that consumption would *increase*. This is the multiplier relationship.

REFERENCES

Aftalion, A. (1927), 'The theory of economic cycles based on the Capitalistic technique of production', *Review of Economic Statistics*, 9, pp. 165–70.

Balke, N.S. and Gordon, R.J. (1989), 'The estimation of prewar national product: methodology and new evidence', *Journal of Political Economy*, 97, pp. 38–92.

Baran, P. and Sweezy, P.M. (1966), *Monopoly Capital*, New York: Monthly Review Press.

Blanchard, O. and Fischer, S. (1989), *Lectures on Macroeconomics*, Cambridge, Mass.: MIT Press.

Caskey, C.T. and S. Fazzari (1992), 'Rising debt in the private sector: A cause for concern?', in D.B. Papadimitriou (ed.), *Profits, Deficits and Instability*, London: Macmillan, pp. 202–18.

Chandler, A. (1977), *The Visible Hand: The Managerial Revolution in American Business*, Cambridge, Mass.: Harvard University Press.

Chandler, A. (1990), *Scale and Scope. The Dynamics of Industrial Capitalism*, Cambridge, Mass.: Harvard University Press

Clark, J.B. (1899), *The Distribution of Wealth*, New York: Macmillan.

Coutts, K., W. Godley and W. Nordhaus (1978), *Industrial Pricing in the United Kingdom*, Cambridge: Cambridge University Press.

Duesenberry, J. (1958), *Business Cycles and Economic Growth*, New York: Mc Graw Hill.

Dunlop, J.T. (1938), 'The movement of real and money wage rates', *Economic Journal*, **48**, pp. 413–34.

Eichengreen, B. (1992), *The Gold Standard and the Great Depression, 1919–1939*, Oxford and New York: Oxford University Press.

Eichner, A.S. (1976), *The Megacorp and Oligopoly*, Cambridge, Mass.: MIT Press.

Gallman, R. (1966), 'Gross national product in the United States, 1834–1907', *Studies in Income and Wealth*, **90**.

Gemmell, N. (1993), *The Growth of the Public Sector: Theories and International Evidence*, Aldershot: Edward Elgar.

Hayek, F.A. (1933), *Monetary Theory and the Trade Cycle*, London: J. Cape.

Hicks, J. (1950), *A Contribution to the Theory of the Trade Cycle*, Oxford: Clarendon Press.

Hicks, J. (1989), *A Market Theory of Money*, Oxford: Clarendon Press.

Hoffmann, W.G. (1965), *Das Wachstum der deutschen Wirtschaft seit der Mitte des 19. Jahrhunderts*, Berlin: Springer.

Howell, P. (1992), 'Stages, technical advance, industrial segmentation, and employment', in E.J. Nell et al. (eds) *Economics as Worldly Philosophy. Essays in Honour of Robert Heilbroner*, London: Macmillan.

Kalecki, M. (1971), *Selected Essays on the Dynamics of the Capitalist Economy*, Cambridge: Cambridge University Press.

Keynes, J.M. (1930), *A Treatise on Money. Vol. II: The Applied Theory of Money*, London: Macmillan.

Keynes, J.M. (1939), 'Relative movements of real wages and output', *Economic Journal*, **49**, pp. 394–412.

Kindleberger, C.P. (1978), *Manias, Panics, and Crashes. A History of Financial Crises*, New York: Basic Books.

Kurihara, K. (1956), *Introduction to Keynesian Dynamics*, New York.

Kuznets, S. (1961), *Capital in the American Economy: Its Formation and Financing*, Princeton: Princeton University Press.

Lavoie, M. (1992), *Foundations of Post Keynesian Economic Analysis*, Aldershot: Edward Elgar.

Lowe, A. (1965), *On Economic Knowledge: Toward a Science of Political Economics*, New York: Harper & Row.

Lowe, A. (1976), *The Path of Economic Growth*, Cambridge: Cambridge University Press.

Lowe, A. (1987), *Essays in Political Economics: Public Control in a Democratic Society*, edited and introduced by A. Oakley, Brighton: Wheatsheaf Books.

Maddison, A. (1982), *Phases of Capitalist Development*, Oxford and New York: Oxford University Press.

Maddison, A. (1984), 'Origins and impact of the welfare state, 1883–1983', *Banca Nazionale del Lavoro Quarterly Review*, no. 148, pp. 55–87.

Maddison, A. (1991), *Dynamic Forces in Capitalist Development*, Oxford and New York: Oxford University Press.

Matthews, R.C.O. (1959), *The Trade Cycle*, Cambridge: Cambridge University Press.

Michie, J. (1987), *Wages in the Business Cycle. An Empirical and Methodological Analysis*, London: Frances Pinter.

Mill, J.S. (1848), *Principles of Political Economy*, London: John W. Parker.

Moore, B. (1988), *Horizontalists and Verticalists. The macroeconomics of credit money*, Cambridge: Cambridge University Press.

Neild, R.R. (1963), *Pricing and Employment in the Trade Cycle*, Cambridge: Cambridge University Press.

The Economy in Traverse

Nell, E.J. (1988), *Prosperity and Public Spending*, London: Unwin & Hyman.
Nell, E.J. (1992a), *Transformational Growth and Effective Demand*, London: Macmillan and
New York: New York University Press.
Nell, E.J. (1992b), 'Transformational growth, mass production and the multiplier', in: J. Halevi,
D. Laibman and E.J. Nell (eds.), *Beyond the Steady State. A Revival of Growth Theory*,
London: Macmillan, pp. 131–74.
Nell, E.J. (1993), 'Transnational growth and learning: developing capitalist technology into
scientific mass production', in: R. Thomson (ed.) *Learning and Technical Change*, London:
Macmillan.
Nell, E.J. (1994), 'Minsky, Keynes and Sraffa: investment and the long period', in. G. Dymski
and R. Pollin (eds.), *New Perspectives in Monetary Macroeconomics: explorations and the
tradition of Hyman P. Minsky*, Ann Arbor: The University of Michigan Press.
Nell, E.J. et.al. (1996), *Transformational Growth and the Business Cycle*, London: Routledge.
Nell, E.J. and Semmler, W. (eds.) (1991), *Nicholas Kaldor and Mainstream Economics.
Confrontation or Convergence?*, London: Macmillan.
Ochoa, E.M. (1986), 'An input–output study of labor productivity in the US economy, 1947–72',
Journal of Post Keynesian Economics, 9, pp. 111–37.
Okun, A.M. (1981), *Prices and Quantities: A Macroeconomic Analysis*, Oxford: Basil Blackwell.
Osiatynski, J. (ed.) (1990), *Collected Works of Michael Kalecki. Vol. 1: Capitalism, Business
Cycles and Full Employment*, Oxford: Clarendon Press.
Patinkin, D. (1965), *Money, Interest and Prices*, 2nd edition, New York: Harper & Row.
Pedersen, J. and Petersen, O. (1938), *An Analysis of Price Behaviour*, London: Humphrey
Milford and Oxford University Press.
Penrose, E. (1954), *The Theory of the Growth of the Firm*, Oxford: Basil Blackwell.
Penrose, E. (1974), *The Large Multinational Firm in Developing Countries*, London: Allen &
Unwin.
Phelps Brown, H. and S.V. Hopkins (1981), *A Perspective of Wages and Prices*, London and
New York: Methuen.
Pigou, A.C. (1927), *Industrial Fluctuations*, London: Macmillan.
Robinson, E.A.G. (1931), *The Structure of Competitive Industry*, Cambridge: Cambridge
University Press.
Romer, C. (1989), 'New estimates of prewar national product and unemployment', *Journal of
Economic History*, 94, pp. 341–52.
Schoeffler, S. (1955), *The Failures of Economics: A Diagnostic Study*, Cambridge, Mass.:
Harvard University Press.
Semmler, W. and Franke, R. (1992), 'Expectation dynamics, financing of investment and
business cycles' in D.B. Papadimitriou (ed.), *Profits, Deficits and Instability*, London:
Macmillan, pp. 330–48.
Steindl, J. (1976), *Maturity and Stagnation in American Capitalism*, New York: Monthly Review
Press.
Sylos-Labini, P. (1984), *The Forces of Economic Growth and Decline*, Cambridge, Mass.: MIT
Press.
Sylos-Labini, P. (1989), 'The Changing Character of the so-called Business Cycle, *Atlantic
Economic Journal*, 17, pp. 1–14.
Sylos-Labini, P. (1993), *Economic Growth and Business Cycles*, Aldershot: Edward Elgar.
Tarshis, L. (1939), 'Changes in Real and Money Wages', *Economic Journal*, 49, pp. 150–54.
Urquhart, M.C. (1965), *Historical Statistics of Canada*, London: Macmillan.
Wolfson, M.H. (1986), *Financial Crises: Understanding the Postwar US Experiences*, Armonk,
N.J.: Sharpe.
Wood, A. (1975) *A Theory of Profits*, Cambridge: Cambridge University Press.
Wray, L.R. (1990), *Money and Credit in Capitalist Economies: The Endogenous Money
Approach*, Aldershot: Edward Elgar.

9. Value and Distribution in the Lowe–Mathur Model

Ian Steedman

In his *The Path of Economic Growth* (1976), Adolph Lowe was concerned largely with the physical expansion of the economy, with changes in labour supply and natural resources, and with technical change. Moreover, his focus was on the complex topic of the 'traverse', rather than on the simpler matter of semi-stationary growth. It is understandable therefore that he not only employed a relatively simple three-sector model of production but rendered it especially tractable by assuming 'equal proportions' between sectors with respect to their capital/wage bill ratios. We shall be less ambitious than Lowe and use his three-sector model to examine certain issues in the theory of value and distribution which can arise when the proportions are not equal but the economy is stationary or semi-stationary. Before we turn to our central concern, however, it may be helpful to compare Lowe's three-sector model with two other models of production to be found in the literature.

1   THREE MODELS COMPARED

Perhaps the simplest and most familiar 'multi-commodity' model of production is that associated with the names of Samuelson, Hicks, Spaventa and others, in which a machines and b units of labour can produce one machine in one year, while α machines and β units of labour can produce one unit of the consumption commodity in one year. If the machine constitutes circulating capital in each use, as we shall assume throughout for simplicity, then

$$ap(1 + r) + bw = p \tag{9.1}$$
$$\alpha p(1 + r) + \beta w = 1 \tag{9.2}$$

where p is the price of a machine in terms of the consumption commodity, r is the yearly rate of profit (interest) and w is the real (consumption) wage rate, paid *ex post*.

We may now set out Lowe's model in a notation which facilitates comparison with the above. In one year, a_1 basic machines and b_1 units of

labour can produce one basic machine, a_2 basic machines and b_2 units of
labour can produce one non-basic machine, and α non-basic machines and
β units of labour can produce one unit of the consumption commodity. If p_1
and p_2 are the (consumption commodity) prices of the basic and non-basic
machines, respectively, then

$$a_1p_1(1+r)+b_1w=p_1 \tag{9.3}$$
$$a_2p_1(1+r)+b_2w=p_2 \tag{9.4}$$
$$\alpha p_2(1+r)+\beta w=1. \tag{9.5}$$

It will be clear from (9.3) and (9.4) that in the special case $(a_1/a_2) = (b_1/b_2) = t$, say, $p_1 = tp_2$ and hence (9.4) may be rewritten as

$$a_2t\,p_2(1+r)+b_2w=p_2. \tag{9.4'}$$

Then the system (9.4') and (9.5) is equivalent to the system (9.1) and (9.2).
Thus the familiar Samuelson–Hicks–Spaventa model is a special case of
the Lowe model of production.

On the other hand, Lowe's model is a special case of that employed in
Gautam Mathur's *Planning for Steady Growth* (1965). (Neither Lowe nor
Mathur appears to refer to the other.) In its most general 'n machines' form,
Mathur's model involves a basic machine which, with labour, can produce
either basic machines or a 'second' machine; the latter, with labour, can
produce a 'third' machine – and so on until we reach the 'n-th' machine
which, with labour, can produce the consumption commodity. (See Mathur,
1965, especially pp. 48–59, 338–44; the five-machine case is set out on p.
56.) As in Lowe's model, Mathur's basic machine can be used to produce
two alternative products but Mathur always insisted that the 'basic
machine–labour' ratio should be taken to be the *same* whichever of the two
products is being produced. (He once said to me that he disliked the
Samuelson–Hicks–Spaventa model precisely because it is only interesting
when $a\beta \neq \alpha b$ and yet, in his view, rigid machine–labour ratios are the
'realistic' case.) Consider, then, the Mathur model with three machines. In
an obvious notation

$$a_1p_1(1+r)+b_1w=p_1 \tag{9.6}$$
$$a_2p_1(1+r)+b_2w=p_2 \tag{9.7}$$
$$a_3p_2(1+r)+b_3w=p_3 \tag{9.8}$$
$$\alpha p_3(1+r)+\beta w=1 \tag{9.9}$$

where $(a_1/a_2) = (b_1/b_2) = t$, say. It will be clear from (9.6) and (9.7) that
$p_1 = tp_2$ and that (9.7) may be rewritten as

$$a_2t\, p_2 \, (1 + r) + b_2 w = p_2. \tag{9.7'}$$

Now system (9.7'), (9.8) and (9.9) is equivalent to system (9.3), (9.4) and (9.5), so that there is no important difference between the *three*-sector Lowe model and the *four*-sector Mathur model. (Of course the Lowe model is still a special case of the Mathur model with four or more machines.) The Samuelson–Hicks–Spaventa model is a special case of Lowe's model, which is equivalent to Mathur's four-sector model which is, in turn, a special case of Mathur's most general model. The following analysis deals with Lowe's model and thus also, in effect, with Mathur's case of three machines.

2   THE WAGE–PROFIT RATE FRONTIER

It is readily deduced from (9.3), (9.4) and (9.5) that

$$w = \frac{\left(1 - a_1\rho\right)}{\beta + \left(ab_2 - a_1\beta\right)\rho + \alpha\left(a_2 b_2 - a_1 b_2\right)\rho^2} \tag{9.10}$$

where $\rho \equiv 1 + r$. The wage–profit rate frontier (9.10) is linear if and only if $a_1 b_2 = a_2 b_1$ *and* $\alpha b_2 = a_1\beta$. (Note that the second part of this double condition refers to all three sectors.) Of course, we are not interested here in the case $a_1 b_2 = a_2 b_1$ since that yields, in effect, the familiar Samuelson–Hicks–Spaventa model; hence we may suppose throughout that the wage–profit rate frontier is nonlinear. It is downward sloping whenever $1 \le \rho \le a_1^{-1}$. (If $a_1 b_2 > a_2 b_1$ then $dw/d\rho$ is never zero; if $a_1 b_2 < a_2 b_1$ then it is zero for two values of ρ, one being less than zero and the other being greater than $2a_1^{-1}$.) What can be said about the curvature of the frontier?

Before seeking to answer this question, let us simplify (9.10) by rewriting it as

$$w = \frac{\left(1 - a_1\rho\right)}{\beta + \beta_1\rho + \beta_2\rho^2} \tag{9.11}$$

where the definitions of β_1 and β_2 are obvious. It may usefully be noted that β_1 and β_2, like β, are dimensionally 'amounts of labour per unit of consumption commodity'. It is to be noted also that nothing important is lost by reducing the six technical coefficients appearing in (9.10) to the four appearing in (9.11), since in the former b_1 and b_2 only appear in the products $\alpha a_2 b_1$ and αb_2. (And indeed $\alpha a_2 b_1 = \beta_2 + a_1\beta_1 + a_1^2\beta$, while $\alpha b_2 = \beta_1 + a_1\beta$, so that a knowledge of $(a_1, \beta, \beta_1$ and $\beta_2)$ is sufficient for the determination of $(\alpha a_2 b_1)$ and (αb_2). Techniques with the same a_1 and β but different α, a_2, b_1 and b_2 have identical wage–profit rate frontiers if the products $(\alpha a_2 b_1)$ and (αb_2) are each the same as between the techniques.)

What then are the curvature properties of (9.11) within the economically relevant range? A simple first clue is readily obtained by considering when the genuine frontier (9.11) intersects the hypothetical frontier defined by

$$w^* = \frac{1 - a_1\rho}{\beta + \beta_1 + \beta_2}. \tag{9.12}$$

By construction the hypothetical frontier (9.12) is linear and intersects the genuine frontier at both $\rho = 1$ $(r = 0)$ and $a_1\rho = 1$ $(w = 0)$. It will be clear that there is just *one* further intersection, at $\rho + 1 = -\beta_1/\beta_2$. This third intersection will, of course, lie in the economically relevant range if and only if

$$2 < -\beta_1/\beta_2 < 2 + R \tag{9.13}$$

where R is the maximum rate of profit. For 'reasonable' values of R, such as 25 per cent, (9.13) is a tight constraint and it seems clear that 'most' combinations of b_1, a_2, b_2, α, β will not satisfy it. It is thus 'likely' that the genuine wage–profit rate frontier will not cross the line running from the point on it at $r = 0$ to that at $w = 0$. (In the relevant range, that is: it *must* cross it at one point other than $r = 0$ and $w = 0$, of course.) An economically relevant 'crossing' is possible, however, as in Figure 9.1; such a curvature of the frontier is of course impossible in the Samuelson–Hicks–Spaventa model.

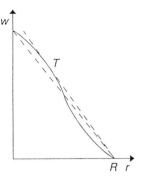

Figure 9.1   The wage–profit rate frontier

The reader who is familiar with Edward Nell's 'Appendix' to Lowe (1976, pp. 289–325) may already have noticed that our finding in the last paragraph – that the genuine and hypothetical frontiers have one and only one intersection, other than those at $r = 0$ and at $w = 0$ – is inconsistent with the figure given by Nell (ibid., p. 323), which exhibits two such intersections, both within the economically relevant range. This discrepancy, which cannot, of course, arise from the fact that Nell's figure refers to the consumption–growth rate frontier (since that coincides with the wage–profit rate frontier), must naturally be explained. The figure in question summarizes Nell's discussion of inflexion points in the frontier, a discussion which is vitiated by his clearly incorrect derivation of, in our notation, $d^2w/d\rho^2$. (See his II.28, p. 321.) This incorrect derivation leads Nell to the conclusion that $d^2w/d\rho^2 = 0$ is a quadratic in ρ, whereas the correct conclusion is that it is a cubic in ρ. Hence, there can be either one real value of ρ, or three real values of ρ, which yield inflexion points but there can never be just two such values. Given this error in Nell's argument, it is, of course, not surprising that his figure is inconsistent with the finding of our previous paragraph.

It would naturally be possible to pursue here the analysis of the cubic in ρ which determines the inflexion points of the frontier and to establish under what conditions the number of such points is one, or is three, and whether that point (or those points) lie(s) in the relevant range. That analysis would be very tedious, however, and we simply assert the conclusions that if $\beta_1^2 < 4\beta\beta_2$ then there are three inflexion points, only one of them occurring when $dw/d\rho < 0$, while if $4\beta\beta_2 < \beta_1^2$ there is only one inflexion point. (Hence Nell's figure is quite impossible.) Since we already know that the genuine and hypothetical frontiers can intersect in the relevant range, we know that there *can be* one inflexion point in that range (see Figure 9.1). Rather than pursue the explicit study of inflexion points, we shall now take up the question where a point such as T, in Figure 9.1, can be located, T being defined as a point from which the tangent line passes through $r = R$, $w = 0$. Fortunately, the condition $-dw/d\rho = w/R - r$ leads to the very simple result $\rho = -\beta_1/2\beta_2$. Hence, there is always exactly one such point. Of course it only lies in the economically relevant range if

$$2 < -\beta_1/\beta_2 < 2 + 2R \qquad (9.14)$$

Comparison of (9.14) with (9.13) shows at once that the former is a little less strict – but still seems to be 'unlikely' to be met for plausibly small values of R. (Within the relevant range, the existence of a point such as T is sufficient but not necessary for the existence of an inflexion point.) It would naturally be possible to ask when there is a point analogous to T from which the tangent passes through $r = 0$, $w = $ maximum wage, but this is equivalent to asking when the value of capital per worker, in a stationary economy, is (instantaneously) not changing with respect to ρ; see below.

3   PRICES

From (9.3), (9.4) and (9.11) it follows that

$$p_1 = \frac{b_1}{\beta + \beta_1\rho + \beta_2\rho^2} \tag{9.15}$$

$$p_2 = \frac{b_2 + \alpha^{-1}\beta_2\rho}{\beta + \beta_1\rho + \beta_2\rho^2}. \tag{9.16}$$

Clearly the derivative of p_2/p_1 with respect to ρ has the same sign as $\beta_2 = \alpha(a_2b_1 - a_1b_2)$. (This result is incorrectly formulated by Nell, in Lowe, 1976, p. 318, line six.) As for p_1 itself, relation (9.15) clearly has a turning-point at $\rho = -\beta_1/2\beta_2$, that is, at the very ρ which defines the point T referred to just above; hence condition (9.14) is also relevant here. This turning-point is a maximum or minimum of p_1 according as β_2 is positive or negative. The relation (9.16), determining p_2, has two real turning-points but it is not clear that anything very useful can be said about the values of ρ at which they occur.

4   THE VALUE OF CAPITAL

It may readily be shown that, in a stationary economy, the vertically integrated (direct and indirect) requirements for the basic and non-basic machines, per unit of consumption commodity output, are $\alpha a_2(1 - a_1)^{-1}$ and α, respectively. It follows at once that the capital–output ratio in a stationary economy is given by, say,

$$v = \left(\frac{\alpha\, a_2}{1 - a_1}\right) p_1 + \alpha\, p_2$$

where p_1 and p_2 are as given in (9.15) and (9.16). Hence,

$$v = \frac{\beta \, v_0 + \beta_2 \rho}{\beta + \beta_1 \rho + \beta_2 \rho^2} \qquad (9.17)$$

where v_0 is the value of v at $\rho = 0$. Differentiation of (9.17) appears not to lead to any very interesting result. It is more interesting to consider when $v = R^{-1} = a_1/1 - a_1$. One solution is, of course, $a_1\rho = 1$; the only other solution is

$$\rho = -\frac{\beta_1 + \beta_2}{\beta_2}.$$

This second solution can naturally be seen as nothing other than a confirmation of the result, immediately above (9.13), concerning the 'interesting' intersection of the genuine and hypothetical wage–profit rate frontiers. The reader wishing to consider when $vR = 1$ if the economy is growing at the steady rate g may analyse the relevant equation, which is

$$\left(a_1\rho - 1\right)\left[\beta_2\rho + \left(\beta_1 + \beta_2\right)\right] = \left(\alpha a_2 b_1\right) g.$$

5   CHOICE OF TECHNIQUE

When Samuelson introduced his 'surrogate production function' (1962) his point was to show how, under certain (very strong) assumptions, the familiar aggregate production function could be consistent with an economy characterized by the presence of indefinitely many heterogeneous capital goods. To this end, it was natural to suppose a one-to-one correspondence between techniques and kinds of capital good. Since every one of the infinitely many capital goods can be produced *only* by itself and labour, it follows at once that the 'surrogate' economy is a peculiarly inappropriate vehicle for the study of the 'traverse' from one semi-stationary state to another. In the absence of foreign trade, such an economy simply cannot make the traverse from one technique (one kind of capital good) to another (with its qualitatively different capital good). It is clear enough, then, why an economist such as Lowe who is concerned to analyse paths of traverse should consider economies with a basic machine and not economies of the 'surrogate' type. (Mathur, 1965, was also much concerned with the *approach* to steady growth paths.) As we turn now to consider the choice between alternative techniques, it must be recognized that it would hardly be in the spirit of the Lowe model to focus on the choice between techniques which are such that a traverse from one to the other would be technologically impossible.

Consider, then, two techniques which have in common a basic machine, produced by a_1 such machines together with b_1 units of labour. They differ, however, in that alternative non-basic machines can be produced (their production involving the coefficients a_2 and b_2, or a_2^* and b_2^*) and then used, with labour, to produce the consumption commodity (with coefficients α and β, or α^* and β^*). Equations such as (9.10), (9.15) and (9.16) will, of course, hold for each technique – but there would be no significance to comparing what we may call (9.16) and (9.16*), since the two non-basic machine prices, p_2 and p_2^*, are non-commensurable. The wage–profit rate frontiers for the two alternative techniques will naturally have the point $a_1\rho = 1$, $w = 0$ in common. They will also intersect, implying both the same wage w and the same value of p_1 whichever technique be used, when

$$\left[\left(\beta - \beta^*\right) + \left(\alpha b_2 - a^* b_2^*\right)\rho\right]\left(1 - a_1\rho\right) = b_1\left(\alpha^* a_2^* - \alpha a_2\right)\rho^2. \quad (9.18)$$

The quadratic equation (9.18) can have no solution, or one solution, or two solutions in the relevant range $a_1 < a_1 \rho < 1$: ignoring the uninteresting first case, then, we may say that either single-switching or double-switching can occur. It will be clear that further alternative non-basic machines could now be introduced, allowing the possibility of 'capital-reversing without reswitching on the economy wage–profit rate frontier' and so on. One could even allow for infinitely many such distinct non-basic machines, so as to create 'anti-surrogate' models in the presence of the common basic machine – but this will be left to the interested reader to pursue.

Perhaps the basic machine could itself be produced with alternative combinations of basic machines and labour (say a_1 and b_1 or a_1^* and b_1^*)? After all, it has been assumed already, throughout the above, that $a_2 b_1 - a_1 b_2 \neq 0$ and hence that basic machines and labour can be combined in different proportions as inputs, albeit to produce different outputs. It is not such a big step then to allow the possibility that either a_1 and b_1 or a_1^* and b_1^* could produce one basic machine. (Mathur would none the less have disapproved of taking this step.) If we do consider this possibility, allowing for only one kind of non-basic machine, we must be careful *not* to proceed by comparing two equations such as (9.10), or (9.11), and jumping to the hasty conclusion that there are up to three switchpoints, determined by a cubic equation in ρ. Rather, we must recall that both w and p_1 must be the same for both techniques at a switchpoint; there is really only one such point, determined by

$$\frac{w}{p_1} = \frac{1 - a_1\rho}{b_1} = \frac{1 - a_1^*\rho}{b_1^*}$$

and being of economic relevance only if

$$1 < \frac{b_1^* - b_1}{a_1 b_1^* - a_1^* b_1} < min\left[\frac{1}{a_1}, \frac{1}{a_1^*}\right].$$

Hence this element of 'variable proportions' in production adds little of interest to what was said above about the choice of technique.

6 CONCLUDING REMARKS

Lowe's three-sector model – or, equivalently, Mathur's three-machine model – may certainly be preferred by the value and distribution theorist to the more widely used Samuelson–Hicks–Spaventa model, which is a special case of the Lowe model. The Lowe–Mathur model is a little more complicated to analyse but, in compensation, it allows one to consider reswitching, capital-reversing, and so on, in a framework which does not render technologically impossible the very idea of a 'traverse' from one technique to another. It has been seen too that the wage–profit rate frontier has a more flexible shape in this more general model, permitting a point of inflexion to occur (a possibility which cannot arise in the Samuelson–Hicks–Spaventa special case).

REFERENCES

Lowe, A. (1976), *The Path of Economic Growth*, Cambridge: Cambridge University Press.
Mathur, G. (1965), *Planning for Steady Growth*, Oxford: Basil Blackwell.
Nell, E.J. (1976), 'An alternative presentation of Lowe's basic model', in Lowe (1976), pp. 289–325.
Samuelson, P.A. (1962), 'Parable and realism in capital theory: the surrogate production function', *Review of Economic Studies*, **29**, pp. 193–206.

10. Structural Analysis of Development and Underdevelopment

Joseph Halevi

1   INTRODUCTION

This chapter will discuss Adolph Lowe's (1956, 1976) contributions by positioning them in relation to the accumulation and crisis debate developed by Russian and German Marxism at the turn of the century (Section 2), to the question of the traverse in a mature economy (Section 3), and to the quasi-structural theories of development of Maurice Dobb and of the Indian school of planning (Section 4).

The reference to the well-known Marxist debate seems to be a useful vehicle to single out the essential differences between a developed and an underdeveloped economy. Indeed, in the next section it will be shown that the tendency towards an unlimited, crisis-free, expansion idealized by Tugan-Baranowsky either will break down because of an excessive accumulation of machines relative to the available workforce, or will require a substantial surplus of labour *vis-à-vis* the production of equipment. The formation of a stock of capital large enough to employ the whole of the working population is then taken to be the factor which differentiates developed from developing economies.

The third section constitutes the centrepiece of the chapter. The conditions for the fulfilment of a mature traverse will be described by means of a model incorporating the essential features of Lowe's framework. Methodologically, the traverse process shows the stringency which the problem of capital formation and liquidation imposes upon sectoral relations. Thus, in the fourth section, after a detailed presentation of Dobb's and the Indian contributions, Lowe's stringency will be applied to a critical examination of those models. Finally, in the conclusions, we shall address the question of the cultural framework in which the structural approach to both growth and development was devised and we shall point out the limitations, also cultural, inherent in their treatment of the links between technical and social relations.

2   FROM TUGAN-BARANOWSKY TO LOWE

Lowe's notion of structure is explicitly linked to Marx's schemes of reproduction whereby the economy is divided into two separate sectors one producing capital goods and one producing consumption goods. This analytical construction has led Marx to raise, in the second volume of *Capital*, the issue of the relation between accumulation and sectoral proportions. After Marx, most Russian and German Marxian thought was influenced by the sectoral approach to accumulation and crisis, rather than by the one-sector cyclical analysis propounded in Chapter 25 of the first volume of *Capital* (Colletti and Napoleoni, 1975). The shift in emphasis was largely due to the impression made on the leaders of the Social Democratic movement in Germany by the nature of Bismarckian growth based on the rapid expansion of the capital-goods sector. German Social Democracy then became concerned, except for the evolutionist wing represented by Bernstein, with whether or not the expansion of the capital-goods sector could continue regardless of consumption demand. Within this framework Marx's two-sector schemes of reproduction formed the analytical foundations of the debate and determined the bifurcation between those stressing the role of consumption demand and those stressing the causal relation between sectoral disproportions and economic crises. The latter strand focused on the way in which, with falling consumption demand, the surplus could be distributed between the two sectors without engendering any slowdown in accumulation. The specification of sectoral flows becomes paramount to the analysis of accumulation. In so doing, the disproportionality school correctly understood the fact that in a two-sector framework the expansion of profits can come only from the expansion of the capital-goods sector.

The significance of structural analysis in Lowe, however, goes farther than the disproportionality approach adopted by Central European and Russian Marxism, which we will henceforth call the *Russian current*.[1] In the latter strand, sectoral analysis matters only in so far as it highlights the separability of the elements serving as means of consumption from those serving as means for capital accumulation. Sectoral analysis does not matter, however, in relation to the specific character of capital goods, since machines can always be freely allocated between the two sectors.

Such is not the case with Lowe, where a specific machine is produced for the consumption-goods sector. The economy is, therefore, formed by a capital-goods sector producing machines for the consumption-goods sector and by a capital-goods sector producing machine tools for itself as well as for the production of the consumption-goods sector's machine.[2] Furthermore, in the system of reproduction used by the Russian current there is no complementarity between machinery and labour, not even for a limited sequence of periods. It is precisely the lack of any form of complementarity which allowed Tugan-Baranowsky to argue for a smooth increase in the number of machines operated by each worker.

The objective of the Russian current was to demonstrate that investment can be realized independently of the dynamics of consumption. In a nutshell, the reasoning put forward by the Russian current consists in assuming that whenever technical progress reduces the quantity of labour necessary to produce one unit of output, the composition of the latter will shift to the capital-goods sector exactly by the amount of productive capacity released from the consumption-goods sector.

The gist of Tugan-Baranowsky's thought can be formulated in terms of physical quantities instead of labour values. Consider a two-sector Marxian model of the following kind:

$$K_{(0)} = K_{i(0)} + K_{c(0)} \tag{10.1}$$
$$E_{(0)} = n_{i(0)} K_{i(0)} + n_{c(0)} K_{c(0)} \tag{10.2}$$
$$\lambda_{(0)} = K_{i(0)}/K_{(0)} \tag{10.3}$$
$$\alpha\lambda_{(0)} = 1 + G_{(0)} \tag{10.4}$$
$$zE_{(0)} = \gamma K_{c(0)}. \tag{10.5}$$

In the above model, equation (10.1) describes the total capital stock K at time $t_{(0)}$ as being equal to the sum of the capital stock installed in the investment- or capital-goods sector K_i and the stock installed in the consumption-goods sector K_c. Likewise, following equation (10.2), employment E is distributed between the two sectors according to the employment capacity of each machine installed in the capital-goods sector – n_i – and the corresponding employment capacity in the consumption-goods sector – n_c. Equation (10.3) defines the share λ of the stock of capital installed in the capital-goods sector over the total stock at time $t_{(0)}$. Equation (10.4) states that the growth rate of total capital G plus replacement, is equal to the output coefficient of the capital-goods sector α multiplied by the sector's share of total capital. The model assumes that capital is of a fully circulating nature. Finally, equation (10.5) describes the Marx–Robinson–Lowe condition whereby the real wage z multiplied by the level of employment E must be equal to the amount of consumption goods produced by the stock of capital installed in the consumption-goods sector. The parameter γ is, therefore, the output coefficent per machine in the consumption-goods sector.

If we assume a given real wage z, the value of λ is determined by substituting equations (10.2) and (10.3) into (10.5) and then solving for λ:

$$z(h\lambda + n_c) = \gamma(1 - \lambda), \tag{10.6}$$

where $h = (n_i - n_c)$ and

$$\lambda = (\gamma - zn_c)/(zh + \gamma). \tag{10.7}$$

Tugan-Baranowsky worked out his mechanism of boundless accumulation in terms of labour values, which imply, just like in Lowe's model, a uniform labour–machine ratio for both sectors. Hence, in our model, $h = 0$ and equation (10.7) reduces to:

$$\lambda = (\gamma - zn)/\gamma, \quad n = n_c = n_i. \tag{10.8}$$

Tugan-Baranowsky's story can be now conceptualized as follows. At time $t_{(0)}$, the economy is characterized by a distribution $\lambda_{(0)}$ of the share of the capital stock installed in the capital-goods sector. This value of λ will carry a growth rate determined by equation (10.4). With fully circulating capital, we can assume that the new machines coming into being at time $t + 1$, will have a new uniform employment coefficient of:

$$n_{(t + 1)} = n_{(0)}(1 - \varepsilon), \tag{10.9}$$

where ε is the discrete rate of automation from time (0) to time $t + 1$. From equation (10.8) we know that λ is inversely related to n, so that a fall in n will increase the new value of λ and, with it, the growth rate of capital stock. As long as labour is available there is no problem in obtaining the new value of λ. Whether or not the negative employment effect of the decline in n is offset by the positive effect caused by the growth rate of the stock of capital depends upon the value of the ratio $E_{(t+1)}/E_{(0)}$. Translated in terms of the coefficients pertaining to the stock of capital we have:

$$E_{(t + 1)} = \alpha\lambda_{(0)}K_{(0)}n_{(0)}(1 - \varepsilon).$$

Thus:

$$E_{(t + 1)}/E_{(0)} = \alpha\lambda_{(0)}(1 - \varepsilon). \tag{10.10}$$

If the value of (10.10) is unity, the decline in n will not bring about industrial unemployment because enough machines have been produced to keep everyone employed. By virtue of equation (10.8) the new value of λ will be greater than $\lambda_{(0)}$, but proportions will be maintained in such a way that no equipment remains unused. By substituting $G + 1$ into $\alpha\lambda_{(0)}$ and setting (10.10) equal to, or less than, unity, we obtain the relationship between Tugan-Baranowsky's *feasible* rate of automation and the rate of growth G:

$$\varepsilon \geq G/(1 + G). \tag{10.11}$$

In Tugan-Baranowsky's analysis, there is no reference to surplus labour originating from the hitherto non-capitalistic segments of the economy, since he considered a fully industrialized system which is encompassed by the two-sector reproduction schemata. Thus, abstracting from demographic growth, the value of ε cannot be smaller than $G/(1 + G)$. If it were so, an overproduction of machines would take place. In this context, excluding the blissful case in which the two sides of k are equal, Tugan-Baranowsky's mechanism can occur only if $\varepsilon > G/(1 + G)$. In other words, the creation of industrial unemployment allows for a reallocation of equipment towards the capital-goods sector without idling any machine. This result confirms Tugan-Baranowsky's theory, according to which the decline in consumption demand due to the fall in the level of employment is not, *per se*, a cause of economic crisis.

Yet, within the Marxian approach adopted by Tugan-Baranowsky, the creation of a reserve army of labour will have an additional effect upon the upward shift of λ because of the negative impact of unemployment on the real wage rate. Equation (10.8) shows that the rise of λ will now be determined by the fall in n and by the fall in the real wage rate z. As a consequence, the growth rate G will rise, lifting the $G/(1 + G)$ ratio relatively to ε. Unless ε increases further, and in such a way as to guarantee a persistent gap *vis-à-vis* the ratio $G/(1 + G)$, the geometric expansion of the output of machines generated by Tugan-Baranowsky's mechanism tends to bring the economy closer and closer to a crisis caused by an excessive production of machines relative to available labour, well before full automation is completed.[3] Obviously, this danger can be postponed as long as the society contains a natural economy generating an almost unlimited supply of labour.

In bringing about the possibility of a crisis generated by an overproduction of machinery relative to the employable labour force, we have moved from a Tugan-Baranowsky world, where proportionality is determined by the *value* of the flows between the capital and the consumption-goods sector, to a Lowe world, where proportionality is contingent upon the relationship between the sectoral *physical* composition of the stock of capital and the available labour force.

The only context in which the Tugan-Baranowsky process can be maintained over time is that of an economy having a virtually unlimited supply of labour so that it can move smoothly towards full automation without its hyperaccumulation being blocked by a bottleneck in the supply of workers. This is indeed quite a paradoxical outcome of Tugan-Baranowsky's theory, once looked at through Lowe's structural prism.

3   ECONOMIC MATURITY AND THE TRAVERSE

The likely outcome of the Tugan-Baranowsky process, confirms the perception about the historical evolution of capital accumulation developed by economists such as Kalecki (1976) and Kaldor (1956). For these authors, the productive capacity installed in advanced capitalist countries is such that the possibility of an overproduction of machinery dominates over the euthanasia of wage labour resulting from automation. A similar position is also to be found in Lowe's (1955, 1976) work but not as a result of a superimposed stylized fact. Lowe's model does not describe the evolution through time of economic life, say from primitive to industrial accumulation. It is, instead, concerned with the study of the process of building up and of wearing down equipment in a morphologically self-contained system. Once this system is defined as an industrial one, then the labour force cannot but work with produced capital goods. There are no other forms of material sustenance in a system so defined. Hence, if there are too many people of working age relative to the employment capacity of installed equipment, the explanation must be sought either in an exogenous influx of labour, or in a prior change in the rate of accumulation which might have led to a dearth in capital formation.

3.1   From Kalecki to Lowe

During the discussion of the Dobb–India models, to be conducted in Section 4, it will be shown how important is the maintenance of a coherent morphological structure for the study of development paths. In this section, I shall take Kalecki's approach as the starting-point of the study of the traverse. We might begin with Kalecki's definition of the *differentia specifica* between the advanced and the underdeveloped capitalist economies:

> The main problem of a developed capitalist economy is the adequacy of effective demand. Such an economy possesses a capital equipment which more or less matches the existing labour force, and therefore it could generate a rather high income per capita provided that its resources are fully utilised. (Kalecki, 1976, p. 20)

In this context, Kalecki believed that advanced capitalist economies tend to a situation of underinvestment since if 'investment falls short of savings of capitalists then a part of the product will remain unsold, and thus goods will accumulate on stock' (ibid., p. 21). Kalecki took the full-employment traverse of a socialist planned economy as an instrument with which to highlight the reasons why such a traverse would not occur in a capitalist society. In the latter, employment is seen as determined by the relationship between investment and national income. He wrote:

> During a slump the fall in investment also causes a reduction in consumption so that the fall in employment is larger than that arising directly from the curtailment of investment activity. In order to bring into focus the nature of this process in the capitalist economy it is useful to consider what the effect of a reduction in investment in a socialist economy would be. The workers released from the production of investment goods would be employed in consumption goods industries. The increased supply of these goods would be absorbed by means of a reduction in their prices. Since profits of the socialist industries would be equal to investment, prices would have to be reduced to the point where the decline in profits would be equal to the fall in the value of investment. In other words, full employment would be maintained through the reduction of prices in relations to costs. In the capitalist system, however, the price–cost relationship ... is maintained and profits fall by the same amount as investment plus capitalists' consumption through the reduction in output and employment. (Kalecki, 1971, pp. 96–7)

Kalecki did not specify, however, why investment ought to be reduced. The only rational motivation for a curtailment in investment can come from structural analysis. More specifically, the objective (that is, social) justification of such a measure must be seen in a decline in the supply of labour relative to available equipment. This hypothesis is consistent with the Kaleckian view that an advanced capitalist economy possesses a level of capital equipment which, at full capacity, can employ the whole of the working population. Under these circumstances, it is equally reasonable to assume that the productive capacity of the capital-goods sector is such that it can easily generate an amount of machines whose aggregate employment capacity exceeds the level of full employment. If those two assumptions are accepted, the socially meaningful traverse is, for an advanced industrialized economy, that of a structural adjustment following a decline in the supply of labour (Lowe, 1976, Ch. 18).

The formal structure of Lowe's theoretical apparatus enables us to say that Kalecki's full employment–full capacity 'socialist' traverse cannot, by and large, be generalized quite independently of whether or not prices are flexible in relation to costs. In particular, the economy can hardly escape the formation of unused capacity during the downward adjustment.

3.2   Lowe's Downward Traverse

Consider a simple Lowe-type model based on two capital-goods sectors and on a sector producing a single homogeneous consumption-good's sector. We then have:

$$K_{k(0)} = K_{m(0)} + K_{i(0)} \qquad (10.12)$$
$$\lambda_{(0)} = K_{m(0)}/K_{k(0)} \qquad (10.13)$$
$$\alpha\lambda_{(0)}K_{k(0)} = K_{k(0)}(G_{k(0)} + d) \qquad (10.14)$$
$$\beta(1 - \lambda_{(0)})K_{k(0)} = K_{c(0)}(G_{c(0)} + d), \qquad (10.15)$$

where K_m is the stock of capital in the machine-tool sector. This machine can either reproduce itself, or be installed in the intermediate investment sector made up by the stock K_i which, in turn, produces the specific machine for the production of consumption goods. K_c is, therefore, the stock of capital in the consumption-goods sector; α and β are the coefficients giving the output for each machine installed in the K_m and K_i sectors, respectively, and d is the given uniform rate of depreciation. The λ coefficient is the two-sector Feldman coefficient of industrialization applied to Lowe's tripartite scheme.

In contrasting Kalecki's hypothetical traverse with Lowe's actual traverse, the difference between the two approaches will hinge on the different sequential mechanisms set in motion by changing λ in equation (10.15), compared to a change in λ in equation (10.3) of the previous section where λ applies to a two-sector model.

Following Lowe's assumption that each sector has a uniform machine to labour ratio, total employment E is given by:

$$E_{(0)} = n(K_{k(0)} + K_{c(0)}) \qquad (10.16)$$

where n is the labour to machine ratio.

At full-capacity employment levels, the unit money wage multiplied by the level of employment must be equal to the value of consumption goods. Hence:

$$wE_{(0)} = p_c\gamma K_{c(0)}, \qquad (10.17)$$

where γ is the output coefficent in the consumption-goods sector, w is the money wage and p_c is the unit price of consumption goods. Setting $K_{c(0)}/K_{k(0)} = q_{(0)}$, and substituting (10.16) into (10.17) we have:[4]

$$z = \gamma q_{(0)}/(1 + q_{(0)}). \qquad (10.18)$$

where $z = w/p_c$.

With the economy ready at time $t_{(0)}$ to grow at a uniform rate, the growth of the two stocks of capital is: $G_{k(0)} = G_{c(0)} = G_{(0)}$.

At this point we can address Kalecki's description of the adjustment mechanism. He maintains that in a socialist economy the adjustment to a fall in investment would not be through the reduction of employment and output via unused capacity. Instead, workers would be moved to the consumption-goods sector and the increase output of consumption goods would be met by reducing prices relative to wages. This is, however, only a virtual not an actual traverse. Both would indeed coincide in a two-sector model. A reduction of investment would mean a fall in the λ coefficient and a rise in the proportion of investment goods allocated to the consumption-goods sector. The fall in investment will cause unused capacity in the investment-goods industries. The unused equipment, and the workers associated with it, would be transferred to the production of consumption goods since, in a two-sector model, capital goods are homogeneous. The increased output of consumption goods would then be purchased by the same number of workers earning the same money wage as before. Now, if the new value of the two-sector λ coefficient is such that the growth rate of the stock of capital is equal to that of population (and of productivity), the system would have adjusted to the new full-employment growth rate.[5]

In a Lowe context the adjustment mechanism is far more complex. To begin with, a cut in investment decisions allows a transfer of machinery only from the sector producing machine tools (primary equipment) to the secondary equipment sector producing machines for the consumption-goods industry (see equation (10.13)). This means that labour is mobile only between the two equipment sectors and not throughout the whole spectrum of the economy. As a consequence, the ratio between the stock of capital in the consumption-goods sector and the combined stock of the two equipment-producing sectors will not change simultaneously with a change in λ. In fact, at any point of time, the ratio K_c/K_k is determined by the value of λ prevailing in the previous period. From equations (10.14) and (10.15) we have:

$$q_t = [K_{c\tau}(1 - d) + \beta(1 - \lambda_\tau)K_{k\tau}]/[K_{k\tau}(\alpha\lambda_\tau - d + 1)], \qquad (10.19)$$

where $\tau = t - 1$. It follows that $q_{(0)}$ is invariant to any change in λ effectuated at time $t_{(0)}$.

A fall in the value of λ at time $t_{(0)}$ would only modify the composition of the labour force within the two equipment sectors, leaving unaltered the ratio between the labour force employed in the two capital-goods sectors and that employed in the consumption-goods sector. Thus equation (10.18) will not change in the wake of a change in λ, which means that, contrary to Kalecki's conclusion, consumption-goods prices will not change either.[6] Kalecki's reliance on the price mechanism to achieve balanced proportions under modified investment conditions does not, therefore, appear to be warranted. According to Kalecki, price flexibility ought to be a constituent element of an advanced socialist economy. He concluded his example of a reduction in investment in a socialist economy by stating that:

> It is indeed paradoxical that, while the apologists of capitalism usually consider the 'price mechanism' to be the great advantage of the capitalist system, price flexibility proves to be a characteristic feature of the socialist economy. (Kalecki, 1971, p. 97)

It is true also that in Lowe's case prices of consumption goods will have to fall in a subsequent phase, but this, too, is secondary to the structural changes which would have to be considered following a decline in the λ coefficient, which, in the three-sector model, applies only to the distribution of equipment between the two capital-goods sectors. Let us develop the argument step by step.

Assume that at time $t_{(0)}$, λ is reduced relative to the value it had at time τ. Let us call this new value λ^*. Between period $t_{(0)}$ and $t + 1$, the growth rate of the stock K_k will now be equal to $(\alpha\lambda^* - d)$ which is less than the growth rate existing between period τ and $t_{(0)}$. The growth rate of the stock of capital in the consumption-goods sector will, however, be higher than that prevailing in the previous period. The new intraperiod growth rate of K_c is given by:

$$(\beta\sigma^*/q_{(0)}) - d, \tag{10.20}$$

where $\sigma^* = (1 - \lambda^*) > \sigma_\tau$.

Equation (10.20) is derived from equations (10.15) and (10.19), the latter showing that $q_{(0)}$ is invariant to a change in λ. Hence, the growth rate of K_c will be higher relative to the period τ, the lower the value of λ^* relative to λ. Obviously, this higher growth is not permanent since the lower the value of λ, the smaller will be the difference between the output of machine tools, forming the K_k stock, and the wear and tear of K_k machines. Consequently, the sector producing secondary equipment will not be able to feed the higher growth rate of K_c in the long run. This is, however, a long-term result; in between there will be structural changes which may well alter the course of the traverse, unless they are strictly controlled by means of non-market institutional measures.

To elucidate this point, consider the case in which the fall in λ from λ_τ to λ^* has been brought about by a decision to reduce investment as a result of an estimated decline in the supply of labour. Clearly, if the new value of λ is such that the growth rate of K_k exceeds the new growth rate of the labour force, overall excess capacity will ensue. However, if the new value of λ^* is brought to the level equal to the new growth rate of labour supply, K_k will expand in line with it but, by virtue of equation (10.20), K_c would still expand at a higher rate than the supply of labour. Unused capacity becomes inevitable at this point.

What kind of unused capacity? At first glance, unused capacity would have to be wholly concentrated in the consumption-goods sector because the new value of λ has put the capital-goods sectors in a position to grow just in line with the new rate of labour supply. It follows that the capital-goods sectors will have to hire the number of workers needed to operate their machinery at full capacity, while the consumption-goods sector will have to absorb the rest. This means that the operational capital stock in the consumption-goods sector would *ipso facto* expand at the same rate as the K_k stock, which is tantamount to saying that the q ratio must become a parameter. If this rule is accepted, the economy will never be able to attain the new normal value of q which is given by equations (10.13) and (10.15):

$$q^* = \beta\sigma^*/\alpha\lambda^*. \tag{10.21}$$

The crucial problem here lies in the fact that the consumption-goods industries have to disregard all the equipment which, if fully operated, will bring the value of q to rise towards q^*. The practical, iterative, working Lowe's model implies that a reduction in the value of λ will swell the intermediate capital-goods sector K_i by an amount of machinery which will be able to produce equipment for K_c in excess of the level consistent with full employment.

In this context, the hypothesis of turning the initial value of q into a parameter is not acceptable. This is so because only at the new value q^* will the stock of capital K_i be able to supply all the replacement requirements for K_c and a net amount of machinery consistent with the new growth rate of the economy. By contrast, if, after a reduction in λ, q remains below q^*, the K_i sector will persistently produce excess capacity for the consumption-goods sector. To avoid such an outcome it is necessary to reverse the logic followed so far and consider the possibility of putting on the capital-goods sectors the whole burden of unused capacity. In this case, the main problem consists in how to distribute unused capacity between the two sectors during the traverse. Since no general rule exists *a priori*, we will present only the main outlines of two possible trajectories based on the condition that the consumption-goods sector must always be kept at full capacity. This will suffice to show how crucial is the decision concerning the sectoral distribution of unused capacity during the planned traverse. A numerical example of both trajectories is provided in the appendix to this chapter.

The first and very simple trajectory stems from fixing the value of λ at the new lower equilibrium level λ^*. The consumption-goods sector's growth rate swells, while the machine-tools sector K_m produces exactly the right amount of equipment to keep the expansion of the K_k stock in line with the new equilibrium growth rate. In this context, if the consumption-goods sector is kept at full capacity, workers will have to be withdrawn from the capital-goods sectors. The ensuing unused capacity in the capital-goods sectors will reduce the ability of the intermediate investment-goods sector to sustain the overexpansion of the stock of capital in the consumption-goods sector. In particular, if the proportion of the operational K_k stock devoted to the production of machine tools is kept at the value λ^*, the excess capacity accumulated in the capital-goods sectors is unlikely to be reabsorbed. The institutions guiding the process of adjustment will have to keep allocating the influx of machine tools coming into the K_k sector according to λ^*, regardless of the existence of unused equipment. This result is shown in Model A of the appendix. It is shown there that holding on to λ^* and keeping the consumption-goods sector at full capacity will lead, unlike the case in which unused capacity falls entirely on the consumption-goods sector, to a once-and-for-all accumulation of unwanted equipment.

The second possible trajectory is illustrated in Model B of the appendix. This assumes that, in the wake of an expected reduction in the supply of labour, the shift in the initial distribution of the K_k stock is so drastically in favour of the K_i stock that K_m is reduced to zero for a time span of two periods. This means that the wear and tear of the K_k stock at time $t_{(0)}$ cannot be replaced, while the K_c stock expands by:

$$\beta K_{k(0)}(1 - dq_{(0)}) = K_{c(t+1)} - q_{(0)}K_{k(0)} \qquad (10.22)$$

Equation (10.22) gives the maximum expansion feasible for K_c in one period. Meanwhile, the stock of capital K_k will have lost, by time $t + 1$, d per cent (10 per cent in Model B) of its effectiveness because of a zero replacement investment. Yet, the maximum expansion of the K_c stock still creates a situation in which the combined employment capacity of the economy exceeds the number of available workers. As a consequence, the consumption-goods sector can function at full capacity by drawing workers from the capital-goods sectors, thereby concentrating in the latter all the unused capacity. Since the dearth of capital in the K_k sector is allowed to continue for one more period, the further depletion of the K_k stock will require to bring back into commission part of the accumulated unused capacity. In Model B, this happens in the second period, at which point it is assumed that the operational part of the K_k stock is distributed between K_m and K_i according to the value λ^*, $1 - \lambda^*$. The example then shows that full capacity and balanced proportions are restored at the beginning of the fourth period. The difference between the first and the second trajectory lies in the fact that in the second all the intraperiod adjustments are sustained by the capital-goods sectors, which undergo, initially, a phase of depletion followed by a gradual reabsorption of unused equipment.

3.3   Lowe and Uzawa

The traverse exercise was conducted in terms of Lowe's assumption of uniform machine–labour ratios in each sector, which is also consistent with Kalecki's description of the adjustment mechanism. On this basis, the formation of unused capacity appears as an inherent characteristic of the structural traverse in a developed economy, where 'developed' means the ability of the capital-goods sectors to produce an amount of equipment in excess of full-employment requirements. Consequently, the planned distribution of unused capacity becomes inseparable from the planning of sectoral proportions. Now, from the standpoint of attaining a balanced growth path while minimizing the amount of unused capacity, the second trajectory is preferable to the first, at least if the comparison is made between Model B and Model A. The first trajectory is better than the second if consideration is taken of the necessity to store up capacity in the light of unexpected events. Finally, the imposition of the burden of unused capacity on the consumption-goods sector, which means accumulating undesired K_c equipment at a steady rate, is meaningful only if the fall in the growth rate of labour is deemed to be temporary. In this way, the accumulation of unused consumption-goods equipment will prove beneficial for absorbing workers when the supply of labour begins to rise again, Yet the crucial adjustment will depend, even in this case, on the system's capacity to liberate capital in the K_m sector.

Lowe's theory of structural changes highlights the qualitative, not quantitative, supremacy of the capital-goods sectors. The total stock of capital constitutes the engine of the system, the proportions between K_m and K_i give the direction at which the system can and should travel. The degree of unused capacity in the K_k sectors gives the degree of freedom avaible in mapping out the adjustment path (Model B) or the degree of flexibility relatively to an unforeseeable expansion in the supply of labour (Model A).

Adolph Lowe's formulations are based on the explicit assumption that the economy possesses the sectors needed to undertake a process of structural change. Thus, his approach is more oriented towards the problem of capital liberation and capital liquidation of an advanced economy. When Lowe first presented his hypotheses in the mid-1950s, there existed a number of publications which tended to emphasize some of the crucial elements of his analysis. Interestingly enough, these contributions came from different intellectual roots. Masao Fukuoka (1955), by using a Leontief model of fixed production coefficients, showed that full employment attained by means of Keynesian policies may not necessarily bring about full capacity. During the same period, an Austrian-inspired book (Lachmann, 1956), devoted entirely to the structure of capital, stressed the specificity of capital goods.

Yet, none of these works addressed the twin issues of specificity and complementarity in relation to growth conditions. The uniqueness of Lowe's approach resides in having combined the heterogeneity of the composition of capital, with complementarity and flexibility in a macroeconomic framework which, *inter alia*, is the only framework in which accumulation and growth can be analysed. During the 1960s, a number of growth models – such as Uzawa's – were developed, incorporating, implicitly, traverse-type aspects (Gandolfo, 1970; Foley and Sidrauski, 1970); but their neoclassical orientation did not allow questions to be raised which Lowe considered to be of crucial importance for the study of capital formation in advanced economies.

Model C of the appendix shows a Lowe version of the Uzawa model. It assumes the same convergence conditions of the neoclassical two-sector fixed coefficient growth model, with the difference that in Lowe they apply to the two capital-goods sectors K_m and K_i only. The absence of structural analysis surfaces, in the neoclassical case, from the fact that sectoral relations are the passive outcome of inertia: in the Lowe version of Uzawa's model, the value of λ is, period by period, determined as the solution to the allocation problem. Indeed, given the labour–machine ratios in the three sectors and given the initial stock of K_k and K_c and their respective output coefficients, the appropriate momentary equilibrium value of λ can be found for a particular growth rate of labour. Such a result requires a ranking of labour–machine ratios of the two capital-goods sectors, K_i ought to be the least labour intensive. Model C, then, shows that, within feasible values, such a ranking in intensities does lead to a steady reabsorption of the unemployment stemming from structural changes. Just the same, in our Lowe version of Uzawa's model, the value of λ has to fluctuate significantly in order for stability to be kept through time. By contrast, in the two-sector Uzawa model, once stability is attained the value of λ stabilizes as well. But the highly cyclical nature of the behaviour of λ from period to period, just to keep the system at full employment, empties Uzawa's conditions of any substantive content, even if they can be applied in a Lowe framework.

As a consequence, Lowe's procedure of treating λ as a policy, or instrumental variable, seems to determine the difference between the purely passive sectoral adjustments of an Uzawa model, where only the relative values of the coefficents matter, and the traverse conditions outlined by Lowe where the planned, thus active, determination of the value of λ defines the phases of the transitional path. The proof that, in Lowe, λ is not determined endogenously is given by the fact that uniform labour–machine ratios within the K_k sector imply a vanishing determinant of the capital-goods sector's matrix. It therefore makes perfect sense to tackle directly the issue of sectoral relations without being absorbed by the question of relative factor intensities. Furthermore, in Lowe labour–machine ratios can be uniform within the K_k sector, but they can still differ between K_k and K_c. This means that the economy is not characterized by uniform labour–machine ratios. When labour–machine ratios differ between K_k and K_c, but not within K_k, Lowe's traverse does not change analytically but only quantitatively.[7]

The emphasis put by neoclassical theorists on factor intensities, as a way to smooth out any form of Harrodian instability, explains why from the mass of the growth-theoretic literature of the postwar period, Lowe's contribution intersects directly only with Hicks's celebrated chapter on the traverse in *Capital and Growth* (Halevi, 1992b).

4   STRUCTURE AND UNDERDEVELOPMENT

A radically different situation prevailed as far as the development literature was concerned. An objective convergence towards a Lowe-type *Fragestellung* emerged from different areas of the world as shown, for instance, in Merhav's book where the theses of the Latin American School of dependency are tied to Lowe's sectoral analysis (Merhav, 1969).

It is, however, from a particular and composite developmentalist orientation that a direct analytical connection with Lowe's approach is most evident. This composite school originated largely in Great Britain and India. In Great Britain, Maurice Dobb's (1960) *Essay on Economic Growth and Planning* explicitly used Lowe's 1956 version of the three-sector model in order to discuss the problem of the choice of techniques for a development strategy constrained by a limited surplus of wage goods, as well as by an initial lack of machine tools. In India, a number of scholars (Raj and Sen, 1961; Naqvi, 1963) produced a set of models which are identical to that expressed by equations (10.12) to (10.15). Here the main difference *vis-à-vis* Lowe's approach lies in that raw materials requirements are taken into account and that machines have an infinite life.

Neither Dobb's nor the Indian models consider the question of the traverse because the economy is supposed to be dominated for a very long time by a large reservoir of labour. The sectoral allocation of machines and of labour is not, therefore, gauged on the basis of the terminal traverse, but on the basis of the growth patterns which can be obtained by allocating labour and machines to the machine-tools, intermediate investment-goods and consumption-goods sectors.

The Dobb–India models are based on the view that the growth-cum-modernization mechanism must take place according to the principle of the *accelerator in reverse*. That is, by the need to expand the production of capital goods well in advance of any market demand for them. This approach was justified by reference to a basic stylized fact, which, at that time, seemed self-evident. The structure of exports inherited from the colonial period was dominated by products having a low demand elasticity relative to income. As in the case of the Latin American school, accumulation and growth were thought to be constrained by limited foreign exchange earnings. In this way, the structural weakness of domestic capital stock was a mirror image of the qualitative inconsistency between the type of global effective demand and the need for domestic development. If these stylized facts are accepted, developing economies would face the task of giving priority to the investment sector precisely when they do not have the necessary machine tools to build it up.

Later it will be pointed out that of the two approaches to development mentioned above, the Indian one is, by far, the closest to Lowe's method of analysis. In fact Dobb's model is akin to Lowe's only in the very general description of the sectors but not in their structural specifications, or in the way the system functions.

4.1   Dobb and Lowe

Dobb's purpose was to show that a choice of technique involving a higher capital intensity in the capital-goods sectors is compatible with the maximization of the growth rate under conditions of abundant labour supply. He then proceeded to construct a model where, for a given real wage, the number of workers employable by the investment sectors is constrained by the limited surplus of wage goods. It follows that the total surplus of wage goods divided by the real wage rate determines the level of employment in the two equipment sectors.

Making the further assumption that machines do not depreciate, he then discussed the possibility that all the investment effort is put in the sector producing machines for the consumption-goods sector. Since equipment has an infinite lifetime, the growth rate of the economy is determined by pouring all the output of capital goods into the consumption-goods sector. Hence, the increments in the stock of capital for the economy as a whole take place in the consumption-goods sector. This is possible only because no machines are used to produce machines and those produced have an infinite lifetime.

From the above illustration it is evident that, conceptually, Dobb's model is only marginally related to Lowe's. For Adolph Lowe, the description of the economy in terms of equations (10.12) to (10.15) is a prerequiste for the analysis of modern production processes even when applied to development conditions. First, in Lowe, no commodity, let alone a machine, can be produced without the utilization of a stock of capital equipment. Second, production is characterized by structural lags which are also connected to the replacement requirements of the capital stock. Thus, in Lowe's approach the mechanism of productivity gains outlined by Dobb cannot take place instantaneously, nor can it be separated from the technological traverses generated by changes in production coefficients (Hagemann, 1992).

From a Lowe perspective, there is in Dobb's analysis an idealistic–romantic element expressed by the drastic hypothesis that a strategy for planned development can be conceptualized in terms of modern industrialization starting from scratch without any prior machine requirement.

4.2   Lowe and Feldman

Paradoxically, Dobb's analysis does not set a structural constraint to the production of capital goods. A completely different typology of development can be deduced from Lowe's approach. To begin with, if development means modern industrialization, then the basic structural interconnections which dominate in an advanced economy must characterize especially the capital-goods sectors of the industrializing economy. Lowe's structural approach allows for the identification of a crucial limiting condition for development called 'cannibalization' (Lowe, 1976, Ch. 16). This is nothing but the decision to forgo replacement investment, so that machine tools can be put to the exclusive function of reproducing themselves. The significance of cannibalization does not lie in its actual feasibility, but in that it sheds light on constraints arising from the capital goods themselves. It is safe to say that, had Dobb fully grasped Lowe's 1956 paper, the exceptionally fluid and unstructural choice of technique story contained in the *Essay on Economic Growth and Planning* would not have been produced. Furthermore, the cannibalization case, or maximum expansion from within, highlights an important morphological difference between Lowe's concept of structure and that of Feldman.

A central feature of Lowe's process of structural change in an upward direction is given by the conditions governing the maximum expansion from within the K_m sector.

The condition for maximum expansion from within is given by setting the value of λ in equation (10.13) equal to unity. In equation (10.22) the process of maximum expansion of the K_c stock during the downward traverse is immediately slowed down if the maximum expansion of K_c is kept for more than one period. In fact, once the K_m stock is shifted entirely towards the K_i sector, the K_i stock ceases altogether to receive replacement equipment. K_i will thus shrink in absolute terms, thereby reducing the absolute supply of machinery to the consumption-goods sector (Model B in the appendix). The limits to maximum feasible expansion of the K_c stock are, therefore, structurally determined by the lack of replacement equipment flowing to the K_i sector.

In the case of maximum expansion from within, the technical limits are not so sharply defined. The limits are first and foremost social in character. With λ set equal to unity, the K_i stock is shifted entirely to the K_m sector. K_c will no longer receive replacement equipment and it will shrink absolutely. This process is called by Lowe cannibalization of equipment. It is clear that the process can continue as long as enough force is brought to bear upon the population to make it accept a sharp reduction in real consumption. In economic terms, this also means that the state must confiscate all the (declining) surplus produced by the consumption-goods sector. That surplus is, indeed, transferred to the workers operating the K_m stock, but no goods are obtained in return. Thus, no price equation can be written for the unidirectional flow of consumption goods to the machine-tools sector, so that the transfer can be enforced only through confiscation.

Now, leaving aside the social aspect of the process, an economy which can undertake a process of cannibalization is by no means an underdeveloped one (Lowe, 1976, Ch. 16; Erlich, 1960). In other words, such an economy does possess a self-expanding core, although it may not yet be large enough to affect the whole economic stratification of the society. The 'cannibalization' perspective on industrialization brings out simultaneously the difference between Dobb and Lowe as well as that between Feldman and Lowe.

In Feldman, the degree of industrialization is defined as the ratio between the share of investment going back to the investment sector and the share going to the consumption-goods sector. Thus, an underdeveloped economy ought to be marked by a low percentage of capital goods' output reinvested into the capital-goods sector itself. Notice that this percentage is nothing but the ratio $\lambda/(1-\lambda)$ applied in a two-sector context (see equation (10.3) in Section 2). In Lowe's approach, the crucial ratio is $\lambda = K_m/K_k$, namely the proportion of machine tools which is reallocated to the production of machine tools.

The Lowe ratio is more relevant than Feldman's for reasons related to the social description of the economy. Indeed, if the rate of industrialization is conceived only in terms of the ratio between investment in the capital-goods sector and investment in the consumption-goods sector, the latter, when referred to a predominantly agrarian society, must include all types of consumption items. In a socially underdeveloped economy the consumption-goods sector may include a great number of commodities which are not produced by modern industrial means. Thus, Feldman's definition of investment in the consumption-goods sector, especially when applied to Soviet Russia of the late 1920s, *de facto* encompasses investments which do not stem from the modern industrial sectors. It is obvious, then that in such a society the share of investment going to the consumption-goods sector would appear to be disproportionately large. The Lowe model, by contrast, establishes a strict homogeneity within the industrial sector itself. The homogeneity is given by the existence of two capital-goods sectors operated by a homogeneous capital good called machine tool. The *modern* consumption-goods sector is spawned by the chosen value of the λ coefficient applied to the K_k stock, where $K_k = K_m + K_i$. It follows that the Lowe ratio, and not the Feldman ratio, is the appropriate variable for the planning of industrialization paths. An economy which cannot operate on the Lowe-based λ coefficent will not be in a position to determine any meaningful growth strategy.

4.3   Lowe and the Indian School

The Indian models of structural development due to Raj and Sen (1961) and elaborated upon by Naqvi (1963), addressed precisely this kind of question. As already noted, the models are formally close to Lowe's except for the fact that the Indian contributions contain a coefficient specifying the use of raw materials, while keeping the assumption of machines with an infinite lifetime.

As shown in Section 3 during the discussion of the downward traverse, the behaviour of the system is always determined by the particular value of

λ. This is so because the economy is supposed to be sustained by its own machine-tools sector. As in Dobb's case, the Indian approach assumes the K_m sector to be initially non-existent or negligible. Machine tools come into being through the expenditure of a given amount of foreign exchange earnings, and/or a given amount of foreign grants. In the case of the Raj and Sen contribution, the structural vacuum manifests itself through the inability to operate upon λ, so that the planning authorities can only fix the share of consumption over national income.

With a negligible K_m sector, the grant – or given amount of foreign exchange – can be used to import either I or M machines. The possibility of importing the machines constitutes the condition for an undeveloped economy to become a Lowe-type structurally advanced system. Raj and Sen did not discuss the case in which the imported M machines are used for their own reproduction. Consequently, their model does not describe a full transition to a Lowe economy.

The need to adopt a conceptually homogeneous approach to the study of industrial production and of structural transformation emerges quite vividly from Naqvi's (1963) modification of the original Raj and Sen model. Naqvi analysed the case in which the given amount of foreign exchange is allocated to the importation of M machines which can then be allocated either to produce additional M machines and/or to produce I machines, thereby leading to a gradual development of the K_m and K_i sectors. In so doing, Naqvi discovered the Lowe coefficient λ (equal to K_m/K_k) and used it as a closure of his system. As in Lowe, the higher the value of λ, the higher the long-run growth rate. Unlike Lowe, however, he stuck to the assumption of machines with an infinite lifetime, which is an absurdity especially in a developing context, where no functioning modern resources are readily available.

The Indian models assumed, quite correctly, that the economy is so poorly endowed with industrial capital stock that cannibalization of equipment is unfeasible. The maximum expansion from within can come only from using the imported M machines to produce additional M machines. In this vein, Naqvi advocated quite a high value for λ obtained by curtailing the demand for modern, non-essential, consumption goods arising from the wealthy classes. It might seem reasonable, at this point, to neglect replacement requirements, since the imported M machines are new and are used to produce additional new M machines.

Common sense, not formal modelling, suggests the opposite. A developing economy has a higher rate of replacement requirements in its nascent modern sector than a mature industrial one. For one thing, such an economy has a poor receiving infrastructure for attending to the imported machines and an equally poor transportation system. The value of λ will be constrained by the need to use part of the imported machines for the construction equipment with which to build the required infrastructure. Meanwhile, because of the underdeveloped conditions of the society, the imported machines will suffer from a rate of wear and tear much higher than that prevailing in the country which has produced them. As a consequence, the actual value of λ will in great part be tied to produce the machines necessary to replace those being scrapped.

Within the structural approach adopted here, the only way in which an economy with little modern capital equipment can sustain a process of K_m expansion is by a constant stream of imports of M machines and of the equipment needed to build the receiving infrastructure. To achieve this, either a very large amount of international public expenditure is needed and/or export markets have to be guaranteed.[8] The inability to utilize modern equipment because of structural bottlenecks in obtaining imported inputs and because of lack of proper maintenance was, indeed, a characteristic of the developing countries choosing inward-oriented industrialization. The situation has changed in the case of South-East and North-East Asian growth because the capacity to import capital goods (from Japan) has been tied to institutionally-arranged agreements concerning the capacity to export to the richer markets, especially to the United States (Lim, 1985; Woo, 1991; O'Brian, 1990; Halevi, 1993).

In conclusion, comparing the Dobb–India models to that of Adolph Lowe we can see that they are structural in form but not so much in content. In the case of Dobb (1960) the choice of technique result is obtained through the formidable assumption that machines are produced only by labour and by omiting structural discontinuities altogether (Halevi, 1987). After specifying structural relations in a consistent manner, the Raj–Sen–Naqvi models whittle them away by neglecting the socio-morphological constraints which in developing countries may lead to the simultaneous formation of a high rate of unused capacity and a high rate of decay through poor maintenance. Instead, these contributions take a romantic flight into the future by assuming that a given, once-and-for-all amount of grants, spent on the purchase of machine-tools M, can trigger the mechanism of endogenous industrialization. As will be pointed out in the concluding section, the Dobb–India approach is an expression of a specific developmentalist culture of the 1950s.

In the approach followed by Lowe, the morphological structure is homogeneous. The whole economy, and the societal relations sustaining it, is contained within the framework of the three-sector system of production. Once this framework is defined, structural relations govern each movement of the system through time. Thus, a developing economy is also subject, in its industrial component, to exactly the same structural processes as a mature one. Indeed, it is by sticking to Lowe's tight and coherent definition of structure that we were able to point out the limitations inherent in the models developed both by Dobb and by the Indian school.

5   CONCLUSIONS

In this chapter Lowe's approach has been put at the centre of the analysis of structural processes in both advanced and developing economies. As far as the former are concerned, the importance of Lowe's notion of complementarity and flexible specificity has been singled out by pointing to the limitation of Tugan-Baranowsky's theory of unlimited accumulation. Once Tugan-Baranowsky's reasoning is cast in terms of the physical conditions linking the two sectors of production, it is quite likely that his idealization of boundless growth will, sooner or later, meet the barrier represented by the degree of complementarity between workers and machines, thereby leading to an overproduction of equipment *vis-à-vis* the existing labour force. This situation has, then, been taken to represent an inherent characteristic of a developed economy.

The third section, therefore, analysed the downward traverse by using Lowe's tripartite scheme. The main lesson is that even in a planned system, it is virtually impossible to secure full capacity during the transitional phase. In this context, the need for planning emerges from the necessity to stipulate a macro-objective constituted by the idea of full employment. Planning has also been associated with the price flexibility that would be missing in a mature capitalist economy (Kalecki). The traverse section argues, however, that price flexibility is not the central factor in the adjustment process, thereby confirming Hicks's view that prices cannot give much guidance about the planning of production and about the path to equilibrium (Hicks, 1985, p. 142).

At this point we may ask why full employment should be taken as a postulated macroeconomic goal if it does not constitute a natural objective of the system. The answer to this query must be found in the specific cultural framework in which growth theories were constructed in the first two decades of the postwar period. As Pasinetti observed long ago, the analysis based on a constant reference to full employment is justified 'because full employment is the situation that matters, and that, indeed, now-a-days forms one of the agreed goals of any economic system' (Pasinetti, 1974, pp. 119–20). In the same vein, Lowe stated that 'full employment has become the universally adopted aim of public policy in mature countries' (Lowe, 1976, p. 9). Twenty years later, there is enough political evidence for doubting the contemporary validity of those statements.

Just the same, within a cultural context which assumed full employment to be the real purpose of policy-makers, Lowe has succeeded in showing that in a system deemed to be dominated by the large size and the technical specificity of inputs, problems of capital formation and of capital liquidation (the downward traverse to full employment) govern the stages of the actual adjustment path. At this point the structural characterization of the economic system raises another question related to the separation of the technical relations from the social relations of the system.

The strict distinction of the material basis from the social framework has been a main feature of Marxian-inspired structuralist approaches. From Tugan-Baranowsky, to Lenin, to Feldman and to Preobrazhenski, intersectoral quantitative relations completely dominated over the social framework. In Lowe, instead of having the former guiding the latter, the study of structural movements is accompanied by the analysis of the motorial (behavioural) factors which are bound to prevail in any particular institutional setup. This is certainly an advancement over the material determinism which has permeated Marxian economic thought. Moreover, Lowe has shown that the objective of full employment cannot be pursued in terms of aggregate demand policies but only through a structural approach. However, if full employment has ceased to be the 'agreed goal of any economic system' (Pasinetti), this was certainly due to factors connected to the social framework itself and the way in which structural transformations and social contexts mutually influenced each other. As a consequence, it seems to us impossible, today, to keep the institutional–behavioural study of the capitalist system on a separate, albeit parallel, plane from the quantitative-structural one. The need to rescue the great methodological teachings of Max Weber and of Werner Sombart – in which social stratification, political and institutional forms strictly interact with the phases of economic evolution – appears in all its importance precisely with the fading away of full employment as a guiding principle of public policy.

If in the mature economy full employment was seen to be firmly embedded in the objectives of policy-makers, in the formerly colonial areas *endogenous* developmentalism appeared to be the agreed goal of any country which achieved independence. The common element of this culture, which embraced nations comprising the vast majority of the planet's population, was the Soviet experience of industrialization. Regimes as different as those prevailing in China, India and Indonesia thought in terms of an economic takeoff based upon the severance of the colonial pattern of trade and on the priority which had to be assigned to domestic-oriented growth. The high point of this pathos was reached in

1955 at the first non-aligned nations' conference in the Indonesian city of Bandung, marked by the presence of Nehru, Chou En Lai, Sukharno, Nasser and Tito, which advocated a form of development oriented towards the expansion of the internal market.

The models produced by Dobb and the Indian school can be said to represent the political economy of the Bandung conference. They are not a replica of the Soviet model, since, unlike Feldman's, they do not posit the prior existence of a capital-goods sector. Instead, they focus on how to start a process of growth without a sizeable machine sector and without a substantial flow of foreign exchange earnings. Heavily influenced by the type of structural approach developed by Lowe, these models fail twice. On the one hand they were not capable of taking full account of the structural relations which a Lowe-type method demanded, and on the other hand they did not offer any analysis of how those societies can traverse from the previous mode of production to the new desired one.

The importance of the study of the social framework is once more highlighted by the fading of that kind of economic culture. The developmentalism of the Bandung conference certainly did not fail because this or that model was not implemented correctly. Its demise was rather due to a much more complex array of social factors pertaining to the nature of intermediate regimes in developing countries (Kalecki, 1976; Halevi, 1992b).

In the light of the foregoing observations, Adolph Lowe's coherent morphological system, although suffering from a too strict separation between the technical–structural and the socio-motorial features of modern societies, has a significant cognitive dimension in relation to those processes which ushered in the demise of the Dobb–India perception of development. The cases of Japan and of East and South-East Asia, can be taken as examples of where Lowe's methodology has cognitive validity. These, however, are not examples of endogenous developmentalism in the sense of Bandung and of the Dobb–India models, but of the formation, through capital accumulation, of structural hierarchies at the international level.

A major feature of Japan's economic expansion during the era of high-speed growth was the allocation of industrial inputs on the basic of structural priorities. Steel output, for instance, was first planned in order to provide inputs to the metal and mechanical industries; later a new plan was devised aiming at producing steel suitable to the consumption-goods industries (Kosai, 1986). Protected by a set of international institutional arrangements guaranteed by the United States (Nester, 1990), Japan developed its industrial apparatus with a relatively low share of exports over national income, hovering around 10 per cent in 1956 and 11.3 per cent in 1970. This allowed Tokyo's authorities to focus on internal accumulation, thereby developing a vast array of machine-tools industries.

In the early 1970s, with the end of accelerated domestic growth, such a situation enabled Japan to become the dominant supplier of capital goods to the rest of Asia, a phenomenon aided also by Japanese direct investment abroad. The possession by Japan of a much wider core machine-tools industry is the single most important factor in generating a persistent balance-of-payment deficit towards Tokyo by high-export performers such as South Korea, Taiwan, Thailand and Singapore, and, more recently, China. The particular role acquired by Japan through its machine-tools sector in providing basic commodities to the region's industries is demonstrated also by the fact that Asia has become the largest source of Tokyo's balance-of-payment surpluses.

The analytical understanding of this historical development, truly the most significant in the evolution of capitalist formations during the present century, does demand a conceptualization of production *à la* Lowe where a strategic sector, the machine-tool one, determines the transition between different growth paths. In this sense, Lowe's traverse analysis represents the didactical exercise which enables the reader to grasp the structural roots of hierarchical relations.

NOTES

1. The analysis of accumulation and consumption in terms of Marx's two-sector scheme influenced first Germany's and then Austria's Social Democrats, beginning with Karl Kautsky and ending (tragically) with Rudolf Hilferding. Yet, in Tsarist Russia and in its empire, it gave rise to a veritable school of thought represented by Bulgakov, Tugan-Baranowsky and Lenin. The last of the disproportionality crisis theorists was Preobrazhenski, who published a formidable piece in Moscow by the end of the 1920s (Preobrazhenski, 1985).
2. This tripartite characterization of production is not alien to the *Russian current*, either. Lenin used it for descriptive purposes to argue against the *Narodniki*, that the impoverishment of the proletariat was not a symptom of crisis but an integral part of the capitalistic transformation occurring in Tsarist Russia (Lenin, 1893; Halevi, 1992a).
3. The above is nothing but a formalization and an adaptation to Tugan-Baranowsky's case of a verbal argument developed by Kaldor in 1938 on the basis of a two-sector model. Kaldor argued that even with technical progress, an economy producing at full capacity can hardly escape the possibility of investment crisis due to an overproduction of equipment (Kaldor, 1938).
4. The value of q represents the ratio between two heterogeneous stocks: the number of machines K_c already installed in the consumption-goods sector and the number of machines installed in the two capital-goods sectors. This is a perfectly meaningful ratio. If the number of machines in the consumption-goods sector is known and if β, α and d are also known we can determine the size of K_i and K_m necessary to keep the system in a stationary state.
5. A numerical example will help clarify Kalecki's reasoning. Assume a two-sector model where 80 machines are installed in the consumption-goods sector and 20 in the capital-goods one. Each machine employs one worker and the rate of depreciation is 10 per cent. Each machine in the capital-goods sector produces one machine. Thus, with $\lambda = 0.2$, the growth rate of capital stock is 10 per cent. Assume now that investment decisions in the capital-

goods sector are such that only 15 machines are used. According to Kalecki's argument, the remaining five machines, and their related workers, ought to be transferred to the consumption-goods sector. It follows that the new value of λ will be 0.15. The growth rate of capital will then be 5 per cent. At the beginning of the new period, the total stock of machines will be made up of 105 units. If, meanwhile, the labour force has also grown by 5 per cent, and this rate is expected to continue for some time, the economy will be on a new full-employment growth path, provided λ remains at 0.15. This outcome is possible only because, as in Lowe's approach, each machine employs the same number of workers irrespective of its sectoral allocation. Assume now that a unit of equipment in the capital-goods sector employs one worker, but that two workers are employed by the machine installed in the consumption-goods industry (this is just a paradox, since if machines are homogeneous, it stands to reason to assume that they have the same degree of complementarity regardless of the sector where they are installed). In this case, the transfer of five machines to the consumption-goods sector would lead to a shortage of labour, engendering unused capacity there. By contrast, if the machine in the capital-goods sector were to employ two workers and that of the consumption-goods sector only one worker, the transfer would involve full capacity and unemployment because of insufficient equipment in the consumption-goods sector.

6. Kalecki's argument applies only to a two-sector model with uniform machine to labour ratios.
7. We will use Model (10.12) to (10.16), but with different labour–machine ratios, to prove our point. In this case equation (10.16) becomes:

$$E_{(0)} = [(n_m - n_i)\lambda_{(0)} + n_i]K_{k(0)} + n_c q_{(0)} K_{k(0)}, \quad \text{call: } n_m - n_i = h. \quad (10.\text{A})$$

Assume that from $t_{(0)}$ to $t + 1$ the labour force has grown by a rate g, less than the previous own growth rate and less than the growth rate of capital $\alpha\lambda_{(0)} - d = G$. For full employment to be maintained we have from (10.A):

$$E_{(t+1)} = E_{(0)}(1+g) = (1+g)[(h\lambda_{(0)} + n_i) + q_{(0)} n_c]K_{k(0)}. \quad (10.\text{B})$$

This equation expresses the available supply of labour at time $t + 1$ in terms of the stock of capital at $t_{(0)}$ multiplied by the rate of growth g of labour. Now, by time $t + 1$ total equipment would have grown by $G > g$. Hence:

$$K_{k(t+1)} = K_{k(0)}(1 + G), \quad K_{c(t+1)} = K_{k(0)}q_{(0)}(1 + G), \quad (10.\text{C})$$

adding up gives:

$$K_{k(t+1)} = K_{k(0)}(1 + G)(1 + q_{(0)}) \quad (10.\text{D})$$

The expression in bold in (10.D), must fetch the quantity of workers resulting from the expression in bold in equation (10.B). Thus, writing Φ for the bold part of (10.B), we have:

$$\Phi = K_{k(0)}(h\lambda_{(t+1)} + n_i + q_{(0)}n_c)(1 + G), \text{ call the right-hand side of (10.E), } \Omega. \quad (10.\text{E})$$

In Lowe, as shown in Model (10.12) to (10.16) in the text, the possibility for changing q when the growth rate of labour changes depends on the ability to change λ. Thus $\lambda_{(t+1)}$ is the unknown to be found. Endogenously this can happen only if h is positive or negative. An Uzawa result requires a positive h. If h is zero, the value of $\lambda_{(t+1)}$ cannot be found by equating Φ with Ω. In fact, with $h = 0$, λ vanishes in both Φ and Ω, yet the coefficient n_c is still different from the uniform labour–machine coefficient of the K_k sector.

8. Little attention has been paid to the fact that the industrialization of South Korea in the 1960s was indeed based on the priority given to heavy industry sustained by very particular conditions heavily determined by American international public expenditure. On the financial plane, its external debt was absorbed by the United States; US expenditure during the Vietnam War generated military procurements directly and exports indirectly, through US aid to South Vietnam. Throughout the 1960s more than 90 per cent of the steel and more than 50 per cent of the transportation equipment exported by South Korea was shipped to South Vietnam (Halevi, 1993; Woo, 1991).

REFERENCES

Bhaduri, A. (1973), 'A Study of agricultural backwardness under semi-feudalism', *Economic Journal*, **83**, March, pp. 120–37.

Colletti, L. and C. Napoleoni (1975), *Il marxismo e il crollo del capitalismo*, Rome: Laterza.

Dobb, M. (1960), *An Essay on Economic Growth and Planning*, London: Routledge and Kegan Paul.

Erlich, A. (1960), *The Soviet Industrialization Debate*, Cambridge, Mass.: Harvard University Press.

Foley, D. and M. Sidrauski (1970), *Monetary and Fiscal Policy in a Growing Economy*, London: Macmillan.

Fukuoka, M. (1955), 'Full employment and constant coefficients of production', *Quarterly Journal of Economics*, **69**, pp. 23–44.

Gandolfo, G. (1970), *Mathematical Methods and Models in Economic Dynamics*, Amsterdam: North-Holland.

Hagemann, H. (1992), 'Traverse analysis in a post-classical model' in J. Halevi, D. Laibman and E. J. Nell (eds), *Beyond the Steady State. A Revival of Growth Theory*, London: Macmillan, pp. 235–63.

Halevi, J. (1987), 'Investment planning', in J. Eatwell, M. Milgate and P. Newman (eds.), *The New Palgrave. A Dictionary of Economics*, London: Macmillan, Vol. 2, pp. 994–7.

Halevi, J. (1992a), 'Accumulation and structural disequilibrium', in J. Halevi, D. Laibman and E. J. Nell (eds), *Beyond the Steady State. A Revival of Growth Theory*, London: Macmillan, pp. 264–88.

Halevi, J. (1992b), 'Asian capitalist accumulation: from sectoral to vertical integration', *Journal of Contemporary Asia*, **22** (4), pp. 444–70.

Halevi, J. (1993), 'Croissance Asiatique et demande effective' (Asian growth and effective demand), *Revue Tiers Monde*, **34** (135), pp. 531–43.

Hicks, J. (1985), *Methods of Dynamic Economics*, Oxford: Clarendon Press.

Kaldor, N. (1938), 'Stability and full employment', in N. Kaldor (ed.), *Essays on Economic Stability and Growth*, London: Duckworth, 1960, pp. 103–19.

Kaldor, N. (1956), 'Alternative theories of distribution', *Review of Economic Studies*, **23**, pp. 83–100.

Kalecki, M. (1971), *Selected Essays on the Dynamics of the Capitalist Economy*, Cambridge: Cambridge University Press.

Kalecki, M. (1976), *Essays on Developing Economies*, Hassocks: Harvester Press.

Kosai, Y. (1986), *The Era of High Speed Growth*, Tokyo: Tokyo University Press.

Lachmann, L. (1956), *Capital and its Structure*, London: London School of Economics and Political Science.

Lenin, V. (1893), 'On the so-called market question', in *Collected Works*, Vol. 1, Moscow: Progress Publishers, 1968.

Lim, H. (1985), *Dependent Development in Korea*, Seoul: Seoul National University Press.

Lowe, A. (1955), 'Structural analysis of real capital formation', in M. Abramovitz (ed.), *Capital Formation and Economic Growth*, Princeton: Princeton University Press, pp. 60–106.

Lowe, A. (1976), *The Path of Economic Growth*, Cambridge: Cambridge University Press.

Merhav, M. (1969), *Technological Dependence, Monopoly and Growth*, New York: Pergamon.

Naqvi, K.N. (1963), 'Machine tools and machines. A physical interpretation of the marginal rate of saving', *Indian Economic Review*, **6**, February, pp. 19–28.

Nester, W. (1990), *Japan's Growing Power over East Asia. Ends and Means*, London: Macmillan.

O'Brian, L. (1990), 'Indices of industrialization: capital goods production in Malaysia', *Journal of Contemporary Asia*, **20** (4), pp. 509–21.

Pasinetti, L. (1974), *Essays on Growth and Income Distribution*, Cambridge: Cambridge University Press.

Patnaik, P. (1972), 'Disproportionality crisis and cyclical growth – a theoretical note', *Economic and Political Weekly*, **7**, Annual Number, February, pp. 329–36.

Preobrazhenski, E. (1985), *The Crisis of Capitalism*, Armonk, NY: Sharpe.

Raj, K.N. and Sen, A.K. (1961), 'Alternative patterns of growth under conditions of stagnant exports earnings', *Oxford Economic Papers*, **13**, February, pp. 43–52.

Woo, J. (1991), *Race to the Swift. State and Finance in Korean Industrialization*, New York: Columbia University Press.

APPENDIX

Models A and B

Assume a Lowe system which at time $t_{(0)}$ is characterized by 400 machines in the consumption-goods sector and by 100 machines in the K_k sectors capable of reproducing one machine each. Assume also a rate of depreciation of 10 per cent and a uniform machine to labour ratio of one. Total employment will be 500 persons. Consider now the case that from any period leading up to $t_{(0)}$ the system was growing at a rate of 10 per cent annually. If this rate were to last, the stock of 100 machines in the K_k sector would have to be distributed in a proportion of 0.2 to the K_m sector and of 0.8 to the K_i sector. But, assume that at time $t_{(0)}$ information is obtained that the growth rate of labour declines from $t_{(0)}$ onwards from 10 per cent to 5 per cent per annum. We then have from equation (10.21) the new value of q $= q^* = \beta\sigma^*/\alpha\lambda^* = (1 - 0.15)/0.15$. The economy will now traverse towards this ratio on the basis of the following strategy: all the capital goods in the consumption-goods sector are kept fully utilized, at $t_{(0)}$ the K_m machines are shifted towards the K_i sector so as to raise the latter to 0.85 of the total K_k stock. This case corresponds to Model A; whereas if it is assumed that all the K_m stock is shifted for two periods to the K_i sector, we obtain Model B. In both instances, the output–capital ratio in the K_m and the K_i sectors is one and the rate of depreciation d is equal to 10 per cent. E is employment and n is the uniform labour–machine ratio.

Table 10A.1 The traverse in the Lowe model

	Model A periods			Model B periods			
	$t_{(0)}$	$t + 1$	$t + 2$	$t_{(0)}$	$t + 1$	$t + 2$	$t + 3$
E	500	525	551	500	525	551	579
K_m	15	$\lambda*80$	$\lambda*83$	0	0	11	13
K_i	85	$\sigma*80$	$\sigma*83$	100	65	61	74
K_c	400	445	468	400	460	479	492
Unused equipment	0	25	26	0	25	11	5

Notes: $\lambda^* = 0.15$; $\sigma^* = 0.85$; $n = 1$; $(\alpha, \beta) = 1$; $d = 10$ per cent; growth of E is 5 per cent from $t_{(0)}$.

The numerical example in Model A shows that by distributing at time $t_{(0)}$ the K_m and K_i components of the K_k stock according to the new estimated growth rate of employable population E, the system will pile up a given quantity of K_k equipment without being capable of reabsorbing it. In Model

B, after withdrawing the stock of machines from K_m altogether for two periods, the system is capable of reabsorbing virtually all the unused equipment within three periods.

Model C

A third model, Model C, can be labelled neoclassical because it is based on the same assumption as Uzawa's famous two-sector model. In order to obtain convergence in the neoclassical two-sector model it is necessary that the capital-goods sector be more labour intensive than the consumption-goods sector. In a Lowe context, this assumption requires that the intermediate investment sector K_i be more capital intensive. Furthermore, the higher the degree of automation in the consumption-goods sector the better, precisely because the capital goods installed in it are heterogeneous. Thus, we built a Lowe–Uzawa model in which, as in A and B, there are 500 machines of which: 400 are in the consumption-goods sector each employing one worker, 80 are in the K_i sector employing two workers each, and 20 are in the K_m sector employing three workers each. All the other parameters, α, β, d and the new growth rate of E are the same as in Models A and B. However, the neoclassical modification of Lowe's model does not yield the same results as Uzawa's. In the Uzawa model, whenever there is a disequilibrium between equipment and labour, the homogeneity of capital allows for a reshuffling of the stock according to relative factor intensities. This is not possible in a Lowe model, where the capital goods produced by the intermediate sector K_i cannot be shuffled around. Thus, even the neoclassical Lowe economy has to anticipate in advance the fall in the supply of labour. Model C assumes that the economy begins its adjustment at $t_{(0)}$, that is one period before the fall in the growth rate of E shows up. We start with the assumption that all the K_m stock is shifted to the K_i sector, which will initially create unemployment because of the lower labour–machine ratio in the K_i sector. This unemployment is of no consequence for the structural evolution of the model. Call n_m, n_i, n_c the employment capacity of one machine installed in the K_m, K_i and consumption-goods, K_c, sectors, respectively. We then have: $n_m = 3$, $n_i = 2$, $n_c = 1$; furthermore the economy arrives at $t_{(0)}$ with 620 workers, the latter being the expression of a previous growth rate of 10 per cent. The adjustment to 5 per cent is as follows.

Table 10A.2 The traverse in the Uzawa–Lowe model

Model C Uzawa + Lowe		periods			
		$t_{(0)}$	$t+1$	$t+2$	$t+3$
L = labour force	L	620	651	683	718
$E_m = n_m K_m$	K_m	0	11	6	10
$E_i = n_i K_i$	K_i	100	79	86	79
$E_c = n_c K_c$	K_c	400	460	493	530
$L - \Sigma E$ = unemployment	U	20	0	0	0

In this model, unlike Models A and B, the value of λ emerges, from period to period, as the solution to the allocation of capital goods and it is determined in each period as follows. For full employment to be attained, it is necessary that once workers have been allocated to operate the specific machine of the consumption-goods sector, the rest will find jobs in the two capital-goods sectors:

$$L - E_c = E_m + E_i = E_k \quad (10A.1a) \qquad E_k \le (L - E_c), \qquad (10A.1b)$$

where L is total labour force.

$$E_k = [(n_m - n_i)\lambda + n_i]K_k \qquad (10.A.2)$$

$$h = n_m - n_i. \qquad (10.A.3)$$

Substituting (10A.2) and (10A.3) into (10A.1) and solving for λ, we obtain:

$$\lambda = (L - E_c - n_i K_k)/ hK_k. \qquad (10.A.4)$$

In (10A.4), L is known as well as E_c and K_k. In a Lowe framework, E_c and K_k are determined by the stocks existing in the previous period. Thus, given n_C employment in the consumption-goods sector, E_c, is determined by the total amount of K_c in the previous period less its own wear and tear plus the amount of equipment produced by the K_i sector of the previous period. Likewise, today's K_k is equal to the previous period's K_k plus the output of the previous period's K_m less the wear and tear of the previous period's K_k.

If in the Uzawa version of Lowe's model λ comes out as the solution to the allocation problem, its value is likely to fluctuate heavily. This can be checked by extending the above numerical example over many periods, while keeping the growth rate of labour at 5 per cent. To attain an Uzawa solution such an economy will have to be hyper-planned, since it will not be able to sustain a high rate of fluctuation in the value of λ and yet remain stable. In this context it seems better to stick to Lowe's assumption of uniform labour–machine ratios which implies that λ is a strategic variable. In fact, in Models A and B, λ does not emerge as the solution, the new growth rate and the coefficients of production give us the new terminal value of λ. Its attainment is determined simply by weighing different possible adjustment paths, as shown in Model A and Model B.

11. Hierarchy of Production Activities and Decomposition of Structural Change: An Essay in the Theory of Economic History

Roberto Scazzieri

1   INTRODUCTION

The relationship between history and theory is still one of the 'unsettled questions' of political economy. The pre-classical attention for the historical framework of civil society (see Ferguson, 1767; Steuart, 1767) was gradually superseded by the identification of economic laws to be derived on the basis of particular characterizing assumptions (see Smith, 1776; Say, 1803; Ricardo, 1817; Mill, 1848), and quite independently of a direct consideration of processes of historical change.[1]

Later contributions have emphasized either the axiomatic structure of economic reasoning, or the consideration of historical and institutional features. The analytical integration between economic theory and economic history has seldom been a central theme of investigation. Adolph Lowe has been, with John Hicks, one of the few modern scholars who have attempted the construction of a theory of economic history, in the sense of a coherent set of abstract propositions regulating the utilization of economic theories in the explanation of historical processes.

The purpose of this chapter is to take up a number of themes connected with Lowe's work and to develop a conceptual framework useful in assessing, from a theoretical point of view, historical processes that may influence the organization and dynamics of production phenomena.

Section 2 discusses the concept of 'form of production organization' and the multiple roots of dynamic processes affecting the network of production activities.

Section 3 emphasizes the need to identify the 'hidden hierarchy' associated with any given form of production organization, and introduces the connection between the hierarchy within any given production network and the 'hidden organization' of structural change over time.

Section 4 develops the latter theme by discussing the different decompositions of economic dynamics that may be associated with alternative hierarchies of organizational layers within any given form of production organization. Here, the issue of the speed of structural change is considered, and different speeds are associated with different 'dominant layers' within productive organizations.

Section 5 introduces the discussion of qualitative structural change and outlines its analytical treatment by means of a suitable decomposition of production techniques. Section 6 draws the chapter to a close by considering a number of themes pertaining to the relationship between economic theory and economic history. Here, special emphasis is laid upon the relationship between the hierarchical structure of production organizations and the specific historical form that a process of structural change may take in terms of shift in dynamic poles and temporal lags.

2   ECONOMIC HISTORY AND CHANGING FORMS OF PRODUCTION ORGANIZATION

A form of production organization may be considered as a relatively permanent set of coordination devices by which the different dimensions of productive activities become consistent with each other from an organizational point of view (see Landesmann and Scazzieri, 1996a). The historical evolution of productive structures may be analytically reconstructed as the evolution of forms of productive organization, quite independently of the technical devices that provide the material basis of productive units (establishments, establishment networks, industries). (See also Hagemann and Landesmann, 1991.)

Industrial organization may thus be considered as a field in which technological evolution interacts with established or emergent practices and moulds historical dynamics in terms of discontinuous jumps (see, for example, Unwin, 1904).

A first approximation to the analysis of the historical evolution of productive organizations suggests that the *continuum* of organizational changes is punctuated by a relatively small number of cases in which there is a real switch from one form of production organization to another. It may be useful to distinguish between pure and mixed forms of production organization. The former directly reflect a given organizational logic, such as the job-shop and the straight-line models of organization.[2] The latter may be a combination of pure forms according to a variety of coordination devices, such as those underlying the putting-out system or the new forms of manufacturing organization (just-in-time production and flexible manufacturing systems) (see also Landesmann and Scazzieri, 1996a).

Any given form of production organization may be considered as a set of coordination devices ensuring some degree of coherence between the three fundamental levels of operation of a production process, that is, tasks, agents' capabilities and materials-in-process (see Scazzieri, 1993; Landesmann and Scazzieri, 1996a). Each level of the production process is associated with a specific set of coordination devices, and the general coherence between different levels is normally achieved by means of an adjustment process that runs through a sequence of stages. First, change takes place at the level in which adjustment is easier, then more rigid constraints will also be removed until the previous organizational structure is completely adjusted to a new set of parameters.

Different forms of production organization may be associated with different constraints, and different time sequences according to which of these constraints may become binding. For example, artisan production following the job-shop organizational logic tends to be flexible in the product mix and in the relative size of each product lot, but relatively rigid in the capabilities to be used and the tasks to be executed. On the other hand, modern factory production in its classical form is associated with a rigid sequencing of fabrication stages over time, whereas capabilities may be flexible and any given task may, in principle, be associated with a variety of elementary processes.

The organization of production processes entails a hidden organization of structural change over time. For the coexistence, within any given organization, of rigid and flexible ties generally makes structural transformation a *process* requiring that certain fabrication stages be modified before other stages can adjust. Structural change cannot be instantaneous if production processes entail a complex hierarchy of relative motions. The analytical decomposition of economic structure (and of the productive structure in particular) shows that structural change is a historical process and that context may influence economic dynamics by modifying the locus of change and the speed of transformation.

3   HIERARCHICAL REPRESENTATIONS OF PRODUCTIVE STRUCTURE

The analytical representation of the production process considered in this chapter distinguishes between three fundamental levels of description: tasks, agents' capabilities and flows of materials-in-process.

Each level corresponds to a particular pattern of interdependencies. Any historical form of production organization generally entails a definite hierarchy of these levels according to strong or weak structural ties (see

Granovetter, 1973). Strong structural ties determine the locus of binding organizational constraints; weak structural ties determine the locus of higher flexibility and thus the dimension at which structural change is most likely to occur.

A simple formalization of hierarchies within a productive structure may be based upon the consideration of pairwise combinations of primitive elements of the production process at the level of tasks, capabilities and materials-in-process.

Let us consider first the relationship between capabilities and tasks. Given the set of capabilities embedded into existing agents (such as human beings and machines) and the set of tasks that may be associated with them, capability relationships may be represented as follows:

$$
C = \begin{bmatrix}
c_{(a,a)} & c_{(a,b)} & \cdots & c_{(a,r)} \\
c_{(b,a)} & c_{(b,b)} & \cdots & c_{(b,r)} \\
\vdots & \vdots & & \vdots \\
c_{(r,a)} & c_{(r,b)} & \cdots & c_{(r,r)}
\end{bmatrix}
$$

Matrix $\mathbf{C} \equiv [c_{ij}]$ describes the capability space in which the various agents may be identified as pools of capabilities. Any *task–capability relationship* c_{ij} denotes that task j may be executed by means of capability i. Any column of $\mathbf{C}$ shows the composition of the set of capabilities by which a certain task may be executed. Any row of $\mathbf{C}$ shows the number and types of tasks that a given capability is able to execute.

Hierarchical, one-way relationships between capabilities and tasks may be introduced as a result of the fact that semi-independent subsets of capability relationships may be distinguished from one another:

$$
\mathbf{C} = \begin{bmatrix}
\mathbf{C}_{gg} & 0 & 0 & 0 & \cdots & \mathbf{C} \\
0 & \mathbf{C}_{kk} & 0 & 0 & \cdots & \mathbf{C} \\
0 & 0 & \mathbf{C}_{ii} & 0 & \cdots & \mathbf{C} \\
0 & 0 & 0 & \mathbf{C}_{pp} & & \mathbf{C} \\
0 & 0 & 0 & 0 & 0 & \mathbf{C}
\end{bmatrix}
$$

Each element of matrix $\mathbf{C}$ is a 'capability subset', which includes the capabilities required in executing only a limited number of tasks and delivered by some agents only. For example, subset $\mathbf{C}_{gg}$ includes tasks that cannot be performed by capabilities $g+1$, ..., r. On the other hand, no capability belonging to subset $\mathbf{C}_{gg}$ is required to execute the tasks $g+1$, ..., *r*. It is reasonable to assume that matrix **C** is incompletely decomposable. This implies that there will be 'universal' agents (that is, agents not specific to particular task groups, such as labour), and that certain 'general tasks' will also be associated with specialized subsets of capabilities.

Each capability subset could be interpreted as a cluster of capabilities whose performance is relatively independent of other skills within the capability space. We may assume that a certain degree of operational independence is always associated with the existence of separate 'agents' (that is, of clearly distinguishable capability clusters). In this way, the identity of any given agent would always be associated with some degree of operational complementarity, which could show itself either directly (as with the joint performance of capabilities) or indirectly (as when the non-performance of a given capability makes performance of another capability possible).

In a similar way, we may identify hierarchical relationships between capabilities and materials. In this case, our starting-point may be the general representation of capability–material relationships provided by matrix **R** below:

$$\mathbf{R} = \begin{bmatrix} r_{11} & r_{12} & \cdots & r_{1k} \\ r_{21} & r_{22} & \cdots & r_{2k} \\ \vdots & \vdots & & \vdots \\ r_{n1} & r_{n2} & \cdots & r_{nk} \end{bmatrix}$$

Matrix $\mathbf{R} \equiv [r_{ij}]$ describes a transformation space in which the different capability–material relationships (each one corresponding to a particular element r_{ij}) may be so rearranged as to form 'blocks' of relationships in which any given element is always on the 'active' side of the relationship (that is, always a capability and never a passive material), except if another element *of its own group* is on the active side.

After such a rearrangement, matrix **R** would look like the one below:

$$\begin{bmatrix} \mathbf{R}_{gg} & 0 & \mathbf{R}_{gk} \\ 0 & \mathbf{R}_{hh} & \mathbf{R}_{hk} \\ 0 & 0 & \mathbf{R}_{kk} \end{bmatrix}$$

We may note that submatrices $\mathbf{R}_{gg}$, $\mathbf{R}_{hh}$ and $\mathbf{R}_{kk}$ contain 'symmetrical' relationships between productive elements of type G, H and K, respectively (so that any given element may appear both on the active and on the passive side).

On the other hand, submatrices $\mathbf{R}_{gk}$ and $\mathbf{R}_{hk}$ contain 'asymmetrical' relationships in which elements belonging to categories G and H, respectively, are 'original' productive funds (they are never 'acted upon' except by elements of their own group).

It is worth noting that the existence of 'original' productive elements (that may be identified from matrix $\mathbf{R}$) is associated with the same mathematical feature that reflects the existence of 'universal' agents in the structure of matrix $\mathbf{C}$. In both cases, incomplete matrix decomposability is associated with the identification of a hierarchical structure within the productive system.

Each submatrix of $\mathbf{R}$ could in this case be interpreted as a 'transformation subset', that is as a cluster of productive transformations whose realization is relatively independent of other capabilities and materials within the overall transformation space $\mathbf{R}$. Clearly distinguishable transformation subsets presuppose the existence of separate 'productive funds', that is, some degree of technological complementarity, which could operate either directly (joint utilization of materials in different transformation processes, as with the standard case of mutton and wool), or indirectly (when the non-utilization of a given material in a certain transformation process makes another transformation process feasible).

The organization of production activities on the basis of primitive elements such as capabilities, tasks and materials leads to productive structures centred upon the relationship between *agents* and *productive funds*. In both cases (agents and funds) capabilities are essential. However, the identity of funds has a material side that is often more binding than the operational side constraining the identity of agents (see above). This suggests that agents (identified by a set of task–capability relationships) may often be a source of flexibility, whereas productive funds (identified by a set of material–capability relationships) are often at the root of rigidities and constrained structural change.

Hierarchies may be identified at each organizational level and across different levels of organization.

In the former case, a hierarchy may be detected by means of a rearrangement of the rows and columns of the appropriate matrix in order to single out semi-independent blocks of relationships. The hierarchical arrangement of these blocks would suggest the existence of hierarchies among tasks, capabilities or materials-in-process. However, such hierarchies would essentially be of a 'logical' type, in the sense that they would be associated with the individual characteristics of tasks, rather than with a descriptive account of the relationship *between* different elements of any given production process.

The identification of hierarchies across different organizational levels, on the other hand, is based upon a descriptive rather than a logical criterion. That is to say, the 'primacy' of certain organizational levels may be derived from factual and statistical material reflecting the historical features of any given form of production organization.

The actual course of structural change generally shows a combination of causation due to historically specific constraints and causation due to the 'internal logic' of any given set of productive relationships.

4 DECOMPOSITION OF ECONOMIC DYNAMICS AND THE SPEED OF TRANSITION

The overall dynamics of any given economic system result from a multiplicity of forces and impulses that interact one upon the other, as well as with the existing structure of the economic system.

Specification of the behavioural and material structure of the economic system is an essential logical step in the analysis of its dynamics. In particular, the specification of the temporal characteristics of economic linkages is a necessary condition of the identification of a 'dynamic structure', that is, of a space of virtual (feasible) transformations in which the different economic magnitudes may be related to one another by a ranking of relative motions (see also Landesmann and Scazzieri, 1990, pp. 96–7).

The hidden hierarchy of any historical form of production organization (see above) entails that a particular dynamic structure is embedded in each productive setup. The time sequencing of structural change reflects the ranking of motions associated with any given structure: weak ties are generally superseded more easily and rapidly than strong linkages. As a result, the organizational features of a productive system suggest the way in which such a system may be affected by structural change in the course of historical time.

Decomposition of economic structure is a necessary condition for the identification of the dynamic potential of any given economic system. And decomposition of higher degree is associated with a better identification of the ranking of relative motions that influences the resilience or flexibility of any given economic setup. The fine structure of economic dynamics may be better identified if economic magnitudes are decomposed into a sufficiently high number of 'primitive' components, for in this case the ranking of relative motions will be more complete, and the analytical process nearer to the historical one.

The above argument entails that the speed of transition of any given economic system from an initial to a terminal state may depend in a critical way upon the hidden hierarchy existing among the different components of the system. In particular, a ranking of relative motions characterized by a limited number of precedence relations is likely to lead to a higher speed of transition than a ranking in which many different motions are related to each other by a precedence relation.

The hierarchical structure of any given economic system is thus inherently connected to its dynamic behaviour, and the degree to which such a system undertakes structural change reflects the *relative* resilience of its component parts.

An economic system in which relative motions (that is, motions of certain parts with respect to others) are excluded is either a stationary system or a system in which motion leaves the structure unchanged. On the other hand, a system in which relative motions are possible lends itself to various patterns of structural change.

We may define a historical process of structural change as a process in which the relative motion of certain subsystems takes place, so that their relative growth (or decline) may be modified. This implies that the same principles explaining structural change are also at the basis of the speed at which an economic system undergoes a transformation. For relative motion introduces a hierarchy between subsystems; and an impulse (or a dynamic force) affecting a subsystem that cannot move alone is likely to induce a slow transition process. On the other hand, relatively independent subsystems may be the locus of more rapid processes of transformation.

The specification of structural change in terms of relative motion makes dynamic decoupling an essential factor in explaining the relative speed at which economic systems undergo changes of structure.

5   'EMERGENT STRUCTURES' AND THE SHIFT OF DYNAMIC POLES

Economic history, if considered from an analytical point of view, offers a rich opportunity to blend conceptual tools and *ad hoc* interpretative judgement.

Adolph Lowe has been, with John Hicks, one of the twentieth-century economists most acutely aware of the need to address economic history with appropriate analytical tools and appropriate methodology.

Lowe developed to this purpose his 'instrumental' approach to economic analysis, which is based upon the identification of fictive (but realistic) states of the world, and attempts to build from them a picture of feasible dynamics. An early presentation of the instrumental approach may be found in Lowe's *Economics and Sociology* lectures (originally delivered at the London School of Economics):

> [the instrumentalistic approach] picks out imaginable constellations of data and deduces therefrom movements and states of rest under varying hypotheses. Any such constellation implies a set of sociological premises. But the conditions of the origin and persistence of these constellations are intentionally disregarded, and equally their connection with the system as a whole and any influences which might arise from outside the particular set of data under consideration ... We call [this method] instrumentalistic, because it does not directly depict real structure, but tries to build up possible types of market order by pursuing individual movements under the assumption of a typical constellation of the whole. (Lowe, 1935, p. 140).

More recently, Lowe has introduced a distinction between the technological level and the institutional level of economic analysis. At the technological level, the instrumental approach identifies the conditions that must be satisfied 'if the transformation of the initial into the stipulated terminal state is to be achieved' (Lowe, 1976, p. 17). At the institutional level, the same approach allows for the analysis of the *plurality* of behavioural and motivational setups that may be consistent with the transition from one dynamic equilibrium to another. And alternative historical setups may entail transitional paths very different from each other: '[o]ne path maximizes speed of adjustment, another minimizes waste of resources, and a third minimizes the impact on consumption during the interval of capital formation' (ibid, p. 106).

Economic history is considered by Lowe essentially as a field for conceptual experiments, some of which may be relevant from the point of view of planning and policy-making. As a matter of fact, the instrumental analysis of dynamic paths makes it possible to assign a specific normative value to particular clusters of historical circumstances. As Sukhamoy Chakravarty has recently argued: 'growth models generally help us in 'characterizing' the class of paths that can be regarded as optimal in regard to the different types of preference function related to the levels of output, consumption and investment' (Chakravarty, 1993, p. 213; lecture delivered in 1988).

Quite clearly, economics appears to Lowe to be located at the edge of 'history' and 'theory' in a sense different from Hicks's. In Hicks's view, economic theory ought to be able to provide what he called a 'theory of economic history' (see Hicks, 1969). In other words, economic theory should provide a conceptual framework in terms of which a rational reconstruction of historical experiences may be attempted. This is indeed what Hicks himself tried to achieve in his *Theory of Economic History*

(1969) and in the two later papers, 'The Mainspring of Economic Growth' (1977a) and 'Industrialism' (1977b).

In Hicks's view, not all features of economic history may be elucidated in terms of a single theoretical framework. Thus the expansion of market networks is partially reconstructed in terms of the theory of competitive markets (with the notable exception of the Industrial Revolution). But other features (from the Industrial Revolution to important aspects of technical innovation and the trade cycle) are interpreted in terms of a theoretical framework that emphasizes the interdependence of production processes rather than that of markets (the neo-Austrian framework presented in Hicks's *Capital and Time*, 1973).

It may be argued that a unifying theme of Hicks's interpretation of historical processes is the consideration of the relationship between free choice and determinism, that is, between economic rationality and processes of an irreversible type (see also Scazzieri, 1994).

In Hicks, economic theory is essentially a free conceptual construction that may be used to 'illuminate' (this is a characteristic Hicksian word) the real processes of history. In contrast to Hicks, Lowe approaches economic theory directly as an exercise in the interpretation of economic history, that is to say, as an attempt to disentangle 'objective' and 'subjective' features, and to locate their respective explanatory roles according to the type of questions that are raised. (In Lowe's later work, 'objective' factors such as technological dynamics determine the set of feasible paths from one fully adjusted position to another, whereas 'subjective' factors, such as the institutional and legal setup, may determine the specific transitional path that is followed.)

It may be argued that both Lowe and Hicks, in spite of the different perspective adopted on the relationship between economic theory and economic history, did in fact share the view that structural decomposition is essential in order to identify endogenous sources of structural change. In Hicks's *Capital and Time* (1973), structural change on a traverse path is associated with the decomposition of the productive structure between old and new processes. In Lowe's *Path of Economic Growth* (1976) the speed of structural change is associated with the 'hierarchy' between productive sectors and reflects the critical role of machine tools (see also Hagemann, 1990). A closer look at historical processes of structural change suggests a distinction between changes in economic structure and changes in the 'rules' according to which structural transformation takes place. For example, the slow and continuous absorption of technical innovations into an existing form of production organization would leave the 'hidden hierarchy' of dynamic structure unchanged (see Section 4, above). But the switch from one organizational form to another is likely to change the ranking of relative motions within the economic system. As a result, the endogenous emergence of new structures would possibly follow a different course.

We may consider the above switch of regime as an instance of 'qualitative' structural change, that is, of structural change associated with new rules of structural formation.[3]

In general, this type of structural change would be associated with the emergence of new 'dynamic poles', that is, of new clusters of activities exerting a critical influence upon the speed and form of economic transformation. (See also Perroux (1955) for the related concept of '*pole de croissance*' (growth pole) and Ricottilli (1976) for the identification of 'dynamic subsystems' derived by pooling together activities associated with a given growth rate.)

For example, the transition from a 'wood economy' to an 'iron economy', such as the one associated with the first industrial revolution (see Wrigley, 1962 and 1988), entails the substitution of one constraining subsystem (the subsystem of iron-based machine tools) for another (the subsystem of wood-based materials and tools). Such a transition is clearly more fundamental than the standard Ricardian switch from one set of land-based constraining subsystems to another (see Ricardo, 1817; see also Quadrio-Curzio, 1986). For the former transition implies the switch from one dynamic structure to another; whereas in the latter case the set of transformation paths that are feasible from the technological point of view is unchanged, and the economic system is simply moving from one feasible path to another as a result of behavioural or institutional changes (which may include demographic changes and changes in consumption patterns).

Qualitative structural change may thus be reconstructed (at least to a certain degree) by means of structural decomposition. For the distinction among component parts of any given economic system allows the identification of the fine structure of motion, which is often based upon the 'hierarchical coordination' of spontaneous changes.

In this way, the ranking of relative motions is a factor influencing the form and speed of structural change. And a change in *ranking criteria* entails structural transformation of a fundamental kind.

6   CONCLUDING REMARKS

This chapter has attempted a preliminary investigation into the 'analytical structure' of economic dynamics, that is, into the primitive analytical components of the historical processes that shape economic systems in the course of time. In particular, the decomposition of economic structure has been considered as a preliminary step essential in disentangling the fundamental dynamic components of any given economic system.

Structural decomposition leads to the substitution of an aggregate representation of the economic system with one based upon a variety of interrelated subsystems (see also Baranzini and Scazzieri, 1990 and Landesmann and Scazzieri, 1996b). The relative motions of subsystems are considered as the starting-point for the analysis of the form and speed of structural change. It has been argued that the fundamental pattern (form) of structural change reflects the 'hidden hierarchy' of relative motions within the economic system, whereas the speed of transformation depends upon the temporal lags embedded in such a hierarchy.

In particular, qualitative structural change may be considered as a process characterized by the emergence of new hierarchies among elements of the productive system. This would generally involve the formation of new dynamic poles and the operation of a 'law of motion' quite different from the one associated with the previous hierarchies.

In this way, critical features of economic history (such as the transition from one growth regime to another) may be understood in terms of economic theory, on condition that the latter is based upon a flexible and 'open' representation of economic structure and its internal asymmetries.

NOTES

1. As recently argued by Michio Morishima 'characterizing assumptions are those which remove extraneous factors so that we can isolate the special characteristics of an economy' (Morishima, 1984, p. 135).
2. The job-shop organization is characterized by multiskilled productive factors (workers, machines, materials) and a flexible assignment of tasks to such factors. The straight-line organization, on the other hand, is characterized by specialized factors and a relatively rigid assignment of tasks to particular agents or materials (see Scazzieri, 1993, particularly pp. 87–93, for a discussion of the job-shop and straight-line models).
3. In this way, there will be a change in the set of new structures that may be generated by historical processes. 'Emergent structures' may continuously appear but their formation is constrained by technological or institutional bounds. (See Arthur, Landesmann and Scazzieri, 1991.)

REFERENCES

Arthur, B., M. Landesmann and R. Scazzieri (1991), 'Dynamics and structures', *Structural Change and Economic Dynamics*, **2** (1), June, pp. 1–7.
Baranzini, M. and R. Scazzieri (1990), 'Economic structure: analytical perspectives', in M. Baranzini and R. Scazzieri (eds), *The Economic Theory of Structure and Change*, Cambridge: Cambridge University Press, pp. 227–333.
Chakravarty, S. (1993), 'The development of development thinking', in S. Chakravarty, *Selected Economic Writings*, with an Introduction by Amit Bhaduri, C.H. Hanumantha Rao and S.N. Raghavan, Delhi: Oxford University Press, pp. 204–33.

Ferguson, A. (1767), *An Essay on the History of Civil Society*, London: A. Millar & T. Cadell; Dublin: B. Grierson.

Granovetter, M.S. (1973), 'The strength of weak ties', *American Journal of Sociology*, **78**, pp. 1360–80.

Hagemann, H. (1990), 'The structural theory of economic growth', in M. Baranzini and R. Scazzieri (eds), *The Economic Theory of Structure and Change*, Cambridge: Cambridge University Press, pp. 144–71.

Hagemann, H. and M. Landesmann (1991), *Sombart and Economic Dynamics*, Discussion papers series, University of Hohenheim, Stuttgart, no. 62.

Hicks, J. (1969), *A Theory of Economic History*, Oxford: Clarendon Press.

Hicks, J. (1973), *Capital and Time. A Neo-Austrian Theory*, Oxford: Clarendon Press.

Hicks, J. (1977a), 'The mainspring of economic growth', in J. Hicks, *Economic Perspectives. Further Essays on Money and Growth*, Oxford: Clarendon Press, pp. 1–19 (first delivered as Nobel Lecture and published in 1973).

Hicks, J. (1977b), 'Industrialism', in J. Hicks, *Economic Perspectives. Further Essays on Money and Growth*, Oxford: Clarendon Press, pp. 20–44.

Landesmann, M. and R. Scazzieri (1990), 'Specification of structure and economic dynamics', in M. Baranzini and R. Scazzieri (eds), *The Economic Theory of Structure and Change*, Cambridge: Cambridge University Press, pp. 95–121.

Landesmann, M. and R. Scazzieri (1996a), 'The production process: description and analysis', in *Production and Economic Dynamics*, Cambridge: Cambridge University Press, pp. 191–228.

Landesmann, M. and R. Scazzieri (1996b), 'Coordination of production processes, subsystem dynamics and structural change', in M. Landesmann and R. Scazzieri (eds), *Production and Economic Dynamics*, Cambridge: Cambridge University Press, pp. 304–43.

Lowe, A. (1935), *Economics and Sociology: A Plea for Co-operation in the Social Sciences*, London: Allen & Unwin.

Lowe, A. (1976), *The Path of Economic Growth*, Cambridge, Cambridge University Press.

Lowe, A. (1987), *Essays in Political Economics. Public Control in a Democratic Society*, Brighton: Wheatsheaf Books.

Mill, J.S. (1848), *Principles of Political Economy with Some of their Applications to Social Philosophy*, London: John W. Parker.

Morishima, M. (1984), *The Economics of Industrial Society*, Cambridge: Cambridge University Press.

Perroux, F. (1955), 'Note sur la notion de "pole de croissance"' (Note on the notion of growth pole), *Economie Appliquée*, **8**, (1–2), pp. 307–20.

Quadrio-Curzio, A. (1986), 'Technological scarcity: an essay on production and structural change', in M. Baranzini and R. Scazzieri (eds), *Foundations of Economics. Structures of Inquiry and Economic Theory*, Oxford and New York: Basil Blackwell, pp. 377–407.

Ricardo, D. (1817), *On the Principles of Political Economy and Taxation*, London: J. Murray.

Ricottilli, M. (1976), 'Autonomous expenditure, output, growth: a sector approach', *Economic Notes*, **5**, pp. 59–80.

Say, J.B. (1803) *Traité d'économie politique*, (*A Treatise on Political Economy*), Paris: Deterville.

Scazzieri, R. (1993), *A Theory of Production. Tasks, Processes and Technical Practices*, Oxford: Clarendon Press.

Scazzieri, R. (1994), 'Economic theory and economic history. Perspectives on Hicksian themes', in H. Hagemann and O.F. Hamouda (eds), *The Legacy of Hicks*, London: Routledge, pp. 225–40.

Smith, A. (1776), *An Inquiry into the Nature and Causes of the Wealth of Nations*, London: W. Strahan & T. Cadell.

Steuart, Sir J. (1767), *An Inquiry into the Principles of Political Oeconomy:* London: A. Millar & T. Cadell.

Unwin, G. (1904), *Industrial Organization in the Sixteenth and Seventeenth Centuries*, Oxford: Clarendon Press.

Wrigley, E.A. (1962), 'The supply of raw materials in the Industrial Revolution', *Economic History Review*, 2nd series, **XV**, pp. 1–16.

Wrigley, E.A. (1988), *Continuity, Chance and Change. The Character of the Industrial Revolution in England*, Cambridge: Cambridge University Press.

12. Traverse Analysis and Flexibility of the Production System

Christian Gehrke

---

1   INTRODUCTION

To the present day, Adolph Lowe's study of traverse processes in *The Path of Economic Growth*, first published in 1976, is often referred to as a seminal contribution to the analysis of growth, accumulation and structural change by many economists who view themselves as working within a framework of a classical origin.[1] So far, however, Lowe's painstaking investigation can hardly be said to have inspired many new contributions to traverse theory, and it seems that the interest in this part of his *œuvre* has expressed itself mainly in going over the same ground again rather than in advancing the argument beyond his own presentation. The majority of the more recent contributions to the field of traverse theory have rather come from authors who have attempted to elaborate on the so-called *neo-Austrian* approach to traverse analysis, drawing on ideas originally developed by John Hicks (see particularly Hicks, 1973, Part II).[2]

The purpose of the present chapter is to investigate (some of) the possible reasons for this development in the field of traverse theory. Traverse analyses are concerned with studying the path that the (model) economy will – or, in Lowe's instrumental approach, should – follow after a major change in data has disturbed the tranquil conditions of a steady-state growth path. In traverse analyses the economic system is generally envisaged as being confronted with an unexpected major change in the long-run data, such as a 'technology shock', that is, the availability of a hitherto unknown method of production, or a sudden change in the availability of labour or of natural resources. The major problem for an economic system exposed to such changes is the inappropriateness of the structure (and/or the volume) of the existing real capital stock and, hence, the need for an adaptation of the latter to the new set of conditions. Broadly speaking, traverse studies concentrate on the problems involved in changing over from one particular configuration of the productive apparatus of an economic system to another one. These studies are therefore especially concerned with structural adjustment problems arising from 'rigidities' inherent in the production system. It is clear, then, that the modelling of the production system forms a key element of all traverse studies.

As has already been noted, the recent literature on traverse theory is clearly dominated by contributions making use of neo-Austrian models of production. This approach to traverse analysis was first introduced by John Hicks (1973, Part II), after the latter had become dissatisfied with his earlier formulation of the traverse problem in the context of a two-sectoral model of production (see Hicks, 1965, Ch. XVI).[3] His major objection to traverse studies that are based on multisectoral production models was the representation of structural adjustments of the existing capital stock by means of an intersectoral reallocation of the capital equipment. His opinion, according to which sectoral models of production are bound to give a distorted picture of the 'real' adjustment processes, was later echoed in various other contributions developing the neo-Austrian approach to traverse analysis. Authors advocating the use of neo-Austrian production models in traverse theory have repeatedly pointed out that capital equipment is generally highly specific and hence not easily transferable among different lines of production (see, for example, Amendola and Gaffard, 1988, p. 29). The modelling of short-period adjustment processes on the assumption of *non-specific*, and thus *shiftable* capital goods in multisectoral traverse models is therefore regarded as an exercise producing highly misleading results.

Interestingly, a similar opinion was also expressed in various recent contributions attempting an integration of the modern reformulation of the surplus approach to value and distribution with the Keynesian principle of effective demand in the long run.[4] Thus Pierangelo Garegnani, a major contributor to this line of research, has recently argued that 'in a short period, capacity is generally given in a highly specialised form. The short-period possibility to accommodate increased investment by lowering consumption would therefore seem in any case small or non-existent' (Garegnani, 1992, p. 63).[5] However, while apparently sharing with the former group a dissatisfaction with the representation of short-period adaptation processes by intersectoral shifts of the existing productive equipment, these authors have generally not denied the existence of a high degree of flexibility in the production system. These contributions have generally emphasized the relevance of the *variability in the degree of capacity utilization*, rather than the *non-specificity of equipment*, for the adaptability of the production system.

The purpose of this chapter is to clarify the role of the flexibility of the production system, which arises from the variability in the rate of utilization of fixed capital, in the context of an analysis of traverse processes. It will be argued that neo-Austrian production models, which emphasize the specificity of capital goods, are not superior to multisectoral production models, and that the neo-Austrian approach to traverse theory cannot be considered to provide a more accurate model of the adaptation process by which the production apparatus of an economic system may be envisaged as changing its form over time. This is due to the fact that these studies have generally proceeded from the assumption of *full performance* of the economic system – a hypothesis that could only be retained in these models because of the introduction of drastic simplifications with regard to production technologies. We shall further argue that for a proper analysis of traverse processes it seems indispensable that the possibility of variations in the rate of utilization of fixed capital is explicitly taken into account. Moreover, once the necessity of integrating an analysis of deviations from normal degrees of capacity utilization into traverse models is acknowledged, it is immediately recognized that the attempt to determine the volume of investment by the volume of full-capacity savings must be dispensed with. As a consequence, a clear-cut analytical separation of 'structural adjustment problems' and 'Keynesian effective demand problems' will be seen to be impossible.

The structure of the chapter is as follows. Section 2 starts with a discussion of major sources of (short-period) flexibility and of rigidity in the production system, and then briefly examines two major objections that have been raised against Lowe's approach to traverse analysis. Section 3 describes the main features of the approach commonly used in traverse studies based on neo-Austrian models of production. It is shown that the attempted generalization of this approach, by way of introducing a *non-vertically-integrated* version of the neo-Austrian production model, reveals the deficiencies of traverse studies based on the *vertically-integrated* version. Section 4 contains a discussion of Hicks's and Lowe's views on the implications of acknowledging variability in the degree of capacity utilization in traverse models. Section 5 contains a summary of the main argument and some concluding remarks.

2   OBJECTIONS TO LOWE'S APPROACH TO TRAVERSE ANALYSIS

In this section we want to examine two major objections that have been raised against Lowe's traverse analysis and, more generally, against traverse studies based on sectoral production models. The first criticism, already mentioned above, consists in the charge of a misrepresentation of the adjustment processes by which the structure (and volume) of a system's real capital stock can be changed. The significance of this criticism will be discussed in Section 2.1, which also contains some general remarks on different sources of flexibility and of rigidity in the production system. The second major criticism, which will be examined in Section 2.2, concerns Lowe's analytical treatment of the introductory phase of a new technique. It will be contended that these objections, although not entirely unwarranted, should not be taken to imply that sectoral representations of the production system must be dispensed with in the analysis of traverse processes.

2.1   Sources of Flexibility and Rigidity in the Production System

In order to become clear about the significance of different elements affecting the short-period adaptability of the productive structure of an economic system we shall first attempt to discuss what may be considered major sources of flexibility and of rigidity of a production system. Before entering into this discussion it should perhaps be noted that the standard adjustment mechanism contemplated in neoclassical economics, which operates via 'input factor substitutability', provides no clue for an analysis of the process in the course of which a preexisting real capital structure is adapted to a new set of long-run conditions. As Lowe makes clear, 'such variations [in input proportions] ... are of a long-period nature insofar as they require the previous formation and transformation of real capital' (Lowe, 1976, p. 115). We should perhaps also remark that we shall not proceed by referring to empirical facts about the characteristics of actual production systems but rather by referring to the theoretical models that are meant to capture the former.

Specific and non-specific commodities

The adaptation of an existing structure of the capital stock to a change in the long-run data is of course easily analysed in models where all goods can be used indiscriminately either as consumption goods or as capital goods, so that an increase (decrease) in whatever capital goods are required for the transition to a new capital structure can be accomplished simply by a corresponding decrease (increase) in consumption.[6] Introducing heterogeneity by distinguishing between commodities which can only be consumed and others which can only serve as capital goods implies, of course, a first element of rigidity.[7] However, as long as capital goods are modelled as being *non-specific*, the fundamental 'adjustment mechanism' does not have to change drastically. When the capital goods, because of their non-specificity, are easily transferable among sectors, any increase (decrease) in the production of capital equipment can always be accomplished by simply reallocating productive capacity from the consumer-goods sector(s) to the capital-goods sector(s) (or *vice versa*).[8]

Specific and non-specific capital goods

The adaptation of the capital structure to a new set of data becomes of course more difficult when specificity of capital goods is taken into account. The possibility of envisaging the adjustment process as a 'reallocation' of existing capacities among different lines of production clearly becomes more limited, if one assumes that each type of capital equipment can only be used in the production of a limited number of commodities. But while it is certainly sensible to suppose that in modern production systems many equipment goods are highly specialized, and that a 'realistic' production model should capture this fact, it should also be clear that a production system cannot sensibly be modelled as containing completely specific capital goods only, that is, capital goods which can serve in the production of a single commodity only. For if all capital goods were assumed to be completely specific, there could not be circular relations of production.[9] Hence an adequate model of a production system would seem to require the incorporation of both specific and non-specific capital goods.[10]

We may now take a closer look at Lowe's production model (see Figure 12.1) to see whether Amendola and Gaffard's criticism is justified.[11] It should first be noted that Lowe's complete 'analytical schema of production' comprises not only three sectors but also four successive stages within each sector. Each of these stages represents a specific industry.

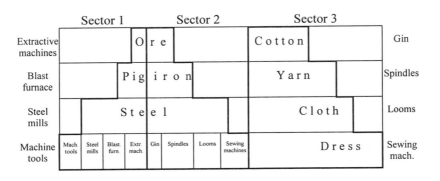

Figure 12.1   Lowe's analytical schema of production[12]

In Lowe's schema the category of equipment-good industries includes not only the industries producing fixed capital goods but also the preceding stages of mining, pig iron and steel production. Similarly, the consumer-good sector comprises not only the making of finished dress ready for sale but also the preceding stages of cultivating cotton, spinning yarn and weaving cloth. It should also be noted that in Lowe's schema the equipment-goods *industries* are grouped in both sectors 1 and 2. The distinction between different 'sectors' is a purely analytical device, and the fictitious 'sectors' are not to be identified with concrete industries. Hence in Lowe's schema all types of equipment goods but one (the 'machine tools') are *specific* and *non-shiftable* among industries. The full significance of Lowe's analytical schema of production can be illustrated by examining, for example, his analysis of the 'phase of partial capacity liberation', in which capacity is 'liberated' in sector 2 and 'transferred' to sector 1. What happens during this phase is that *a part of the output* of those industries which comprise the first three stages of the two equipment goods sectors (that is, the 'extractive industry', the 'iron industry' and the 'steel industry'), which before had served as an input in the production of secondary equipment is now directed towards those segments of the 'machine-tools industry' which produce primary equipment. Thus, from an analytical point of view *a part of the capacity* of these industries is 'transferred' from sector 2 to sector 1, while, in fact, this equipment is still used in the production of the same industry-specific output as before. In Lowe's schema there is only one group of industries which uses non-specific equipment: the 'machine-tools industry'. The process of adapting the economy's real capital stock is thus *not* visualized simply as a process of shifting *non-specific* equipment among different industries. Similarly incorrect is also Amendola and Gaffard's further claim that there is a 'strict relation between the sectoral representation of the economy (with its synchronic representation of the process of production) and the hypothesis of transferability' (Amendola and Gaffard, 1988, p. 29).

Variability in the degree of capacity utilization

The hypothesis of intersectoral transferability of capital equipment is of course not the only possibility of providing for short-period flexibility of the production system in multisectoral production models. A restructuring of the system's capital stock can also be accomplished through changes in the utilization of the sectoral production capacities, that is, through above- or below-normal degrees of capacity utilization in some or all of the industries. So far, however, this 'adjustment mechanism' has received only scant comments from traverse theorists (see below, Section 4), and it has not been integrated into sectoral traverse models.[13]

Other sources of short-period flexibility

Finally, some other sources of flexibility should be mentioned briefly. A first possibility of coping with the problem of a temporary shortage of equipment goods immediately suggests itself, if the analysis is based on a fixed capital model with durable equipment with a finite lifetime. One may then introduce the possibilities of postponing (anticipating) the scrapping of equipment, or of a reactivation of equipment that is worn out but has not yet been scrapped. Further elements of flexibility emerge, of course, if the assumption of a closed economic system is abandoned. In an open-economy framework the possibility of increased imports opens up a variety of different ways to overcome a (temporary) shortage of equipment goods. If, for example, particular equipment goods are in short supply, additional imports can be used to close the gap. This can take the form of importing directly the required equipment goods, or of importing equipment goods which are necessary to produce additional amounts of the particular capital goods which are in short supply, or of importing other goods (possibly also pure consumption goods) in order to liberate productive capacity for the production of the required equipment goods.[14]

What emerges from the above considerations is admittedly no more than a (perhaps rather incomplete) list of various elements that may be envisaged as either decreasing or increasing the degree of flexibility of a production system. However, our purpose was not to arrive at a complete taxonomy, but rather to provide the reader with some idea about the complexity of the issues involved in an analysis of the adaptation of the real capital structure. Clearly, any study of traverse processes would seem to require, in order to be interesting at all, a production model that takes some elements of rigidity into account. On the other hand, however, it is, of course, also necessary to allow for some elements of flexibility, for otherwise an adaptation of the existing capital stock would be precluded for purely technical reasons.

2.2. The Introduction of a New Technique

A more serious objection to Lowe's approach to traverse theory concerns his analysis of traverse processes that are caused by process innovations. The issue under consideration can best be explained by taking a brief look at Lowe's analysis of a 'pure labour displacing' innovation. The starting-point of Lowe's analysis is a state of the system, in which

a capital stock equal to the original one in terms of wage units can now produce the original output with less labour input, because either the given physical stock is more efficiently organized or a new more efficient stock was built after the original stock was fully depreciated. (Lowe, 1976, p. 256)

Hence Lowe does not consider that phase of the traverse in which the diffusion of the new production method occurs, that is, in the course of which the new method is gradually replacing the old one. The analysis presented by Lowe concentrates exclusively on the requirements for an efficient compensation of labour displacement that is *assumed* to have occurred during the diffusion phase. Moreover, Lowe for simplicity supposes the diffusion process to result in a state of the system where, 'after the displacement has occurred, the system as a whole, excluding the displaced, is again in equilibrium' (ibid., p. 257).[15] That the initial phase of the traverse, in which the construction and incorporation of the new equipment takes place, is largely left in the dark, is no doubt a major shortcoming of Lowe's analysis of traverse processes that are caused by the introduction of new production methods. Moreover, we must also acknowledge Amendola and Gaffard's further criticism that in Lowe's analysis a process innovation, which generally involves the introduction of qualitatively different equipment, is reduced to a purely quantitative change in production coefficients.[16]

3   THE NEO-AUSTRIAN APPROACH TO TRAVERSE ANALYSIS

This section contains a brief outline of the neo-Austrian approach to traverse theory initiated by John Hicks (1973). In the present context the most important characteristic of the Hicksian traverse model is the assumption that capital goods are fully specific to each technique, that is, the 'new' technique uses capital goods that are qualitatively different from those of the 'old' technique. More recently an attempt was made to substantiate the results derived by Hicks and others within the framework of the *vertically-integrated* neo-Austrian production model by extending the Hicksian approach to traverse theory to a so-called *non-vertically-integrated* version of the neo-Austrian production model (see Belloc, 1980, and Violi, 1982). In the following it will be argued that this attempt cannot be considered to have been successful, but, on the contrary, may be viewed as demonstrating the limited scope of the Hicksian analysis. The main reason for this is that the assumption of *full performance*, on which Hicks had based his analysis, loses its significance in the context of a more general framework.

3.1   The Analysis of a Transition Between Techniques in a *Vertically-integrated* Neo-Austrian Model

In *Capital and Time* (1973), Hicks proposed to analyse the transition process by considering two different 'scenarios', each determined by a different set of hypotheses. In the first scenario the real wage rate is assumed to adjust instantaneously in the course of the traverse to keep the available labour force continuously fully employed ('full employment path'), while in the second scenario the wage rate is assumed to be rigidly fixed, so that the non-steady growth of the flow of consumption goods output results in variations in the level of employment ('fixwage path'). The two different hypotheses with regard to wage flexibility are then combined with the so-called *full performance* hypothesis, according to which the activity levels for the start of new processes will always be chosen such as to absorb the remaining part of the full-capacity output of the existing processes (that is, after deducting the consumption requirements of the labour force employed on the existing processes plus the so-called 'take-out' for capitalists' consumption). Hence both of Hicks's scenarios are based on the principle of Say's Law: the level of aggregate investment is determined by the level of full-capacity aggregate savings.[17] Hicks motivates the introduction of the full performance hypothesis by reference to the well-known method of 'isolation by abstraction'. Since the purpose of the analysis consists in tracing the macroeconomic effects of the gradual introduction of a new technique, that is, in studying its impact on employment, income distribution and so on, it seems appropriate to set aside the Keynesian problem of aggregate effective demand.

According to Hicks, the Austrian view of the production process as a transformation of original factors into consumer goods is especially suited to the study of non-steady growth paths involving changes in techniques, because it relegates the role of the means of production to that of intermediate products, integrated and subsumed within the elementary production process without explicitly showing up. In a vertically-integrated neo-Austrian production model an elementary production process is represented by a sequence

$$\{l(u),b(u)\}_0^D,$$

with: $l(0) > 0$ and $l(u) \geq 0$ $\forall u \in [0, D]$
          $b(u) = 0$ $\forall u \in [0, d]$ and $b(u) \geq 0$ $\forall u \in \,]d, D]$,

where $l(u)$ denotes the input flow of labour and $b(u)$ the output flow of a (composite) consumption good; D gives the physical life of the process; d separates the primary phase (which may be conceived as the 'construction phase of a machine') and the secondary phase (which may be conceived as the 'utilization phase of a machine') of the elementary process.

When $x(t - u)$ represents the rate of starts of elementary processes at date $(t - u)$, and g denotes the steady growth rate, a steady-state growth path is described by $x(t - u) = x(0)e^{g(t - u)}$. Under steady-state conditions, the total output of consumption goods, $B(t)$, total employment, $L(t)$, and capitalists' take-out, $C(t)$, at time t will then be given by

$$B(t) = \int_0^D b(u)x(t - u)du = \int_0^D b(u)x(0)e^{g(t-u)}du, \tag{12.1}$$

$$L(t) = \int_0^D l(u)x(t - u)du = \int_0^D l(u)x(0)e^{g(t - u)}du, \tag{12.2}$$

$$C(t) = B(t) - w*L(t). \tag{12.3}$$

The steady state is supposed to be disturbed, at time $t = 0$, by the emergence of a new elementary process whose introduction pushes the economy on to a traverse path. Following Zamagni (1984, p. 139), we may consider the special case of a 'mechanization' of production, that is, we suppose the newly available process to exhibit increased input requirements in the construction phase and reduced input requirements in the utilization phase, relative to the old process. Moreover, the new technique differs from the old technique in terms of the duration of both the construction and the utilization phase (variables with an asterisk refer to the old technique, those without to the new one):

$$b(u) = b*(u) \qquad \forall\, u \in [\max (d, d*), \min (D, D*)]$$
$$l(u) > l*(u) \qquad \forall\, u \in [0, k[$$
$$l(k) = l*(k)$$
$$l(u) < l*(u) \qquad \forall\, u \in [k, \min (D, D*)].$$

In order to determine the rate of starts of the new process along the fixwage traverse path, the full performance hypothesis is of crucial importance. On the Hicksian assumption that there is an unchanged take-out, that is, that $C(t) = C*(t)$, we have

$$C*(t) = B(t) - w*L(t). \tag{12.4}$$

Given the *full performance* condition, the volume of final output and of employment along the traverse path is determined, for $t > 0$, by the activity levels of 'old' processes that are still operated, and by the activity levels of 'new' processes that have been started from $t = 0$ onwards. If we define $q(u) \equiv b(u) - w^*l(u)$ and $q^*(u) \equiv b^*(u) - w^*l(u)$, and denote the activity levels referring to the new processes by $x(t)$ and those referring to the old processes by $x^*(t)$, equation (12.4) can be written as

$$C^*(t) = \int_{t-D^*}^{0} b^*(t-u)x^*(0)\,e^{gu}du + \int_{t-\min(t,D)}^{t} b(t-u)x(u)du$$

$$- w^*\left(\int_{t-D^*}^{0} l^*(t-u)x^*(0)\,e^{gu}du + \int_{0}^{t} l(t-u)x(u)du \right)$$

$$= \int_{t-D^*}^{0} q^*(t-u)x^*(0)\,e^{gu}du + \int_{0}^{t} q(t-u)x(u)du \qquad (12.5)$$

$$\text{for} \quad 0 < t \le \min (D, D^*), \text{ and}$$

$$C^*(t) = \int_{t-D}^{t} b(t-u)x(u)du - \int_{t-D}^{t} w^* \, l(t-u)x(u)du$$

$$= \int_{t-D}^{t} q(t-u)x(u)du \qquad (12.6)$$

$$\forall t > \max (D, D^*).$$

The rate of starts of the new elementary process, $x(t)$, is (uniquely) determined from (12.5) and (12.6), and it is thus possible to study the development of total output and total employment along the traverse path. The evolution of $x(t)$ along the fixwage traverse path is seen to be primarily dependent on the time shape of the net output profiles, $q(u)$ and $q^*(u)$, that characterize the old and the new technique, respectively. Without a further specification of the latter, the occurrence of negative solutions for $x(t)$ during some time interval of the traverse path cannot generally be excluded. Its emergence would indicate that the output currently forthcoming falls short of the input requirements of the already existing processes, that is, not only can no new process be started but also the existing capacity cannot be fully utilized.[18]

Violi (1984) has provided a rather general proof of the (asymptotic) convergence of the fixwage traverse path to a new steady-state growth path by using the method of Laplace transforms. However, as Violi also pointed out, it is meaningless to prove convergence for the 'late phase' of the traverse path, if the latter exhibits negative solutions for the rate of starts during its 'early phase'. A sufficient (but not necessary) condition for non-negative solutions is given by $q'(u)/q(0) \leq 0$. Since $q(0) < 0$ by definition,[19] the sufficiency condition reduces to $q'(u) \geq 0$. This means that the net output profile of the new process must be assumed to be *non-decreasing* in order to exclude the possibility of negative rates of start along the traverse path. Clearly, such an assumption would be extremely restrictive, as is readily admitted by authors who studied traverse processes in *vertically-integrated* neo-Austrian production models.

3.2   The Analysis of a Transition Between Techniques in a *Non-vertically-integrated* Neo-Austrian Model

The representation of the production structure by means of a vertically-integrated neo-Austrian model of production is extremely restrictive. As Burmeister (1974), Belloc (1980) and, more recently, Baldone (1984) have shown, the association of a consumption-good flow with a finite flow of labour inputs is only possible, if (i) the input matrix is assumed to be superior-triangular; (ii) fixed capital is only involved in the production of the consumption good; (iii) no circulating capital is involved in the production of the consumption good, that is, the production of the latter requires fixed capital and direct labour only.

Two advocates of the neo-Austrian approach to traverse analysis, Belloc (1980) and Violi (1982), have therefore suggested generalizing the Hicksian approach by introducing a generalized version of the neo-Austrian model of production. The model proposed by these authors allows for 'assisted labour' in all stages of the production process and, hence, for circular relations in production and a mechanized production of intermediate inputs. Even though it is impossible, in this case, to associate a consumption flow with a finite labour input flow, it is still possible to associate a flow of a finished commodity[20] with a temporal sequence of input vectors, whose elements denote the requirements of commodities and labour that are necessary to obtain the particular product flow under consideration. The underlying production model is a time-phased input–output model comprising n elementary production processes, each of which is described by dated input and output streams extending over time:

$$\{\mathbf{A}\,(u),\,\mathbf{B}\,(u)\} = \{a_{ki}\,(u),\,b_{ki}\,(u)\}$$

with:

$k = 1, 2, \ldots, n$
$i = 0, 1, 2, \ldots, n$
$u = 0, 1, 2, \ldots, D_k$.

The elementary production process of some commodity, say commodity j, is described by the set of the j-th column vectors of the matrices $\mathbf{A}(u)$ and $\mathbf{B}(u)$, that is, $\mathbf{A}_j(u)$ and $\mathbf{B}_j(u)$. Each of these column vectors consists of $n + 1$ elements, the first of which denotes labour inputs, so that, clearly, $b_{k0}(u) = 0$ for all u must hold. D_k denotes the maximum lifetime of the elementary process k.

Suppose, for simplicity, that commodity n is the only consumption good and, consequently, that commodities $1, 2, \ldots, n - 1$ are pure capital goods. Let us consider the conditions of reproduction of an economy along the balanced growth path at rate g. Denoting with $x_k(t - u)$ the rate of starts of process k at time $t - u$, a steady-state growth path is described by $x_k(t - u) = x_k^* e^{g(t-u)}$ Continuous equilibrium requires that the amounts of each commodity i that are produced at time t (by processes of different 'vintages' of the i-th elementary process) exactly equal the quantities absorbed by all those processes that are active at time t:

$$\sum_{k=1}^{n} \int_{t-D_k^*}^{t} a_{ik}^*(t - u)x_k^*(0)e^{gu}du = \int_{t-D_i^*}^{t} b_{ii}^*(t - u)x_i^*(0)e^{gu}du \quad (12.7)$$

for $i = 1, 2, \ldots, n - 1$.

Moreover, if (in analogy with the vertically-integrated model) a given wage rate, denoted by w^*, and zero savings by workers are assumed, capitalists' take-out on the steady-state growth path is determined by the balance between the supply of and demand for the consumption good:

$$C^*(t) = \int_0^t b_{nn}^*(t - u)x_n^*(0)e^{gu}du - w^* \sum_{k=1}^{n} \int_0^t a_{0k}^*(t - u)x_k^*(0)e^{gu}du \quad (12.8)$$

Suppose now that at $t = 0$ an economic system in such a dynamic equilibrium is disturbed by the emergence of a new elementary process for the production of commodity h,

$$\{\mathbf{A}_h(u), \mathbf{B}_h(u)\} \neq \{\mathbf{A}_h^*(u), \mathbf{B}_h^*(u)\},$$

the adoption of which allows extra profits to be obtained at the ruling wage rate and prices.

With full performance the produced amounts of commodities $i = 1, 2, ...,$ $n - 1$ would have to be completely absorbed along the traverse path, so that

$$\sum_{k=1}^{n} \int_{t-\min(t,D_k)}^{t} a_{ik}(t-u)x_k(u)du \; + \; \sum_{k=1}^{n} \int_{t-D_k^*}^{0} a_{ik}^*(t-u)x_k^*(0)e^{gu}du$$

$$= \int_{t-\min(t,D_i)}^{t} b_{ii}(t-u)x_i(u)du \; + \; \int_{t-D_i^*}^{0} b_{ii}^*(t-u)x_i^*(0)e^{gu}du \qquad (12.9)$$

for $i = 1, 2, ..., n - 1$.

Since the reference path is characterized by

$$\sum_{k=1}^{n} \int_{t-D_k^*}^{0} a_{ik}^*(t-u)x_k^*(0)e^{gu}du \; + \; \sum_{k=1}^{n} \int_{0}^{t} a_{ik}^*(t-u)x_k^*(0)e^{gu}du$$

$$= \int_{t-D_i^*}^{0} b_{ii}^*(t-u)x_i^*(0)e^{gu}du \; + \; \int_{0}^{t} b_{ii}^*(t-u)x_i^*(0)e^{gu}du, \qquad (12.10)$$

the impact of the introduction of the new technique can be studied by referring to the difference between the traverse path and the reference path,

$$\int_{t-\min(t,D_i)}^{t} b_{ii}(t-u)x_i(u)du \; - \; \sum_{k=1}^{n} \int_{t-\min(t,D_k)}^{t} a_{ik}(t-u)x_k(u)du$$

$$= \int_{0}^{t} b_{ii}(t-u)x_i^*(0)e^{gu}du \; - \; \sum_{k=1}^{n} \int_{0}^{t} a_{ik}^*(t-u)x_k^*(0)e^{gu}du \qquad (12.11)$$

for $i = 1, 2, ..., n - 1$.

With the definitions $q_{ik}(u) \equiv b_{ik}(u) - a_{ik}(u)$ and $q_{ik}^*(u) \equiv b_{ik}^*(u) - a_{ik}^*(u)$ this can be rewritten as

$$\sum_{k=1}^{n} \int_{t-\min(t,D_k)}^{t} q_{ik}(t-u)x_k(u)du = \sum_{k=1}^{n} \int_{0}^{t} q_{ik}^*(t-u)x_k^*(0)e^{gu}du. \qquad (12.12)$$

The equation system (12.12) is a system of $n - 1$ Volterra integral equations of the first kind, with n functions $x_k(u)$, denoting the activity levels of the k elementary processes along the traverse path, as the variables to be determined. The n-th equation is obtained from the equilibrium between supply and demand of the n-th commodity – the pure consumption good. With the Hicksian hypothesis of an unchanged take-out one obtains

$$\int_{t-\min(t,D_n)}^{t} b_{nn}(t-u)x_n(u)du \;-\; w^* \sum_{k=1}^{n} \int_{t-\min(t,D_k)}^{t} a_{0k}(t-u)x_k(u)du$$

$$= \int_0^t b_{nn}(t-u)\dot{x}_n(0)e^{gu}du \;-\; w^* \sum_{k=1}^{n} \int_0^t a_{0k}^{\cdot}(t-u)\dot{x}_k(0)e^{gu}du \,. \tag{12.13}$$

Using the definitions $q_{ik}(u) \equiv b_{ik}(u) - w^*a_{0k}(u)$ and $q_{ik}^*(u) \equiv b_{ik}^*(u) - w^*a_{0k}^*(u)$, with $b_{nk}(u) = 0$ and $b^*_{nk}(u) = 0$ for $k \ne n$, gives

$$\sum_{k=1}^{n} \int_{t-\min(t,D_k)}^{t} q_{nk}(t-u)x_k(u)du = \sum_{k=1}^{n} \int_0^t q_{nk}^{\cdot}(t-u)\dot{x}_k(0)e^{gu}du \,. \tag{12.14}$$

Combining (12.12) and (12.14), one obtains a system of n Volterra integral equations, which determines the activity levels $\mathbf{x}(t) = [x_1(t), x_2(t), ..., x_n(t)]$ along the fixwage traverse path. In analogy with the *integrated* model, where $q'(u)/q(0) \le 0$ is a sufficient condition for non-negative solutions for $x(t)$, a sufficient condition for non-negative solutions in the *non-integrated* model would be given by $[\mathbf{Q}'(u)\,\mathbf{Q}^{-1}(0)] \le 0$. However, as opposed to the integrated model, where $q(0)$ is a scalar with negative sign, $\mathbf{Q}(0)$ is a matrix containing semi-negative elements. Sufficiency conditions for non-negative solutions can only be formulated by introducing restrictions on the technology set. If one assumes, for example, that $\mathbf{Q}(0)$ can be reduced to a diagonal matrix, that is, if one assumes that each elementary process requires a specific input in the starting phase, then a sufficient condition for non-negative solutions for the activity levels would be given by $\mathbf{Q}'(\mathrm{u}) \ge 0$ (which, of course, is the analogue of $q'(u) \ge 0$ in the integrated model).

However, this latter hypothesis – which was indeed introduced both by Belloc (1980, pp. 144–6) and by Violi (1982, p. 252) in order to preserve the formal analogy with the integrated model – has severe effects for the attempted generalization of the Hicksian approach. Supposing that $\mathbf{Q}(0)$ is a diagonal matrix implies that one of the process-specific inputs which is used in the starting phase of one of the elementary processes consists of direct labour (since the n-th commodity was assumed to be a pure consumption good) and hence that the elementary production process of one of the commodities is started by 'unassisted labour'. Without this hypothesis, on the other hand, it cannot be excluded that negative 'solutions' for some elements of the activity vector may be obtained already for $t = 0$. The economic implication of this would be that the new process cannot even be activated, and hence that the transition to the new technique cannot even be started, without violating the full performance condition.

Next, let us consider the phenomena which would give rise to such results. A first case where the traverse process could not be started without violating full performance occurs whenever the start of the new elementary process in sector h requires a positive amount of some input which was not required to start the corresponding processes of the old technique, that is, whenever the vector $\mathbf{A}_h(0)$, and consequently also the matrix $\mathbf{A}(0)$, contains a positive input requirement of a commodity which is not contained in the matrix $\mathbf{A}^*(0)$. In this case, because of the full performance condition, the existing amounts of the input under consideration would be entirely absorbed by the full-capacity input requirements of those processes that were started before $t = 0$. A similar problem arises whenever the starting activities of the new technique do *not* require a positive amount of some input which was required by the starting activities of the old technique, that is, whenever the matrix $\mathbf{A}(0)$ does *not* contain any input requirements of some commodity which was contained in the matrix $\mathbf{A}^*(0)$. In the first case the new process cannot be introduced because the full performance hypothesis implies the non-availability of the input under consideration, while in the latter case it could not be introduced because the existing amounts of the input under consideration cannot be fully absorbed.

Given that the approach followed by Belloc (1980) and Violi (1982) of introducing *ad hoc* restrictions on the technology set is considered inappropriate, one may then ask what other possibilities exist in order to determine the traverse paths. Baldone (1984) has suggested the above-mentioned difficulties to solve by introducing an appropriately modified version of the full performance hypothesis into the analysis. In each period in which it is not possible to use all the resources that are available for investment, full performance is defined as a situation, where the activity levels of the starting phase of the n processes are determined in such a way that the activity level of any process cannot be increased without lowering that of another process. With regard to the treatment of the 'residuals', the surplus amounts of inputs which emerge when this modification is adopted, Baldone has proposed two different solutions. One may either assume that inputs which cannot be absorbed in the start of new processes are immediately (and costlessly) discharged, or, alternatively, that the surplus amounts of inputs can be 'transferred over time' in order to be absorbed at a later date.[21] Baldone rightly points out that this modification would, in general, deprive the neo-Austrian approach to traverse analysis of its capacity to determine *unique* solutions for the evolution of the economic system outside of the steady state. His conclusion is that neo-Austrian models of production cannot be considered to be better suited for the analysis of traverse processes than input–output models.

While Baldone's proposal allows one to overcome the difficulty of starting the traverse path in the second case, in which the problem lies in an incomplete absorption of the existing amounts of inputs, it is of no avail in the first case, where the problem consists in the non-availability of particular inputs. In this case it is only if the full performance hypothesis is dropped that positive amounts of these inputs can be made available for the start of the new process.[22] Moreover, although Baldone's proposal is capable of solving the problems encountered in the second case from a formal point of view, the economic content of this solution is rather dubious. It attempts to preserve the full performance hypothesis (albeit in a modified form) and, consequently, the determination of the volume of investment by the volume of full-capacity savings in a situation, where the commodity structure of full-capacity savings is incompatible with the commodity structure of the investment requirements. The economic implication of following Baldone's suggestion would be that along the traverse path surplus amounts of some commodities are (perhaps permanently) produced – and consequently labour and other inputs are used up – not because there is demand for these commodities, but only in order to avoid any deviation from normal capacity utilization. It is perhaps also worth noting that the problems encountered in the non-vertically-integrated version of the neo-Austrian traverse model appear to be closely related to the so-called 'dynamic instability problem' encountered in the dynamic input–output model proposed by Leontief (1953). As is well known, in this model the attempt to determine investment residually, by requiring the continuous full utilization of the existing capacities, also results in the emergence of negative 'solutions' of the activity vector.[23] Similarly, the proposal to allow for variability in the degree of capacity utilization in traverse models may be seen to be closely related to the solution proposed by Duchin and Szyld (1985) for dynamic input–output models.[24]

Even if one were prepared to accept the full performance hypothesis as an appropriate starting-point for the analysis of traverse processes and were only interested in tracing out the further development of the economic system after an 'overinvestment crisis' has occurred, it would be necessary to provide an analysis of over-/underutilization of productive capacity. The attempt to determine the level of investment by the level of full-capacity savings, in order to exclude Keynesian effective demand problems in a study of traverse processes, is therefore bound to falter even in the context of the integrated neo-Austrian model of production. However, the inappropriateness of the full performance hypothesis in the context of a study of traverse processes is put into sharp relief when the analysis is extended to the framework of a non-vertically-integrated neo-Austrian model of production.

Clearly, once it is acknowledged that any attempt to preserve the full performance hypothesis in the context of traverse models with more general production structures is bound to fail, it becomes necessary to specify an *independent* investment hypothesis of some kind in order to determine the traverse paths. This, however, also necessitates acknowledgement of the possibility of varying degrees of capacity utilization. Moreover, it would seem to render obsolete the idea of strictly separating the analysis of 'technological unemployment', which is consequent upon the introduction of a new technique, from that of 'Keynesian unemployment', which is caused by an insufficiency of aggregate effective demand.[25]

4 HICKS AND LOWE ON THE ROLE OF VARIABILITY IN THE DEGREE OF CAPACITY UTILIZATION IN THE CONTEXT OF TRAVERSE ANALYSES

Even though both Lowe and Hicks based their analyses on the assumption of fixed technical coefficients, they both also considered the modifications that in their view would result from introducing further elements of flexibility, and particularly from introducing variable degrees of capacity utilization, into the analysis.

4.1 Lowe's Views on Flexibility

According to Lowe, a transition to a path of higher steady-state growth would cause hardly any adjustment problems, if either all resources were 'by and large non-specific', or 'the normal state of the system is one of underemployment' (Lowe, 1952, p. 30). However, in Lowe's opinion the first possibility must be rejected on grounds of realism, while the second would be removed with the success of Keynesian policies of demand management:

> The greater the success of this policy of stabilization, the smaller the flexibility of the system, and the greater the difficulties in achieving a smooth expansion path. Growth can then no longer feed on pools of idle capital and labor and, more than ever before, becomes conditional on the shift of employed resources and, especially, on capital formation. (Lowe, 1976, p. 9)

It is for this reason that Lowe felt justified in 'assuming more or less full utilization' of the capital stock and given technical coefficients of production throughout most parts of his study (ibid., p. 10). Yet he also devoted a special chapter of his *Path* to a discussion of the implications resulting from taking into account variability of production coefficients (see ibid., Ch. 13). As Lowe makes clear, this variability must refer to a short-period context. He therefore dismisses the standard textbook adjustment mechanism which operates via extensive capital–labour substitutability on the ground that 'such variations of the capital–labour ratio are of a long-period nature insofar as they require the previous formation and transformation of real capital' (ibid., p. 115). What is at stake is variability with regard to the existing capital stock in its given form and here Lowe sees 'at least three instances in which considerable variability seems to prevail: underutilization of the available capital stock; a margin between the optimum and the maximum utilization of the initially given equipment; and the working of equipment over more than one shift' (ibid.).

However, in Lowe's view there are also a number of elements that considerably limit the possibilities of an overall expansion of output, employment and capacity along this route. First, Lowe maintains that 'the feasible margin for such expansion of output and employment varies considerably among different fields of production' (ibid., p. 116). A proportionate increase of output and employment would therefore be constrained by the expansion possibilities in the 'smallest-margin' industry. Second, 'rapidly diminishing marginal returns and, thus, rapidly rising marginal costs keep the *economically* exploitable margin within still narrower limits' (ibid.; emphasis added). Third, overutilization of equipment will raise the effective rate of wear and tear, and will therefore be associated with increased replacement requirements for the fixed capital items involved.

According to Lowe, the important question is therefore whether it is possible to have a proportionate expansion of output in all sectors, by way of above-normal degrees of capacity utilization, which can serve as an effective substitute for a process of new capital formation via internal restructuring. His (rather tedious) numerical calculations lead him to conclude that a process of real capital formation via overutilization of equipment 'more than suffices to absorb any empirically relevant *once-over* increase in labor supply' (ibid., p. 118). He questions, however, the possibility of adapting the capital stock of the economic system to a *permanently* increasing supply of labour via this route. Lowe maintains that a successful transition to a higher growth path is only possible if the *gross* surplus of the increment in the output of primary equipment resulting from overutilization is devoted to the production of additional primary equipment, that is, only if the capital stock of the primary equipment sector is expanded more rapidly than the capital stocks in the other sectors.

In our view Lowe's argument in Chapter 13 of the *Path*, and hence also the inference of his calculations, is not fully convincing. First, it may be noted that what Lowe termed the 'technically feasible margin' for an expansion of output in a particular industry obviously depends on the prevailing mode of operation of plant and equipment under *normal* conditions.[26] Second, while Lowe's assumption that overutilization of equipment will generally raise the effective rate of wear and tear of the fixed capital items involved is rather plausible, he apparently does not take into account an aspect that was particularly emphasized by Hicks (see below): the increased replacement requirements resulting from above-normal degrees of capacity utilization do not arise immediately but only in subsequent periods.[27] Third, it should be noted that Lowe's analysis of a proportionate expansion of output and employment in all sectors via above-normal degrees of capacity utilization involves a reduction in per-capita consumption, contrary to what Lowe suggests.[28]

4.2   Hicks on the Role of Variability in the Utilization of Capacity

Hicks has also repeatedly discussed the possibility of introducing variability in the degree of capacity utilization into his two-sectoral *Capital and Growth* model.[29] He conjectured that the negative results with regard to convergence properties were largely due to a number of 'unrealistic' assumptions upon which his analysis was based. Among these it was particularly the assumption of rigidly fixed technical coefficients of production which he considered inappropriate. Acknowledging the existence of some degree of variability in input proportions would, in Hicks's view, render the production system more flexible and would thus make possible a smoother adjustment to any change in the long-run data. The relevant passage in *Capital and Growth* also contains an interesting remark with regard to Lowe's opinions about the consequences of above-normal degrees of capital utilization:

> In the case of circulating capital goods, over-utilization means reducing stocks below normal. There is a limit beyond which this process cannot be carried, and (even short of that limit) the deficiency must, sooner or *later*, be made up. In the case of fixed capital, there will also be some tendency to more rapid wear and tear; the *future* need for replacement will, at least to some extent, be increased. (Hicks, 1965, p. 194; emphasis added)

For Hicks, then, an important aspect of acknowledging the possibility of above-normal degrees of capacity utilization (in combination with a reduction of input stocks) consists in the possibility of temporarily reversing the normal sequence of producing additional inputs *before* additional outputs are obtained. This aspect is again stressed by Hicks in his concluding statement, where he argues that

> even if one grants that over-utilization means 'borrowing from the future', it does facilitate greater flexibility. ... if it is possible to postpone it [that is, the 'normal' replacement of equipment] so that resources which would be used for it can be (temporarily) employed elsewhere, bottlenecks which would otherwise have been cramping may be more speedily broken. (Ibid., p. 194)

It will be noticed that Hicks's concern in these passages is only with the breaking of bottlenecks, and hence, with *over*utilization of equipment.[30] Hicks's conjecture that admitting variability in the degree of capacity utilization will generally facilitate the adjustment processes thus appears to be based on a complete omission of the possibility of *under*utilization of productive equipment. Apparently, Hicks wants to proceed in two steps. First, a traverse path is determined on the assumption of full performance. Only if the evolution determined by full performance results in bottleneck problems, one should introduce, in a second step, the possibility of *above*-normal degrees of capacity utilization in order to overcome the impasse. However, Hicks nowhere considers the implications of this modification for his approach to the determination of the volume of investment.[31]

5   CONCLUDING REMARKS

In this chapter we have considered the role of the flexibility of the production system for the analysis of traverse processes, which arises from the possibility of varying degrees of capacity utilization. It was argued that the attempt to determine the level (and structure) of aggregate investment in traverse analyses by postulating full performance of the economic system is generally bound to falter unless the analysis is confined to extremely simplified representations of the production structure of an economic system. Hence it would seem to become necessary to introduce an independent investment hypothesis in traverse models (in a positive analysis) or to stipulate an appropriate level and structure of investment according to some pre-specified criteria (in normative or instrumental analyses), and to allow for the possibility of above- and below-normal degrees of utilization of productive capacity. In view of these considerations 'an integration of the workings of the Keynesian principle of effective demand in the longer run into ... traverse analysis' (Hagemann, 1992, p. 260) would not only appear desirable, but would rather seem to be an unavoidable step in the further development of traverse theory.

NOTES

1.   Statements to this effect can be found in various essays in a volume on the theory of non-steady growth that was recently edited by Halevi, Laibman and Nell (1992); see particularly the contribution by Walsh (1992, p. 31).
2.   It is noticeable, however, that more recently there have been various contributions to traverse theory that are based on Kaleckian models; see, for example, Lavoie and Ramírez-Gastón (1994) and the literature cited there. The main focus of these studies is, however, the relation of short-period and long-period theories of pricing, prices and income distribution rather than the analysis of technological change.
3.   It is perhaps noteworthy that a preliminary account of Adolph Lowe's approach to the study of traverse problems was published prior to Hicks's first analysis of the path from one steady-state to another in *Capital and Growth*; see Lowe (1955).
4.   For contributions to this line of research see, among others, Garegnani (1992) and Kurz (1986; 1990; 1992).
5.   Unlike the comment by Amendola and Gaffard, Garegnani's statement is not referring specifically to traverse models, but more generally to models of growth and accumulation attempting an integration of short- and long-period analysis considerations.
6.   With *non-specific* commodities there is, obviously, a rather direct link between 'capital accumulation' and 'abstention from consumption'. For a traverse model based on *non-specific* commodities see, for example, Solow (1967).
7.   'To put it plastically, it is no longer possible to increase the number of bulldozers by merely accumulating the abstained consumption of, say, yogurt' (Georgescu-Roegen, 1978, p. 437).
8.   This intersectoral reallocation of equipment is the standard adjustment mechanism in many two-sector growth models, including the famous 'corn-tractor model' of Hicks's 1965 contribution to traverse theory. It will be observed that the 'reallocation of capital goods adjustment mechanism' envisaged in these models preserves the direct link between making additions to the capital stock, that is, between '[increments in] capital accumulation', and 'abstention from [producing] consumption [goods]'.
9.   It is worth noting that the necessity of *non-specific* capital goods for the existence of circularity in the production system had already been pointed out in the early 1930s by one of Lowe's former collaborators, Fritz Burchardt (1931–32). The same idea was formulated again in the 1960s by Gautham Mathur, who termed it the 'principle of versatility'; see Mathur (1965, pp. 44–5).
10. It should further be noted that equipment goods could, of course, also be conceived of as non-specific before they have been installed in particular industries, and as specific and non-transferable capital goods afterwards. It should further be clear that the question of whether or not a piece of equipment is transferable *ex post* is not a purely technical but an economic question. What emerges from these considerations is the inadequacy of maintaining a rigid classification of capital goods that only distinguishes between 'specific' and 'non-specific' capital goods.
11. For a more detailed account, see Gehrke and Hagemann (1996, Section 4).
12. See Lowe (1976, p. 32) and Lowe (1987, p. 38).
13. Considering the case of a fall in demand, underutilization can have different meanings. It is possible *either* to utilize all of the existing equipment below normal, *or* to work part of the existing equipment at the normal degree of capacity utilization, while the remaining part of the capital stock can be left idle, or scrapped, or transferred to another sector.

14. For traverse studies based on multisectoral models in an open-economy framework, see Mathur (1965) and Merhav (1969). For an analysis based on a neo-Austrian production model, see Ricottilli and Cantalupi (1987).

15. Clearly, then, the precondition for a successful compensation is a process of additional capital formation, and, not surprisingly, Lowe's structural analysis reveals a close analogy with an adjustment process to a higher rate of growth of the labour supply.

16. That Lowe was aware of this gap in his analysis can be seen from his statement that 'the normal case is a replacement of the original type of machinery by a new type' (Lowe, 1976, p. 266). According to Amendola and Gaffard, multisectoral models involving circular relations in production encounter difficulties when the effects of innovations are to be studied which involve the introduction of new capital goods. In our view, the major obstacle would not appear to lie in the existence of circular relations in production. Since 'any improved equipment good must initially be produced with the help of preexisting, that is, nonimproved equipment goods' (Lowe, 1976, p. 238), a new equipment good can enter into its own production only *after* it has first been produced by a production method in which it is neither directly nor indirectly required as an input.

17. Since in Hicks's vertically-integrated neo-Austrian model the start of elementary production processes is assumed to require no capital goods, 'investment' reduces to the provisioning of workers who are engaged in the starting-up of new production processes with consumption goods.

18. The source of the underutilization of capacity is, however, not an insufficient demand, but rather an insufficiency of supply. The phenomenon is therefore very similar to a Hayekian 'overinvestment crisis'; for details, see Zamagni (1984).

19. This follows from the properties defining the elementary production process given above.

20. Finished commodities are final consumption goods and all those commodities that are subject to interindustry exchange.

21. In the latter case it would of course be necessary to introduce 'intertemporal transfer processes', together with some hypothesis about the costs of 'transferring inputs over time'.

22. Without full performance, there are two different ways to accomplish the availability of those input amounts: either they could be additionally produced by means of overutilization of existing equipment, or they could be liberated by means of underutilization of some other equipment.

23. There is, however, no one-to-one correspondence between the standard dynamic input–output model and a discrete version of the non-vertically integrated neo-Austrian traverse model. Unlike the latter model, the former assumes the non-specificity of capital equipment, and it allows for an *ex post* intersectoral transfer of capital goods.

24. Another way to overcome the 'dynamic instability problem' consists in the introduction of input substitutability at the industry level (see Jorgenson, 1960–61).

25. It should perhaps be noted that the idea of an analytical separation of these phenomena is not only common among authors working in the Hicksian tradition, but also advocated by many of those who propose to analyse the economic consequences of technological change in terms of multisectoral models. For a recent statement, see, for example, Clauser et al. (1992, p. 9), who maintain that 'the problem of technological unemployment should be carefully distinguished from other types of unemployment, namely Keynesian and structural'.

26. This can be exemplified with regard to the shift system. Clearly, comparing the existing margins in two industries, one of which operates its equipment in a treble-shift system for seven days a week, under *normal* conditions, while the other industry operates its equipment only in single shifts during normal working days, it would appear sensible to suppose that the latter industry has a larger 'technical margin' for increasing its output via above-normal degrees of capacity utilization.

27. Lowe's calculations in Chapter 13 are carried out on the assumption of *immediate* increases in replacement requirements.

28. On Lowe's assumption that above-normal degrees of capacity utilization are associated with a reduction in labour productivity, the relative increment in consumer-goods output must be smaller than the relative increment in employment, so that an expansion process via overutilization must necessarily be associated with a reduced per-capita consumption of the employed workforce.

29. See Hicks (1965, pp. 193–7) and also Hicks (1985, pp. 139–42). Apparently Hicks later became convinced that he should have attached much more importance to this possibility, as may be inferred from the statements in his contribution to the Sraffa Conference (1990, pp. 101–2).
30. This is also the case in his later contributions; see Hicks (1985, pp. 139–42, and 1990, pp. 101–2).
31. Interestingly, there is no explicit discussion of variability in the degree of capacity utilization in Hicks's *Capital and Time* (1973). Yet Hicks may be interpreted as implicitly referring to this possibility when he introduces, in a chapter entitled 'Ways ahead', the notion of 'minor switches', which he explains as follows:

> What I mean by *minor switches* is much the same as what Marshall meant by short-period adjustments. ... Minor switches are changes made, in mid-course, to *old* processes. ... The process has been chosen as that which appeared most profitable at the time when it was started; but in the course of its execution conditions change. If that change had been foreseen, a different technique would have been adopted *at the start*; but it is too late for that. All that can be done is to adapt the 'tail' of the process to the new conditions. (Hicks, 1973, pp. 138–40)

It is not entirely clear, however, whether an adaptation of the 'tail' of an elementary production process must necessarily involve a change in the degree of capacity utilization. According to Hicks, the normal effect of a rise in the interest rate consists in the adoption of process tails, which, compared to the formerly chosen process tails, exhibit higher net outputs earlier and lower net outputs later. Obviously this can mean the adoption of above-normal degrees of utilization in earlier periods, but also that, for example, maintenance activities are no longer carried out. Hicks does not enter into a discussion of which kind of phenomena he had in mind. It is important to recognize, however, that the introduction of 'minor switches' (irrespective of whether the latter are meant to refer to variability in capacity utilization or not) would not change the character of the Hicksian model. As the choice of a new process tail is supposed to be made immediately after the change in relative prices occurred, the traverse path can still be determined, and the model still be supposed to be working, at full performance.

REFERENCES

Amendola, M. and J.L. Gaffard (1988), *The Innovative Choice. An Economic Analysis of the Dynamics of Technology*, Oxford: Basil Blackwell.
Baldone, S. (1984), 'Integrazione verticale, struttura temporale dei processi produttivi e transizione fra le tecniche' (Vertical integration, the temporal structure of production processes and transition between techniques), *Economia Politica*, 1, 79–105. English translation forthcoming in M. Landesmann and R. Scazzieri (eds) (1996), *Production and Economic Dynamics*, Cambridge: Cambridge University Press, pp. 81–104.
Belloc, B. (1980), *Croissance économique et adaptation du capital productif*, Paris: Economica.
Burchardt, F. (1931–32), 'Die Schemata des stationären Kreislaufs bei Böhm-Bawerk und Marx', *Weltwirtschaftliches Archiv*, 34, pp. 525–64, and 35, pp. 116–76.
Burmeister, E. (1974), 'Synthesizing the neo-Austrian and alternative approaches to capital theory: a survey', *Journal of Economic Literature*, 12, pp. 413–56.
Clauser, O., P. Kalmbach, G. Pegoretti and L. Segnana (eds) (1992), *Technological Innovation, Competitiveness, and Economic Growth*, Berlin: Duncker & Humblot.
Duchin, F. and D. Szyld (1985), 'A dynamic input–output model with assured positive output', *Metroeconomica*, 37, pp. 269–82.
Garegnani, P. (1992), 'Some notes for an analysis of accumulation', in J. Halevi, D. Laibman and E.J. Nell (eds), *Beyond the Steady State. A Revival of Growth Theory*, New York: St. Martin's Press, pp. 47–71.

Gehrke, C. and H. Hagemann (1996), 'Efficient traverses and bottlenecks: a structural approach', forthcoming in M. Landesmann and R. Scazzieri (eds), *Production and Economic Dynamics*, Cambridge: Cambridge University Press, pp. 140–66.

Georgescu-Roegen, N. (1978), 'Dynamic models and economic growth', in G. Schwödiauer (ed.), *Equilibrium and Disequilibrium in Economic Theory*, Dordrecht and Boston: D. Reidel.

Hagemann, H. (1992), 'Traverse analysis in a post-classical model', in J. Halevi, D. Laibman and E.J. Nell (eds), *Beyond the Steady State. A Revival of Growth Theory*, New York: St. Martin's Press, pp. 235–63.

Halevi, J., D. Laibman and E.J. Nell (eds) (1992), *Beyond the Steady State. A Revival of Growth Theory*, New York: St. Martin's Press.

Hicks, J. (1965), *Capital and Growth*, Oxford: Clarendon Press.

Hicks, J. (1973), *Capital and Time. A Neo-Austrian Growth Theory*, Oxford: Clarendon Press.

Hicks, J. (1985), *Methods of Dynamic Economics*, Oxford: Clarendon Press.

Hicks, J. (1990), 'Ricardo and Sraffa', in K. Bharadwaj and B. Schefold (eds), *Essays on Piero Sraffa. Critical Perspectives on the Revival of Classical Theory*, London: Unwin Hyman, pp. 99–102.

Jorgenson, D. W. (1960–61), 'Stability of a dynamic input-output-system', *Review of Economic Studies*, **28**, pp. 105–16.

Kurz, H.D. (1986), '"Normal positions" and capital utilization', *Political Economy – Studies in the Surplus Approach*, **2**, pp. 37–54.

Kurz, H.D. (1990), 'Effective demand, employment and capital utilization in the short run', *Cambridge Journal of Economics*, **14**, pp. 205–17.

Kurz, H.D. (1992), 'Accumulation, effective demand and income distribution', in J. Halevi, D. Laibman and E.J. Nell (eds), *Beyond the Steady State. A Revival of Growth Theory*, New York: St. Martin's Press, pp. 73–95.

Lavoie, M. and P. Ramírez-Gastón (1994), 'Traverse in a two-sector Kaleckian model of growth with target return pricing', unpublished manuscript (July 1994), 40 pp., University of Ottawa, Ottawa.

Leontief, W. (1953), *Studies in the Structure of the American Economy*, New York: Oxford University Press.

Lowe, A. (1952), 'A structural model of production', *Social Research*, **19**, pp. 135–76.

Lowe, A. (1955), 'Structural analysis of real capital formation', in M. Abramovitz (ed.), *Capital Formation and Economic Growth. A Report of the National Bureau of Economic Research*, Princeton: Princeton University Press, pp. 581–634.

Lowe, A. (1976), *The Path of Economic Growth*, Cambridge: Cambridge University Press.

Lowe, A. (1987), *Essays in Political Economics: Public Control in a Democratic Society*, ed. by A. Oakley, New York: New York University Press.

Mathur, G. (1965), *Planning for Steady Growth*, Oxford: Basil Blackwell.

Merhav, M. (1969), *Technological Dependence, Monopoly and Growth*, New York: Pergamon.

Ricottilli, M. and M. Cantalupi (1987), 'A development strategy with foreign borrowing', Working Paper Series of the Dipartimento di Scienze Economiche, Università degli Studi di Bologna, No. 35, Bologna.

Solow, R.M. (1967), 'The interest rate and transitions between techniques', in C.H. Feinstein (ed.), *Socialism, Capitalism and Economic Growth. Essays presented to Maurice Dobb*, Cambridge: Cambridge University Press, pp. 30–39.

Violi, R. (1982), 'L´economia della traversa: struttura del capitale e crescita non uniforme', laurea thesis: Università di Parma.

Violi, R. (1984), 'Sentiero di traversa e convergenza', *Giornale degli Economisti ed Annali di Economia*, **43**, pp. 153–96.

Walsh, V. (1992), 'The classical dynamics of surplus and accumulation', in J. Halevi, D. Laibman and E.J. Nell (eds), *Beyond the Steady State. A Revival of Growth Theory*, New York: St. Martin's Press, pp. 11–43.

Zamagni, S. (1984), 'Ricardo and Hayek effects in a fixwage model of traverse', in D.A. Collard, D.R. Helm, M.F.G. Scott, and A.K. Sen (eds) *Economic Theory and Hicksian Themes*, Oxford: Clarendon Press, pp. 135–51.

PART IV

Balancing Freedom and Order:
Modern Society and its Analysis

13. Spontaneous Conformity in History

Bertram Schefold

1 THE SELF–DESTRUCTION OF SOCIETY

The continuity of Adolph Lowe's thinking in his published writings over a timespan of nearly 80 years is most remarkable. Prior to the First World War, he wrote a study on the relationship between unemployment and criminality; he analysed the connection between economic necessity and social living conditions. His last book *Has Freedom a Future?* appeared in 1988, the German translation, revised by the author, in 1990. Lowe admits, indeed he postulates, emancipation as a human goal. A better future is one in which there is more scope for freedom. But a stable economic and social development is impossible without controls, and if these are not to be authoritarian, people have to submit *voluntarily* to a general order. There has to be, in Lowe's terms, 'spontaneous conformity'. But precisely the forces of voluntary social cohesion are undermined by the process of emancipation. High tax rates which are meant to help redistribution lead to embezzlement, and public financial support for the old, meant to facilitate a dignified life in retirement, may tempt a reduction in filial care. The growth of affluence leads not only to ecological damages in industrial production but also in consumption. Traditional habits of making parsimonious use of materials are replaced by wasteful expenditure, and if everybody wants to have exotic adventures, the wilderness will disappear.

We may speak of spontaneous conformity in the political, social and economic sphere. The leading modern example of spontaneous conformity in the political realm is tolerance as an essential value, helping to avoid authoritarian regimes. In the social domain, we first remember the duties in the family according to age and the tasks of education. Some form of spontaneous conformity is also required in economic transactions. It is topical nowadays to think first of the environment: the dispositions to protect plants or to recycle waste, rather than to throw it away, are regarded as desirable attitudes. But it seems to be a relatively recent phenomenon to see conflicts with economic goals primarily in the perspective of the preservation of nature. In the history of thought, the deliberation of why one should conform to established rules of behaviour is an aspect of ethics and often illustrated by means of examples taken from the core of economic activity, that is, the trading in different markets, a domain which today is largely controlled by the legal system. In earlier times, people were simply expected to trade honestly, to honour contracts, to avoid usury and to be fair to subordinates. In such matters, it was thought that conformity ought to be spontaneous even if it often was not. Roman law marks a transition in that unfair practices (for example, the *laesio enormis*) can be brought to court (Gordon, 1975, pp. 123–4, 132).

As is well known, Lowe's primary concern is with spontaneous conformity in the political sense. His writings on this topic, dating from the time of his emigration to Great Britain, prior to his appointment at the New School in New York, were inspired by the contrast between the political consensus which characterized English society on the one hand and the extreme individualism, especially among intellectuals, in Germany on the other. Tolerance, fairness and the respect for certain basic rules allowed the English people a large degree of private freedom and of independent political activity, within certain conventional bounds, while the claim to greater, almost unlimited independence in Germany provoked more stringent controls.

Lowe has traced the origins of this difference back to the conditions of modernization. Without repeating the details of his argument, suffice it to recall here the essential contrast in the period when the nation state was formed in Britain. The gradual political emancipation of the middle class, the adoption of middle-class values by other strata of society, went hand in hand with economic development and the slow transition of absolute monarchy to democracy, favouring the emergence of a basic consensus on the rights and the duties of the citizen. By contrast, he emphasized the narrow limits to political emancipation in the small German states prior to unification. The miracle of Weimar will always be remembered as a world historical example of what the cultural emancipation of the individual can achieve in a small community. But its ideals provided no model for the political constitution of the German empire, as was felt by the generation of Schmoller (Schefold, 1989).

Lowe (1988, p. 56) cites Pericles' celebrated speech for the dead in the second volume of Thucydides' *History of the Peloponnesian War* to illustrate the pride of a community in which the individuals are free and politically equal, as citizens, and yet held together by their common concern for independence, power and their cultural achievements. Let me quote another passage from the oration, which emphasizes more the spontaneous conformity of the Athenians, while the passage chosen by Lowe refers to the 'unwritten laws': 'We strive for beauty, without extravagance, and like to philosophize, without weakness'.

Pericles, in Thucydides (1882, Book II, Ch. 40) continues, adding a characterization of democratic participation to that of cultural pursuits:

wealth we employ more for use than for show, and place the real disgrace of poverty not in owning to the fact but in declining the struggle against it. Our public men have, besides politics, their private affairs to attend to and our ordinary citizens, though occupied with the pursuits of industry, are still fair judges of public matters; for, unlike any other nation, regarding him who takes no part in these duties not as unambitious but as useless, we Athenians are able to judge at all events if we cannot originate, and, instead of looking on discussion as a stumbling-block in the way of action, we think it an indispensable preliminary to any wise action at all.

This famous text alludes to several aspects of the Athenian polity and contains subtle implications which I try to render explicit, with possibly some exaggeration: the love of art but not of luxury (such as is found in the orient), the passion for knowledge which is supposed not to weaken the state (as the Spartans would have believed), a spirit of enterprise (both cultural and economic, rather than a mere display of riches), recognition also of poor citizens (the logical contradiction of the 'not shameful ... more shameful' indicates some disdain for the working poor, however), the praise for those who care both for their private estate and for the state at large (these are the well-to-do, the real statesmen, according to Plato), the recognition of some political involvement even of those in other occupations (such as artisans, who do not have as much leisure as the estate owners) and the conclusion: not to cooperate would be parasitic, all are actively involved in doing something positive (without leaving decisions to a political class).

Modern liberalism lives with a different conviction. Society is not integrated by some idea of a common good, only by the rights and constraints which law assigns. The constitution guarantees the realm of individual liberty, without prescribing ends or substantial contexts to social and political intercourse. But periodically, this position has been criticized, Hegel being a prominent early example, as being devoid of realism. There must at least be a common ground of moral values inherited from the past without which the intercourse would be impossible and society dissolved. A modern form of this critique is that of the communitarians (Honneth, 1993).

The liberals argue that modern democracy is essentially different from the participatory democracy of the Greek *polis* state. The communitarians reply, without denying that such differences exist, that liberalism will dissolve unless it is based on liberal ideals which tend to remain vague or only formally precise, as abstract concepts, unless reference is made to their historical roots and to the forms of life in which they are to be realized.

The contrast between the two conceptions of liberalism can be traced back to Adam Smith himself in so far as the *Wealth of Nations* interprets the economic process as governed by the self-interest of independent individuals who will be able to achieve their economic reproduction through the mediation of the market, with a remuneration in proportion to what each has to offer, while the model of social intercourse in the *Theory of Moral Sentiments* makes reference to a differentiated collection of moral values which guide individual behaviour, either because they are simply accepted or because the individual fears to lose prestige by not following them. In his *Lectures on Jurisprudence* we find the contention that the market produces even moral values. 'Whenever commerce is introduced into any country, probity and punctuality always accompany it. These virtues in a rude and barbarous country are almost unknown ... This is not at all to be imputed to national character ... it is far more reducible to self-interest' (Smith, 1978, p. 538).

If Lowe's conception of spontaneous conformity is reconsidered in the light of the Rawlsian discussions on the foundations of liberalism, it may appear poor because it does not reflect the philosophical ramifications of the debate; moreover, no systematic sociological account is given of the forms of behaviour which might be said to be governed by spontaneous conformity. Nevertheless, two advantages of Lowe's approach are also clear: the complexities of moral theory are avoided and the lack of specificity as to the behavioural domains allowed Lowe to formulate an interesting general historical hypothesis. Spontaneous conformity is a complex phenomenon, with some of its roots being traced back to the Middle Ages (Lowe, 1988, pp. 20, 66), in which education plays a crucial role (ibid., p. 61). Yet it remains one of those concepts which elude attempts at formal definition; it appeals to the intuition of the reader who is invited to add his or her own examples. It seems to owe more to the traditions of the Historical School than is acknowledged.

A challenge to Lowe's thesis consists in the proposition that what he calls spontaneous conformity may be interpreted as a behaviour dictated by self–interest – a self-interest which is perhaps not reflected upon in each single instance but which emerges in the form of customs in an evolutionary process: it must become customary to observe contracts in a society based on market exchange. Parents will teach respect and care for the old in a rural society where the old can only be supported by the young, and within the family. To avoid waste is more in the direct and obvious interest of the individual and the collective, the poorer the society is.

Lowe himself stresses causal factors which generate conformity but they are various – he even mentions geography (p. 65), and private interest, of course, is not absent (p. 114). He appears to be cautious when he invokes the opposite of economic determinism, that is, the forces of culture and belief; his idea of spontaneous conformity is not a derivative of a Weberian sociology of religion. At any rate, it is not useful for his purpose to invoke it:

> But ... a religion cannot be manufactured, and social integration is not its primary function. Therefore, if at the present stage we search for the precepts of a communal ethic, we must do so within the confines of a secular universe of discourse, admitting that its first principle is a product of 'intuition' ... . (Ibid., p. 137)

In what follows I shall not try to discuss the notion of spontaneous conformity by embarking on the discussion of the philosophical foundations of liberalism but I shall try to illustrate the concept by means of historical examples which will, I hope, show that the economic perspective is insufficient to explain what we observe, although it is certainly not devoid of truth. Lowe does not want to deny that self-interest plays a role in the constitution of spontaneous conformity but his point is that self-interest as generated by the modern economic system is by itself not able to produce and reproduce the moral code which supports it. He insists that we have to go back to the past in order to understand the genesis of our morals. Their preservation thus acquires a value of its own, like a cultivated landscape or other resources which must be tended to be kept but cannot be reproduced at will.

There are differences of rules of spontaneous conformity in different economic systems, but it would imply economic determinism to postulate a precise correspondence. After all, spontaneous conformity was first invented to characterize differences between German and British capitalism. It seems more appropriate to postulate that spontaneous conformity characterizes an economic style, with its different dimensions: specific forms of rationality and economic dynamism, with an economic and social order, and based on a certain level of technological development (Schefold and Peukert, 1992).

2   SPONTANEOUS CONFORMITY IN THE ECONOMIC DOMAIN AMONG HUNTERS AND GATHERERS

Even in the absence of the formal legal system, not all behaviour following a regular pattern is controlled by spontaneous conformity. It is meaningful to speak of spontaneous conformity where people act voluntarily according to norms. It does not really matter whether their actions are dictated by a sense of duty or whether the norms have been internalized to the extent that people follow their inclinations, as long as people obey the norm without being forced to do so. Spontaneous conformity refers to actions between two extreme motivations: if the action is entirely dictated by a sense of duty and quite against the inclination of the actor, the spontaneity of the action is doubtful. If the action is entirely from inclination, there is not much meaning in the word conformity unless the action follows a pattern dictated by tradition and enforced by education. As far as primitive societies are concerned, one hesitates to speak of spontaneous conformity where actions or non-actions are strictly prescribed by the religious system, in such a way that a lack of conformity is threatened by an automatic sanction. On the other hand, the term does not seem appropriate where actions simply follow the impulse of a short-run interest. The behavioural patterns relevant to us are in between.

Sharing and gift-giving among hunters and gatherers seem to be primary examples where spontaneous conformity regulates economic distribution. Sharing and gift-giving also occur in more-developed societies but they are only of marginal importance economically today. They are central to the lives of hunters and gatherers. Often, the women collect plants, berries, roots and so on, and distribute them within the family while the men go hunting in groups where success is more spasmodic. More elaborate rules are then required to divide the booty. But since the prey varies and since the composition of the group of hunters is not always the same either, the rules for sharing cannot provide an exact description of who is to get what: a feeling for fairness is indispensable to the process of sharing.

Sharing is essential for the collective for fairly obvious reasons. Individuals might not be able to sustain themselves if each had to rely on his or her own catch. Occasionally, the killed animal may be too large to be consumed by one family alone before the meat rots, and there are other considerations. The existence of sharing may thus be interpreted as the result of an evolutionary process in societal development. The generality of the phenomenon of sharing supports such a hypothesis.

Nevertheless, sharing presupposes differentiated forms of spontaneous conformity. The details of the norms do not follow from general principles and are not enforced by hierarchical authority; hunters and gatherers typically form small and egalitarian societies. On each occasion, a distributional frame must be proposed by someone who must control his or her impulse to take more than a 'fair' share.

A number of other activities among hunters and gatherers could be considered which reflect spontaneous conformity: when a hunt is to be prepared and undertaken, when to break camp and so on. A lack of consensus on what is to be done is, of course, possible. If talks do not settle the dispute, the band may split, with some individuals or families leaving it and joining other bands. Conformity may have limits.

A major institution helping to integrate archaic societies is that of gift–giving. As Malinowski has shown, networks of gift–giving may extend widely between different tribes over vast geographic distances, but the institution also exists within individual units. 'The Kula exchange has always to be a *gift*, followed by a countergift; it can never be a barter, a direct exchange with assessment of equivalence and with haggling' (Malinowski, 1978, p. 352).

In the leading examples of gift-giving in Malinowski, the contrast between gift-giving and commodity-exchange is stark. In *Gifts and Commodities,* Gregory (1982) has provided different schemes for gift-exchange and commodity-exchange. Relevant distinguishing features concern not only the absence of haggling.

The objects of market-exchange have a common dimension of value which implies that, to each quantity of a commodity of one kind, there is, for each commodity of another kind, a definite second quantity which can be exchanged for the first, in conditions of regular reproduction where normal prices rule, or where market prices are defined. In the absence of an organised market, economic agents can individually conceive of such exchange ratios which would satisfy them. The ultimate expression of this common dimension is the existence of money as a general equivalent for all commodities.

The objects circulating in an extended system of ceremonial gift-exchange such as the Kula-ring described by Malinowski, typically move in different spheres. It is characteristic for them that they are not generally commensurable. The gift of a necklace may require a specific counter-gift (perhaps another necklace), or the original necklace may be returned to the donor, after having been passed on by one or several intermediate persons, but other objects would not represent appropriate gifts, whatever quantity would be given. Gifts are ranked in different classes.

With regard to spontaneous conformity, the most important difference, however, seems to be this: one commodity (or money) pays for the other so that the contracting parties are under no lasting obligation, once the exchange has been concluded. Gift-giving is different in that it creates a bond between the exchanging partners. Of course, both market-exchange and gift-exchange create a temporary obligation till payment is made or the gift is returned. But after the event, no obligation remains in the case of market-exchange, except in so far as a recollection may remain that the partner is a person one can trust in trade. The situation turns out to be different in the case of gift-exchange as becomes most clear if the same object is eventually returned. Such a transaction would serve no purpose if it did not create a social bond between the partners. It is therefore a means to ensure peace, to create a federation, to confirm friendship or, as in marriage-exchanges, to reinforce a standard family relationship. Gift-giving therefore occurs in more rudimentary forms among hunters and gatherers and develops into more elaborate systems in more complex archaic societies. (For a textbook statement of these matters, see, for example, Harris, 1983.)

The conceptual distinction between gift-giving and commodity-exchange is rigorous and clear and does not preclude the existence of all sorts of intermediate forms in reality. The situation is particularly bewildering with regard to the use of money as the general equivalent in commodity transactions. It may be the case that different kinds of money circulate in the same society, with none of them being 'the' general equivalent in pure form, and such money may partly be used in gift-exchanges. Moneys may not only be used as means of exchange and of payment, but also as displays of wealth which can be exhibited; ornamental and other subsidiary uses are made of it (*Fremdes Geld*, nd). Some authors, who emphazise the special character of gift-giving, nevertheless count objects as money which are frequently used in gift exchanges. In his famous essay *Sur le don,* Mauss writes: 'After having reached the stage of making goods circulate, within the tribe and outside it, humanity has found that these instruments of purchase could be used as means of counting (numeration) and for the circulation of wealth' (Mauss, 1983, p. 179, my translation). Ambiguous uses of the term 'money' should not obscure the conceptual difference between commodities and gifts, however.

Commercial society presupposes peace in order to allow each individual to engage in transactions. Conversely: 'The gift is the primitive way of achieving the peace that in civil society is secured by the state' (Sahlins, 1972, p. 169). The primitive order is one in which law is absent. The danger arises that each will try to make his own, thus entering into open conflict with others. Gift-exchange is a symbolic interaction which helps to foster an alliance, to overcome isolation and to create customary intercourse. This is the rationality of a behaviour which also presents irrational aspects, not only because feelings are involved and, if possible, affection results, but also, because gift-giving is embedded in complex systems of religious belief which we cannot discuss here but which are the subject of extensive debates in the literature (regarding the spiritual side of counter-gifts, see, for example, Sahlins, 1972, p. 165). Mauss insists that to refuse a gift, to fail to invite, or to reject a gift may be equivalent to a declaration of war. Hence one finds oneself forced to give, and magic beliefs reinforce obligations. In an example pertaining to Australia, a son-in-law owes all the products of his hunting to his father-in-law and his mother-in-law. He is not allowed to consume his prey in front of them for fear that their breathing might poison what he is eating (Mauss, 1983, p.

163). And the obligations to give extend to the religious sphere, with sacrifices being gifts to gods.

Systems of gift-giving are none the less expressions of an underlying rationality which helps to preserve order. It is further clear that this order will be preserved best if it is observed spontaneously. Those of us who doubt the potential of witchcraft to operate as a sanction, but recognize the stability of traditional societies, are compelled to believe all the more in the spontaneity of the observance of traditions.

There are still limit situations in our lives where we may ponder whether it would be more appropriate to organize exchange around the gift relationship or the laws of the circulation of commodities. It has been argued that the human blood needed in hospitals for operations should be collected as a gift rather than bought, in order to avoid the hazard of obtaining contaminated blood (Titmuss, 1970), but this is a rather exceptional case. Modern society is characterized by a clear demarcation between a public sphere of commodity circulation and compulsory redistribution on the one hand and the private world, which is not monetized, on the other. Some forms of charity are the only major remaining instances of the more archaic form of organization for society at large.

3 SPONTANEOUS CONFORMITY: AN ARISTOTELIAN THEME?

If people greet each other friendly, or if they tell the truth – not for fear of admonition but because they are disposed to do so – their spontaneous conformity is historically not very specific; such values are almost universal. Others, or the forms in which they are expressed, are very specific. Should a man take off or put on his hat when he enters a holy building? Specific are also designations of those values, and the relationships between them. What is the traditional name for the qualities of a person who is regarded as well-behaved? A person, say, who is nice and agreeable, kind and friendly, but also honest and outspoken, endowed with that courage which is sometimes necessary to tell the truth, sufficiently pacific to discern what peace-making conformity really means in complex situations: as we extend the list, we realise that spontaneous conformity presupposes, in the language of traditional moral philosophy, the possession of certain virtues. Virtues seem to be ordered, but not always in the same ways. A medieval knight ought to be both polite and belligerent – a problematic combination not required from others.

Spontaneous conformity, a catchword of modern sociology, thus refers us back to a traditional, difficult, often forgotten notion of ancient philosophy. And yet this should come as no surprise if we remember that Lowe got an important inspiration from a speech by Pericles. I propose to reconsider the Aristotelian teachings on virtue, as a reflection of generalized principles of communal life in the *polis* state; for a wider perspective on the relation between politics and economics in classical Greece and in modern Liberalism see, for example, Bürgin (1993), Koslowski, (1993); for a comprehensive representation of Greek economic thought, see Lowry (1987). The philosophy of 'virtue' has not yet been adequately integrated into this discussion.

When we open Aristotle's *Nicomachean Ethics*, with Lowe's question in mind, we realize that spontaneous conformity was, in different guise, a central theme of his philosophy. Moreover, I believe that it can be demonstrated that Aristotle's aim was not to create new standards of behaviour but on the contrary to provide a systematic account for the rationale of traditional behaviour in Greek society, with some of the most important themes being age-old and having found a clear and most influential expression as early as in Homer. The same may be said of the economic motives of this tradition, their origin in archaic epic and early classical poetry, their expression in classical drama and their systematic representation in late classical philosophy: they are not overthrown, not even drastically revised, but ordered and expressed in the language of the then 'modern' philosophy in Aristotle (Schefold, 1992, pp. 13–89).

According to Aristotle, the person acting virtuously comes closest to the state of happiness (ευδαιμονία – *eudaimonia*): by acting, not for the sake of pleasure, or exclusively from a sense of a duty, but with the wisdom, knowledge, comprehension and the artistic faculties which are necessary to do what is appropriate, to live in friendship and to pursue what is good and beautiful. Virtue is therefore not contrary to the interests of the individual, if that is well understood, but it may often seem to be contrary to short-run pleasures and interests. 'To act virtuous is not, as Kant was later to think, to act against inclination; it is to act from inclination formed by the cultivation of the virtues' (Macintyre, 1985, p. 149).

Macintyre's 'cultivation of the virtues' is a social activity, hence historically specific, and Aristotle knows this, but in the *Nicomachean Ethics* he tries to isolate some values which he regards as universal, while historical relativism is more emphasized in his *Politics*. We shall soon see how even his limited universalism founders.

Relativism is obvious in the hierarchy of virtues. Do we not have good arguments to defend parsimony because that helps accumulation? Do we not also have other arguments to defend generosity and spending in order to realize philanthropic aims and to create employment? What is really helpful and good, very much depends on circumstances, however much such a conclusion may disappoint those who look for a foundation of moral principles which is both general and able to yield concrete implications. Aristotle is more on the side of generosity than of parsimony; spending is mentioned in his *Politics* as a populist measure of tyrants to enlarge their political base (Pol. 1313 b 25). The aim of reaching individual *eudaimonia* is the primary concern, but the ways to reach it are partly social, involving friendship, for instance. Thus what is good is not only a matter of private evaluation. An intermediate goal is to support a harmonious social development which is agreeable to all. Some basic rules must be observed, the common principles of which constitute 'goods', in the language of traditional philosophy. And if moral values are attached to the communal life, individuals must be supposed to be dedicated to it.

Clearly, we are back at Lowe's opposition between spontaneous conformity and private emancipation, as it appeared in the *polis* state. Let us first consider Aristotle's idea of justice which occupies a central place in the *Nicomachean Ethics*. He called justice the most perfect virtue because it has to be used in practising virtue, not only in one's private affairs but also in relation with others (Aristotle, EN 1129 b 31–35).

There are then particular forms of justice. Distributive justice shows how each shall get his or her due. This presupposes some social order; the officer and the private soldier do not have the same claims. There is corrective justice which has to find a compromise between opposing private claims (this is the task of a judge). There is the principle of reciprocity which in itself is not always just (it would not be appropriate for a soldier to return a punishment which has justly been inflicted on him by an officer) (Aristotle, EN 1132 b 29).

But in the interchange of services Justice in the form of Reciprocity is the bond that maintains the association: reciprocity, that is, on the basis of proportion, not on the basis of equality. The very existence of the state depends on proportionate reciprocity; for men demand that they shall be able to requite evil with evil – if they cannot, they feel they are in the position of slaves – and to repay good with good – failing which, no exchange takes place, and it is exchange that binds them together. (Aristotle, EN 1132 b 31, p. 281)

This remarkable passage shows that Aristotle interprets 'exchange' in the spirit of reciprocity in gift-giving: it is the condition which allows the intercourse between free and equal individuals to be distinguished from that between persons in authority and their dependants. It is what creates a social bond between the association of the free. 'Exchange' is actually a bad translation here, since the Greek word is 'μετάδοσις – *metadosis*' which also means private or public gift. This interpretation is reinforced by the passage which follows and which is even more remarkable:

> This is why we set up a shrine of the Graces in a public place, to remind men to return a kindness; for that is a special characteristic of grace, since it is a duty not only to repay a service done one, but another time to take the initiative in doing a service oneself. (Aristotle, EN 1133 a 3, p. 281)

The Graces are the goddesses of grace in the sense of beauty, thankfulness and recognition. The Greek word 'χάρις – *charis*' also came to mean 'mercy' which touches the religious sphere. To be able to be generous, to be first in giving, is a faculty which transcends ordinary human abilities according to a tradition which could easily be traced back to the oldest ancient sources, indeed, using etymology, to Indo-European origins (Benveniste, 1969, pp. 65–79). The cardinal virtue of justice here links up with the general idea of gift-giving which is interpreted by Aristotle in essentially the same way as by modern anthropologists. They do not seem to be aware of their precursor.

Immediately after this passage, Aristotle goes on to illustrate commercial exchange in a series of paragraphs which have often been interpreted as embodiments of the Aristotelian theory of just price. The technical term now changes; he speaks of 'ἀντίδοσις – *antidosis*', the (just) counter-gift.

The aim, however, is not to provide a quantitative explanation of relative price but to indicate the conditions under which the exchange of gift and counter-gift does not violate the established order, even if the transaction is of a commercial character, as the examples show (a house is paid for in terms of shoes, or, eventually, in terms of money). My interpretation of the details of the argument have been given elsewhere (Schefold, 1989b); the point is that the relative standing of the people effecting the exchange must not be reversed in the process.

It is interesting to note that Aristotle here seems to be at some distance from individual justice as a virtue, in that he does not say that it is typically the virtuous person who will buy and sell at the just price (an expression which he does not use himself but which is implied by his analysis). He only hints at a condition under which the price would be just. The condition is perhaps best expressed by saying that the remuneration must be such that it does not upset the status relationship. But this condition is an anachronism. It helps to illustrate justice in distribution according the Homeric tradition: the gift to the leader of the army, Agamemnon, must suit his rank, just as that to the greatest hero, Achilles, must correspond to the honour of the latter, or else the social order will be disrupted, as the beginning of the *Iliad* shows. Aristotle succeeds in formulating the condition that a traditional social order will not be disrupted by the exchange of commodities if that exchange preserves status but he utterly fails to explain how the exchange could be so organized as to achieve this aim in the market.

So, precisely at the point of Aristotle's analysis which has most attracted the attention of economists, we are at a dead end: Aristotle's theory of justice is illuminating in various ways but its application to commercial activity provides neither standards of individual conduct for the trading partners, nor an economic norm for the terms of exchange which could be translated into quantitative terms. He has no theory of relative prices. It is true that distributive justice involves a 'mathematical' proportion: an individual who deserves more will get more, and he explains that exchange is just if it does not upset this principle. But the persons and their remunerations are not commensurate, hence his 'proportions' are only useful as metaphors. The later Aristotelian tradition attached strong moral commandments, although in vague forms, to the idea of a just price (such as the prescription not to claim an outrageously high price on the supply side). Even hotter became the debate on the existence of just forms of interest. Modern theory has moved away from such a conception of morality in economics. In fact, there are other elements in Aristotle which are more interesting to economists, at least in our context. We now move to a less abstract level of the discussion to enquire which virtues were listed by Aristotle and why.

4   GREEK VIRTUES

Rackham, the English editor of the Harvard edition of the *Nicomachean Ethics*, perceived an analogy in the values governing English spontaneous conformity and Aristotelian doctrine. At any rate, he formulated the amusing phrase: 'Both in its likeness and its difference it is a touchstone for that modern idea of a gentleman, which supplies or used to supply an important part of the English race with its working religion' (Aristotle 1968, p. xxviii). History teaches us something about ourselves.

The first virtue discussed by Aristotle is courage, which is not surprising in view of the history of the Greek *polis*. Courage in battle – and in politics, too – is clearly often not in the immediate interest of the man who displays it. The courageous man will be honoured if he survives but survival is not certain. So why should one be courageous? For the sake of beauty, says Aristotle, 'τοῦ καλοῦ ἕνεκα' (Aristotle, EN 1115 b 13 and 23) or, as Rackham translates it, because it is noble. The example shows that the exercise of virtue is not pleasant in every case (Aristotle, EN 1117 b 15).

Nevertheless, there are people who are courageous: inspired by spirit (θυμός – *thymos*) and reinforced by what courage is for (Aristotle, EN 1117 a 6). The influence of education or of the social environment is not discussed. There is probably some regard for courage in all societies. But the special emphasis, given to it by Aristotle, seems to be founded on a consensus which does not need the support of further arguments. This surprises us, since neither the transhistorical concept of duty, nor that of inclination, is in itself sufficient to explain the display of courage.

We are here less interested in those virtues which are rather obviously in the long-run interest of the individual than in those which are not so easily reconciled with egocentric motives and perhaps cannot even be based on some form of the Kantian imperative. Omitting temperance, we turn to Aristotle's discussion of liberality. The liberal man (ἐλευθέριος – *eleutherios*) observes the mean in relation to wealth; he is neither stingy nor extravagant. There are good ways and bad ways of using whatever there is a use for. Riches belong in the category of the useful, and he who knows best how to use them has virtue in relation to riches (Aristotle, EN 1120 a 6–8). Liberality, the virtue in relation to riches, is for Aristotle not a matter of parsimony, as classical and neoclassical economists believe. Nor is it the virtue of the entrepreneur. On the contrary, liberality pertains more to the art of individual spending than saving. The liberal gives for the same reason for which the courageous man displays courage: because it is beautiful (or noble). He gives to the right people, in appropriate amounts. It is found, says Aristotle, that those who inherit a fortune are often more liberal than those who created it. He therefore appears to agree with the theory of the cycle of generations, but whereas the nineteenth century takes sides with the parsimonious parents, he sides with the generous descendants (Aristotle, EN 1120 b 11–14). The liberal man is easy to deal with in money matters and is easily deceived. It is easier to cure prodigality which is less bad than the other extreme, meanness. But meanness is more common.

Next, Aristotle discusses magnificence (μεγαλοπρέπεια – *megaloprepeia*), which is also concerned with wealth. Unlike liberality, it is not a matter of spending small sums but of the big gift. The magnificent therefore is also liberal, but not vice versa. Magnificence is in between paltriness and vulgarity; the magnificent is an artist in spending: he spends considerable sums with good taste, to good purpose, without mean calculation and in a noble fashion.

As we approach Aristotle's examples, we begin to understand what this strange discourse is about. Honourable are gifts for the gods, like votive offerings and sacrifices, the founding of public buildings, or the provision of a choir in tragedies or of a warship or of a public feast. In short, the magnificent person is primarily the one who provides 'liturgies' which are gifts to the public of a character which is somewhere in between a voluntary donation and a luxury tax. Everybody, and especially the rich, was expected to provide for the community. If one person had given more and believed himself to be poorer than another, then he could challenge a rival in the courts. Athens, the city which for long periods led the others in the artistic and the intellectual, in the military and the economic fields, thus retained an archaic institution for the financing of public expenditure which relied on spontaneous conformity.

Aristotle's further discussion of magnificence may be read as a reflection of how opinion exerted subtle pressure. The pauper who tries to be magnificent is foolish. Magnificence befits the rich and high-born. The magnificent live in beautiful houses and provide hospitality. They know how to produce a splendid effect even when they give small things like toys to children. Aristotle also gives examples of tasteless exaggeration, such as the giving of a dinner to one's club, which is as sumptuous as a wedding meal.

A climax is reached as he moves on to discuss greatness of the soul (μεγαλοψυχία – *megalopsychia*): the character of one who 'claims much and deserves much' (Aristotle, EN 1968, p. 215); he is the one who has the right disposition with regard to honours and graces, 'since it is honour above all else which great men claim and deserve' (Aristotle, EN 1968, p. 217). This virtue is the crowing ornament of all the others. Greatness of the soul is not simply pride. It implies that one prefers to give rather than to take, that one gives more than one receives and that one nevertheless remembers rather what one had received than what one has given. The great souled person likes to own beautiful and useless things rather than useful things that bring in a return, since the former show his or her independence more (ibid, p. 225). This virtue then comes in between smallness of soul and vanity. If it was part of Rackham's 'working religion for the English race', he must have meant Oxford, not Manchester.

We need not go on to discuss other virtues such as good temper and modesty. After the long digression on justice, Aristotle recalls that some virtues are of a moral, others of an intellectual kind (τὰς μὲν εἶναι τοῦ ἤθους ἔφαμεν, τὰς δὲ τῆς διανοίας) (Aristotle, EN 1139 a 1). The intellectual virtues such as knowledge, prudence, wisdom and intelligence are usually rendered more extensively in discussions about Aristotle than the moral virtues, some of which we mentioned. The discussion of the intellectual virtues is philosophically a good deal more sophisticated and their systematic ordering has a better claim to generality than that of the moral virtues. However, even the identification and ordering of the intellectual virtues reflects specific traits of Greek thought and life.

Aristotle puts great stress on prudence or practical wisdom – something one acquires later in life, he says. Young people may be good mathematicians but they do not have prudence. Related virtues are deliberative excellence, good understanding and consideration. Prudence concerns the choice of the right means, but one can also be clever in the pursuit of dead ends. Prudence, therefore, is more than cleverness; it is a prerequisite of being good, and there is no prudence without moral virtue (Aristotle, EN 1144 b 33). For Aristotle, practical wisdom is not a value–free pursuit. Ultimately, theoretical wisdom is the prerequisite of happiness; in this the Aristotelian discourse culminates.

But we are not concerned with a confrontation of these strikingly anti-modern conceptions with modern ones. They show that, for Aristotle, even the intellectual virtues are faculties helping to attain the good life and, therefore, not completely dissociated from ethics. But spontaneous conformity, especially in the economic sphere, is, according to Greek thought, primarily a question of the acceptance of certain moral virtues. Their system provides an image of the functioning of the private and the public sphere of the Greek economy which, although incomplete, refers to a market economy with peculiar features. And here, the sceptical economist must start to ask questions. Does the outcome of the market process really depend on the moral behaviour (the virtues) of agents? Can gift-giving and liturgies really play an essential role for the economic life of a community? Is this image of the economy only a fantasy of Greek philosophy? Is it, in fact, perhaps only a fancy of Aristotle alone, with other Greek thinkers taking substantially different positions?

To begin with the last question, it could be shown, as already indicated, that the Aristotelian doctrine on virtue is, so to speak, in the mainstream of Greek thought on virtue. Differences with other philosophers concern the theoretical argument more than the broad ideas about the attitudes and intellectual faculties which, partly acquired, partly natural gifts, constitute virtues. The debate about difficult moral issues such as whether it is better to suffer evil than to do it, as Plato's Socrates maintains, and the arguments concerning the logical relationship between a general good and individual virtues should not detract us from the observation that essential values, characteristic for the Greek thinking about the *polis* state, were common to all. The broad ideas about virtues derived from an aristocratic tradition which is modified but not eliminated in the transformations of Greek democracy in the fifth and even in the fourth century. Magnificence and magnanimity are aristocratic ideals which continue to command respect down to the latest stage of the *polis* state in which Aristotle writes, even if they are challenged politically by egalitarian currents and intellectually in the satirical characterizations of Greek comedy. But all this only implies that the great ideal is worn down, not lost. According to the Greek and more specifically the Aristotelian conception of the good, beauty and virtue are always a question of the right measure, they should be found in moderation. In fact, the comedy reabsorbs conservative old ideals by its ironic critique of the deviations, for instance of pusillanimity and vanity which are the deviations from magnanimity, and of niggardliness and vulgarity, the deviations from magnificence.

This interpretation is confirmed by the fact that Aristotle's philosophical successor, Theophrastus, wrote a book on characters which represents anecdotally how people may fall short of virtue by adopting extreme behaviour. As an example, 'the man of petty ambition' (μικροφιλοτιμία) is the one who, when invited for dinner, takes care to eat reclining next to the host himself. For the ceremony of cutting his son's hair, he takes him to Delphi (the hair of youths coming of age would customarily be dedicated to a *local* deity; Theophrastus, 1993, pp. 123–5). Other amusing details follow. Similarly the ungenerous man: 'when emergency contributions are announced in an assembly ... either remains silent or gets up and leaves their midst' (in difficult times, the wealthiest citizens were asked to pledge voluntary payments to the government; ibid., p. 129). The earlier epic and tragic poets create intuitive images of virtuous persons, like Homer's depiction of the intelligent Odysseus and Sophocles' of the courageous Antigone. The emphatic positive ideal of virtue in earlier philosophy eventually survives in a weaker form in the negative characterization of Theophrastus.

It is a great deal more difficult to determine the extent to which the image thus created of Greek economic life corresponded to reality. The cultural heritage is there to be seen, the liturgies are known to have been a working institution. Raymond Goldsmith has attempted a quantitative assessment of the distribution of wealth in Athens in Periclean times. He found that about 45 per cent of wealth was privately held and 55 per cent in public possession. He comments on the astonishingly high share of public wealth as follows:

> it is doubtful, whether as high a ratio can be found anywhere else except in some of the theocracies of the Ancient Near East. The ratio of cult buildings and objects in particular is astonishingly high, possibly reaching as much as 1/8 of national wealth. The high ratio of public property is significant because virtually all of it was economically unproductive even though it may have provided psychic satisfaction to the inhabitants ...' (Goldsmith, 1987, p. 22)

The concentration of property in the hands of the state is often the expression of autocratic power. In the democratic epoch of Athens it was the result of a singular participation of the citizens in political, cultural and economic affairs, of a participation which was clearly voluntary in juridical terms but much enforced by public opinion, and thus it provided the outstanding example of spontaneous conformity.

There is no room here to look for further characterisations of the common traits and the variants of Greek *polis* states. The Greeks themselves were intensely interested in the differences between their political constitutions and lifestyles; it was topical to contrast liberal Athens, and Sparta with its more pronounced participation of the government in the task of education. The Greek city states, as well as later the Roman republic, were eventually absorbed by monarchical empires which helped to extend economic integration, and probably led to further economic growth for some time but which eliminated the economic institutions of participatory democracy.

Their is no evidence that the Aristotelian denunciations of usury had much impact on classical Greek reality, with its emerging early forms of money-lending and banking; it was a late reflection of the aristocratic disdain for commercial activities. It is even less clear how the Aristotelian idea of a rank-preserving exchange could be realised in the market, i.e. beyond the sphere of gift-exchange. As Smith observed in Scotland, the slow historical effect of the exchange between the ancient nobles and the rising merchants was to lower the prestige of the former and to enhance the status of the latter. Even liturgies in Athens gradually ceased to be voluntary contributions; the term eventually meant a service which was due.

But there were more possibilities to interfere with credit and to regulate prices in a stratified society, with some degree of hierarchical control, as developed in the Middle Ages. At their end, the emergence of liberalism was associated with the justification of the free play of the market, hence also of interest-taking, and the medieval project of regulating the economy according to principles with Aristotelian roots was replaced by the programme of controlling only the adherence to the rules of free exchange, and not the market process itself. The role both of authority and of spontaneous conformity in the market domain was reduced accordingly.

5   FUTURE PERSPECTIVES

Macintyre ends his book with something like an Aristotelian confession:

> My own conclusion is ... that on the one hand we still, in spite of the effort of three centuries of moral philosophy and one of sociology, lack any coherent rationally defensible statement of a liberal individualist point of view; and that, on the other

hand, the Aristotelian tradition can be restated in a way that restores intelligibility and rationality to our moral and social attitudes and commitments. (Macintyre, 1985, p. 259)

But the communitarian spirit, if it can be rekindled at all, concerns political and social intercourse more than the economic sphere. This is also true of the thoughts of Adolph Lowe, who favours more direct controls to stabilize the economy. Some spontaneous conformity on the part of economic agents is helpful: honesty in the payment of taxes, a cooperative attitude at the workplace, fairness in the direction of enterprise. The interplay of such values and attitudes with the formal institution in which the market process develops still characterizes the economic styles of the economies in different countries and periods. But institutions and formal controls have grown so strong that changes in the degree of spontaneous conformity are not felt to be a direct threat to the working of the economic system while historians of antiquity amaze us because they attributed the decline of the entire Roman empire primarily to the loss of traditional virtues. If economic growth has been less fast in the last two decades than earlier in Western Europe (the reversed phenomenon is to be observed in EastAsia) the crucial reasons are probably not to be sought in a loss of spontaneous conformity. Growth will resume once the economies have adapted to the structural conditions in the world economy.

Economists, therefore, are seldom worried about the loss of spontaneous conformity, while others note the phenomenon, calling it by other names, and shrug their shoulders. Sociologists are at a loss when they try to indicate countervailing tendencies to the disintegration of traditional familial and social ties, which seems to be the price of the process of emancipation of the individual (Beck, 1986). The state continues to create institutions which provide formal compensation, but limits to the provision of finance for such extensions of the welfare state have become more and more obvious. One suggestion is to hope for the potential of integration within smaller groups which solve their problems. However, we are moving towards larger, not smaller, entities, in a process of continental, if not global, integration. History cannot teach recipes but it can lead to a better understanding of what this might mean: a further loss of spontaneous conformity, not its revival.

I was surprised to find that Hayek, the stern defender of the market, seemed to share Lowe's concern:

the fact that the tradition of moral rules contains adoptions to circumstances in our environment which are not accessible by individual observation or not perceptible by reason, and that our morals are therefore a human equipment that is not only a creation of reason, but even in some respects superior to it because it contains guides to human action which reason alone could never have discovered or justified, explains why the value of traditional morals as an autonomous equipment is unintelligible to those intellectuals who are committed to a strict rationalism or positivism. (Hayek, 1984, p. 320)

The difference between Lowe and Hayek seems to be that one has but little and the other no hope to restore morality by political design.

The moral consensus is never perfect, and what moral consensus we find is the outcome of extremely complicated historical processes, subject to economic and political influences, but also to autonomous cultural developments. Marx emphasized the role of force in the creation of the proletariat in the period of mercantilism (the laws against idleness, enforced mobility and so on) for the acceptance of disciplined work in the factories. Weber emphasized the role of religion in the emergence of the capitalist spirit. Modern research points to the role of competition between nations in the creation of institutions which foster economic growth. If this is the case: are nations not also induced to educate morally?

Aristotle asked the same question, and James Bonar, one of the most perceptive historians of the relation between economic thought and philosophy noted (in the year of Adolph Lowe's birth), as a summary of Aristotle's conclusions:

> There are three ways ... in which men become good; they are good by nature, or by precept, or by custom. The first is a happy chance that we cannot control; the second is uncertain unless the minds of the hearers have been prepared beforehand so that the seed is sown on good ground. Hence it is the last way, the way of custom, that must be used by the legislator. Nothing but a general and thorough system of moral education will give us a virtuous community. We must have laws for the whole of life from infancy upwards. (Bonar, 1967 [1893], p. 43)

Such has always been the hope of the reformist intellectual: to call for enlightened government and for the recognition of its powers to emancipate, in an educated society. Conformity is now to be imposed. Aristotle himself voices various doubts as to who should teach the legislators and whether private persons would not be more appropriate as educators, and the attempt to find the right balance then leads him to undertake the comparative study of constitutions: the end of the *Nicomachean Ethics* is the introduction to his *Politics*. A society in pursuit of knowledge and wisdom will thus find its way, perhaps, to the restoration and development of its moral system. It then turns out that different virtues are required, and in different degrees, under different constitutions. Aristotle's normative intentions eventually give way to the realism of a positive description of the regularities of political processes.

Revolutionary movements usually attack both conventions and the state which enforces them, without knowing the dilemma that the undermining of the former creates a need not to reduce but to increase the power and the interference of the latter. Lowe's concept of spontaneous conformity provided a happy formula not only to illustrate the opposition between individual emancipation and the subordination to social needs, but also to let this conflict appear as something new. He thus gave a fresh impetus to the debate. It is, in fact, one of the oldest of humankind, and one for which each generation has to work out its own solution.

REFERENCES

Aristotle (1968), *Nicomachean Ethics*, ed. with an English translation by H. Rackham, Cambridge, MA: Harvard University Press [1926, 1934]. Bekker's pagination refers to the Greek text, page quotations to Rackham's translation.
Aristotle (1972), *Politics*, ed. with an English translation by H. Rackham, Cambridge, MA: Harvard University Press [1932, 1944].
Beck, U. (1986), *Risikogesellschaft. Auf dem Weg in eine andere Moderne.* Frankfurt am Main: Suhrkamp Verlag.
Benveniste, E. (1969), *Le vocabulaire des institutions indo–européennes*, Vol.1, Paris: Ed. de Minuit.
Bonar, J. (1967 [1893]), *Philosophy and Political Economy in Some of Their Historical Relations*. London: Allen & Unwin.
Bürgin, A. (1993), *Zur Soziogenese der politischen Ökonomie*, Marburg: Metropolis.
Fremdes Geld (nd), *Fremdes Geld, Tauschmittel und Wertmesser außereuropäischer Gesellschaften.* Ausstellungskatalog zur Ausstellung der Commerzbank zusammen mit dem Museum für Völkerkunde, Frankfurt am Main: Commerzbank und Völkerkundemuseum.
Goldsmith, R.W. (1987), *Premodern Financial Systems*, Cambridge: Cambridge University Press.
Gordon, B. (1975), *Economic Analysis before Adam Smith*, London: Macmillan.
Gregory, C.A. (1982), *Gifts and Commodities*, London: Academic Press. (Studies in Political Economy, vol. without numeration).
Harris, M (1983), *Cultural Anthropology*, New York: Harper & Row.
Hayek, F.A. von (1984), *The Essence of Hayek*, ed. by C. Nishiyama and K.R. Leube, Stanford, CA: Hoover Institution Press.
Honneth, A. (ed.) (1993), *Kommunitarismus. Eine Debatte über die moralischen Grundlagen moderner Gesellschaften*, Frankfurt am Main: Campus Verlag.
Koslowski, P. (1993), *Politik und Ökonomie bei Aristoteles*, Tübingen: Mohr.
Lowe, A. (1988), *Has Freedom a Future?*, New York: Praeger.
Lowry, S.T. (1987), *The Archaeology of Economic Ideas.* Durham, NC: Duke.
Macintyre, A. (1985), *After Virtue – a Study in Moral Theory*, 2nd edn, London: Duckworth.
Malinowski, B. (1978 [1922]), *Argonauts of the Western Pacific*, London: Routledge.
Mauss, M. (1983), *Sociologie et anthropologie*, Paris: Presses Universitaires.
Sahlins, M. (1972), *Stone Age Economics*,Chicago: Aldine.
Schefold, B. (1989a), 'Normative Integration der Einzeldisziplinen in gesellschaftswissenschaftlichen Fragestellungen', in *Gustav Schmoller oggi/Gustav Schmoller heute*, ed. by M. Bock, H. Homann and P. Schiera, Bologna: Il Mulino and Berlin: Duncker & Humblot, pp. 251–69.
Schefold, B. (1989b), 'Platon und Aristoteles', in J. Starbatty (ed.), *Klassiker des ökonomischen Denkens*, München: Beck Verlag.
Schefold, B. (1992), 'Spiegelungen des antiken Wirtschaftsdenkens in der griechischen Dichtung', in B. Schefold (ed.), *Studien zur Entwicklung der ökonomischen Theorie XI, Schriften des Vereins für Socialpolitik*, Neue Folge 115/XI, Berlin: Duncker & Humblot, pp.13–89.
Schefold, B. and H. Peukert. (1992), 'Wirtschaftssysteme im historischen Vergleich: ein Projekt', in *Jahrbuch für Wirtschaftsgeschichte*, N.S. 1, pp. 243–54.

Smith, A. (1976), *An Inquiry into the Nature and Causes of the Wealth of Nations*, ed. by R.H. Campbell, A.S. Skinner and W.B. Todd, 2 vols, Oxford: Clarendon. (Vol. 2, in two parts, of the Glasgow edn).

Smith, A. (1978), *Lectures on Jurisprudence*, ed. by R.L. Meek, D.D. Raphael and P.G. Stein, Oxford: Clarendon (Vol. 5 of the Glasgow edn).

Smith, A. (1979), *The Theory of Moral Sentiments*, ed. by D.D. Raphael and A.L. Macfie, Oxford: Clarendon (Vol. 1 of the Glasgow edn, second printing).

Theophrastus (1993), *Characters, with other works and with translation*, ed. by J. Rusten et al., Cambridge, MA: Harvard University Press.

Thucydides (1882), Greek text, with comments, ed. G. Boehme, Leipzig: Teubner.

Titmuss, R.M. (1970), *The Gift Relationship. From Human Blood to Social Policy*, London: Allen and Unwin.

14. Lowe and Tillich on the Church and the Economic Order*

Betsy Jane Clary

1 INTRODUCTION

In the summer of 1937 an ecumenical conference of Christian churches was held at Oxford University under the auspices of the Universal Christian Council for Life and Work. The subject of the conference was the Church, Community and State, and it was primarily concerned with the relationship of the Church to the outside world. The conference was divided into five sections, and each section made recommendations in a written report. Paul Tillich was one of more than four hundred representatives attending the conference, and he was assigned to the section dealing with the Church, Community and State in Relation to the Economic Order. Tillich was a member of the drafting committee for this section. While Adolf Lowe did not participate in the conference, he reported that

> Tillich, a close friend since the early post-war days in Germany, ... was an American delegate to the conference, assigned to the section that dealt with Christianity and the Economic Order, and had been asked to draft a summary statement of the proceedings to be included in the final report. Then at Manchester University, I received an urgent call from my old friend Tillich asking me to help draft the summary statement. (Vickers, 1991, p. 8)

The statement they wrote was opposed by the American delegation as an unjustified attack on business (ibid.). Because the statement was supported by the organizer of the conference and because time did not permit an alternative statement to be written, the statement written by Lowe and Tillich was included in the final conference report (ibid.).

The purpose of this chapter is to explore this early contribution of Lowe and Tillich to social economics. This alliance between a Jewish social scientist and economist and a Protestant theologian and philosopher resulted in important ideas for social economics. The friendship and collaboration between Lowe and Tillich will be examined, beginning with their work in prewar Germany and continuing with their collaboration after each was expelled from Germany by the Nazi government. The report of the Oxford Conference concerning the economic order will be closely examined. Finally, the later contributions of Lowe to social and political

257

economics will be reviewed in the light of the influence of the early collaboration with Tillich. Many of the topics with which social economics is concerned today were dealt with by Tillich and Lowe as early as the 1920s, and both men continued to address these concerns throughout their respective careers, Tillich as a theologian and Lowe as an economist.

2   THE FRIENDSHIP AND COLLABORATION BETWEEN TILLICH AND LOWE

Tillich, born in Germany in 1886, had served as a Lutheran chaplain in the German army in the First World War, and upon his discharge from the army in 1919 he went to Berlin where he first served as a vicar to the Bishop of Berlin and later became a *Privatdozent* with the opportunity to establish himself as a scholar and lecturer.[1] It was during this time immediately after the war that Tillich became interested in politics and political analysis. In May 1919 Tillich addressed the Independent Socialist Party on 'Christianity and Socialism', and for this he was reprimanded by the Church. Tillich asserted that Christianity implied a duty to shape humanity in terms of justice and liberty and that the Protestant Church in Germany identified itself with the feudal–capitalist order and remained anti-democratic and anti-socialist after the war. Tillich was warned by the Church to attend no more radical, socialist meetings. Tillich, however, wrote to his friends that he wanted a new order of society, born of the Christian religion and socialism, by which the destructive powers of capitalism and nationalism could be overcome. To realize these hopes, Tillich founded the religious socialist movement in Germany.

In 1920, Tillich joined a small group of academicians in Berlin, known as the *kairos* circle, which saw the defeat of Germany as a sign and as an opportunity to create a new social order. Among the regular members of the group were the economists Eduard Heimann and Adolph Lowe, both Jewish and who both held government positions in the Weimar Republic. The group met regularly in Berlin until 1925. Heimann, the son of one of the leading Social Democrats of the German Empire, had begun his career working with the commission entrusted with the socialist reconstruction of the German economy in 1918. The efforts of the commission failed (Lowe, 1967, p. 610). This group of friends were very conscious of the breakdown of the old order, but they gave no support to those who wished to restore the former system of feudalism, capitalism, the monarchy, and the division of social classes. The German Lutheran Church was increasingly seen as an ally of the old order and as opposed to democratic and social action. The members of the *kairos* circle concluded that social action should be determined by justice, both social and economic, and they became convinced that the period after the First World War provided the setting for the fulfilment of the new order. They viewed socialism as the best vehicle for constructing a new social order. It was in this group that Tillich learned socialist theory, and out of this group, attempting to rethink socialist fundamentals, was born the Religious Socialism of post-First World War Germany. Tillich gave the movement the name *kairos*, from the Greek, because it expressed the feeling that post-First World War Germany was at a period in its history in which changes to the existing social, economic and political order were possible. This idea became the central point upon which this group based its proposals for reform and action. The idea of a *kairos* became a cornerstone for Tillich's theology.[2]

Lowe was working in Berlin when he met Tillich and became involved in the religious socialist movement. Lowe and Tillich became fast friends, and Tillich was stimulated by the debates he had with Lowe. When Tillich often discussed the friendships he maintained with the Jews, he was referring primarily to Lowe. Later in his life Lowe remembered Tillich's desire to baptize him as fulfilment of Tillich's life mission. Tillich later came to realize the possibility that some people outside the Church might speak more clearly than those within the Church concerning God's relation to humankind, and he was persuaded, largely because of his friendship with Lowe, that it was a useless task to attempt to convert a Jewish believer to Christianity (Pauck and Pauck, 1976, p. 194).

The *kairos* group disbanded in 1925 when many of its members left Berlin for other posts. Tillich had left Berlin in 1924 for a teaching position at Philipps University in Marburg. He was offered his first full professorship in 1925 at the Dresden Institute of Technology, where he taught religious studies until 1929, when he was appointed to the chair of philosophy at the University of Frankfurt am Main. In 1931 Lowe was appointed to the same faculty as Professor of Political Economy, where he resumed working with his friend Tillich.

The University of Frankfurt am Main had been established in 1914 around several scientific institutes. After the First World War new faculties were formed, and the privately-funded university rapidly became very progressive and liberal. Many, if not most, of the faculty were Jewish, and Tillich was sometimes jokingly called 'Paulus among the Jews'. Professors in the different faculties visited each other's classes and worked together, and Tillich and Lowe resumed their discussions on politics and socialism in discussion groups and sessions with colleagues throughout the University.

It was during this time in Frankfurt that Tillich became well known in Germany and that his reputation was established. He developed a large and enthusiastic following among his students and colleagues, and he delivered lectures and attended conferences throughout Germany. His book, *The Socialist Decision*, the result of many of his lectures, was published early in 1933. Becoming increasingly distressed about the rise of the National Socialist movement and its strength in Germany and in order to have greater influence on the socialist movement, Tillich had joined the Social Democratic Party in 1929, although he disagreed with its reformist policies. *The Socialist Decision* was mostly written during the summer of 1932 when Tillich and his wife were on vacation in Switzerland with Adolf Grimme, the religious socialist who had been Minister of Education from 1930 to 1932, the sociologist Karl Mannheim who was on the faculty at the University of Frankfurt, and Lowe. Lowe reported that Tillich would go into the woods and write in the morning and that in the afternoon Tillich and Lowe would discuss what had been written. In the Foreword, Tillich dedicates the book to the economist Eduard Heimann and mentions his indebtedness to Lowe. Tillich also mentions in the book that he could not have written the final chapter, entitled 'Nature and Planning in the Economic Order', without the special assistance of Lowe.

The Socialist Decision became a symbol of courage, as well as resistance to the Nazis, for Tillich's socialist friends (Tillich, 1933: 1977, p. xxiv). In Tillich's eyes Germany faced a choice between nationalism and socialism. Tillich clearly came down on the side of socialism when he wrote that if 'militant nationalism proves victorious, a self-annihilating struggle of the European peoples is inevitable. *The salvation of European society from a return to barbarism lies in the hands of socialism*' (ibid., p. 161).

The situation at the University deteriorated rapidly in 1933. Fights and riots between Nazi and Jewish students occurred, and Tillich publicly defended the Jewish students, demanding that the Nazi students be expelled. Soon after Hitler came to power early in 1933, *The Socialist Decision* was banned, and the book was little circulated and had little influence. Tillich was attacked in a Frankfurt newspaper for his defence of Jewish students and for his socialist writings, especially his statement concerning the salvation of Europe via socialism. In April 1933 the Nazi-led government launched the 'Restoration of Civil Service Act', which gave pseudo-legal support to the removal of 'undesirable' people with civil service status, among them German professors with their assured tenure. Two categories of enemies were named on the dismissal lists: first were members of the Communist and the Socialist parties and left-wing intellectuals, and second were the Jews, or the 'racially suspect'. Tillich and Lowe were both named on the first list, despite Lowe's being Jewish.

Lowe, fearing imprisonment, had left Germany for Switzerland on 2 April with his family just before the publication of the lists and just before all Jews were to have turned in their passports. That Lowe's name appeared on the first list, as a political threat, instead of on the second list of Jews, and that he was expelled for political rather than for racial reasons was a source of pride to him. After unsuccessfully trying to secure a job in Switzerland and in France, he was offered a position at the University of Manchester in England where he was appointed Special Honorary Lecturer in Economics and Political Philosophy in 1933.

Tillich remained in Germany. He and his wife left Frankfurt for a brief interval and returned in May in time to watch the burning of books on the Nazi blacklist in the city square. *The Socialist Decision* was one of the books burned. Few copies survived, and those that did were quietly passed around among those opposing Hitler. A second edition was published in German in 1948, but it received little attention. The book was, after many years, translated into English, and the English edition was published in 1977. Later in life, Tillich remarked that of all his books, he was most proud of *The Socialist Decision* (ibid, 1977, p. xxv), and Lowe called the book Tillich's 'most prophetic' (ibid.).

Early in the summer, 1933, Tillich received an invitation from Reinhold Niebuhr on behalf of Union Theological Seminary and Columbia University to join the faculties in New York. The faculty at Union, in the midst of the Depression, had voted that each professor would give 5 per cent of his salary toward that of Tillich. He and his family arrived in New York in early November 1933.

Tillich remained in the United States for the rest of his life. He retired from Union Theological Seminary in 1955, at which time he was appointed University Professor at Harvard. In 1962 he moved to the University of Chicago where he held a chair as Professor of Theology. In the spring of 1965, Tillich was invited and accepted the invitation to join the faculty at the New School for Social Research in New York to become the first occupant of the Alvin Johnson Chair of Philosophy.[3] He died in Chicago in October, before he was able to take up the position in New York.

Lowe remained in England at the University of Manchester until 1940. He recognized his opposition to the prevailing opinion in the economics department as well as that department's opposition to his unorthodox views. He became a naturalized British citizen at the beginning of the war, but wartime regulations prevented foreigners from actively engaging in the war effort. Lowe increasingly found that his views were neither accepted nor shared at the Department of Economics in Manchester, and he accepted an invitation to become Professor of Economics at the New School for Social Research in New York. He continued to be active at the New School after his retirement in 1963 as Professor Emeritus until he returned to Germany in 1983, where he lived with his daughter until his death in 1995.

Tillich and Lowe were colleagues, first in Germany in Berlin and Frankfurt and later in New York, for more than forty years. That they influenced each other is beyond doubt. In 1936 when Tillich celebrated his fiftieth birthday, Lowe was living in England. At that time Tillich was travelling in Europe performing work for the preparatory commission for the Oxford Ecumenical Conference to which he had been invited by J.H. Oldham, the organizer of the conference, who had heard Tillich deliver a paper in New York. Tillich was in Switzerland for his birthday when he received many letters and tributes from his friends in America and Europe in response to his wife's arrangements that they be written. Included among the birthday letters was one written by Lowe in which he described the unique sociological aspects of English society. The letter was published the following year by Virginia and Leonard Woolf at the Hogarth Press as *The Price of Liberty*.[4] Later in the summer of 1936, Tillich travelled to Manchester where negotiations were under way for him to come to Manchester to join the University as a lecturer. The offer remained unrealized, and Tillich returned to Union (Pauck and Pauck, 1976, p. 193). In the summer of 1937, Tillich returned to England to participate in the Oxford Conference during which he called upon his friend Lowe to assist in writing the summary report for the section dealing with the Church and the Economic Order.

3   THE OXFORD CONFERENCE AND THE CHURCH AND THE ECONOMIC ORDER

The Oxford Conference was a successor to one held in Stockholm in 1925, out of which grew a movement known as the Life and Work Movement. A second conference was held in Edinburgh in August 1937, which had as its primary concern the relation of the churches to each other, and which was a successor to an earlier conference held in Lausanne in 1927. The World Council of Churches was created out of the Oxford and Edinburgh Conferences of 1937. Both conferences and the World Council of Churches were indications of a growing ecumenical movement among the Christian churches.

Four hundred and twenty-five delegates attended the Oxford Conference. Of those, three hundred were appointed by the different churches represented, one hundred were lay people appointed by the Universal Christian Council on the advice of the different sections of the conference, and twenty-five delegates represented other ecumenical movements as well as the officers responsible for the preparation of the conference. In addition to the official delegates, four hundred visitors and associate delegates participated. At the conference were delegates representing all the principal Christian churches of the world with the exceptions of the Church of Rome, which sent no official delegate, and the Protestant Church of Germany, of which Tillich had been a minister before 1933. The German situation was of special interest at the conference, and the extent to which extreme nationalism, imperialism and racism were usurping the place of religion in that situation were of special concern.

The delegates were divided among the five sections of the conference: the Church and the Community; the Church and the State; Church, Community and State in Relation to the Economic Order; Church, Community and State in Relation to Education; and the Church Universal and the World of Nations. The section on the Church and the Economic Order had approximately seventy members. Preparatory work, in which Tillich had played a part, had taken place over the preceding year. When the section first met in July it had before it the sixth draft of a preliminary report written by a drafting committee, some of whose twelve members were, in addition to Tillich, Reinhold Niebuhr, Professor R.H. Tawney and T.S. Eliot. Lowe is mentioned in none of the reports on the conference. The only reference to Lowe's participation with Tillich in writing the report is by Mrs Jeanne Vickers in her introduction to the correspondence between her father-in-law, Sir Geoffrey Vickers, and Lowe. Lowe discussed the conference and his participation in writing the report with Mrs Vickers in an interview at Lake Thun where he was vacationing in Switzerland in 1990.[5] The extent to which Lowe and Tillich participated in writing the report can only be surmised from Lowe's statements.

A few of those in attendance at the 1937 Conference formed a group called the Moot which meet in England three or four times each year to continue discussions begun at the conference. Members of this group of lifelong friends were Joe Oldham, convener of the Oxford Conference, Karl Mannheim, Reinhold Niebuhr, Middleton Murray, T.S. Eliot, Michael Polanyi, Sir Walter Moberly, Geoffrey Vickers, Lowe and Tillich (Vickers, 1991, p. 8).

The report of the section dealing with the Church and the Economic Order is divided into six parts. The first explains why and on what basis the Church is concerned with the economic order or the economic system. The second part analyses the present (1937) economic situation. Part III describes the economic assumptions and the results of the economic order which the Church finds offensive and with which the Church takes issue. The report in Part IV discusses the Church's proposals for reform or reconstruction of the existing economic system and points out the kinds of social decisions which Christians, as citizens, must make. In Part V the report discusses what the teaching of the Church, as a church, should be concerning the economic order. The final part describes immediate actions, based on Christian teaching, that the Church and its members can take in reforming and changing the existing economic order. Following is a summary of each of these six parts of the section report.

3.1   Part I: The Basis of the Christian Concern for the Economic Order

The section report begins with a discussion of the reasons why and on what grounds the Church is concerned with the economic order of society and concludes with the assertion that the Church is opposed to any economic system which gives one person undue advantage over another. The basis for such concern rests with the Christian obligation that we love our neighbours as ourselves. This obligation, recognized in all systems of morality, rests on the 'native worth and dignity of man as made in the image of God' (Oxford Conference Report, 1937a, p. 10). Christianity, however, also recognizes that, because of sin, man's worth and dignity are largely obscured, and that the obligation rests primarily on 'duty towards God and continues to be operative even when the neighbour does not obviously demand or deserve respect' (ibid., p. 10). Because the world is sinful and because behaviour falls short of the ultimate standard of Christian conduct of loving one's neighbour as oneself, the Christian must discover the best possible means of increasing the possibilities of this standard being practised in the world. The relative standard for 'social arrangements and institutions, all the economic structures and political systems', is the principle of justice (ibid., p. 11). Justice attempts to keep in check the 'tendency of one life to take advantage of another' (ibid., p. 11) with both positive and negative significance. Of negative significance are those principles of justice that 'restrain evil and the evildoer' by preventing 'men from doing what sinful ambition, pride, lust, and greed might prompt them to do' (ibid., p. 11). While these negative principles of justice are embodied in systems of coercion, and while coercion involves power which tempts the possessor to wrongly use that power, the use of coercion and power is ultimately not desirable. Christian love alone, however, will never 'obviate the necessity for coercive political and economic arrangements' (ibid., p. 11). Of positive significance are those principles of justice that extend the 'principle of love beyond the sphere of purely personal relations' and 'beyond the requirements of economic and social institutions' (ibid., p. 11).

While individual acts of love, or charity, may 'mitigate ... injustices and increase ... justice' these acts are 'no substitute for law, for institutions, or for systems' (ibid., p. 11). The Christian has the responsibility of 'seeking the best possible institutional arrangement and social structure for the ordering of human life' and of securing the 'best possible social and economic structure' (ibid., pp. 11–12).

The 'relation of the commandment of love to the justice of political and economic systems' is both an ideal and a standard 'by which various schemes of justice may be judged' (ibid., p. 12). Because all systems fall short of the ideal, that ideal may be used as a 'principle of indiscriminate judgment upon' all systems, giving the 'advantage' in making decisions about those systems 'to established systems as against the challenge of new social adventures and experiments', tempting 'Christians to make no decisions at all', with the result of reserving decision becoming 'in practice decisions in favour of the *status quo*' (ibid., p. 12). In using the relation of the commandment of love to the justice of a particular system as a standard by which a political and economic system is judged, one may make the error of identifying 'some particular social or economic system with the will of God' (ibid., p. 12). Any attempt to identify a particular system with the 'Kingdom of God' is 'essentially heretical from the point of view of Christian faith' (ibid., p. 12).

Instead, the 'law of love ... is properly regarded ... not only [as] a criterion of judgment in all the fateful decisions which men must make in history, but also [as] an indictment against all historical achievements' (ibid., p. 12). As such, the 'law of love gives positive guidance, in terms of justice ... and places clearly under condemnation all social and economic systems which give one man undue advantage over others', when, for example, it

> denies children, of whatever race or class, the fullest opportunity to develop whatever gifts God has given them and makes their education depend upon the fortuitous circumstance of a father's possession or lack of means to provide the necessary funds. It must challenge any social system which provides social privileges without reference to the social functions performed by individuals, or which creates luxury and pride on the one hand, and want and insecurity on the other. It makes the conscience of Christians particularly uneasy in regard to the deprivation of basic security for large masses of human beings. (Ibid., p. 13)

In summary, the basis of the Christian concern for the economic order is the commandment that we love our neighbours as ourselves, and, based on that commandment, any social and economic system which gives one person undue advantage over another is condemned. While the commandment prescribes no particular system as representing the 'Kingdom of God', it does serve as a 'criterion of judgement upon the relative merits of economic arrangements and social structures' (ibid., p. 13).

3.2.   Part II: Analysis of the Present Economic Situation

While the section recognized that the ecumenical Christian movement faced no one particular economic order and that there were even various differences among the many types of capitalism, it was the capitalist economic system on which the section dealing with the economic order chose to concentrate its efforts at analysis.

It was recognized that the 'dawning of the capitalist age' was a 'definite step forward in the progress of humanity' because it set free the 'development of human potentialities' which had been restrained by the restrictions of the Middle Ages (ibid., p. 13). Through technological advancement the system of free enterprise was responsible for overcoming economic scarcity, raising the standard of living and, through mechanization, reducing the necessary physical labour of workers. Technology had brought the different parts of the world closer together, making the idea of the unity of humankind a possibility.

The report further recognized, however, that the new economic order brought with it not only improved material conditions but also social injustices, such as greater inequality and insecurity, and 'subjected all members of modern society to the domination of so-called independent economic "laws"' (ibid., p. 14). The traditional society of craftsmen and farmers was destroyed by large-scale production, resulting in the concentration of great wealth alongside the poverty of the urban masses. Increasingly, large numbers of workers were subjected to long periods of unemployment, resulting in 'poverty in the midst of plenty' (ibid., p. 14). In addition, in the capitalist system human labour is treated as a commodity, 'bought at the lowest possible price and ... utilized to the greatest possible extent', and the 'predominance of the profit motive ... deprived the worker of the social meaning of his work and ... encouraged hostility between the members of different groups in their economic relationships' (ibid., p. 14).

The report analysed the colonization of the nineteenth century which allowed the more advanced industrial countries to mitigate some of the worst evils brought about by the rise of capitalism by expanding markets and reducing social and economic pressures in the industrial countries, thereby making possible the rise in real wages and the passage of social legislation. Many Western governments enacted legislation providing for progressive taxation and social insurance programmes, helping to lessen the results of social evils accompanying the rise of capitalism.

The report reached the conclusion that, partly because of expansion and technical progress, the free-trade and competition characteristic of the early stages of capitalism have largely been replaced by protectionist measures and monopolies. The political consequence was more state control, on the one hand aimed at controlling the economic process and on the other hand aimed at protecting the particular interests of certain industrial and financial groups. Out of the conflict between free competition, and monopoly and state control, have emerged 'social and economic systems ... which contain elements of both tendencies in varying proportions' (ibid., p. 15).

The report concludes that as a consequence of the development of capitalism, socialism and communism emerged, and both movements represented a 'protest against the evil results of the capitalist economic order from those who suffered chiefly from it' (ibid., p. 16). In several cases, this protest included a denial of 'Christianity, the Church, and belief in God ... *partly* due to the fact that the Churches had become deeply involved in the social and cultural attitudes of the wealthier members of society, upon whom they were frequently dependent, politically and economically' (ibid., p. 16). A division developed between the Church, which did not seem to recognize the social injustices, and those who were struggling for social justice on non-religious grounds, resulting in the persecution of the Christian Churches, on the one hand, by communism and the persecution of communists and socialists, on the other hand, with the support, or at least without protest, of the Church.

In conclusion, while the Church must acknowledge social injustice it must reject certain elements of communism which are in conflict with Christian truth. These elements include *Utopianism*, which 'looks for the fulfilment of human existence through the natural process of history, and which presupposes that the improvement of social institutions will automatically produce an improvement in human personalities'; *materialism*, which 'derives all moral and spiritual values from economic needs and economic conditions, and deprives the persona and cultural life of its creative freedom'; and the *disregard for the dignity of the individual*, which is present in communism as well as in other totalitarian movements (ibid., p. 16).

In summary, capitalism, while overcoming scarcity, increasing the general standard of living, and reducing the hardship of physical labour through technological improvements, has resulted in social injustices, such as the concentration of wealth and widespread unemployment, and in hostility and conflict among the members of different economic groups. In addition, the further development of capitalism has resulted in the adoption of protectionist policies and monopolies, giving rise to increased control and interference by the state. As a protest against social injustice, socialism and communism developed as alternative systems. The Church must recognize and acknowledge social injustice but it must also reject those elements of communism which it judges to be anti-Christian.

3.3   Part III: Points at Which the Christian Understanding of Life is Challenged

Before discussing four features of the economic system of the industrialized world which the writers find offensive, the third part of the report explains how such a system has the potentiality for good. The authors accept the possibility that, because of technology and the release of human resources, poverty, which denies the physical necessities of life, can and is being overcome. Instead of being dependent on natural factors and conditions, the abolition of poverty is seen as dependent on the organization of economic activity. As such, the possibility of 'economic "plenty"' achieves moral importance in that the persistence of poverty is a matter of human responsibility (ibid., pp. 16–17). The report argues that poverty continues to exist not because of natural necessity and scarcity but because of man's shortcomings in organizing economic activity in areas of both production and distribution. Technological advance has made the modern period different from all others in which Christian thinking about economic matters was formulated, and Christian effort concerning economic activity 'should henceforth be turned from charitable paternalism to the realization of more equal justice in the distribution of wealth' (ibid., p. 17) not only within national boundaries but also among different nations.

The first feature of the economic system with which the report takes issue is the system's enhancement of acquisitiveness. The preoccupation with the attainment of riches has several important implications for individuals and society. In the first case, this economic system results in a 'danger that the finer qualities of the human spirit will be sacrificed to an over-mastering preoccupation with a department of life which, though important on its own plane, ought to be strictly subordinated to other more serious aspects of life' (ibid., p. 17). Second, when society makes the 'acquisition of wealth the chief criterion of success it encourages a feverish scramble for money, and a false respect for the victors in the struggle', and '[i]n so far as the pursuit of monetary gain becomes the dominant factor in the lives of men, the quality of society undergoes a subtle disintegration' (ibid., p. 17), resulting in a society in which a perpetual conflict of interests between economic groups exists. Unless people are united by a common purpose superior to the individual interests, they do not and cannot cooperate. Finally, the economic system cannot be 'recognized as properly fulfilling its social purpose' if it is organized for the purpose of producing purely financial gain for some of its members instead of for the service of the community.

The second feature of the economic system with which the report takes issue is that of inequality, both the inequality in the distribution of income and wealth and the inequality in the distribution of opportunity. The report points out that while Christianity does not teach that all people are equally endowed and that identical provision should be made for all irrespective of difference of capacity and need, Christianity does require that they should all be treated with dignity and that any natural differences among them are trivial. Any system which treats 'some men as ends and others as means' and 'which obscures the common humanity of men by emphasizing the external accidents of birth, or wealth, or social position, is *ipso facto* anti-Christian' (ibid., p. 18). The report in this part deals with the particular plight of children in such an economic order. The health and education of children is discussed as a Christian duty, and differences among that afforded to different groups often is a function of differences in income among the parents and of race.

The third feature of the economic system with which the report takes issue is that a few individuals or groups, who are not responsible to any particular organ of society, wield power which creates in individuals and in society characteristics which are difficult to reconcile with Christianity. For example, the 'leaders of the world of finance' make decisions which 'raise and lower the economic temperature' (ibid., p. 19). The 'controllers of certain great key industries' make policies which 'vitally affect the lives of millions of human beings', and the masters of 'a mass of economic undertakings' exercise 'power over the few hundred, or few thousand, persons dependent on each of them' (ibid., p. 19). This economic power which escapes the control of the state 'tends to create in those who wield authority, and in the agents through whom they exercise it, a dictatorial temper, which springs ... from the influence upon them of the position which they occupy' (ibid., p. 19). Further, the effect of this power on those over whom it is exercised 'makes them servile; fear of losing their jobs, and a vague belief that, in the end, the richer members of society always hold the whip-hand, tends to destroy their spiritual virility' (ibid., p. 19). Economic autocracy results in an outlook on life which is contrary to that of Christianity.

The final point with which the report takes issue is that of the conflict which results when the Christian worker is required by the economic system to perform work which is contrary to what he or she sees as his or her Christian duty in his or her daily work. While most employees are '*directly* conscious of working for the profit of the employer', they are 'only *indirectly* conscious of working for any public good' (ibid., p. 19). Many workers find themselves having to produce things which are of inferior quality or which are destructive. Salesmanship which involves deception is recognized as a threat to the integrity of the worker. The threat of unemployment produces a feeling of insecurity, and prolonged unemployment creates a sense of uselessness, or of being a nuisance. An economic system which does not provide meaningful work and significant activity tends to destroy human self-respect.

The Christian understanding of life is challenged by the economic system of the industrialized world by at least four points discussed in the report: the enhancement of acquisitiveness; inequalities; irresponsible possession of economic power; and the frustration of the sense of Christian vocation. These aspects of the economic system are in conflict with the Christian understanding of the moral and spiritual nature of humankind.

3.4   Part IV: Christian Decisions in Response to this Challenge

This part of the report discusses proposals for reform of the economic system which would alleviate at least part of the struggle among various social groups. It is pointed out that Christianity is a social religion, with its teaching directed towards people as members of a community, insisting that the only life in which they can find peace and happiness is the life of service and self-sacrifice. Relationships among people are determined largely by economic interests, and it is the duty of Christians to evaluate the institutional framework of society in the light of their Christian beliefs, neither taking the economic system for granted nor dismissing it as irrelevant to spiritual life. It is the duty of the Christian to examine the moral credentials of the economic system, and, when that system fails to satisfy the criterion of the Christian doctrine, it is the duty of the Christian to change, amend, or supersede that system.

The report recognizes that Christians, united by common religious convictions, differ in their conceptions of political obligations. The two most prevalent political systems recognized in the report which can address the four challenges discussed in the previous section are a system of private enterprise and a system based on social ownership of the means of production. While the report recognizes that differences between the two systems will not be resolved, it stresses that attitudes which either complacently defend exclusive privilege or practise self-righteous fanaticism are both incompatible with membership in the Christian Church.

The report in this section offers three proposals for economic reform of a system of private enterprise, all of which had already been adopted to some degree by modern industrial nations. The first kind of reform is that which seeks to exercise a greater degree of social and political control on the holders of economic power, demanding a greater degree of social responsibility from those who hold that power. The second type of reform is that which attempts to diminish economic inequalities through taxation and social legislation. The third type of reform seeks to prevent the centralization of economic power by government destruction of monopoly. All three proposals for reform recognize that the main dangers of an economic system based on private enterprise are irresponsible power and inequality.

Instead of reforming the system of private enterprise, the report recognizes that some would change the economic system to one of social ownership. There was general agreement in the report that this could be done by a gradual democratic political process. While the proponents of socialization differed in their opinions of the degree to which property should be socialized, the report recognized that basic industries and natural resources are those for which socialization is generally demanded.

The report further recognized that there are some proposals which fall between those of reforming a system of private enterprise and of socialization, citing specifically the proposals for the socialization of money and credit and for the extension of voluntary cooperative enterprises, both of which have strong Christian support on the grounds that they can be implemented with little social conflict and that they provide the means of eliminating the evils of the present (1937) system.

In summary, the report in this section offers various proposals for reform, some maintaining the system of private enterprise and others resulting in a system of socialization of economic means. All, however, are aimed at alleviating conflict among social and economic groups.

3.5   Part V: Christian Teaching in Relation to the Economic Order

This part of the report attempts to describe what the teaching of the Church concerning the economic order should be. The authors suggest three areas in which the Church should play a role through its teaching about economic life.

First, Christian teaching should present standards and principles '*in the light of which every concrete situation and every proposal for improving it must be tested*' (ibid., p. 24). Five such standards by which an economic situation can be tested are given as examples. The implications of these standards involve significant changes in economic life.

1.   Since man must be in fellowship with his fellow man in order to be in fellowship with God, any economic arrangement which frustrates that fellowship among men must be modified. Any ordering of economic life that 'tends to divide the community into classes based upon differences of wealth and to occasion a sense of injustice among the poorer members of society' must especially be changed. Further, '[t]o every member of the community there must be made open a worthy

means of livelihood', and '[t]he possibilities of amassing private accumulations of wealth should be so limited that the scale of social values is not perverted by the fear and the envy, the insolence and the servility, which tend to accompany extreme inequality' (ibid., p. 24).

2. Every child, regardless of race or class, should have the opportunity of education suitable for its full development, free from health and environmental handicaps, and 'the protection of the family as a social unit should be an urgent concern of the community' (ibid., p. 24).

3. People who are unable to perform economic activity, whether because of sickness, infirmity, or age, would be the 'object of particular care' (ibid., p. 24) and should not be economically penalized, and here, too, the safeguarding of the family is an issue of importance.

4. Since labour has intrinsic worth, the 'duty and the right of men to work should therefore alike be emphasized', and 'labour should never be considered as a mere commodity' (ibid., p. 24). In his work man should be able to fulfil his Christian vocation, and labour is entitled to 'a living wage, wholesome surroundings, and a recognized voice in the decisions which affect his welfare as a worker' (ibid., p. 24).

5. The resources of the earth, since they are the gifts of God to the whole human race, should be protected for the needs of both the present generation and for future generations.

In addition to these five standards, the report in this section addresses the question of property, recognizing that any action affecting property rights would also affect the application of the principles explained above. Christian thinking must be reconciled with the development of the institutions of property in modern economic conditions, and the report suggests some directions in which Christian thinking about property should move. Because 'all human property rights are relative and contingent only in virtue of the dependence of man upon God as the giver of all wealth and the creator of man's capacities to develop the resources of nature' (ibid., p. 25), the Christian must be willing to 'examine accumulations of property in the light of their social consequences' (ibid., p. 25). Further, because the present (1937) distribution of property and the system of property rights were developed by 'largely non-moral processes' (ibid., p. 25), that system and that distribution must be criticized. Also, Christian teaching should affirm that 'individual property rights must never be maintained or exercised without regard to their social consequences or without regard to the contribution which the community makes in the production of all wealth' (ibid., p. 25). Finally the Church should make a distinction between the different forms of property, for property in the form of personal possessions has a clearer moral justification than does property in the form of the means of production and land. The latter give the owner power over other persons while the former do not, and '[a]ll property which represents social power stands in special need of moral scrutiny, since power to determine the lives of others is the crucial point in any scheme of justice' (ibid., p. 25).

The second area with which the Christian can expect to receive guidance from Christian teaching is in the examination of the existing economic situation and in an evaluation of the human consequences of that situation. Constructive change is brought about through a process of a critical analysis of facts, and that sort of critical analysis must be part of the message of the Church. The human consequences of economic activity are within the province of the Church in part because the clergy have the opportunities of 'knowing what the present economic situation does to the character, the *morale*, the true welfare of men, women, and children, and to family life' (ibid., p. 26). Through Christian insight one can 'see more deeply into the effects of an economic situation' (ibid., p. 26). The Church has not only the obligation to make facts available to its members, both lay and clergy, but also an obligation to assist in securing facts. Not only is it the business of the Church to 'catalogue particular cases of poverty and exploitation or to call attention to specific cases of selfish and irresponsible conduct on the part of those in power', but the Church must also 'point out where the economic institutions of our time are in themselves infected with evil' (ibid., p. 27). Further, while there are many Christian employers and businesspeople who preserve high standards of personal integrity within their spheres of influence and whose conduct is inspired by praiseworthy human motive, 'the presence of such conscientious Christians in places of responsibility should not create the expectation that, with changes in institutions and legal relationships, they will be able to overcome the evils set forth in Part III' (ibid., p. 27).

The third area in which Christian teaching can offer guidance for economic life is in making clear the obstacles to economic justice which exist within the individual. Through the teaching of the Church, the individual can gain self-knowledge which can help him or her understand to what extent his or her attitudes are 'moulded by the position which they hold in the economic order' (ibid., p. 27). The Church can help individuals understand

> how far their opinions on economic issues are controlled by the interests of the group or class to which they belong, how far they are deceived by false slogans and rationalization, how far they are callous to 'evil at a distance' or evil experienced by another national or class group than their own – evil to which they may consent, for which they may vote or by which they may profit. (Ibid., p. 27)

The different parts of the Church must address especially their various particular constituencies. For example, those parts of the Church which contain the 'comfortable middle classes should create an atmosphere in which it is most likely that the peculiarly middle-class illusions will be punctured' (ibid., p. 28). These classes tend to take the existing property system for granted and to 'regard as unjust changes which alter the present distribution of property or the present rights of owners' (ibid., p. 28). The Church, in its teaching, has an obligation to address these issues and to dispel these illusions. The Church must also help this class to

> come to see how one-sided those conceptions of Christianity are which assume that, because Christianity is a spiritual religion, economic conditions do not greatly matter, or that it is enough to leave it to the grace of God to save souls in all varieties of external circumstances. (Ibid., p. 28)

In addition, 'to be complacent in the face of existing obstacles to the personal development of others' because of a religious belief 'is to turn religion into an opiate for the conscience' (ibid., p. 28). Finally, the Church must help the middle class come to realize that they are as controlled by class interests as are the working class. The Church must further attempt to puncture the 'assumption that the interest of the middle classes are identical with the interests of the community' which is an illusion which 'unconsciously blinds many of the most sincere Christians and makes them unfair and self-righteous in their attitude towards those classes which at present are the chief sufferers from the economic order' (ibid., p. 28). Each group, both the middle class and the working class, must be brought under the criticism of the Church in order to increase the self-knowledge of its members. Each must be able to understand, to think, and to feel the position of the other if suspicion and distrust are to be broken down. The Church must seek to bring under its moral control the attitudes of its members concerning economic relationships just as it does the attitudes of its members concerning personal relationships.

To summarize, this part of the report outlines three areas in which the Church, through its teaching, can give guidance concerning the economic order. First, Christian teaching should outline standards and principles by which an economic system can be judged. Second, Christian teaching must examine the actual facts and consequences of the existing economic order through critical analysis of those facts. Finally, Christian teaching must help individuals gain self-knowledge so that they can better recognize and understand those obstacles to economic justice which exist within the human heart.

3.6   Part VI: Immediate Christian Action

The final part of the report describes what immediate actions, by churches and by individuals, can be taken in order to increase economic justice in society. The churches were implored to 'set their own houses in order' regarding 'the sources of income, methods of raising money, and administration of property, as well as in the terms on which [they] employ men and women' (ibid., p. 30). The report also addressed pay equity, proposing 'a reasonable uniformity in the payment of those who hold the same spiritual office', that the church should pay those who work for it 'according to the real need of themselves and their families' (ibid., p. 30). The report further addressed the issue of redistribution of income among individual churches, stating that '[i]t is not tolerable that those who minister to the rich should be comparatively well-off and those who minister to the poor should be poor for that reason alone' and 'churches in poor and depressing districts should [not] be handicapped by an inefficient and unlovely plant, which would not be tolerated in the assemblies of the rich' (ibid., p. 30). The report asserts that a church with such 'defect in its organization' will 'prejudice its witness in the world' (ibid., p. 30).

The report urges the churches to provide for study and research for their ministers so that they might become better acquainted with economic facts. In addition, the churches were urged to encourage cooperation between their ministers and laity engaged in industry and commerce. Finally, the churches were urged to help 're-establish in the experience of men and women a unity of work and worship' so that there would be no 'discontinuity' between the church and life and work (ibid., p. 31).

In addition to outlining those actions which the church can immediately take to improve economic justice, the report also outlines actions which individual Christians can take. Individuals are implored to carry their faith into their daily business and personal relationships and to enter into government service in order to encourage and foster social action. Individuals are urged to join with others of similar conviction to bring about social change. Finally, individuals are, according to the report, responsible for changing the economic and political system 'through their membership of political parties, trade unions, employers' organizations, and other groups' (ibid., p. 32).

The report ends with a reaffirmation of Christian doctrine and states that God can and will use man to achieve God's purpose for mankind, a just society.

4   THE RELATIONSHIP OF LOWE'S ECONOMICS TO THE OXFORD REPORT

Lowe's last work, *Has Freedom A Future?* (*HFF*), published in 1988 when Lowe was ninety-five years old, grew out of Lowe's desire to apply to the present and to the American situation the ideas expressed in *The Price of Liberty* (*TPL*), first written as a letter to Tillich on the occasion of Tillich's fiftieth birthday in 1936 (Vickers, 1991, pp. 95, 97, 131, 225). Lowe points out that in both works the theme is that freedom, or liberty, is a 'value of the highest order,' but that this '*freedom is safe only so long as it is associated with certain constraints*' (Lowe, 1988, p. xxvii). These constraints are necessary to ensure economic, social, and political order and stability. People's freedom, or emancipation, to realize their 'constructive potential' is the goal of all contemporary societies, and this freedom, 'understood as self-determination', exists 'only where everyone has access to the means on which the attainment of his or her chief ends depends. Such access is greatly reduced in a class structure with large inequalities of income and wealth' (ibid., pp. 4–6). These hindrances to freedom, however, are not laws of nature, but are subject to removal, and, as such, are '*legitimate targets of public control*' (ibid., p. 6). Thus Lowe argues that freedom is possible only in a stable society, that social stability depends on some control of and constraint on individual and class conduct, and that the price of freedom is the willingness to be subject to certain constraints. Real freedom is possible only through control and what Lowe calls 'spontaneous conformity,' or the spontaneous consensus among the members of society of a code of conduct, the standards of which are accepted and obeyed by the individual members of society. Lowe had written to Tillich in *TPL* that

> England's social conformity is the spontaneous achievement of individuals. Neither a central political body nor a representative social group enforces its constant realization. Conformity is of course a product of education, and all social institutions are focused on its maintenance. But if we disregard the handful of rebels, this conformity is felt not as a compulsion but as the genuine form of self-realization. The thought and emotion of the average Englishman is ruled by a social code whose standards of fairness and common decency have become indisputable axioms for all classes. (Lowe, 1937, p. 15)

The concept of 'spontaneous conformity' as the foundation of both personal liberty and social stability and the search for institutions and agencies which induce and foster spontaneous conformity became the focus of Lowe's work in this area. In both *TPL* and *HFF?*, Lowe points to the political, social and economic institutions necessary to bring about the spontaneous conformity required for stability and thus for freedom.

Lowe used the example of the English social order to explain his concept of a social order for the future. The 'reformist optimism' of the *kairos* group which had been active in Berlin only ten years earlier had been replaced with 'frustration ... over the collapse of a social order which once appeared ... as the starting-point of genuine progress' (ibid., p. 7). Lowe, Tillich and their friends had reached the 'conclusion that the supreme principle for the reorganization of the Western world must be a new integration of society, that is social stability based on justice' (ibid., p. 8). In order to attain this goal, however, Lowe asserted that freedom must be 'at least second in the table of social values' (ibid., p. 7). Only by 'renouncing' freedom could social stability based on justice be attained. In Lowe's view, English society had at least in part accomplished this task. The English example showed that 'at least once in history a mass-society resolved the inherent conflict between freedom and order without recourse to autocracy or anarchy', and the English example 'corroborates the possibility of a large-scale society held together by voluntary agreement' (ibid., p. 42). The fact that such a society once existed in history proved to Lowe that such a society is possible and that the realization of such a society again can be recognized as a goal towards which policies can be directed. Social institutions can be devised and a programme of social control and reform can be worked out in order to achieve this goal (ibid., pp. 42–3).

Lowe, however, ended *The Price of Liberty* with these ideas. His programme for social reform remained to be worked out over the next approximately fifty years, with much of it suggested in *Has Freedom A Future?*. Many of the reforms suggested in the Oxford Conference Report on *The Church and the Economic Order* appear to be ones which are aimed at achieving a just and stable social order. A few examples will serve to demonstrate the continuity of Lowe's thought concerning these issues and the unifying themes contained in his work.

First is the primary importance of the goal of social stability based on justice. Tillich worked out a system of justice based on the four principles of adequacy, equality, personality and liberty (Clary, 1994, p. 370). Lowe, Tillich and others had reached the conclusion that 'the supreme principle for the reorganization of the Western world must be a new integration of society, that is, social stability based on justice' (Lowe, 1937, p. 8). The Oxford Conference Report for the section dealing with the economic order stated that '[t]he standard for all the social arrangements and institutions, all the economic structures and political system, by which the life of man is ordered, is the principle of justice' which is the 'ideal of a harmonious relation of life to life' (Oxford Conference Report, 1937a, p. 11). In the later work, *HFF?*, Lowe demonstrates that true freedom, or emancipation, is possible only in a stable and just society, and he shows in this work, as he had shown before in *On Economic Knowledge*, that the factors which served to make for a stable and just society in the past were no longer applicable in the second half of the twentieth century. The unifying theme, therefore, of Lowe's work, beginning with *TPL* in 1937 and concluding with *HFF?* in 1988 is a desire to find ways to achieve a stable and just society in which people can achieve freedom in order to realize their potential.

Some of the economic means of achieving a stable and just society proposed by Lowe in the 1930s, as well as fifty years later, are the equality of income and wealth, planned domestic colonization, and the ability of the economy to provide full employment for all of its members. All are discussed, at different levels of detail, in *The Price of Liberty*, the Oxford Conference Report, and *Has Freedom a Future?*.

In discussing his views on achieving a stable and just society, Lowe, in *TPL* states that 'a new form of spontaneous collectivism' is necessary which must be accompanied by 'an equalization of income and wealth' (Lowe, 1937, pp. 40–41). As shown above, the authors of the Oxford Conference Report discussed throughout the report the concern with acquisitiveness and the resulting inequalities and the effects of this on the achievement of a just society. When Lowe discusses the conditions of achieving a stable society in *HFF?* he lists equity in economic, as well as social, relations, and he explains that he means equality of opportunity as well as equality of outcomes (Lowe, 1988, pp. 89–92). Lowe recognizes also that there will be both gainers and losers in any sort of redistribution of opportunity and outcome and that both must realize that stabilization must take priority over the abolition of privilege (ibid., p. 92). Stability must be in place before equalization can be achieved. However, while freedom in the sense of self-determination can exist only in a stable society, it cannot exist within a society in which large inequalities of income and wealth are present (ibid., pp. 5–6). Lowe's programme of control would thus contain, at least to some degree, the control of the distribution of income and wealth.

A second characteristic of Lowe's system is the necessity of 'planned domestic colonization'. This idea, too, is first discussed in *TPL*. In discussing the special case of English society, Lowe addresses the English reliance on foreign trade as a 'pillar' of 'economic stability', especially the role played by the effective demand of the colonies for English goods (Lowe, 1937, p. 30). This ability of English markets to expand easily also explains 'the more human form of English competition' (ibid., p. 30). Lowe raises the possibility that where no empire exists society must create, through 'perhaps planned decentralization of the population' a 'colonial outlet for the young' (ibid., p. 43). The Oxford Conference Report offers the possibility of controlling demand though the 'socialization of money and credit' (Oxford Conference Report, 1937a, p. 22), and the concept is further developed in *HFF?* when Lowe explains the need 'for a *substitute for the growth mechanisms of the past*' (Lowe, 1988, p. 92). This substitute Lowe calls *planned domestic colonization*, suggesting the idea that 'the mature regions of the West are not fully 'developed', and are in need of collective action in order to consummate their latent potentialities' (ibid., p. 92). This collective action includes the production of non-material goods, such as 'education, health care, and other social services, ... [and] everything that belongs to the dimension of aesthetics and general culture', as well as, at least in the United States, the 'material substructure ... from road building and water supply, slum clearing and other items of urban renewal, and reorganization and extension of public transportation, to a solution of the energy problem' (ibid., pp. 92–3). These 'goods' can be provided through public agencies and can be financed by saving or by the transfer of purchasing power from the private to the public sector (ibid., p. 93). Seen in this sense, Lowe's idea of planned domestic colonization is a sort of domestic imperialism with the purpose of sustaining demand so that stable growth is possible.

The final example of an economic phenomenon necessary for a stable and just society is that the economy must provide full employment for its members and is related to Lowe's idea of planned domestic colonization, for without adequate demand employment opportunities cannot be generated. Lowe is especially concerned with the problem of technological unemployment. The authors of the Oxford Conference Report recognized that the 'progressive mechanization of industry has periodically thrown large numbers of workers into long periods of unemployment,' (Oxford Conference Report, 1937a, p. 14) and that the threat of unemployment creates 'a feeling of extreme insecurity', and prolonged unemployment creates 'a sense of uselessness ... of being a nuisance, ... and empt[ies] ... life of any meaning' (ibid., p. 20). Lowe explains in *HFF?* how technological unemployment has developed and how an uncontrolled market cannot overcome the loss of employment opportunities due to increased technology. His remedies include the extension of part-time work, the abolition of overtime, early retirement and training programmes, all of which are aimed at increasing the overall level of employment (Lowe, 1988, pp. 95–106). While Lowe recognizes the problems associated with technological unemployment, he clearly understands the past achievements and the future necessity of increased and widely dispersed technological development. As pointed out in the Oxford Conference Report, technology had made possible the solution to the problem of the natural scarcity of economic resources and had, at the same time, reduced the amount of physical labour needed to acquire the necessities of life (Oxford Conference Report, 1937a, pp. 13–14).

These few examples, the inequalities of income and wealth, the lack of adequate effective demand, and technological unemployment, all serve to demonstrate the development of Lowe's work in explaining the, especially, economic prerequisites for a stable and just society and, thus, for individual freedom. These ideas were worked out over a lifetime.

5   CONCLUSION

This chapter has attempted to show that Adolph Lowe, a German, Jewish social scientist and economist, and Paul Tillich, a German, Protestant theologian and philosopher, together made important contributions to the study of social economics in the 1920s and 1930s and that Lowe, working in political economics, continued the development of these ideas throughout his working life. His last book, *Has Freedom A Future?*, is the culmination of his more than sixty years' work in outlining the prerequisites, economic, social and political, for a stable and just society. Lowe, Tillich and their group of friends began this work in post-First World War Germany, full of optimism at the prospect of re-forming German society into a socially stable society based on justice. The optimism of achieving such an end soon faded, but both continued, throughout their respective careers and in their respective fields, to work out the details of their just society.

Lowe's contribution to the Oxford Conference Report for the section dealing with the Church and the Economic Order, either through his friendship, collaboration, and influence with Tillich, or because of his direct work in writing the report, seems clear. Many of the ideas expressed in the report are more fully detailed statements, with a Christian emphasis, of the concepts expressed only one year earlier in his letter to Tillich, later published as *The Price of Liberty*. Many of the same ideas, with an emphasis on achieving economic stability, are worked out in even greater detail in his last book, *Has Freedom A Future?*.

The religious influence, especially the Catholic influence, on the social aspects of economics has long been recognized. The contributions of Lowe and Tillich are likewise important for a better understanding of the foundations of social economics. Tillich provides us with the philosophical and theological basis for a just society, and Lowe provides a description of the economic conditions necessary for attaining the just society. The collaboration between Lowe and Tillich presents a possible solution to the problem of designing a social organization in which the economic problem can be efficiently solved within the bounds of an ethical, stable and just society.

NOTES

* The author gratefully acknowledges the helpful suggestions of Professor Hans E. Jensen, Mrs. Jeanne Vickers, and Professor Mathew Forstater.
1. The biographical details were taken from several sources: the biography of Tillich by Wilhelm and Marion Pauck (1976), the autobiography of Hannah Tillich (1973), the autobiographical piece by Tillich (1936: 1966), Tillich's autobiographical introduction to Kegley and Bretall (1952), Lowe's autobiographical piece in the *Biographical Dictionary of Dissenting Economists* (1991), and Vickers's introduction to Sir Geoffrey Vickers and Lowe (1991).
2. For a more detailed description of *kairos*, see Clary (1994).
3. Many of Tillich's German colleagues emigrated to the United States via New York, with several, including Eduard Heimann and Adolph Lowe, taking positions at the New School. Throughout his career at Union, Tillich attended seminars and delivered lectures at the New School.
4. While I have found no record of Lowe having personally known Keynes, Keynes's connection with the Hogarth Press and his close friendship with Leonard and Virginia Woolf are widely known.
5. Mrs. Vickers relates that Lowe's account of this was a very enthusiastic one and that Lowe relished having had input into the document. She states that his reminiscences were imparted with clarity, complete with dates, despite his age at the time of the interview. Schefold makes a similar observation about his interview with Lowe on the business-cycle debates of the 1920s in Germany (Schefold, 1994, p. 327). Professor Harald Hagemann likewise relates that Lowe, in an interview, discussed his participation in writing this report.

REFERENCES

Adams, J.L. (1965), *Paul Tillich's Philosophy of Culture, Science and Religion*, New York: Harper & Row.
Adams, J.L., W. Pauck and R. Shinn (eds.) (1985), *The Thought of Paul Tillich*, New York: Harper & Row.
Clary, B.J. (1994), 'Paul Tillich on the institutions of capitalism', *Review of Social Economy* (Fall), pp. 361–76.
Heilbroner, R.L. (ed.) (1969), *Economic Means and Social Ends*, Englewood Cliffs, NJ: Prentice-Hall.
Heilbroner, R.L. (1978), 'Adolph Lowe', *Challenge*, **21** (September–October), pp. 66–7.
Kegley, C.W. and R.W. Bretall (eds) (1952), *The Theology of Paul Tillich*, New York: Macmillan.
Lowe, A. (1937), *The Price of Liberty*, London: Hogarth Press.
Lowe, A. (1967), 'In memoriam: Eduard Heimann, 1889–1967', *Social Research*, **34** (December), pp. 609–12.
Lowe, A. (1977), *On Economic Knowledge: Toward a Science of Political Economics*, enlarged edn, White Plains, NY: M.E. Sharpe; first published 1965.
Lowe, A. (1980), 'The Veblen–Commons Award', *Journal of Economic Issues*, **14** (June), pp. 241–54.

Lowe, A. (1987), *Essays in Political Economics: Public Control in a Democratic Society*, ed. with an Introduction by Allen Oakley, Brighton: Wheatsheaf; New York: New York University Press.

Lowe, A. (1988), *Has Freedom a Future?*, New York: Praeger.

Lowe, A. (1991), 'Adolph Lowe', in P. Arestis and M. Sawyer (eds), *A Biographical Dictionary of Dissenting Economists*, Aldershot, Hants, UK: Edward Elgar, pp. 323–8.

Oxford Conference Report (1937a), *The Church and the Economic Order*, New York: Universal Christian Council.

Oxford Conference Report (1937b), *The Churches Survey Their Task. On Church, Community, and State*, with an Introduction by J.H. Oldham, London: George Allen & Unwin Ltd.

Pauck, W. and M. Pauck (1976), *Paul Tillich: His Life and Thought*, New York: Harper & Row.

Schefold, B. (1994), 'The revival of economic thought in Germany: the Dogmenhistorischer Ausschuss', *History of Political Economy*, **26**, (Summer), pp. 327–35.

Tillich, H. (1973), *From Time to Time*, New York: Stein & Day.

Tillich, P. (1933), *The Socialist Decision*. Translated by Franklin Sherman, New York: Harper & Row 1977.

Tillich, P. (1936), *On The Boundary*, New York: Charles Scribner's Sons 1966.

Tillich, P. (1952), *The Courage to Be*, New Haven: Yale University Press.

Tillich, P. (1954), *Love, Power, and Justice*, London: Oxford University Press.

Tillich, P. (1967), *Systematic Theology*, three volumes in one, New York: Harper & Row.

Tillich, P. (1971), *Political Expectation*, New York: Harper & Row.

Vaughn, K.I. (1992), 'Theologians and economic philosophy: the case of Paul Tillich and Protestant Socialism', *History of Political Economy*, **24** (Spring), pp. 1–29.

Vickers, J. (1991), *Rethinking the Future, The Correspondence Between Geoffrey Vickers and Adolph Lowe*, New Brunswick: Transaction Publishers.

Vickers, J. (1993), Personal letter to the author.

15. Economics and Sociology: Lowe and Mannheim on Cooperation in the Social Sciences

Heiner Ganßmann

1   ECONOMIC IMPERIALISM

The current debate about the relationship between economics and sociology is mostly about 'economic imperialism'. Should economic modes of reasoning be applied in other social sciences? Gary Becker, receiving the Nobel award, suggested that such applications are gaining more or less official recognition, at least inside economics. From the perspective of sociology, the claim that there are no inherent obstacles to the exclusive reliance on the economist's concept of rational, self-interested action in the explanation of *any* type of social fact, such as marriage, drug abuse, raising children, and so on, is perceived with mixed feelings. One, if not the major, sociological tradition rests precisely on the idea that rational action is a concept too limited to explain what people really do or what holds society together. To a large extent, this tradition historically sprang from a conservative, romantic, or even reactionary distrust against the claims of the enlightenment and, especially, of the French Revolution, to rebuild society from scratch according to rational principles (compare Spaemann, 1959). However, that the *raison d'être* of sociology as a separate social science was based on its opposition to the rationalistic model of man and the corresponding concept of instrumental action characteristic of economics, cannot just be attributed to a tradition-bound spirit of distrust against reason. Modern sociology has had to balance the traditions of enlightenment and romanticism because they appear to be the cognitive counterparts of distinct characteristics of modern society, characteristics most aptly described by the *Vergemeinschaftung–Vergesellschaftung* distinction.

However, this balance is difficult to stabilize. What comes under the heading of sociology has not converged durably towards a paradigmatic mainstream. So it is not surprising to encounter a new[1] type of sociology with an affirmative attitude towards economics and its notion of human agency in recent years. It is busy importing and generalizing economic models to test their explanatory potential in a wide range of 'seemingly non-economic' problems. 'Sociology as general economics' (van Parijs, 1981) is the ideal pursued by the proponents of 'rational choice' sociology. They want to disentangle their work from the conceptual ambiguities of traditional sociological thought.

Currently, there is not much hope for settling the dispute between this new approach and the tradition. It appears to be a fair bet that both will continue to be parts of sociology, since both have some definite strength. On the one hand, the economic concept of action is admittedly limited when, for example, compared to the richness of Max Weber's typology of action. On the other hand, the 'rational choice' framework imported from economics into sociology has the significant advantages of a clear explanatory strategy and of a capacity for formalized reasoning.

But is not the crucial problem with the project of 'sociology as general economics' an old one? Durkheim (1893), and after him most prominently Talcott Parsons (1937), claimed that there are 'non-contractual conditions of contract', or, to put it more generally, non-rational conditions of rational action. Norms cannot be deduced either as implications of individual rationality or as results of strategic interaction among rational agents. Thus, sociologists staked their claim by insisting on the binding (or action-coordinating) quality of shared norms as well as on the tenet that explanations in the social sciences which did not rely on norms were incomplete. From this perspective it is therefore hardly surprising that Jon Elster (1989), after years of rather militantly propagating the rational-choice approach, has recently come up with the proposition that actions following norms cannot be reduced to rational action (rational in the sense of an agent self-interestedly pursuing goals with the most appropriate means). Reinventing the sociological wheel, Elster insists that rational action is consequence-oriented while action following norms is, in the extreme, held to be completely unconcerned about results and solely concerned about conformity with the respective norms. Elster's position implies not only that all attempts to derive norms in a rational-choice framework (Ullmann-Margalit, 1977) are doomed but also that the traditional division of labour between economics and sociology as conceived by classical thinkers such as Durkheim, Pareto or Weber remains roughly intact.

So, following Elster, we seem to return to the old state of relations between economics and sociology: economics spells out the implications of rational action,[2] sociology is concerned with other, complementary types of action (norm-oriented, traditional, affective, and so on).[3] Of course, there is nothing wrong with divisions of labour, in the social sciences and elsewhere. But this way of determining the respective tasks of economics and sociology has repeatedly turned out to be unsatisfactory, if only because it leads to endless confusions between the 'economy' in the technical sense of the language of economics, where it is more or less identified with the realm of rational action (Robbins, 1932), and the 'economy' in the language of everyday life, where it is understood to be the social sphere of material provisioning, the realm of work and exchange, production, distribution, trade, and so on. In addition, the intended division of labour leaves unanswered the need for a synthetic super-science,[4] an instance of coordination between the various separate branches of social science.

2   ECONOMICS AND SOCIOLOGY IN THE 'AGE OF PLANNING'

To avoid reinventing the sociological wheel *à la* Elster, and as a tribute to Adolph Lowe, I want to reexamine the proposals for the division of labour and cooperation between economics and sociology which Adolph Lowe and Karl Mannheim put forward in the mid-1930s. These proposals are contained in two texts which were published in 1935: Mannheim's *Mensch und Gesellschaft im Zeitalter des Umbaus* (an English translation was published in1940: *Man and Society in an Age of Reconstruction*[5]) and Lowe's *Economics and Sociology – A Plea for Co-operation in the Social Sciences*. The two texts have to be read as the fruits of the cooperative[6] attempt to understand the broader social significance of the social turbulences of the 1920s and the Nazi takeover in Germany. Evidently, the texts are also part of their authors' efforts to cope with the experience of forced emigration and to gain some standing in British academia. Seen in this light, the high level of abstraction on which both texts operate may appear less astonishing than it does at first sight. Mannheim and Lowe interpreted their experience in Germany as exemplary for the development of contemporary Western societies. They described German events in a generalizing mode, attempting to convince their Western European audiences: *de te fabula narratur*.

To put it very briefly, the main premise of their argument was that the 'Age of Planning'[7] had arrived. Growing social and economic problems required more coordination, higher consistency of decisions and more knowledge on the part of public authority. As Mannheim put it in one of his lectures at the time: 'We cannot avoid seeing that planning will come, and is already upon us. At this time it is all the more necessary to make up our minds about the kind of planning we want' (Mannheim, 1953, p. 309). Both the Soviet experiment's slide into Stalinism and the fascist dictatorships raised the question (which was to remain a lifelong concern for both authors) of how planning was to be reconcilable with democracy.

Thus, the proposals which Lowe and Mannheim made in 1935 regarding the division of labour and form of cooperation between economics and sociology were driven by practical political concerns while being based on a theoretical premise. The theoretical premise was that the development of modern societies pushed them ever closer to the alternative of increasing social planning or facing social turbulences and chaos. Planning could take on very different political forms, however. The dominant practical concern was to prevent the further advance of dictatorial regimes. This advance would be unavoidable unless the democratic polity took up the tasks of social and economic planning which in turn required the cooperative support of economics and sociology. The dissatisfaction and impatience both authors express with regard to a kind of social science content with description and diagnosis, each in its respective separate field of inquiry, must have had to do with the trauma of the Nazi takeover in Germany. Not least as a result of that experience, they emphasized a new potential role for social scientists. By deliberately taking on the responsibility to use (and further develop) planning tools and resources, social scientists were to contribute to the prevention of the kind of social regression experienced in Nazi Germany. In exile, as early as 1933 Mannheim was nursing the idea of a scientifically constructed therapy for social disorders which he called 'socio-analysis', in analogy to Freud's psychoanalysis (compare Kettler et al., 1984, pp. 80ff.). In retrospect, these designs may appear overambitious,[8] but given the helplessness and failure of the academic community in Germany *vis-à-vis* Nazism (Papcke, 1986), it seems inappropriate to blame Mannheim, Lowe and others for their ambitions to draw practical lessons from that traumatic experience. For them the issue was whether social scientists would take on the responsibility of using whatever (even modest) means and tools they could develop to prevent the slide of modern societies into the kind of economic, political and social chaos which had opened the way for fascist or Stalinist dictatorships (and war). This concern was not coupled to any fantasies of omnipotent planning or perfect social engineering.

This brief sketch should help to explain the setting in which Lowe and Mannheim argued for their project of closer cooperation between economics and sociology. In what follows, I want to examine their argument in some detail in the hope of finding elements of more substantive definitions of and distinctions between the two disciplines than those governing the current debate. This hope is based not merely on the fact that Mannheim and Lowe were highly sophisticated representatives of their disciplines but more so, first, on the circumstance that paradigmatic consolidation had just taken place in economics and not yet in sociology – so the alternatives to what is today the mainstream were still vividly present – and, second, on the circumstance that the extra-scientific pressure to generate socially useful knowledge was extremely high at the time.

3   MANNHEIM

Mannheim sees the common root of the social problems of his time in the conflict-laden coexistence of *laissez-faire* and political regulation. He combines this diagnosis with his project of a sociology of knowledge. In the framework of a highly stylized three-stages theory of the evolution of human thinking (the stages are: finding, inventing and planning) he argues that human thinking has so far failed to come to grips with the new interdependencies which have emerged between previously self-regulating social realms. It is not yet mature enough for planning, where planning means that 'man and society advance from the goal-oriented invention of a particular object or a particular institution to the goal-oriented regulation and transparent control of those interdependencies which rule between those invented particular objects' (Mannheim, 1935, p. 98). This idea of planning implies a critique of the social sciences (and of the sciences in general), in so far as they have been content with observing and explaining their well-distinguished, separate and, as it were, endogenously-developing objects of enquiry.[9] Mannheim maintains that the presumed autonomy of social realms is a fiction drawn from the outdated image of a society developing mostly in evolutionary terms in the direction of increasing functional differentiation. By contrast, vast and increasing realms of society are now organized, planned, consciously directed and, in this sense, rationalized. Mannheim's distinctive and decisive point is that such increased rationalization in various separate social realms results in increased frictions and problems on the level of society as a whole. Why?

> Fields which are unplanned and regulated by natural selection on the one hand and goal-oriented, invented and consciously implanted constructs on the other hand can coexist without friction only as long as the fields of the unplanned remain dominant. The longer the various stretches in the social process become which are already functioning according to predetermined designs, the more difficult will be their coexistence in the totality of unregulated social events. ... This is so for two reasons, first, because any planning destroys the mobility and adaptibility of the individual element, second, because the possibility of sidestepping and the chance of individual adjustment and adaptation in the unplanned intermediate spaces are forever reducing. (Ibid., p. 102)

To cope with these problems, society is in need of 'reconstruction', with the emphasis on 're-', not on 'construction': society cannot be built anew; it has to be changed by taking its existing elements and structures as inputs, as it were, of a process of controlled social change. According to Mannheim, the aimed-for reconstruction of society as an extensively planned society has to start – not surprisingly for the champion of '*Wissenssoziologie*' – on the level of thought. Human thought has not kept pace with real social developments. The sciences are no exception. They still operate in the successful patterns of the past, pushing towards increased abstraction, specialization and isolation. By contrast, the knowledge required for the present has to be interdisciplinary and multidimensional. Why? While most modern sociology holds – since Herbert Spencer – that modernization means increasing functional differentiation,[10] Mannheim argues that a new 'melting' together of social spheres is taking place which must be reflected in a new form of scientific observation and explanation, requiring cooperation across the boundaries of established disciplines:

> As they pursue this tendency of integrated social and economic units to try and establish an internal linkage between the different chains of effects of the social, unions succeed in enforcing a 'political wage', cartels impose 'administered prices' and the great corporate enterprises put consumption needs regulated by advertising in place of the free choice of consumers. In this way, the interference between the economy and the extra-economic world which formerly emerged only occasionally is built into the economic circular flow itself and the separation of economics and sociology in the old sense becomes obsolete. (Ibid., pp. 111ff.)

Pars pro toto, the modern economy shows that the factors tending towards equilibrium have eroded because of increasing interventions, on the one hand, and because of 'the interference between political, technical and psychological chains of effects' (ibid., p.106), on the other hand. These real and relatively recent social developments require for their understanding an increased complexity of thought in order to accomplish a 'multidimensional structural picture of the total social movement' (ibid.). Such complexity can be achieved only in so far as interdisciplinary theory is constructed on the level of *principia media*, placing itself between the tendency of the Historical school to study individual events – losing itself in the infinity of the particulars – and the abstractness of general theories which remain empirically empty.[11] The substantial argument for concentrating on 'theories of the middle range'[12] rests on an assumption about the compatibility and coherence of coexisting social structures.[13] Given high degrees of interdependence and coherence between different social realms, only the elaboration of *principia media* can provide the knowledge required for comprehensive planning. On this middle level, the interdependence of the factors which the specialized social sciences study in isolation can be taken into account. Mannheim's conclusion for the social sciences is clear: they have to start intensive cooperative efforts if they are not to fail in their explanations of ongoing social developments and thus lose their potential therapeutic function.

4 LOWE

Lowe not only shares Mannheim's critical attitude towards contemporary social science, but goes one step further. For him, the problem with economics and sociology already starts with their having a false self-understanding with regard to their presumed autonomy. Lowe therefore sets out to demonstrate that economic theory, once it reaches beyond a theory of individual utility maximizing, rests on implicit assumptions which are of a sociological nature. This can be shown in two ways: first, by demonstrating the historical specificity of markets and of the type of action generated in markets; second, by putting under scrutiny the transition from a theory of individual decision-making to a theory of economic transactions involving the interaction of a plurality of agents.

The underlying idea of limiting the applicability of pure economic theory by making explicit the linkage between its concepts and the specific economic system of nineteenth-century capitalism was not Lowe's invention. Rather, it presents one of the solutions of the '*Methodenstreit*' between the German Historical School and the proponents of pure theory. According to that solution, which proposes a compromise between the two opposed views, pure theory is legitimate as long as it is not mistakenly understood as universal theory – as it often has been.[14] Rather, pure theory's range is limited. Its basic concepts inevitably reflect the specific socio-historical conditions of emerging occidental capitalism. In particular, instrumental rationality as the dominant orientation of economic action is generated in competitive markets only. Max Weber took the decisive step in finding this compromise between the competing claims of the pure theorists and the Historical school of economics by introducing the concept of 'ideal types'.[15] They are simultaneously purely theoretical constructs as well as limited to typifying historically specific structures.

Lowe uses similar arguments to determine the reach of 'pure' economic theory. His primary objection to the standard self-understanding of what economic theorists do does not so much concern the historical relativity of their reasoning, however, but the theoretical transition from a theory of individual decision-making to propositions about social phenomena.

In his later work, Lowe laid out the problem of this transition by distinguishing between man–matter relations and man–man relations, the first concerning the technological core of economic activities, the latter its 'socialization' (Lowe, 1965, p. 18). In 1935, this distinction is not yet developed. Instead Lowe pursues the idea that pure economic reasoning applies to the economic calculus of the isolated individual only and that any move beyond Robinson Crusoe has to rely on sociological concepts. Lowe's specific version of that idea (where, again, in general, it was a shared one, compare von Wieser, 1914) is remarkable. He argues that the advance from the individual economic calculus to a theory of exchange, to the law of supply and demand, to the concept of general equilibrium, in short, to price determination, requires some conceptual ways of restricting the individual 'absolute freedom of choice', the latter being one of the starting postulates of pure theory.

This restriction is achieved in two ways. First, there is the idea of economic man, whereby action is constrained by internalized rules of conduct. Second, there is the idea of perfect competition, defining the constraints inherent in the situation in which economic action is taking place. Interestingly, for Lowe, *homo oeconomicus* is not merely the incarnation of instrumental rationality, an agent relentlessly adapting means to ends. Rather, the concept expresses 'a very formal maxim of behaviour "unconcerned" with the ultimate ends and motives of the economic actions ... because it is not related to the use of the outcome of any bargain, but to behaviour *in* bargaining'.[16] This is so because pure theory 'postulates that in buying and selling we prefer the larger advantage to the smaller one, calculated not in subjective return of pleasure, but in objective quantities of goods or money' (Lowe, 1935, pp. 52ff.). Thus, Lowe asserts, pure theory pictures consumers in exchange as quantity rather than utility maximizers.[17] But it does not have an argument to support this proposition because such behaviour is not implied in the basic twin assumptions of rationality and utility maximizing. If Lowe's assertion is correct, it follows indeed that the idea of *homo oeconomicus* brings 'an unquestionably sociological element into the pure theory of the market' (ibid., p. 53).

What is sociological about this element? It looks archetypically economic. However, Lowe points out that to understand (and explain) action, we need to understand its constraints. On the one hand, there is the claim inherent in economic theory that 'we can strictly deduce bargaining behaviour without caring at all about its ends and motives' (ibid., p. 50), implying that any restrictions on behaviour cannot be derived from the ends as ascribed to the agent. On the other hand, economic reasoning, like all action theory, starts from the postulate of 'free choice of action' (ibid.), which makes it unlikely that actions can be predicted in the first place:

action is contingent. Thus, to predict any results of the market process, some restrictions on the range of (likely) actions have to be introduced. According to Lowe, the restrictions which pure economic theory has to offer, as far as they are 'internal' to the agent, namely utility maximizing and rationality, do not by themselves translate into the exchange behaviour requisite to support the law of supply and demand. Some further constraints on behaviour must be added. 'In theory', says Lowe, 'any substantial rule of bargaining conduct' would do, but 'whatever maxim we choose, it cannot be deduced from pure economics'(ibid., p. 53). Enter sociology.

Lowe uses an analogous argument with respect to the role of the idea of perfect competition. Apart from its functioning as a situational rather than an actor-internal constraint on action, it serves the same purpose, namely, limiting the agents' freedom of choice in such ways that their behaviour realizes the 'laws' of the market as postulated by pure theory. Again, the argument is that the condition of perfect competition cannot be part of the initial set of propositions of a pure, that is universal, economic theory. To make agents behave as price-takers adjusting solely in terms of quantities, the theory relies on the idea of perfect competition. However, in doing so it not only relies on a 'sociological element', but also betrays the rootedness of economic theory in the specific historical setting of nineteenth-century capitalism.

Lowe's argument converges with Mannheim's when he takes up the idea of *principia media*. *Homo oeconomicus* and perfect competition are not only sociological concepts by origin but Lowe also uses them to describe what he calls 'middle principles', relying, as did Mannheim, on John Stuart Mill and Morris Ginsberg. The elegant twist in Lowe's argument is that he uses his critical results in a positive manner: *homo oeconomicus* and perfect competition are the 'middle principles' characteristic of nineteenth-century British capitalism. They are inedaquate for an understanding of the contemporary constellation of economy and society, but as middle principles they can serve as an illustration for what is required today: giving up the quest for universality and for the 'exact calculation of economic movements' (ibid., p. 147) in favour of empirical relevance. For the latter, the interdisciplinary elaboration of 'middle principles' is required, reflecting real and growing social interdependence. 'It is sheer self-deception to think that one can advance one single assertion about any part of society without implying a statement on the order of the whole' (ibid., p. 151).

This is not the standard statement that all things hang together, but a warning against what happened later on in the development of economic theory despite this warning: many economists did not

292   *Balancing Freedom and Order: Modern Society and its Analysis*

'realize that there is only the choice between an unconscious conception of the whole
on the basis of common sense with all its obscure fallacies and prejudices, and a
scientific working hypothesis with its obvious insufficiencies which are at least
accessible to correction in the face of new and inconsistent facts.' (Ibid., p. 152)

Rather than opening to the 'synthetic work of sociology' the economist's
view of the economy was projected 'on the order of the whole' and became
the economist's world view.[18] Society is seen not only as if it functioned
like the economy, but as if it functioned like the economy of nineteenth-
century Britain. As soon as economic theory had centred around the
paradigmatic core of Walrasian equilibrium economics, its development
became more and more self-referential. Its explanatory goals were given,
further broken down and self-imposed by general equilibrium theory with
its quest for formally proving the existence, uniqueness and stability of
equilibrium. As it turned out, the implied tasks – defined in the late
nineteenth century – are formidable enough to keep economic theorists
very busy until today. Ironically (or is it tragically?), as Lowe pointed out,
the Walrasian paradigm at best reflects the economic and social conditions
of the nineteenth century. So general equilibrium theory is an impressive
response to a purely intellectual challenge, but it has no practical relevance
under the changed socioeconomic conditions of the twentieth century. If –
and in so far as – economists want to contribute to the solution of
contemporary socioeconomic problems, they have to do a different kind of
work: theory will have to be constructed with the aim of empirical
relevance, relying on sociological knowledge.

As long as economics claims to be an empirical science, the exactness of its
theoretical generalizations will be judged only by their congruence with the facts.
Whatever it may lose in mathematical elegance, its capacity to depict modern reality
and to explain its causal concatenation will increase to the extent to which it uses the
results of sociology for the constructions of its foundations. (Ibid., p. 148)

5   CONCLUSION

Let us return to the beginning. How can Lowe's and Mannheim's case for
cooperation between economics and sociology be related to the
contemporary debate on economic imperialism? At first sight, there seems
to be a problem. The current juxtaposition of rational and normative action
does not correspond to the point Lowe and Mannheim make in
distinguishing between economics and sociology, namely, that economic
reasoning refers to specific historical societal practices and is therefore
limited in scope and reach and has to rely on sociology to monitor social

change. For Lowe, especially, the point is that economics as a positive science is constructed with nineteenth-century capitalism as its empirical object of reference. The niceties of the law of supply and demand and all the other notions of price formation have emerged in social conditions which ensured stable patterns of economic activity. Only their stability and regular recurrence made economic processes accessible to the standard mode of scientific reasoning. Thus, the object of economic enquiry was not simply constituted by the presumed rationality of economic agents and their actions, bound together by self-interest. Rather, it owed its analysability to a type of competition (atomized) and to technical conditions of production (high flexibility, adaptibility, small units with little fixed capital). One may well concede to Mises and his successors that rational action remains dominant in the modern economic system, but the situation in which this rationality is operative changes in the twentieth century: monopolistic competition, big enterprises units with little flexibility and low mobility of capital, the erosion of traditional norms, and so on. According to Lowe and Mannheim, these factors lead to a destructuration, a loss of order of the economic system. Its mode of operation becomes more erratic, its movements are less and less predictable, the calculability underlying rational action is vanishing. So the point is not that rational action is disappearing, but rather that – despite perhaps increased efforts and capabilities to rationalize actions (more sophisticated calculations, more information gathering, more experience) – the 'objective' conditions which form the situation in which actions take place, the context and the articulation of actions and perhaps the norms governing the selection of ends all lack the stability and regularity required to predict action outcomes successfully. In his *On Economic Knowledge* (1965), Lowe's conclusion will be that positive economic science is no longer possible. In *Economics and Sociology* (1935), the conclusion is not quite as radical: the hope remains that the interlocking of economic and sociological arguments which allow for the elaboration of middle principles can generate scientifically sound and practically relevant reasoning about the socioeconomic conditions of the modern age.

So how can we link this set of ideas to the current debate, revolving around the opposition between rational and normative action? One obvious way would be to insist on the historical boundedness of rational action as it is held to be constitutive of the modern economy. The dominance of rational action in the economy is just as contingent on a certain stage in the development of modern societies as the existence of the economy as a distinct societal subsystem. Another rather arduous way would be to show how normative elements are contained in the very concept of instrumentally rational action as it is used to build economic theory.

The most adequate way consists of reformulating Lowe's challenge: the claim of universality of pure economic theory cannot be combined with the claim of empirical relevance. Lowe's arguments are certainly correct as far as the coupling between nineteenth-century capitalism and economic theory and the inapplicability of nineteenth-century ideas to twentieth-century realities are concerned. In so far as sociology is – and economics is not – able to explain this coupling and specify the 'middle principles' underlying economic reasoning, the conclusion on the necessity of a close cooperation between economics and sociology remains entirely justified – at least as far as economists remain curious about the historical relativity and social boundedness of their reasoning and sociologists of knowledge (in the Mannheim tradition) can come up with some contributions. Lowe's arguments may be more difficult to swallow not only as far as his (1965) proposition on the impossibility of positive economics is concerned, but also his conception of political economics as a planning science. But in view of his challenge to orthodoxy the current debate, rehashing the issue of the division of labour between economics and sociology merely in terms of the types of action involved, appears a bit naive. It does not take into account how economics – dominated by praxeology – has lost its capacity for realistic theory. In Lowe's and Mannheim's terms, the issue is not one that can be clarified by distinguishing types of action which then are taken to constitute the separate objects of enquiry of economics and sociology. The issue is whether we want theories which help to organize our empirical knowledge of contemporary society and are, thereby, practically relevant.

NOTES

1. The basic idea is not new. In postulating the universality of rational action Mises made himself the forefather of modern 'economic imperialism' – with a peculiar twist, however: he saw economics as a part, and the most developed part at that, of sociology (Mises, 1929, p. 465).
2. Whether this happens in a general equilibrium framework or in the more subjectivist/individualist framework of the Austrian tradition is secondary.
3. However, it is not self-evident that both disciplines define themselves on the level of and by distinguishing types of action, thus sharing what Parsons called the 'action frame of reference'.
4. Ambitions to formulate the grand synthetic theoretical framework are not the monopoly of 'economic imperialists' but are also nurtured by sociologists: Parsons's (1937) action frame of reference or a general theory of social systems (Luhmann, 1984) can serve as examples. The rationale behind such efforts is that any division of labour requires coordination, at least as long as there is 'no invisible hand which brings the specialist conceptions of the whole or even of the borderlands into harmony with each other' (Lowe, 1935, p. 151).
5. In what follows, I have relied on the German version using my own translations, as I have with the other German texts cited.
6. This cooperation started with joint seminars in Frankfurt and was continued in exile, for example, in a joint seminar given in the Netherlands in 1934 on 'Economy and Man in the Age of Planning' (compare Kettler et al., 1984, p. 71).

7. This conviction seems to have been shared by many social scientists in the early 1930s. Compare Pollock (1932) and the enormous amount of literature on planning reviewed in the *Zeitschrift für Sozialforschung*, especially by G. Meyer and K. Mandelbaum.
8. 'With Karl Mannheim the idea, propagated in grand style, of sociology as a planning science still had something of a self-fulfilling prophecy; as it turned out it had the advantage of becoming ever truer ... compared to the more modest idea of sociology as an auxiliary science' (Habermas, 1963, p. 225).
9. The opposite insistence on the interdependence of social realms can be exaggerated, however: 'It is evident that in order to understand or manipulate one segment of reality we must know the total reality' (Rumney, 1936, in a review of Lowe, 1935). If this were Lowe's or Mannheim's view, it could be easily discarded. We always manipulate segments of reality and we never know total reality.
10. The proposition that modernization means functional differentiation may simply reflect the attempt to establish and defend the given division of labour between the social sciences: for the sake of peace and order in academia, give each of them a nicely distinguishable societal subsystem!
11. In proposing the elaboration of *principia media* in this way, Mannheim gives an interdisciplinary twist to Ginsberg's (1934, pp. 17ff.) description of the tasks of sociology.
12. In his 'Sociological theories of the middle range' Merton (1968, pp. 39–72) refers to Ginsberg, Mannheim and Lowe as predecessors in designing research strategies which are to avoid both empty generality and the myopia of concreteness. Merton being Merton, he instructively traces back the idea via J.S. Mill and Bacon to Plato.
13. 'When states of society, and the causes which produce them, are spoken of as a subject of science, it is implied that there exists a natural correlation among these different elements; that not every variety of combination of these general social facts is possible, but only certain combinations; that, in short, there exist Uniformities of Co-existence between the states of the various social phenomena'(Mill, 1911, p. 595).
14. Mises, especially, became more and more militant in this respect. After earlier on considering economics as part, if only the most-developed part of sociology (compare note 1, above), he came to see economics as part, if only the most developed part of 'praxeology', the science of 'all human action as such' (1940, p. 3). Characteristically, the English version of his '*Nationalökonomie – Theorie des Handelns und Wirtschaftens*' (1940*)* carried the title '*Human Action – A Treatise on Economics*' (1949). Observing such changes of view on basic issues, one can see that the 1920s and early 1930s in Germany were still a period in which neither economics nor sociology had consolidated paradigmatically (compare Stölting 1986).
15. Weber (1922, p. 190) held that there are three presuppositions underlying the ideal image of the processes on markets as they are depicted by abstract economic theory: exchange society, free competition and strictly rational action. Mises (1929, p. 489) objected (with respect to the first presupposition) that modern economics starts from the isolated economy without exchange. So Lowe responds implicitly to Mises when he focuses on the transition from the isolated agent calculating marginal utilities to problems of interaction. For a discussion of the difference between the Austrian and the other neoclassical schools with respect to that transition from the 'subjective to the social', compare Mayer (1932, p. 224).
16. Note that the distinction between outcome-oriented behaviour and rule-governed behaviour, like 'behaviour *in* bargaining', corresponds to the distinction between rational and norm-oriented action in the rational choice literature (Elster, 1989, p. 98).
17. This argument is not quite clear. Maybe Lowe is referring to the attempts to conceptualize consumer behaviour once the assumption of measurable utility had to be dropped, attempts which later on resulted in the convexity assumption. Its function is to connect maximizing behaviour in exchange to utility maximization, but it is an assumption of a totally different logical order from that of utility maximization itself. ... We must imagine that the individual has the choice of alternative uses of a given stock of goods to maximize his well-being. The preferences for alternative bundles rest then on the *best* use that can be made of each. This preliminary maximization, so to speak, gives rise to the convexity of the indifference curves' (Arrow, 1983, p. 41).
18. The recent disappointment of advocates of shock therapy in post-socialist countries offers a good example of the way encounters between the real world and the 'ideal world' of economists are processed by the latter: if the real world does not behave as theory predicts, then something is wrong with the real world, not with the theory.

REFERENCES

Arrow, K.J. (1983), 'An extension of the basic theorems of classical welfare economics', in *Collected Papers*, Vol. 2, Cambridge: Belknap Press, pp. 13–45.

Durkheim, E. (1893), *De la division du travail social*, 6th edn, Paris: Alcan 1932.

Elster, J. (1989), *The Cement of Society – A Study of Social Order*, Cambridge: Cambridge University Press.

Ganßmann, H. (1984), 'Political economics and social action', *Eastern Economic Journal*, **10** (2), pp. 129–37.

Ganßmann, H. (1988), 'Money – a symbolically generalized media of communication?', *Economy and Society*, **23**, pp.285–315.

Ginsberg, M. (1934), *Sociology*, London: Oxford University Press.

Habermas, J. (1963), 'Kritische und konservative Aufgaben der Soziologie', in *Theorie und Praxis*, Neuwied: Luchterhand, pp. 215–30.

Kettler, D., V. Meja and N. Stehr (1984), *Karl Mannheim*, Chichester: Ellis Horwood.

Lowe, A. (1934), 'Review of "Mises, L., Grundprobleme der Nationalökonomie"', *Zeitschrift für Sozialforschung*, **3**, pp. 312–13.

Lowe, A. (1935), *Economics and Sociology – A Plea for Co-operation in the Social Sciences*, London: Allen & Unwin.

Lowe, A. (1965), *On Economic Knowledge*, New York: Harper & Row.

Luhmann, N. (1984), *Soziale Systeme*, Frankfurt am Main: Suhrkamp.

Mannheim, K. (1935), *Mensch und Gesellschaft im Zeitalter des Umbaus*, Leiden: Sijthoff's.

Mannheim, K. (1951), *Freedom, Power and Democratic Planning*, London: Routledge.

Mannheim, K. (1953), *Essays on Sociology and Social Psychology*, London: Routledge.

Mayer, H. (1932), 'Der Erkenntniswert der funktionellen Preistheorien', *Die Wirtschaftstheorie der Gegenwart*, **II**, Vienna, pp. 147–239b.

Merton, R.K. (1968), *Social Theory and Social Structure*, New York: Free Press.

Mill, J.S. (1911), *A System of Logic*, London: Longmans.

Mises, L. von (1929), 'Soziologie und Geschichte', *Archiv für Sozialwissenschaft und Sozialpolitik*, **61**, pp. 465–512.

Mises, L. von (1940), *Nationalökonomie – Theorie des Handelns und Wirtschaftens*, Geneva: Editions Union; English edition as *Human Action – A Treatise on Economics*, Chicago: Regnery 1949.

Papcke, S. (1986), 'Weltferne Wissenschaft', in S. Papcke (1986) (ed.), *Ordnung und Theorie*, Darmstadt: Wissenschaftliche Buchgesellschaft, pp. 168–222.

Parijs, P. van (1981), 'Sociology as general economics', *European Journal of Sociology*, **22**, pp. 299–324.

Parsons, T. (1937), *The Structure of Social Action*, New York: McGraw-Hill.

Pollock, F. (1932), 'Die gegenwärtige Lage des Kapitalismus und die Aussichten einer planwirtschaftlichen Neuordnung', *Zeitschrift für Sozialforschung*, **1**, pp. 8–27.

Robbins, L. (1932), *An Essay on the Nature and Significance of Economic Science*, London: Macmillan.

Rumney, J. (1936), 'Review of "Lowe, A., Economics and Sociology"', *Zeitschrift für Sozialforschung*, **5**, p. 115.

Spaemann, R. (1959) *Der Ursprung der Soziologie aus dem Geist der Restauration*, Munich: Kösel.

Stölting, E. (1986), 'Soziologie und Nationalökonomie. Die Wirkung des institutionellen Faktors', in S. Papcke (1986) (ed.), *Ordnung und Theorie*, Darmstadt: Wissenschaftliche Buchgesellschaft pp. 69–92.

Ullmann-Margalit, E. (1977), *The Emergence of Norms*, New York and Oxford: Oxford University Press.

Weber, M. (1922), *Gesammelte Aufsätze zur Wissenschaftslehre*, Tübingen: Mohr.

Weber, M. (1975), *Wirtschaft und Gesellschaft*, Tübingen: Mohr.

Wieser, F. von (1914), 'Theorie der gesellschaftlichen Wirtschaft', in *Grundriss der Sozialökonomik*, Vols 1 and 2, Tübingen: Mohr-Siebeck, 2nd edn., 1923. Translated as *Social Economics*, New York 1927: Greenberg.

16. The Traverse as a Problem of Human Agency*

Allen Oakley

1   INTRODUCTION

Adolph Lowe's analyses of the traverse have been set against the backdrop of his critical concerns about the exaggerated scientism of 'positive' economic theory, with its methodologically-driven claims to have emulated the epistemological achievements of the physical sciences. These concerns have been grounded upon the fact that such claims are made in spite of self-evident failure of theory to recognize fully the most essential facet of the nature of its object phenomena, namely that they have their origin in the complex of processes that comprise human agency. The simple fact is that the decisions and actions of human agents have chronically contingent dimensions that are only partially contained by the pressures of the situational conditions through which they must operate.

Lowe reasons from this fact that economic phenomena must lack the two minimum essential qualities required for the legitimate application of 'positive', progressive hypothetico-deductive, scientific methodology: they should have an *autonomous existence* that is independent of any human agent's volition or action, as well as of the time and place of observation; and they should also have an *inherent orderliness* that renders them tractable to logical representation. In the absence of these two qualities, scientists are unable to produce and test any objective theories of how the phenomena are generated. Most importantly, they cannot make reliable predictions based on nomologically-structured cause-and-effect relations. It will be emphasized below that the lack of these qualities in the context of human science stems not merely from any analytical complexity and intractability that would render economics akin to, say, meteorology. It is a consequence rather of the unique character of the origins of its phenomena in the mix of contingent and contained dimensions that comprise the actions of human agents.

By means of a sustained critique of orthodox market theory, in which he exposes the most fundamental and stringent requirements of realizing stable market outcomes, Lowe cogently establishes that these characteristics of autonomy and orderliness are absent in the phenomena of

297

a modern capitalist system (1977, Chs 1–4). Ultimately, though, it is the traverse that is the particular object of his most profoundly original analyses, while the approach he adopts reflects serious critical concerns about the nature of orthodox theories of growth and technological change. Not only do these theories perpetuate the futility of practising a 'positive' methodology in the face of such demonstrably intractable objects, but they also consciously avoid confronting the real exigencies of human agency that are the substance of economic motion by adopting a set of unrealistic assumptions and restrictions.[1] The effect is artificially to impose upon the relevant phenomena just those characteristics that lend themselves to scientistic representation as deductive–logical arguments. In this orthodox neoclassical approach, it is methodological predilection which shapes the represented form of the *Erkenntnisobjekt*. More reasonably, if 'positive' economics is to have any defence, the matter should be inverted, with the correct methodological strategy selected so that it is consistent with the proper representation of the ontological nature of the object. In a moment, we shall see that Lowe's paradoxical alternative is just the opposite: he sets out legitimately to change the *object* in a manner which ensures the relevance of the deductive methodology and its predictive accuracy without resorting to 'positivist' tenets.

In citing these methodological and substantive issues that undermine the validity and relevance of 'positive' economics, Lowe has always been concerned to show that they also have immediate practical import for the well-being of human agents. What the substance of his critique indicates is that the form and direction of the traverse processes will be unreliable if their realization is left to the 'invisible hand' of market forces in a modern capitalist economic system, given that the guidance of the 'hand' in question is ultimately the collective consequence of the capricious conduct of human agents. For both epistemological and pragmatic reasons, then, Lowe has undertaken his bold and radical revision of the methodological strategy to be applied in economic analyses designed for both theoretical and policy purposes.

His alternative strategy is to propose an *instrumental–deductive* method in which the *object* of theoretical representation is consciously provided with the required autonomy and orderliness by dint of its *ex ante* formal establishment as a *known and given goal state* that the economic system may be so directed as to achieve. Given, that is, by virtue of the democratically-based political process (ibid., pp. 311ff.). Also known is a set of empirical generalizations about ideal functional categories of human agents and about the natural, social, institutional and technological structures in and through which they carry out the operations of the system. From these known conditions, Lowe argues that it is possible, as a matter of principle, at least, formally and rigorously to *deduce* the required conduct by relevant categories of agents through which the desired goal state could be realized. In this way, deductive theory is transformed so as to constitute an *instrumental analysis* in his particular sense.[2] Within this analysis, the established *logical* requirements for an efficient, goal-directed traverse are given an operational status as a wholly predictable cause-and-effect sequence by means of a consciously-designed policy strategy.[3] As devised by Lowe, this strategy has its primary emphasis on the control of human agents whose conduct is to give effect to the processes of the intended traverse. Such, then, is the foundation of his *political economics*, or the science of controlled economic systems. Control, as it is to be understood here, is made consistent with freedom by relying on manipulation to elicit voluntary conformity by agents to appropriate action directives, expectations formation and decisions in an otherwise free-market environment. It will be made clear below that the requirement introduced here is for policy-makers so to construct the means by which agents are manipulated that the resort to the presumptions of an unreliable 'invisible hand' is replaced by a reliance on a consciously and carefully designed 'visible hand'. The 'hand' should be one with a gentle touch: one which preserves the essentials of agent freedom while ensuring the securely predictable collective consequences of achieving a goal state of order and stability.[4]

Now if such a radical approach to economic and social policy management is to be successfully developed and applied, a necessary condition is that its *logic* be translated into operational requirements. Such requirements can only flow from analyses that are founded upon a due and proper understanding and representation of those multiple exigencies of human agency that are the result of agents purposively engaging their situational environment. Meeting this condition centres on the formulation of some key theoretical ideas about how these agents interact with and have their conduct directed by their respective situations. Furthermore, as will be explained, agents should be understood as simultaneously constituting and reflexively reconstituting these situations. My intention is to reinforce the view that the motion of economies and societies cannot be fully comprehended or reliably controlled without the relevant analyses being founded upon such a set of ideas. In so doing, I will focus on eliciting and then applying these theoretical tenets to the traverse, giving particular attention to the problematic as it is formulated by Lowe.

After establishing the dimensions of the involvement of human agency in the traverse as a theoretical and practical policy management problem in the next section, I go on in Section 3 to consider the essential nature of human agents in their confrontations with their situational environments.

Section 4 exposes the mix of contingency and containment that characterizes the interaction between agents and their situations with a view to eliciting the *means* and *forms* of conditioning and direction that may be applied in order to manipulate their conduct. The chapter concludes that there exists an agenda for much further research into the nature and significance of human agency in the constitution and policy-induced control of the traverse phenomenon.

2   THE TRAVERSE AND HUMAN AGENCY

The traverse process consists of the sequential and parallel mix of the *qualitative and quantitative* dimensions of interdependent reproduction and change through which an economy is transformed from an initial state to an altered terminal state through real time. Analysis of the traverse gives emphasis to the decomposition of the total process in time from which the terminal state is generated. It exposes the pattern of relative rates of change of relevant quantities and qualities, where these rates are dictated by the inherited structural and institutional qualities of the initial state of the system, along with the interim responses of agents to the progressive demands of the change that is to be absorbed.

One of Lowe's most significant contributions to our understanding of the traverse has been his emphasis that its constituent processes have two *analytically* separable dimensions: one comprising the demands of reproduction and changes that are dominated by a physical–structural-cum-engineering dimension – *vide* Lowe's *structural* analysis; and the other comprising the actual operations that carry into effect the reproduction and change and are the work of systemically situated human agents – *vide* Lowe's *motor or force* analysis. The latter operations are human and social–institutional in their constitution and originate in the initiating and mediating decisions and actions of human agents.[5] As a problem of engineering calculations and reconstruction *per se*, the traverse requirements can, at least in principle, be worked out in objective detail, making due allowance for the practical limitations of such calculation and design that are ever present, even with modern computational techniques. By taking such engineering adjustment requirements as established *per se*, understanding the traverse must then focus on the operations demanded of structurally and institutionally situated human agents in effecting them. It is *these* operations which determine the degree of efficacy with which the physical–technical transformations that would optimally absorb the traverse-inducing changes into the terminal state of the economy are realized (Lowe, 1976, pp. 17, 63).

As the traverse phenomenon is treated by Lowe, it is generated by the assumed desire to bring an economy to a new terminal state of balanced economic growth after it has experienced some change to its motion determining parameters or variables. The renewal of balanced growth effectively becomes a macroeconomic goal state to be realized by means of the proper absorption of the change. It is readily apparent that this realization can only result from the collective decisions and actions of individual human agents who are involved in the traverse. These microeconomic activities must be of such dimensions as ultimately to 'add up' to the macro-goal conditions over the passage of the traverse period. Three very particular requirements must be met if this is to be so, independently of the systemic setting of the processes. First, the microeconomic details of the conduct required of each agent must be identified in all their dimensions: qualitative, quantitative and temporal. It is worth noting in passing that the temporal dimension has been added here because even the most elementary of traverse analyses suggests that agents will be expected to alter their patterns of conduct during the period of a single traverse. Quite probably, these details may only have an implicit status and their identification at this point should be thought of as a matter of principle only. Second, the correct terms of conduct must be communicated to agents as individuals in accordance with the details identified. Third, agents must be induced by whatever means to conform to the conduct demanded by the communication received (Lowe, 1977, p. 25).

Now, as Lowe's own analyses have so graphically revealed, the modern free-market capitalist economic system is especially poorly equipped to meet any of these requirements (ibid., pp. 32ff.). No single agent or group is so placed as to be able to identify the totality of the microeconomic patterns of conduct that would result in the macro-goal of balanced growth being restored by the traverse adjustments. Such requirements thus remain inaccessible to any observers, including the agents of whom the particular conduct is expected. The sole means of communicating the requirements is confined to the price and quantity signals that are sequentially generated as the impact of the traverse-inducing change is diffused through the system of markets for commodities and resources. Under current policy principles, governments endeavour to modify these signals by various interventions to compensate for the distorting nature of the extant market conditions and to impose some redirection of conduct to achieve desired collective outcomes that would otherwise not occur. However, the fact remains, again as Lowe has so cogently demonstrated, even under perfect market conditions, the freely generated signals are not sufficient to ensure that agents' responses are those required. The decisions and actions which agents take are a product of a myriad of diverse influences. Within the market context, they are primarily determined by the agents' respective motivations manifested as their action directives. Even if we can agree that in their economic conduct, agents are dominated by an extremum action directive that dictates the maximization of pecuniary returns and the minimization of all costs associated therewith, our difficulties are not at an end. Agents are required, by the very nature of the decisions that they must make, to depend upon the formation of expectations about future events. And, even if we confine our attention to adaptive expectations concerning prices and quantities, Lowe showed us long ago that the elasticities of these expectations are decisive in determining the market outcomes that follow from particular current signals. And, as the market has no mechanism for ensuring the formation of the particular elasticities required, the laws of supply and demand have no validity or market-stabilizing results that can be taken for granted, even under the most perfect of conditions (Lowe, 1942 and 1977, pp. 37ff.). Once we leave the perfect-market environment, the expectations that agents must form are extended to take in a range of other concerns, not the least of which are the patterns of reactions by other relevant agents to their actions. Conduct thus takes on a strategic dimension that poses exceedingly complex problems of representation.

Lowe devised his instrumental analysis as the theoretical foundation for the design of the 'Controls' that are the core of his political economics. This was originally done in order to render the market mechanism more reliable. It must be realized immediately, though, that this radical revision of theory and policy strategy can in no way avoid confronting the three requirements with which I opened this section. On the contrary, they become even more prominent in the arguments that ensue once we adopt Lowe's alternative. He is, of course, well aware of this himself and has always qualified his analyses so as to emphasize their limitations from just these perspectives. The design of Controls must be premised upon an understanding of precisely what they are to achieve. Most fundamentally, 'the purpose of Control is to induce responses on the part of the controlled which conform with the intention of the controller' (Lowe, 1977, p. 148). This means, in the present context, first of all *identifying* what the agents must do in order to ensure that the goal state of the traverse is realized. Policy analysts and would-be controllers are, therefore, required explicitly to elicit the logic of the traverse by a process of regressive inference. What must emerge from work on this logic is a pattern of agent actions that are goal directed and which ultimately 'add up' to the desired macro-level outcome by means of the market system (ibid., pp. 139ff.). The challenge remains to communicate these actions to the agents concerned and to get them to accept and carry them out. That is, the behavioural logic is to be converted into a set of reliable cause-and-effect relations. If we grant that the policy authority could establish the correct conduct patterns for all the agents, it is these communication and implementation requirements which demand critical scrutiny if we are to be assured that Controls can be designed so as to be accurate and effective.

We must recall first of all that as far as is feasible, the Controls must be such as to cause the agents to act volitionally to carry out the desired actions: that is, to lift *'micro-autonomy itself to the rank of a genuine goal'* (ibid., p. 318, original emphasis). For this to happen, the process can only begin by having the agents correctly interpret and understand, and then accept and approve the desired conduct by virtue of its being that which maximizes, or perhaps satisfies sufficiently, their own micro-objectives (Lowe, 1976, p. 287; 1977, pp. 319–20; 1987, p. 182). As a pressing complication, we should keep in mind that during the traverse, many agents will be required to change the tenor and direction of their conduct as well.

If volition is to be depended upon, the Controls must be attuned to the existing motivations and action directives of agents. Alternatively, the controllers could try somehow to manipulate these in a more apt direction, but this approach has a more long-term perspective about it (Lowe, 1977, p. 154; 1987, pp. 183–4). In addition, the success of linking Controls to actions will still rely on agents forming the correct pattern of expectations, including their elasticities. Achieving the desired expectations will require quite subtle flows of information to be generated and communicated to the relevant agents. And, as expectations are such subjective and fragile things, much will need to be done continuously to control a range of other situational influences on agents that are likely to disturb and distort them. Moreover, in all of this communication with agents, it must be recognized that as receptors, calculators and reactors, agents vary widely in their capacities. That is, it must be an integral condition of the subtle design of the information flows that they are 'agent neutral', so to say, in their impact. Finally, though, it should be added that Lowe does not envisage that the above manipulative Controls will be adequate in practice. Resort to command Controls, linked to 14 unavoidable sanctions, will be needed as a backup means to the realization of public ends accepted as desirable (1977, pp. 148–9).

Most generally, it is apparent that the effectiveness of the Controls will depend upon analysts having a proper understanding of the links between the dimensions of the situational environment which they modify and the reactions of agents to these modifications. Primacy must be given here to understanding the nature of the agents themselves as situated interpreters and actors, for they constitute the essential 'raw material' of the design problem faced by the controllers. How and to what extent can the conduct of agents really be manipulated by environmental controls if responses are left to volition alone? Answers depend upon the limited state of our knowledge of 'social causation ... [as] the manner in which the sociopolitical environment and, especially, public controls affect [the] economic behavior of the microunits'. Lowe nominates this as the weakest link in the formulation of his ideas by virtue of its reliance on an area of psychology that remains poorly developed (1976, p. 286, compare p. 14; and compare 1977, pp. 147ff.; 1987, pp. 182–3). My inquiries will amplify the grounds for Lowe's own suggestion that 'it is not surprising that psychology has not yet presented us with any "laws of social causation" on which instrumental analysis could be safely based' (1987, p. 182).

3   THE NATURE OF SITUATED HUMAN AGENTS

The first of the facts about human agents that we should confront is that they are, in an absolute and ultimate sense, existentially free beings who may choose and act in any way that they may wish. In any exercise of this right, they draw upon their constituent congenital characteristics and capacities, which Lowe refers to as '"internal influences" arising from the psychosomatic structure of the individuals concerned' (ibid., p. 182). These influences are compounded with the acquired profile of qualities and knowledge that are the result of their respective biographies as individual human beings who have internalized the effects of a range of cumulative, externally-imposed experiences. All such qualitative dimensions vary widely and bring to agents' conduct an ever-present element of contingency which Lowe is moved to cite as originating in 'the innate capriciousness of ... economic actors' and as leading to an 'ineradicable spontaneity of human decision making' (1977, p. 57; 1987, p. 182).

Second, in virtually all facets of their life-world, human agents exist, make decisions and do their periodic choosing and acting within and through some particular situation with a multiplicity of dimensions (Lowe, 1987, p.182). In this respect, Lowe is conscious of the influences that 'certain environmental conditions exert on the formation of action directives and expectations' of human agents (1977, p. 62). Such situational exigencies are, for many short-term human imperatives, *given* as effectively inherited from period to period. Their importance is that selectively relevant aspects of them always serve to *constrain, contain direct and/or facilitate* the agents' otherwise free choices, decisions and actions. The effect is to introduce a counterweight of uncertain proportions to the pure capriciousness and spontaneity of human action. A crucial part of my subsequent argument will seek to ascertain the nature and dimensions of this balance between contingency and containment. Most immediately, it is important to note that there are a multiplicity of influences involved here, for it is all too easy rather to treat situational conditions as merely externally imposed *constraints* on human action. That this latter view is seriously misleading will also be a key contention of the argument to follow.

There are several characteristics of the human situation that we should immediately consider. For our purposes, an agent's situation comprises *a complex totality of natural and humanly-created environmental conditions made up of physical, spatial, social and institutional dimensions.* To begin with, though, it should be explicitly recognized that there are physical–technical structures involved in production, with which economic agents must contend in their ongoing operations and in the implementation of change. These structures bring with them certain technological and other quite objective rules to which agents must conform if the basic process of material reproduction is to be effected with optimum efficacy, measured by whatever criteria are deemed appropriate. This is not to suggest that agents *will* so conform, but rather, in the spirit of instrumental analysis, to emphasize that such potentials exist, none the less. They also represent a largely irreversible commitment of resources, the services and value of which are not able to be retrieved in the face of their redundancy consequent upon change.

In the human sciences generally, and in economics especially, then, it is quite inappropriate to ignore the physical dimensions of the structural environment. There is a readily demonstrable sense in which much of the agency of an economy is primarily 'structured' by the absolute need to work with a physical–technical infrastructure as the essential medium of generating human material well-being. And nowhere has this been made clearer than in Lowe's analyses of economic motion with their focus on the traverse as, at root, a physical-cum-engineering adjustment problem that is centred on the process of production. The difficulties to be confronted are illustrated most expressly by his setting out of an elementary traverse sequence required for reestablishing a balanced reproduction and growth path after a disturbance to the existing path strictly in terms of its *physical-engineering requirements alone* (Lowe, 1976, Ch. 12 and passim).[6]

Changes to the physical–technical form of the production structure are strictly of an engineering nature, but they must be decided upon and implemented by human agents and they may well require induced adjustments to the qualitative profile of the labour and managerial services provided by the associated cohort of agents. Just what is done and how it is influenced by the particular *virtual* structural context in which the producing agents operate, depends upon the degree to which those structures facilitate and/or impede the physical and agent profile changes that are deemed necessary. Such virtual structures, as agents are likely to confront them on a day-to-day basis, may be treated as made up of *roles*, *rules* and *resources* and are often manifested in *institutions*. More particularly, the existence of agreed roles and rules facilitates mutual comprehension and assessment of interdependent actions by agents. They should not be envisaged as rigid or immutable, for '*rules and practices only exist in conjunction with one another*' and second, there is no 'singular relation between "an activity" and "a rule"' (Giddens, 1979, p. 65, original emphasis). Rather, they are based upon accepted practices that have evolved because they are functionally efficacious and mutually advantageous to the agents concerned. Moreover, the capacity of agents to adopt roles and to follow rules will depend upon the human and material resources that they possess.

The particular physical and virtual structural forms that are pertinent to a traverse analysis are readily explicated. The processes involved are primarily to be interpreted as centring around the physical–technical production structure, with the very substance of the traverse frequently found in the changes that take place in this structure. These may be of a purely quantitative nature in that along with replacement investment, more means of production of exactly the same type may be added thus increasing only the scale of existing productive operations. More usually, both replacement and net investment will bring qualitative changes of varying degrees to the technology of the means of production stock, together with any scale changes. Required changes to the quantitative and/or qualitative character of the labour force by means of which this stock is made operational, including spatial and skills distributions, may also increase the effective rigidities of the existing production system and thus compound the problematics of traverse adjustments.

To return to the nature of human agents themselves, a third consideration is that as they are self-conscious and autonomous, they *subjectively reason about, interpret and formulate meanings* for their situations. In sharp contrast to the objective function that represents 'economic man' in the rigid 'situational determinism' of neoclassical analyses (Latsis, 1972), Lowe refers to 'purposeful actors who "move" only after they have interpreted their field of action in terms of their goals and their common-sense knowledge' (1977, p. 61). The highly significant and problematical ideas that agents act through interpretation and with purpose in the light of their action directives and goals, and apply their cognitive capacities in so doing, inject a dimension of contingency into the understanding of human agency. It should be explicitly recognized, too, that the cognitive capacity of agents includes their ability to be *creative and originating* in forming in the imagination all the bases upon which choices, decisions and actions are undertaken. This ultimate level of contingency may greatly affect the formation of motivations, action directives and expectations in a manner that pre-empts any external influences, thus compounding the generally subjective and open-ended character of human conduct.

A final facet of the essential nature of human agents is exposed by considering them in the process of confronting their respective situations when undertaking individual economic and social choices, decisions and actions, more or less freely and guided by their personal self-interest, other motivations and objectives. What may be anticipated is that while they have little immediate control over their periodically inherited structural and institutional environments, manifested as immanent rules, directions, facilities and constraints, they may frequently be inclined to reason that it is in their best interests volitionally to cooperate with them. That is, the majority of agents will choose so to orient their freely exercised conduct as to get the best out of the system for them individually, *providing that they are able to make the correct interpretations and calculations about such matters*. And, as is well known, agents' innate and learned abilities, along with their preparedness to apply them to information gathering and processing, vary widely. It is wholly inappropriate to represent agents as homogeneous in this respect, and we need to confront their cognitive limitations and individual differences quite squarely. The idea that agents apply what Lowe refers to as simply as 'common sense' cognitive factors and capacities (ibid., pp. 16–17, 24, 97) requires further investigation and elaboration and needs to be juxtaposed to the potential for certain key agents, at least, to have to deal with complex problems by means of sophisticated methods during the traverse. Not only are agents' capacities variable, then, but also the cognitive demands made upon them differ according to the mode of their participation in economy and society. The importance of these patterns of difference for the traverse is that the collective outcome of individual agents' activities will depend upon them being willing and able to meet the intellectual and skill demands that they confront during its progression (compare ibid., pp. 96ff.).

4   THE CONDUCT OF SITUATED HUMAN AGENTS

The image of agents and the agency processes in which they engage that emerges from the above discussion is one comprising a blend of potentials for contingency and for containment in the determination of their conduct. Lowe's political economics, as it is particularly applied to the traverse, will depend for its practical success on an increase in and extension of the latter potential relative to the former. What will be required is a significant increase in our capacity to define and design efficacious situational means of containing and directing agents' volitional conduct. Agents would, through a process of concurrent 'education' of some sort, also be called upon to understand and accept a reduction in the degrees of freedom open to them in their decisions and choices in exchange for the benefits it would bring (Lowe, 1988, pp. 116ff., 128ff.).

My concern in this section is with explicating some of the means by which the situational environments confronted by agents may simultaneously facilitate, direct, contain and constrain the innately contingent decisions and actions of individuals in a particular socioeconomic context. The perception of human agent conduct as *highly contingent but situationally contained*, rules out the use of any purely subjectivist or voluntaristic ontology of human agency, along with endeavours to account for it by means of the tenets of methodological individualism.[7] At the same time, though, it should not be read as espousing the opposite theses in which agents' actions are *determined* by structural or class positions in or by the so-called functional needs of societies (compare ibid., p. 10). The question of the extent to which it is really appropriate to lift agents out of their functional and structural situations when the intention is to account for their conduct may be examined by recognizing that there is a mutual interdependence between situation and agency, with the former being both facilitating and directing, as well as containing and constraining with respect to the latter. The effect is to reconcile the conscious and active subject agent, often treated as an isolated individual, with the existence of and a need for a context for action so that situational conditions are seen to become the servants of agents rather than their masters. That is, so that situations are not *'conceptualised as a barrier to action, but as essentially involved in its production'* (Giddens, 1979, pp. 69, 70, original emphasis). Agents are thus located securely in a situational complex, but they are still credited with and are free to exercise their own knowledge and capabilities in any engagement with it. Indeed, the crucial aspect of some especially relevant, virtual dimensions of the environment becomes that they are only instantiated in the actions of agents themselves. So it is that such a 'decentring of the subject must at the same time *recover* that subject, as a reasoning, acting being' and 'neither subject (human agent) nor object ("society", or social institutions) should be regarded as having primacy'. This means that: '*Each is constituted in and through recurrent practices*' and that neither can be adequately represented in abstraction from the other (Giddens, 1982, p. 8, original emphasis). This theoretical framework explicitly integrates the operations of human agents and their situational environment as the basis for understanding social and economic reproduction and change.

The particular activities in which individual agents are represented as engaging, are often categorized in social theory as *rules* and *roles*. Care is needed, though, in applying such categories in order to ensure they are not represented as so functionally deterministic in their effect as to pre-empt the consciousness of decision and action that should be the centrepiece of any theory involving human agents. There is, first of all, a lack of any unique correspondence between *rules* and agents' actions because the latter are mediated by their *resources*, the other component of virtual structures to which reference was made above. Resources may be appropriately defined as 'possessions (material or otherwise) [that] actors are able to bring to bear to facilitate the achievement of their purposes in the course of social interaction: that therefore serve as a medium for the use of *power*' (Giddens, 1977, p.118, original emphasis). The important inference here is that in the last instance, the crucial resource used by agents is power to act within the current rules of a particular structural situation. So, power is manifested in some agents' capacities to get things done in their own interest by using their resources and the rules available to them in particular by virtue of the system's structural conditions, a fact of economic life that is nowhere more spectacularly demonstrated than in the conduct of modern corporate capitalists.

What should also be stressed is that: 'It is fundamental to affirm that *social systems are not constituted of roles but of (reproduced) practices*; and it is practices, not roles, which (via the duality of structure) have to be regarded as the "points of articulation" between actors and structures' (Giddens, 1979, p. 117, original emphasis). It is these practices, which emerge from 'role prescriptions' by virtue of agents' actions, on which we should focus while remaining mindful that agents are *attached* to such roles without their conduct being determined by them. Variations in ability and the individual discretion left to agents leaves an ever-present contingent element in the practical operation of all roles, although it should be added that for many well-defined economic functions to be carried out with precision and reliability, little is required by way of agent ability. Moreover, in such cases under normal circumstances, there is little scope or desire for the exercise of agent discretion to a degree that could distort the outcome.[8]

A focus on the practice of role influenced functions, especially where they demand particular agent capacities and the exercise of discretion, involves individual agents in an '[economic or] social identity that carries with it a certain range (however diffusely specified) of prerogatives and obligations that an actor who is accorded that identity (or is an "incumbent" of that position) *may* activate or carry out' (ibid., p. 117, emphasis added). It is also to be recognized, though, that the actually realized actions by agents may not be wholly consistent with their role prescriptions because of the pressure of various types of 'role strain'. First, agents, *qua* existentially free human beings, have a general identity that extends beyond any imposed economic or social identity and this brings with it discretionary desires and needs that are extraneous to, and perhaps in conflict with, the role prescriptions which they face. Second, agents will often find themselves with more than one role prescription to activate within a single identity and tensions may emerge about the relative priorities and emphases to be given to each when deciding how to act, especially where limited resources are available. Third, individuals may be situated in 'positions involving more than one economic or social identity' and again may face several different role prescriptions and the associated tensions. Fourth, tensions can arise because a particular economic or social identity gives an agent certain powers, the exercise of which may be disputed and or resisted by others. In the process of resolving one or more of these categories of tensions, the agents must make choices, the collective consequences of which may well have a significant unintended and unpredicted content and lead to the suboptimal reproduction of an economic or social system.

A further matter concerning agents' roles which requires explicit treatment is that different aspects of economic role prescriptions call for different profiles of agents' capabilities, some innate, some learned, if they are to be serviced optimally. Any population of agents can be expected to conform to the ideal qualitative profile to varying degrees. Agents' role prescriptions will also require them to act strategically in the sense that the potential effects of their decisions and actions can only be assessed *ex ante* in the context of the expected consequent action and response pattern of other effectively relevant agents. As a consequence of all this, the traverse will almost inevitably involve some agent conduct that deviates individually from any given pattern of role prescriptions and thus results in a technically and socially suboptimal set of collective adjustments to the production structure and related economic processes. Such suboptimality may appear, for example, as excessively slow adjustments to the characteristics of particular means of production, overbuilding of productive capacity by certain firms, and socially undesirable changes in the distribution of income through inadvertent shifts in economic (allocational) power relativities.

Understanding human agents in action requires us to give primary emphasis to matters concerning their knowledge and capabilities as situated individuals with particular biographies. First and foremost, we should endeavour to establish as accurately as possible the realities of the intellectual capacities of agents by juxtaposing the sorts of capabilities they *need* alongside those that they are found to *have* in undertaking meaningful economic and social actions as individuals and as members of various groups. Most essentially, the argument must be that the survival of agents themselves and the reproduction of their system, along with the controlled absorption of changes thereto, cannot be accounted for without the assumption that the agents *know* about the conditions of their environment and about the powers and obligations of their functional situations within it, at least to some minimal extent. Thus, it may well be asserted that '*every [economic and] social actor knows a great deal about the conditions of reproduction of the [economy and] society of which he or she is a member*' (ibid., p. 5, original emphasis). The implication is that all agents must be, to an extent, users and interpreters of extant economic and social theory. But, having said this, it is immediately essential to recall two qualifications to any such claim. First, and most obviously, agents' capacities in this respect will vary widely and, as a consequence, the delivery of their agency will be of a variable quality relative to any theoretical ideal.[9] Processes such as the traverse involving complexes of agent participation will be, in essence, all the more contingent as a result. Second, it is problematical rather than self-evident just what knowledge and information individual agents *can actually acquire* about the totality of the reproductive demands of their economy in terms of their particular pattern of participation. A third qualification that should also be noted is that as individuals, agents will rarely know as much about, or even concern themselves as much with, the total conditions of reproduction as the above quotation from Giddens might suggest. Many will confine their understanding to that part of their situational environment which they understand as immediately influencing their pursuit of short-term self-interests. The important implication of the passage then is that *collectively*, as assessed by results, agents appear effectively to 'know' about the required conditions as they affect their particular contribution to the aggregate outcome.

In order to explicate the types of knowledge, aptly represented as an accumulated *stock*, and of the complementary *flows* of information that agents require effectively to participate in traverse processes, it must be understood that so much of what economic agents must decide about has an irremediably future orientation. It is often recognized in economics, but infrequently given sufficient weight, that the future is uncertain in a sense that cannot be legitimately represented by formalized probabilistic mathematical techniques. Indeed, to argue in terms of 'information' about and 'knowledge' of the future is epistemologically illegitimate in a strict sense, even though agents must represent such things to themselves in the form of a set of expectations to which they attribute some imagined degree of confidence. They are obliged to form and apply relevant expectations in order to be able to act at all in the face of an uncertain and perfidious future. Agents act on and through structures in the face of an uncertain future about which they cannot be *informed* at all in the strictest sense of the term. Instead, they must form expectations on the basis of what they *can know*, where such knowledge and information are highly contingent and the expectations so formed are even more so.[10]

Expectations formation behaviour can perhaps be usefully interpreted as involving agents in specifying and consciously gathering the information that they require for all sorts of purposes. But, when it comes to weighing the significance of and combining the selected parts of such information and knowledge with unconscious and other unacknowledged mental premises and abilities in order to form expectations, even agents themselves would probably find it difficult to explicate and justify formally the results. Moreover, agents are faced with the same sort of issue when applying information and knowledge to the reflexive monitoring of the realized consequences of their expectations, decisions and actions in relation to the intended outcome. In subsequently revising their expectations and actions, agents will rely to a great extent on the subjective facets of their consciousness as well. They will be concerned with finding reasons for especially the negative consequences of their actions, most immediately as far as they concern them as individuals. This apparent *ex post* examination and rationalization of action is reflected in 'the chronic *reflexive monitoring of conduct* that social actors routinely carry on' and is 'crucially involved with how those actions are sustained' (Giddens, 1982, p. 29, original emphasis).

Human action, at least that part of it that is of concern to social and economic theorists, is intentional and purposeful and is constantly monitored as to the success or otherwise of its outcomes. It must be recognized, though, that because individual actors exist in a set of less than fully reliable and predictable dependence relations with others, and because their actions are linked to 'unacknowledged conditions of action', including their non-conscious minds, such outcomes will include both intended and unintended elements (ibid., p. 10). We can only conclude that the 'reflexive monitoring' of outcomes by individual agents cannot overcome the ambiguities of decision-making on the basis of expectations, no matter how knowledgeable and capable the agents are. Errors by agents, induced by some lack of knowledge, information and/or capability, and by the impossibility of having 'information' about the future, including about the strategic responses of other agents, bring varying degrees of instability to systems undergoing changes such as those we try to understand as traverses. Moreover, any idea of *learning* to do better is beset with problems because of the ever-changing situations that agents confront and the ever-present uncertainty about the future situations into which their decisions will carry them. How 'long' a time is assumed for learning by agents is really irrelevant and all movement by agents through time brings with it new uncertainties with which to contend.

The fact that reproduction and change never begin *ab initio* mitigates this sort of contingency, however. Knowledge of the past, and the expectations that flow from extrapolating it into the future, provide often substantially correct guidance about key dimensions of the future. That expectations will frequently be falsified is beyond doubt. But the *degree of deviation* may well be small, even if it cannot be predicted with strict accuracy, because much of the change affecting economic systems comes in relatively small increments and impacts on a limited number of sites. Agents have the capacity to learn by experience about their immediate action environment. The sorts of changes that involve similar decision requirements to those confronted in the past can, as a consequence, largely be absorbed with more or less ease and they rarely bring significant disruptions to otherwise routine conduct. Thus, reproduction as a process involving both stability and change relies upon 'tradition and routinization in social life' to ensure the intertemporal preservation of at least the core of structures and operations in any social or economic system (Giddens, 1979, p. 7).

Due recognition should also be given to the fact that much of discursive information and some parts of accumulated knowledge should be treated as commodities in a modern economic system. These things cost resources to generate, disseminate and acquire. The availability to and the use by agents of information and knowledge is itself a matter of economic decision-making and agents may well choose to operate with *technically* suboptimal information and knowledge inputs for these reasons. The effects of this possibility are compounded by the fact that some such desirable input elements may not be available at all, independently of economic considerations. This comes about mostly because some information and knowledge is highly subjective in its form and, therefore, cannot be gathered or processed in any consistent and reliable manner. This applies especially to information about the intentions of the other agents with whom particular agents must deal and upon whom their returns depend. Such information just cannot be gathered at any cost. Moreover, certain information and knowledge is kept secret by individual agents in order to preserve the benefits that they realize therefrom and can only be obtained by resorting to costly and unethical, or perhaps illegal, clandestine means that may be more or less successful.

All in all, these considerations about the information and knowledge needs and uses of agents serve to reveal an exceedingly complex relationship between agents, their roles and all dimensions of their situations in the processes of the traverse. Traverse analysis is very much about trying to understand how chronically situated agents obtain and use information and knowledge, and form expectations, to the extent that their abilities allow, in order to implement, and see absorbed, processes of change. It is an unfortunate fact, though, that our understanding of these things, especially within mainstream economics, has not kept pace with the complexities of the traverses that the modern capitalist system must endure. It is apparent that if Lowe's political economics is to be given any hope of achieving the practical success that it promises as a matter of principle, there is a pressing need for further research into all the matters concerning human agents and agency to which I have drawn attention above.

NOTES

*   Much of the research for this chapter was carried out during my stay at the Institut für Höhere Studien in Vienna. I would like to express my gratitude to Dr Andreas Wörgötter and his colleagues for their kind hospitality. I am also indebted, with the usual proviso, to Adolph Lowe, Robert Heilbroner, Bruce McFarlane and Phil O'Hara for their helpful comments on earlier versions of this chapter.

1.   This imposition is facilitated by the *quite legitimate* expression of economic variables in strictly quantitative terms, most often measured in homogenized monetary units. While such an approach correctly captures the *results of economic activity*, it immediately obscures the vitally human dimensions of it. As well, the approach hides away the physical–technical and durable form taken by, and the consequently inflexible and immobile nature of, most produced means of production and many other productive resources that are the media of economic actions. The consequence is that 'positive' economic analysis fails to represent the intricacy and duration of the adjustment processes that are the very substance of motion. Indeed, this obscurantism ensures that the concept of the traverse itself is rarely accorded even a glance in established growth and cycle theories.

2.   Lowe's use of the concept of *instrumentalism* must be carefully distinguished from the meaning that has become commonplace in discussions of economic methodology, very largely as a result of the influential efforts of Milton Friedman (1953).

3.   Lowe consequently cites a set of specific unknown means to be explicated in logical sequence as the constituents of this analytical strategy: (1) the path or succession of macro-states of the system that would transform the existing state into the goal state; (2) patterns of micro-conduct by agents appropriate to keeping the system on the stipulated temporal path; (3) the micro-motivations, or action directives, of agents that would induce the required conduct; and (4) a situational environment in and through which agents must operate, including a set of suitable controls, that will elicit these motivations and the associated goal-adequate conduct (1977, pp. 249ff.; 1987, pp. 169ff.).

4. Lowe's accompanying *caveat*, that has always been frankly stated, is that while 'freedom is the *power of self-determination* over the range open to human decision making', it must always remain that '*specific constraints on our conduct are a prerequisite of enduring freedom*'. So, he concludes, in the end, the realization and preservation of freedom for all will depend upon the exercise of a constrained freedom by individuals: 'In a nutshell: *The price of public freedom is self-constraint*' (1988, pp. 5, 11, 73, original emphasis).
5. Most generally, because of the clearly social and institutional context in which all economic activity is situated, Lowe's own work on economic theory and policy has always had a strong sociological orientation (compare 1914; 1935; 1988). More specifically, he has always been conscious that it is the involvement of human agents that is the crucial fact which sets economic phenomena apart from those of the physical world as objects of scientific study (1977, pp. 31, 61; 1987, p. 230).
6. It has really been this technical and more or less objective aspect of the traverse, argued as between essentially capitalist-market equilibrium states as the initial and terminal conditions, that has received most of the important critical and developmental attention in the literature on Lowe and the theme generally. For recent examples, see Kriesler (1989), and the papers comprising Part IV of Halevi et al. (1992).
7. This is, of course, a notoriously ambiguous concept and one which I cannot stop to explore (see, for example, Lukes, 1968 and Hodgson, 1986).
8. As an example, think of the mechanics of the postal service between the posting and the subsequent delivery of a letter. Efficacious agency mediations here depend upon strictly functional processes being followed out, with the cognitive demands on and the need for discretion by the agents being minimal.
9. Herbert Simon has frequently drawn attention to the negative difference that it makes to the meaningfulness of orthodox economic analysis if the delimited abilities of agents to calculate and generally to conduct their affairs rationally is given due recognition: see, for example, Simon (1982, Sections VII and VIII). In the argument to follow, Simon's general caveat about the 'bounded rationality' of agents should be kept in mind.
10. It was George Shackle who, over the whole of his intellectual career, continuously prodded us to give due recognition to the problematics of taking agent expectations formation and application seriously (see 1972; 1974; 1979). It is an unfortunate fact that few economists responded.

REFERENCES

Friedman, M. (1953) *Essays in Positive Economics*, Chicago: University of Chicago Press.
Giddens, A. (1977), *Studies in Social and Political Theory*, London: Hutchinson.
Giddens, A. (1979), *Central Problems in Social Theory: Action, Structure and Contradiction in Social Analysis*, London: Macmillan.
Giddens, A. (1982), *Profiles and Critique in Social Theory*, London: Macmillan.
Halevi, J., D. Laibman and E.J. Nell (eds) (1992), *Beyond the Steady State. A Revival of Growth Theory*, London: Macmillan.
Heilbroner, R.L. (ed.) (1969), *Economic Means and Social Ends: Essays in Political Economics*, Englewood Cliffs, NJ: Prentice-Hall.
Hodgson, G. (1986), 'Behind methodological individualism', *Cambridge Journal of Economics*, 10, pp. 211–24.
Kriesler, P. (1989), 'From disequilibrium to the traverse in economic theory', *School of Economics Discussion Paper*, No. 13, University of New South Wales.
Latsis, S.J. (1972), 'Situational determinism in economics', *British Journal for the Philosphy of Science*, 23, pp. 207–45.
Lowe, A. (1914), *Arbeitslosigkeit und Kriminalität. Eine kriminologische Untersuchung*, Berlin.
Lowe, A. (1935), *Economics and Sociology: A Plea for Co-operation in the Social Sciences*, London: Allen & Unwin.
Lowe, A. (1942), 'A reconsideration of the law of supply and demand', *Social Research*, 9, pp. 431–57.
Lowe, A. (1976), *The Path of Economic Growth*, New York: Cambridge University Press.
Lowe, A. (1977), *On Economic Knowledge. Toward a Science of Political Economics*, [1965], Enlarged edition, New York: M.E. Sharpe.

Lowe, A. (1987), *Essays in Political Economics: Public Control in a Democratic Society,* ed. with an introduction by Allen Oakley, Brighton: Wheatsheaf.

Lowe, A. (1988), *Has Freedom a Future?*, New York: Praeger.

Lukes, S. (1968), 'Methodological individualism reconsidered', *British Journal of Sociology*, **19**, pp. 119–29.

Shackle, G.L.S. (1972), *Epistemics and Economics: A Critique of Economic Doctrines*, Cambridge: Cambridge University Press.

Shackle, G.L.S. (1974), *Keynesian Kaleidics: The Evolution of a General Political Economy*, Edinburgh: Edinburgh University Press.

Shackle, G.L.S. (1979), *Imagination and the Nature of Choice*, Edinburgh: Edinburgh University Press.

Simon, H.A. (1982), *Models of Bounded Rationality: Behavioral Economics and Business Organization*, Cambridge, MA: MIT Press.

Published Writings of Adolph Lowe

1914: *Arbeitslosigkeit und Kriminalität. Eine kriminologische Untersuchung*, Berlin: J. Guttentag, Verlagsbuchhandlung.

1915a: 'Zur Methode der Kriegswirtschaftsgesetzgebung', *Die Hilfe*, **21**, pp. 333–5.

1915b: 'Die freie Konkurrenz', *Die Hilfe*, **21**, pp. 385–7.

1916a: 'Die Reichseinkommensteuer im künftigen Steuersystem', in *Parlament und Wissenschaft zu den Kriegssteuern*, Berlin, pp. 10–21.

1916b: *Wirtschaftliche Demobilisierung*, Berlin.

1917a: 'Die ausführende Gewalt in der Ernährungspolitik', *Europäische Staats- und Wirtschaftszeitung*, **2**, pp. 542–6.

1917b: 'Die Massenspeisung im System der Volksernährung', *Europäische Staats- und Wirtschaftszeitung*, **2**, pp. 657–61.

1917c: 'Mitteleuropäische Demobilisierung', *Wirtschaftszeitung der Zentralmächte*, **2**, pp. 563–5.

1917d: 'Rücksiedlung aufs Land', *Heer und Heimat*, **2**, No. 28.

1918a: 'Die Fragen der Übergangswirtschaft', *Die Woche*, **20**, pp. 612–13 and 637–8.

1918b: 'Die rechtliche Entstehung und Ausgestaltung des Kriegsernährungsamtes. Eine Studie zur Entwicklung der verfassungsrechtlichen Ideen im gegenwärtigen Krieg', unpublished dissertation, Tübingen.

1918c: 'Der Entlassungsplan', in *Der Tag der Heimkehr, Soziale Fragen der Übergangswirtschaft, Schriften der Gesellschaft für soziale Reform*, No. 59, Jena, pp. 57–62.

1919a: 'Die Arbeiter- und Soldatenräte in der Demobilmachung', *Europäische Staats- und Wirtschaftszeitung*, **4**, pp. 89–94.

1919b: 'Die neue Demokratie', *Der Spiegel*, **1**, pp. 8–14.

1920: 'Zur Soziologie der modernen Juden', *Der Spiegel*, **2**, pp. 8–12.

1924: 'Zur ökonomischen Theorie des Imperialismus', in R. Wilbrandt, A. Löwe and G. Salomon (eds), *Wirtschaft und Gesellschaft. Beiträge zur Oekonomik und Soziologie der Gegenwart. Festschrift für Franz Oppenheimer zu seinem 60. Geburtstag*, Frankfurt am Main: Frankfurter Societäts-Druckerei, pp. 189–228.

1925a: 'Chronik der Weltwirtschaft', *Weltwirtschaftliches Archiv*, **22**, pp. 1*–32*.

1925b: 'Der gegenwärtige Stand der Konjunkturforschung in Deutschland', in M.J. Bonn and M. Palyi (eds), *Die Wirtschaftswissenschaft nach dem Kriege. Festgabe für Lujo Brentano zum 80. Geburtstag*, Munich and Leipzig: Duncker & Humblot, Vol. 2, pp. 329–77.

1926a: 'Weitere   Bemerkungen   zur   Konjunkturforschung',
Wirtschaftsdienst, **11**, pp. 1271–6 and 1516–17.

1926b: 'Wie   ist   Konjunkturtheorie   überhaupt   möglich?', *Welt-wirtschaftliches Archiv*, **24**, pp. 165–97; English translation 'How is business cycle theory possible at all?' in *Structural Change and Economic Dynamics*, **8**, 1997, pp. 245–70.

1927:   'Zur   Möglichkeit   der   Konjunkturtheorie,   Antwort   auf   Franz Oppenheimer', *Weltwirtschaftliches Archiv*, **25**, pp. 380–84.

1928: 'Über den Einfluß monetärer Faktoren auf den Konjunkturzyklus', in K.   Diehl,   (ed.), *Beiträge   zur   Wirtschaftstheorie*, Part II, *Konjunkturforschung und Konjunkturtheorie, Schriften des Vereins für Sozialpolitik*, Vol. 173/II, Munich and Leipzig: Duncker & Humblot, pp. 355–70.

1929a: 'Das Reparationsproblem', 2 Parts, *Veröffentlichungen der Friedrich-List-Gesellschaft*, Vols 1 and 2, Berlin: Verlag von Reimar Hobbing, Part 1, pp. 89–91, Part 2, pp. 155–6 and 299–303.

1929b: 'Discussion on "Die Konkurrenz"', *Verhandlungen des Sechsten Deutschen Soziologentages*, Tübingen, pp. 107–8.

1929c: 'Discussion on "Die Wanderung"', *Verhandlungen des Sechsten Deutschen Soziologentages*, Tübingen, pp. 203–7.

1929d: 'Kredit und Konjunktur', in F. Boese (ed.), *Wandlungen des Kapitalismus. Auslandsanleihen. Kredit und Konjunktur. Schriften des Vereins für Sozialpolitik*, Vol. 175, Munich and Leipzig: Duncker & Humblot, pp. 355–70.

1929e: 'Sozialismus aus dem Glauben'. *Verhandlungen der sozialistischen Tagung in Heppenheim, Pfingstwoche 1928*, Zürich and Leipzig: Rotapfel, pp. 117–21 and 219–22.

1929f: Review of *Wirtschaftsprognose* by Oskar Morgenstern, *Zeitschrift für die gesamte Staatswissenschaft*, **87**, pp. 419–23.

1930a: 'Fragen   der   Kartellpolitik', *Veröffentlichungen   des   Enquete-Ausschusses über Kartellpolitik*, Berlin, pp. 323–34.

1930b: 'Kapitalbildung und Steuersystem, Verhandlungen und Gutachten der Konferenz von Eilsen', 2 Parts. *Veröffentlichungen der Friedrich-List-Gesellschaft*, Vols 3 and 4, Berlin: Verlag von Reimar Hobbing, Part 1, pp. 76–82 and 428–31, Part 2, pp. 143–4.

1930c: 'Reparationspolitik', *Neue Blätter für den Sozialismus*, **1**, pp. 37–41.

1930d: 'Lohnabbau als Mittel der Krisenbekämpfung?', *Neue Blätter für den Sozialismus*, **1**, pp. 289–95.

1930e: 'Lohn, Zins – Arbeitslosigkeit', *Die Arbeit*, **7**, pp. 425–30.

1931a: Der Sinn der Weltwirtschaftskrise', *Neue Blätter für den Sozialismus*, **2**, pp. 49–59.

1931b: 'Das gegenwärtige Bildungsproblem der deutschen Universität', *Die Erziehung*, **7**, pp. 1–19.

1932: 'Über den Sinn und die Grenzen verstehender Nationalökonomie', *Weltwirtschaftliches Archiv*, **36**, pp. 149*–62*.

1933: 'Der Stand und die nächste Zukunft der Konjunkturforschung', in G. Clausing (ed.), *Der Stand und die nächste Zukunft der Konjunkturforschung. Festschrift für Arthur Spiethoff*, Munich: Duncker & Humblot, pp. 154–60.

1935a: *Economics and Sociology: A Plea for Co-operation in the Social Sciences*, London: Allen & Unwin; 1953: Japanese edition, Tokyo; 1956: Portugese edition under the title *Economia e Sociologia*, Rio de Janeiro.

1935b: 'Some theoretical considerations of the meaning of trend', *Manchester Statistical Society Group Meetings*, pp. 40–45.

1936: 'Economic analysis and social structure', *The Manchester School*, **7**, pp. 18–37.

1937a: *The Church and the Economic Order*, Being the Report of Section III of the Conference on Church, Community, and State, Oxford and London: George Allen & Unwin.

1937b: *The Price of Liberty. A German on Contemporary Britain*, London: Hogarth Press; 2nd edn 1937, 3rd edn 1948.

1937c: 'The social productivity of technical improvements', *The Manchester School*, **8**, pp. 109–24.

1937d: 'The task of democratic education: pre-Hitler Germany and England', *Social Research*, **4**, pp. 381–98.

1938: 'The turn of the boom', *Manchester Statistical Society Group Meetings*, pp. 10–15.

1939a: 'Nationalism and the economic order', in: *Nationalism. Report of the Royal Institute of International Affairs*, London, pp. 217–48.

1939b: 'The crisis in democracy', *The Student Movement*, **42** (2), pp. 29–31.

1940a: 'Social transformation and the war', *The Christian-News-Letter*, No. **29**.

1940b: *The Universities in Transformation*, New York: Macmillan.

1942: 'A reconsideration of the law of supply and demand', *Social Research*, **9**, pp. 431–57.

1944a: 'The study of world affairs', in *The Study of World Affairs. The Aims and Organization of the Institute of World Affairs*. Two Addresses delivered at the Inaugural Meeting on 17 November 1943, New York, pp. 9–24.

1944b: 'The trend in world economics', *American Journal of Economics and Sociology*, **3**, pp. 419–33.

1947: 'Freiheit ist nicht umsonst zu haben', from the brochure 'The Price of Liberty' (1936), *Neue Auslese*, **2**, pp. 1–9.

1951a: 'Cyclical experience in the interwar period: the investment boom of the twenties and business cycles in a planned economy', in National Bureau of Economic Research (ed.). *Conference on Business Cycles*, New York, pp. 222–3 and 390–96.

1951b: 'On the mechanistic approach in economics', *Social Research*, **18**, pp. 403–34.

1952a: 'A structural model of production', *Social Research*, **19**, pp. 135–76; reprinted in Lowe (1987), pp. 27–59.

1952b: 'Lowe's "mechanistic approach". Rejoinder to James Parsons', *Social Research*, **19**, pp. 497–500.

1952c: 'Lowe's "structural model". Rejoinder to Gerhard Colm', *Social Research*, **19**, pp. 503–7.

1952d: 'National economic planning', in B.F. Haley (ed.), *A Survey of Contemporary Economics*, Volume II, Homewood, IL.: R.D. Irwin, pp. 405–7.

1954: 'The classical theory of economic growth', *Social Research*, **21**, pp. 127–58; reprinted in Lowe (1987), pp. 107–31.

1955a: 'Structural analysis of real capital formation', in M. Abramovitz (ed.), *Capital Formation and Economic Growth*, Princeton: Princeton University Press, pp. 581–634; reprinted in Lowe (1987), pp. 60–106.

1955b: 'Technological unemployment reexamined', in G. Eisermann (ed.), *Wirtschaft und Kultursystem. Festschrift für Alexander Rüstow*, Stuttgart and Zürich: Eugen Rentsch Verlag, pp. 229–54.

1959a: 'F.A. Burchardt, Part I: Recollections of his work in Germany', *Bulletin of the Institute of Statistics*, Oxford, **21**, pp. 59–65.

1959b: 'The practical uses of theory', Comment, *Social Research*, **26**, pp. 161–6.

1959c: 'Wirtschaftstheorie – der nächste Schritt', in Zur Ordnung von Wirtschaft und Gesellschaft. Festausgabe für Eduard Heimann zum 70. Geburtstage, *Hamburger Jahrbuch für Wirtschafts- und Gesellschaftspolitik*, **4**, pp. 174–81.

1961: 'Über eine dritte Kraft. Über das Verhältnis von theologischer und politischer Wissenschaft', in K. Hennig (ed.), *Der Spannungsbogen. Festgabe für Paul Tillich zum 75. Geburtstag*, Stuttgart: Evangelisches Verlagswerk, pp. 109–27.

1965a: 'In memoriam Franz Oppenheimer', *Year Book of the Leo Baeck Institute*, **10**, pp. 137–49.

1965b: *On Economic Knowledge: Toward a Science of Political Economics*, NY: Harper & Row; 1977: second, enlarged edition, White Plains, NY: M.E. Sharpe; 1968: German edition under the title *Politische*

Ökonomik, Frankfurt am Main: Europäische Verlangsanstalt; 1984: second, enlarged German edition, Königstein im Taunus: Athenäum; 1969: Portugese edition under the title *A Ciencia da Economia Politica*, Rio de Janeiro; 1973: Japanese edition, Tokyo.

1965c: 'S ist noch nicht P', in S. Unseld (ed.), *Ernst Bloch zu Ehren*, Frankfurt am Main: Suhrkamp, pp. 135–43.

1967a: 'In memoriam: Eduard Heimann 1889–1967', *Social Research*, **34**, pp. 609–12 (German translation: 'Nachruf für Eduard Heimann', *Zeitschrift für die gesamte Staatswissenschaft*, **124**, 1968, pp. 209–11).

1967b: 'The normative roots of economic value', in S. Hook (ed.), *Human Values and Economic Policy*, New York: New York University Press, pp. 167–80 (German translation: 'Die normative Wurzel des wirtschaftlichen Wertes', in *Interdependenzen von Politik und Wirtschaft. Beiträge zur Politischen Wirtschaftslehre. Festgabe für Gert von Eynern*, Berlin, pp. 135–43.

1969a: 'Toward a science of political economics', in R.L. Heilbroner (ed.), *Economic Means and Social Ends. Essays in Political Economics*, Englewood Cliffs, NJ: Prentice-Hall, pp. 1–36; reprinted in Lowe (1987), pp. 157–92.

1969b: 'Economic means and social ends. A rejoinder', in R.L. Heilbroner (ed.), *Economic Means and Social Ends. Essays in Political Economics*, Englewood Cliffs, NJ: Prentice-Hall, pp. 167–99; reprinted in Lowe (1987), pp. 193–225.

1970: 'Toward a science of political economics', in M. Natanson (ed.), *Phenomenology and Social Reality. Essays in Memory of Alfred Schutz*, The Hague: Martinus Nijhoff, pp. 140–73.

1971: 'Is present-day higher learning "relevant"?', *Social Research*, **38**, pp. 563–80.

1975a: 'Adam Smith's system of equilibrium growth', in A.S. Skinner and T. Wilson (eds), *Essays on Adam Smith*, Oxford: Clarendon Press, pp. 415–25.

1975b: 'Hans Philipp Neisser 1895–1975', *Social Research*, **42**, pp. 187–9.

1976: *The Path of Economic Growth*, Cambridge: Cambridge University Press.

1978a: 'Prometheus unbound. A new world in the making', in S.F. Spicker (ed.), *Organism, Medicine and Metaphysics*, Dordrecht: Kluwer, pp. 1–10.

1978b: 'Über das Dunkel des gelebten Augenblicks', in K. Bloch and A. Reif (eds), *'Denken heißt Überschreiten'. In Memoriam Ernst Bloch 1885–1977*, Cologne and Frankfurt am Main: Europäische Verlagsanstalt, pp. 207–13.

1979: 'Die Hoffnung auf kleine Katastrophen', in M. Greffrath, *Die Zerstörung einer Zukunft. Gespräche mit emigrierten Sozialwissenschaftlern*, Reinbek: Rowohlt, pp. 145–94.

1980a: 'Hans Staudinger', *Social Research*, 7, pp. 201–3.

1980b: 'What is evolutionary economics? Remarks upon receipt of the Veblen–Commons Award', *Journal of Economic Issues*, **14**, pp. 247–54; reprinted in Lowe (1987), pp. 226–33.

1981: 'Is economic value still a problem?', *Social Research*, **48**, pp. 786–815; reprinted in Lowe (1987), pp. 132–54.

1982: 'Is the glass half full or half empty?', *Social Research*, **49**, pp. 927–49; reprinted in Lowe (1987), pp. 234–50.

1984: 'Zur Ortsbestimmung der Gegenwart', in H. Hagemann and H.D. Kurz (eds), *Beschäftigung, Verteilung und Konjunktur. Zur Politischen Ökonomik der modernen Gesellschaft. Festschrift für Adolph Lowe*, Bremen: Bremen University Press, pp. 26–33.

1985a: 'Briefwechsel Adolf Lowe – Ernst Bloch 1943–75', in *Ernst Bloch Briefe*, Frankfurt am Main: Suhrkamp, pp. 728–823.

1987: *Essays in Political Economics: Public Control in a Democratic Society*, edited and introduced by A. Oakley, Brighton: Wheatsheaf.

1988a: 'Can Keynes's Theory of Employment be Verified?', in H. Hagemann and O. Steiger (eds), *Keynes' General Theory nach fünfzig Jahren*, Berlin: Duncker & Humblot, pp. 459–64.

1988b: *Has Freedom a Future?*, New York: Praeger; 1990: German edition under the title *Hat Freiheit eine Zukunft?*, Marburg: Metropolis.

1989: 'Konjunkturtheorie in Deutschland in den zwanziger Jahren', in B. Schefold (ed.), *Studien zur Entwicklung der ökonomischen Theorie VIII*, Schriften des Vereins für Socialpolitik, New Series Vol. 115/VIII, Berlin: Duncker & Humblot, pp. 75–86.

1991: 'A Self-Portrait', in P. Arestis and M.C. Sawyer (eds), *A Biographical Dictionary of Dissenting Economists*, Aldershot: Edward Elgar, pp. 323–8.

Name Index

Aftalion, A. xiii, 98, 107–10, 115, 123, 126–7, 138
Amendola, M. 209, 212–13, 215, 229–30
Aristotle xv, 244–51, 254
Arrow, K.J. 64–5, 295
Arthur, B. 206
Aubrey, R. 11–12
Azariadis, C. 58–9

Bacon, F. 295
Bagehot, W. 101
Baldone, S. 219, 223–4
Balke, N.S. 151
Baran, P. 152
Baranzini, M. 127, 206
Barro, R.M. 52, 72
Baumol, W.J. 58
Beck, U. 253
Becker, G.S. 283
Belloc, B. 215, 219, 222–3
Benveniste, E. 246
Bernstein, E. 165
Bertola, G. 72
Beveridge, W. 27
Bismarck, O. von 15
Blanchard, O. 140
Blaug, M. 90
Böhm–Bawerk, E. von 77–8, 90, 118, 121
Bonar, J. 254
Bonn, M.J. 30
Boulding, K.E. xv, xvii
Bouniatian, M. xiii, 98, 104–6, 108, 112, 126
Brentano, L. 8, 30
Bretall, R.W. 281
Bulgakov, S.N. 188
Burchardt, F. xi, 95, 98, 115–18,

120–121, 127, 131, 229
Bürgin, A. 244
Burmeister E. 219

Cantalupi, M. 229
Carver, T.N. 126
Caskey, C.T. 141
Caspari, V. xii, 33–42
Cassel, G. 115, 117, 127
Chakravarty, S. 203
Chandler, A. 138
Chou En Lai 187
Clark, D. 30
Clark, J.B. 138
Clary, B.J. xv, 257–82
Clauser, O. 230
Clausing, G. 30
Cobb, C.W. 47, 49
Cole, H. 70
Colletti, L. 165
Colm, G. xi, 21, 23, 26, 30
Coutts, K. 140

Dahmen, E. 126
Dixit, A. 68
Dobb, M. xiv, 164, 169, 178–81, 183–5, 187
Domar, E.D. 46, 95, 133
Dönhoff, M. Countess xii, 3–6
Douglas, P.H. 47, 49
Drazen, A. 58–9
Duchin, F. 224
Duesenberry, J. 147
Dunlop, J.T. 137
Durkheim, E. 284

Eichengreen, B. 139
Eichner, A.S. 141
Eliot, T.S. 263

Subject Index